THE REIGN OF ETS

The corporation that
makes up minds

by
Allan Nairn
and
associates

The Ralph Nader Report
on the
Educational Testing Service

© Copyright 1980, Ralph Nader.
All rights reserved.

THE REIGN OF ETS: THE CORPORATION THAT MAKES UP MINDS

ERRATA

p. 49	line 6:	Correct title is <u>New York Times Guide to College Selection</u>
p. 51	line 6:	"school" should be "schools"
p. 278	line 15:	add "is": ". . .this is a good use. . ."
p. 289	line 3:	"of" should be "by"
p. 378	line 6:	"close" should be "closed"
p. 405	note 18a:	the author is Karen C. Hegener
p. 408	note 36:	the photo caption should be "Rites of Summer"
p. 440	note 301:	refers to page 337
p. 441	note 322:	title given is for cover memo; title of report is in text
p. 441	note 323:	should be John Fremer, not John Kramer

ACKNOWLEDGMENTS

Many individuals contributed a great deal to produce this report. Without their knowledge, effort, time and persistence, it would never have been completed.

Tom Sutton, my partner in the research and interviews at ETS, played a major role in preparing the report. During the first summer of 1974, Don Bucklin and Hope Cone helped with interviews and research. Peggy Grace, Seymour and Martha Montgomery graciously gave us lodging, work space and encouragement. Chris Burke, Ed Lloyd and Steve DeMicco of the New Jersey Public Interest Research Group (NJPIRG) lent us their office and offered guidance in many ways. Marge Tabankin of the Youth Project gave us access to the files of the Project on Educational Testing (POET), a 1972-73 study directed by James Ghee.

The staff and student members of the New York Public Interest Research Group (NYPIRG), including its director Donald Ross (who began looking into ETS in 1972), testing project coordinator Steve Solomon, Steve Cary, Arthur Malkin, Dennis Kaufman, Gene Russianoff, Gerry Gartenberg, Leslie Haber and Susan Burnett provided information and assistance, and a spirited example of constructive action in their successful campaign for New York State's landmark Truth-in-Testing law.

Perhaps my heaviest debt is to Kerry Barnett, David Bollier, Ron Brownstein, Karen Croft, Ed Hanley, Tim Massad, John Richard and Jim Wheaton; they played crucial roles, variously researching, editing and checking the report. Ron Brownstein helped in writing portions of the report, in particular, parts of Chapter VIII. I am also greatly indebted to Dr. Claire Nader who took the time to review and edit the entire manuscript.

The following people made important contributions with information, reviews of the manuscript, and kinds of support too diverse to mention: Karen Aptakin, David Ayón, Dierdre Baldwin, Judy Brewer, Steven Brill, Dan Clearfield, Bob Chlopak, Vivian Daub, Marjy Fisher, Ruth Fort, Charlie Garlow, John Haber, Mark Harlos, Harvey Jester, David Jones, Sharon Kalemkiarian, Kenzie MacKinnon, Matt McCormick, Bob Mathis, Kimathi Mohammed, Tilt Meyer, Pam Pagliocini, Dan Politi, Richard Rampell, George Riley, Scott Rosenberg, Joel Seligman, Nan Shapiro, David Targan, Bill Taylor, Norman Waitzman, John Weiss, and Parma Yarkin.

E.W. Kelley, professor of government at Cornell University, with teaching experience in psychometrics at the University of Chicago and an adviser on testing to the Department of Health, Education and Welfare and to Congressional committees, read Chapters III and V with care. Dr. Vito Perrone, President of the National Consortium on

Testing, and Dean of the Center for Teaching and Learning at the University of North Dakota, gave a critical reading to Chapter V. Leon Kamin, professor of psychology at Princeton University, and Dr. Hassler Whitney, mathematician at the Institute for Advanced Study in Princeton, New Jersey gave advice and suggestions. Edgar Cahn, Co-Dean of Antioch School of Law, advised on the problems of the law school admission testing process. David White, an attorney and director of a study of law school admissions for the National Conference of Black Lawyers, reviewed Chapter VI in detail.

Many current and former ETS employees have contributed information and observations to this report. Their cooperation has been indispensible. The commentaries of Chuck Stone, formerly Director of Minority Affairs at ETS, were particularly helpful.

Kathryn Borsoni typed the manuscript in its later stages through to its printed version, making constructive suggestions all along. Millie Stearman typed early drafts of the manuscript.

Finally, most of all this report owes its existence to Ralph Nader who long ago recognized ETS as a fundamental power in society and with patience and unrelenting tenacity sponsored and supervised this long and challenging project.

Although many have contributed to this effort, I take full responsibility for any errors or oversights in the report.

Allan Nairn

CONTENTS

Acknowledgments iii

Preface ix

Chapter I: "Hope . . . Will Be Kept Within
                   Reasonable Bounds".   1

Chapter II: Rosedale: Power and Privilege at ETS . 28

Chapter III: Five Percent of Nothing: Aptitude
                   Testing, The Respectable Fraud 55

Chapter IV: "The Worth of Other Men": The
                   Science of Mental Measurement and
                   The Test of Time 161

Chapter V: Class in the Guise of Merit 197

Chapter VI: ETS: Barrier to the Bar 220

Chapter VII: The ETS Way of Doing Business:
                   Student Consumers in Captivity 260

Chapter VIII: Inside ETS: The Soft Institution . . . 294

Chapter IX: Rays of Sunlight, Winds of Change . . 370

Footnotes 399

Appendix I: ETS Candidate Volume 509

Appendix II: ETS Test Development Personnel 513

Appendix III: An Analysis of Questions Exemplifying
                   Cultural Bias from David M. White . . 519

Appendix IV: ETS and College Board Financial
                   Documents 525

Appendix V: Truth-in-Testing legislation 529

Glossary 548

Abbreviations 551

Reader's Comments 554

PREFACE

The conception for this report on the Educational Testing Service began with the victims of standardized testing. Some of these students would come up to me at colleges and universities around the country to express a feeling that they had been unjustly judged by a three hour exam. They would tell me how their educational or career opportunities were damaged or destroyed by their low score on the multiple-choice test, taken one morning in the fall or spring, even though they had done well in their grades and extra-curricular activity. Other students merely expressed a _fait accompli_: Why could they not go to graduate school or law school? They just didn't have the aptitude was their reply. How did they know this? Because they didn't test out. It was not so much an attitude of resignation as one of accepting a kind of revealed truth about themselves.

About eight years ago, during a broader discussion of testing, I was mentioning some of these student reactions to an editor with the _New York Times_. He said he had interviewed a number of ETS officials and staff in Princeton, New Jersey, and they had persuaded him that almost every criticism ever leveled at that institution had been considered and discussed in detail inside ETS.

They made it all seem so very complex, he said--so complex, apparently, that he never completed a lengthy article which had been planned.

His comments were intriguing. When psychometricians, as with other specialists, allege complexity and assert that test consumers are not really qualified to question the testing sovereignty that affects their lives so profoundly, it is time for them to evaluate their testers.

Throughout the past thirty years, the multiple-choice standardized testing industry expanded to judge more people, starting with five-year-olds. It was not only the schools which required such tests; dozens of occupations and professions in all the states conditioned entrance on these kinds of examinations. Alongside the testing industry there developed a coaching school industry which taught students, who could afford to pay, how to improve their test scores. The Educational Testing Service (ETS), the giant testmaker, has long refused to recognize the efficacy of these coaching classes. Even after a Federal Trade Commission study concluded in May 1979 that some students taking these courses can improve their test scores significantly, ETS remained doubtful. After all, if the tests measured aptitude or intelligence, as the ETS claim went, coaching, *a priori*, could not work. For, if coaching did work, then the basic ETS assumption of measuring intellectual constants could be seriously questioned. And, given the price of admission to these coaching schools, so could the assumption that the tests gave equal chances to students from different economic backgrounds.

The bureaucratization and depersonalization of education catered to the ETS type of testing. Its multiple-choice format offered the patina of objectivity and the administrative ease of being machine-scored. Emphasizing its scholarly status and institutional prestige, not as propositions to be examined but as articles of faith to be intoned, ETS made it easy for the schools, colleges and universities to broker the power of these tests over students while passing responsibility for them to the nationally centralized Educational Testing Service.

In listening to student complaints and questions, it became clear that all roads led to the Rosedale "campus" of ETS at Princeton. If there is to be a consumer perspective and analysis of ETS as judge and gatekeeper for millions of young Americans, then, students are the logical ones to prepare a report on the consequences and the worth of the standards by which they are so decisively judged.

During the summer of 1974, a small group came together in Princeton led by Allan Nairn. They formally approached ETS officers for interviews, published materials and other useful information. The response was frosty, to say the least. The executives at ETS initially demanded compensation for executive time spent in interviews, our retaining

a court reporter to take transcripts, and a pledge that
no information we obtained be used in anybody's litigation
anywhere. They also sought the power of reviewing the
manuscript prior to publication. Eventually, after much
negotiation and public controversy, they dropped these
conditions, and finally permitted over fifty hours of
interviews. ETS President William Turnbull granted interviews on three occasions.

In the intervening years as the report matured toward
completion, we spent considerable time writing and speaking
to various consumer and professional groups about ETS.
Together with some media coverage, this activity surfaced
more data and case studies, and helped advance the truth-in-testing movement, which the report describes.

The initiatives taken in this direction by particular
students throughout the country, and especially in New
York state are noteworthy. So are the more quiet initiatives of former ETS employees who contributed new and insightful evidence contained in the pages of this study,
often at risk to their careers. They are the unsung
heroes of the testing establishment.

Perhaps most striking was our finding that for years
many insiders had been criticizing the status quo, challenging the official line and recommending changes.
Yet, so dominant and profitable a status has been accorded
the reign of ETS that a wall of resistance and strong
peer group bonding enveloped to suppress the voices advocating

constructive change. There was no nourishing soil for
these voices to receive a rational hearing--one that was
always mindful of the interests of students who were
supposed to benefit from the ETS tests.

For all its internal speculation, the standardized
testing ideology was quite a closed circle. Their ritualistic
exercises in self-assessment notwithstanding, the theory
had long ago become the practice whose very commercial success, in turn, throttled self-examination of the theory.
Its academic accoutrements aside, ETS has appeared incapable
of applying Alfred North Whitehead's description of the scientific attitude: that of keeping open "options for revision."

Even more extreme is the fear and secrecy which pervade
ETS. The corporation, as befits an almost mystical belief
in its particular brand of testing, could not loosen up.
This tightness reflects a long heritage of closed-door
business practices. One ETS program director, to cite an
episode during our study, addressed a letter to Allan Nairn
and put it in the ETS mail system. Before the letter left
the building, someone noticed the address and reported it
to the public relations director who then called the program
director at home that evening demanding an explanation.
Not long afterward, his supervisor sent him a written repri-
mand. Others were more circumspect. One ETS executive
insisted on dealing with the author through a third party,
so that, when questioned, he could respond that he had
never talked to any of the researchers and wouldn't know

them if he saw them on the street. These instances are recounted with sadness. Having studied such corporations as General Motors, Dupont, and Citibank, we were accustomed to secrecy and intransigence from these powerful profit-making corporations. ETS surprised us with its even greater seige-mentality.

But, then, its long-standing policy to remain hidden from public view, from the audience of affected consumers, has worked to perpetuate its power and world view. Imagine a process of evaluation where the educational and career opportunities of millions of people are significantly determined by multiple-choice examinations, which do not even purport to test their judgment, wisdom, experience, creativity, idealism, determination or stamina. (What ETS _purports_ to measure is discussed in this report.) Small wonder that, as this report documents, such tests fail so badly in their predictive value.

The final tragedy occurs when too many students accept these unreliable test verdicts as a measure of their own self-worth. Because students have no choice but to be judged by such a standard which frequently destroys their self-confidence, they, in effect, become its final enforcers.

To break this vicious circle, knowledge, alternatives and perceived choice are needed. Ending the reign of ETS means adopting other broader, more diverse approaches for assessing individual performance and enabling diagnosis, evaluation and correction. This is another way of testing that allows for options beyond a narrow-gauged "stop or go" verdict; it leads to a multi-criteria, multi-cultural array of evaluations, which can tap the untapped or unique talents of diverse individuals, and away from the false precision of the ETS testing culture.

This report devotes considerable analysis to this testing culture and its historic backdrop. It strives to show, for one thing, that a short, one-time three hour gamble which can determine a life's pathway is simply not compatible with what is known about human personalities, their capacity for growth, their diversity and versatility. It is also inimical to the opportunities--both analytic and normative--which a democracy should provide all its citizens from all classes, races, age groups and genders.

The soaring hubris and jargon of the psychometric community was deflated recently by a leading psycho-metrician and winner of the ETS Award for Distinguished Service to Measurement, the late Dr. Oscar K. Buros: "We don't have a great deal to show for fifty years of work. . . . The improvements--except for the revolutionary electronic scoring machines and computers--have not been of enough consequence to permit us to have pride in what we have accomplished. . . ."

An independent analysis of the dominant testing culture is now coming on the scene. There will be no turning back this time. The shallowness of the ideology and the depth of ETS' political power to preserve its way of testing are apparent to increasing numbers of students, parents, educators, administrators and, most refreshingly, to those deprived people who never made it through the first multiple-choice gate.

Many more Americans need to be aware of a testing system which encourages both teachers and students to prepare for such trivial results--results which predict poorly and perpetuate social biases. Deciding who advances through what schools and careers is an immense power--one that would have produced a furor long ago if a governmental agency possessed it. The presumption to define what is aptitude and manage the allocation of opportunities based on that definition should be directly challenged.

Although this report acknowledges the broader educational and social institutions underpinning the testing apparatus of ETS, it aims, first, to lay the basis for the consumer perspective needed to examine the assumptions and consequences of contemporary standardized testing. The trail of understanding will lead to recognition of the roots of ETS' power. For now, however, a plethora of local and national discussions and initiatives is in order. It is time to reveal the past and explore the future of testing in America. It is time for the specialists who have privately criticized the injustices inherent in the tests to go public, and join with the consumers who no longer are willing to pay the toll for such injustices. It is time for common candor within the testing establishment to cease being viewed as uncommon courage.

Our society is in need of a wide-ranging search for and distribution of human talent. The straightjacket that the reign of ETS has imposed on this need can be lifted when the pattern of ETS's insupportable claims about its tests is widely understood.

>
> Ralph Nader
> P.O. Box 19312
> Washington, DC
> December, 1979

CHAPTER I

"HOPE . . . WILL BE KEPT WITHIN REASONABLE BOUNDS"

"Life may have less mystery but it will also have less disillusionment and disappointment. Hope will not be a lost source of strength but it will be kept within reasonable bounds."[1] Henry Chauncey, Groton '23, Harvard '28, former dean of Harvard and examiner of men for the U.S. Navy,[2] wrote these words in 1950. As the guiding philosophy behind the mission of a new corporation, their effect would eventually be felt by millions of people.

Devereux Colt Josephs, Groton '11, Harvard '15, president of the New York Life Insurance Company and former President of the Carnegie Corporation, did not routinely engage in the management of small enterprises. The corporations on whose boards he served were organizations of obvious wealth and power: J.P. Morgan Company, Consolidated Edison, American Brake Shoe, American Smelting and Refining.[3] Yet, together with colleagues from the worlds of government and education, Mr. Josephs had consented to oversee the assets of a non-profit corporation of only minor material wealth, which had powers that were subtle by comparison.

At its inception, the company had little physical endowment beyond some data processing machines and its offices in Princeton, New Jersey. In contrast to Mr. Josephs' other corporate ventures, the firm was not equipped to command vast amounts of money or labor. But by combining the influence of institutional powers like Devereux Josephs and the vision of social planners like Henry Chauncey, this corporation would deal in commodities of an entirely different kind.

On Friday, December 19, 1947, the New York State Board of Regents granted absolute charter number 5515, incorporating five men and their associates and successors under the name of "Educational Testing Service." The incorporators represented three organizations--the Carnegie Foundation, the American Council on Education, and the College Entrance Examination Board, which had agreed to consolidate their standardized testing programs.[4] Devereux Josephs, according to the official account, "quarterbacked the merger and supplied important initial funds."[5]

IBM (International Business Machines), Pepsi Cola Corporation, the Association of American Medical Colleges, Harvard University, the U.S. Department of State, the U.S. Atomic Energy Commission, and more than fifty leading universities, foundations, government agencies and corporations greeted the new testing firm with advisory services and contracts.[6] In the Educational Testing Service (known as ETS), they were backing an unusual kind of organization. ETS was not in business to make a profit, sell products, teach students, or wield government power. By big business standards a modest-sized corporation (less than $2 million initial capital, 111 employees),[7] ETS had been assigned by its backers a mission of basic social importance.

The Plan

In his 1949-50 Annual Report to the Board of Trustees, Henry Chauncey, the President of ETS, described the "ETS Mission":

first, "To serve American education by providing tests and related services . . . which will aid in the guidance of students and in their self-understanding, and which will lead to proper selection and placement of students, not only within but also at the end of the educational process"; second, "To serve government agencies by providing tests and related services in their educational and training efforts and particularly in time of national emergency to serve the federal government in other activities to which testing and related techniques are applicable"; and third, "Through research, to expand and improve testing theory and techniques thereby advancing the science of testing."

The United States of 1950 did not lack challenges for ETS and the science of testing. Noting that "there is an urgent need for a national census of human abilities," Mr. Chauncey proposed an inventory of "the quality and quantity of our human resources." Chauncey argued that such a census was not only "of critical importance for the National Military Establishment" but would have broader application as well. He saw it as providing "a basis for realistic planning on a nationwide scale in peace or in war." Chauncey believed that the data collected would be helpful to industry, for example, "in relation to the ability difference between men and women, and the trends of employment as between the sexes. . . ." It was in educational planning, however, that Chauncey foresaw the most extensive use of the census of abilities. He wrote:

Data on the abilities of the school-going
population are needed for planning of educational
programs. Obviously, also, such data would be
of the greatest value in the educational and
vocational guidance of individual students whose
abilities would then be compared with reliable
national norms. . . . Such information would
appear to be essential for intelligent planning.

Fortunately, it is entirely feasible to undertake such a census at the present time; tests are
available or can be readily developed to measure
with adequate precision the distribution of
important abilities within the population. . . .
It is, I think, evident that the field of testing
is exceedingly broad and the opportunities for
ETS almost limitless.[8]

The opportunities open to ETS, however, were entirely different from those available to most institutions; pursuit of the ETS mission would actually change the way people think and feel about themselves and others. Chauncey explained:

To many the prospect of measuring in quantitative
terms what have previously been considered
intangible qualities is frightening, if not down-
right objectionable. Yet, I venture to predict
that we will become accustomed to it and will find
ourselves better off for it. In no instance that
I can think of has the advance of accurate
knowledge been detrimental to society, unless it
was misused. And with respect to knowledge of
individuals, the possibilities of constructive
use are far greater than those of misuse.
Educational and vocational guidance, personal
and social adjustment most certainly should be
greatly benefited. Life may have less mystery
but it will also have less disillusionment and
disappointment. Hope will not be a lost source
of strength, but it will be kept within reasonable bounds."[9]

The Plan Becomes Reality

*The Case of Gary Vladik.** More than twenty-five years after Chauncey wrote these words, Gary Vladik, a seventeen year-old from Canton, Ohio, received a letter from the Educational Testing Service. Enclosed was the computer print-out of his Scholastic Aptitude Test (SAT) score. He took the letter and went to a place where he could be alone. "I was scared to look," he explained later.

Gary opened the letter, examined the score, sealed the envelope and put it away. "I hid it. It was in the drawer. No one saw it." When his brother and friends came around asking "how'd you do?", "I would lie," Gary said, "I would sit down and lie."

The score did not surprise Gary. It mirrored his score on another ETS test, the PSAT/NMSQT (Preliminary Scholastic Aptitude Test/National Merit Scholarship Qualifying Test), taken the year before. He knew that the SAT score meant the end of his college hopes: "That was my rejection right there." But, he also knew that it marked the end of a year of waiting for the decisive moment. It had been a year of deep self-doubt and agonizing concealment. "It was a terrible time," he said.

For years Gary had aspired to attend an agricultural school. He wanted to do research in animal science and, perhaps, prepare for veterinary school. With a 95% average, he ranked tenth in his high school class, and was an editor of the yearbook, an

---

*NOTE: Names and identifying information have been changed.

actor in school plays, and a volunteer for community organizations. He worked intensely and, though modest, described himself as "highly motivated."

When the PSAT/NMSQT score arrived the year before, Gary's future was thrown into question. "All those years of school and then this. It all came so fast." Counsellors at his high school suggested he change his plans. "My parents were heart-broken for me." Gary's PSAT score became what he called "my hidden secret."

ETS bulletins emphasize that theirs is no ordinary classroom test score. "The PSAT/NMSQT measures verbal and mathematical abilities important in college work," ETS explains. "Both the PSAT/NMSQT and the SAT*stress reasoning ability rather than ability to remember specific information . . . The chances are about 2 out of 3 that your verbal and mathematical scores are within 4 points of the scores you would receive if it were possible to measure your academic abilities with absolute precision."[10] As the name indicates, it is said to be a test of "aptitude" which helps distribute rewards according to "merit."

The students at Gary's high school took the company at its word. From the day the scores arrived, people viewed them not just as official measurements of thinking and potential, but as rewards and penalties based on merit. Those who scored high were bathed in glory: "He deserves it, he's brilliant," some said. And those who scored low could be reappraised by friends and teachers who had known them for years. A friend who had expected Gary to

---

*According to an ETS technical manual, the PSAT is made of questions formerly used on the SAT. Source: William H. Angoff, ed., <u>The College Board Admissions Testing Program</u>, (New York: College Entrance Examination Board, 1971) p. 45.

do well confided her PSAT score. It was nearly double Gary's score, but he wouldn't admit it. "I wouldn't tell anybody how I did," he said, "it would really mentally cripple me. I was a wreck." Gary had his rationale. "Everybody exaggerated their scores. It was a kind of mental deception you had to play, out of self-deception or more out of shock." It was stated in the ETS literature, and everybody just knew, that the test was an official measurement of deep qualities of your mind. When the scores came in the mail, you could kid yourself, ignore it, look the other way. But, ultimately, what could you say?

Gary took his score for what the authorities said it was. It measured your aptitude, Gary explained, "because it's standard, it's a standardized test. It was stripping us of everything and measuring us as equals." On its face, Gary saw nothing in the test that would lead him to question it, although, "I hadn't seen the vocabulary before." As someone who welcomed challenges, the questions even seemed appealing--at least the first time around. "It was fun, I would have enjoyed taking it, if it didn't count. I like figuring out analogies."

When the PSAT score came back, there was no escaping its verdict. His chance at vindication would come in a year, when he got a chance at the SAT.

Gary's PSAT scores and the impending SAT absorbed him "like a fetish." Objectively, he knew that an important part of his future would be changed by three hours in the test center. "I had to do it. This was it. All or nothing." The night before, he couldn't sleep. When he took the test, he was "in hysterics."

Six weeks later, when ETS mailed Gary his SAT score, the year-long ordeal ended. "For me it took away all my self-worth. Despite all my high school background, it was all the SAT."

Gary went for an interview with an alumni representative from the agricultural school. The alumnus liked Gary's four year record and strong outside activities. "Everything was impressive, he said. But then he stared right at my SAT's and said 'no way.' If I couldn't bring it up 200 points, I wouldn't even be considered."

As the agricultural school recommended, Gary took the ETS College Board Achievement Tests. But, before the achievement scores came back from ETS, Gary received his rejection letter.

Tens of millions of people before Gary had had their thinking assessed and measured by ETS. But, upon opening the envelope and seeing his score, Gary was left alone with himself. The company that produced the test operated a national system which would affect more than six million others that year. For Gary, however, it was a personal matter--there aren't many things more personal than your future and your mind. "I didn't want to seek out any psychological therapy," Gary explained, "because I thought it was justified, I thought it was a valid test."

For many people this might have been the beginning, at age seventeen, of a sharp, long downturn in their self-confidence and aspirations. But Gary was a person of unusual will; more important, he was lucky enough to live near a good, affordable college which did not require an ETS test. He was accepted by the college and with two years of intense work racked up top grades. The agricultural school which had rejected him on the basis of his ETS score accepted him as a transfer student in animal science. Weeks into the term, Gary contracted hepatitis and missed a month and a half of school. He beat the illness, returned, caught up on eighty hours of missed lab work, and finished with a 3.3 average on a scale of 4.0.

Only then, four years after receipt of his first ETS score, did Gary begin to regain the old confidence in himself, marking an end to a rare experience. Gary had been able to overcome the roadblock. His feat provides a rare comparison between predictions made on the basis of an ETS test and real-life performance. His performance disproved the prediction. But for many people the multiple choice test can preclude the performance test. Rejected because of an ETS score, they are denied the chance to show what they can really accomplish.

The case of Frank Washington. Frank Washington went from a black, working class family in the Northeast to a state university which had de-emphasized the use of SAT scores. He became a campus political activist, an athlete, and a passionate student of psychology. In his sophomore year, he began working with a distinguished professor, helping with experiments and, eventually, undertaking original research in physiological psychology. Both Frank and the professor were enthusiastic about his future in this field.

In his senior year, Frank Washington applied to the psychology department for admission as a graduate student, hoping to continue his studies and research with the professors who had sparked his interest. The admissions committee consisted mostly of his classroom professors, one of whom was an ETS consultant. The committee found his grades and recommendations acceptable, but, like all applicants to the department, Frank was required to take the ETS Graduate Record Examination (GRE). The department had a GRE cutoff score below which all applicants would be rejected. Since Frank was applying for financial aid, he had to exceed a cutoff even higher than the regular one. Frank's score was close, but still below the cutoff. Over heated protests from the professor with whom he had worked, and several other faculty members, Frank was rejected. He took the GRE again with only a minor improvement in score. Most psychology departments at private colleges or out-of-state universities were out of his financial league, and at the few to which he applied, his GRE scores disqualified him. By the end of his senior year, Frank began looking for another career.

The case of Mark Simons. Mark Simons came from a moderately wealthy white family and elite suburban high school where high ETS scores were common. He had his sights set on college biology and a career in medicine. Four years of volunteer work in hospital wards and emergency rooms had instilled in Mark a deep concern with the humanistic aspects of patient care. He covered school sports for the local radio station where his graphic descriptions and outrageous sense of humor won him a considerable public following. Mark had an A average in the high school's college-level advanced placement biology course, a grade rank near the top of his 700 member class; he also had a history of low scores on standardized tests.

Having carefully researched the admission requirements of more than twenty colleges, Mark knew he was in trouble when he received his SAT scores. Always an intense and meticulous worker, he embarked on a systematic campaign to master the SAT. He bought all the cram books at $6 to $10 each. He enrolled in a $275 SAT cram course that friends had reported could produce score gains of more than 100 points. Five nights a week he reported to the conference room of a local motel where dozens of teenagers studied simulated SAT questions and worked through practice tests as cram instructors hovered nearby with stopwatches.

The night before his second SAT, Mark was shaking but determined to succeed. Despite weeks of cram school instruction to proceed quickly and use an optimum guessing strategy on the test, Mark still left major chunks of each SAT section unanswered. He knew he had blown it, and the scores confirmed it--they were lower than the first time.

By now the SAT had become Mark's consuming obsession. He grew morose and cynical, making bitter jokes about his mental limitations. College admissions officers told him to look elsewhere unless he came up with better scores. He sent ETS the registration fee for his third SAT. Money was no object. All around him, by investing in cram books, cram courses, and extra test administrations, friends were trying to buy SAT score points. The way Mark and his parents saw it, much of his future was at stake; since they had the money to spend, even a modest ETS score gain was a bargain at any price. They laid out $300 for a second cram course (another company at another motel), and Mark dropped sportscasting and hospital work for evenings with the stopwatch.

On this third try, Mark steeled himself to follow the strategy: skipping quickly from question to question before he had time to digest the reading passage or work out all the equations, forcing himself to guess whenever he could eliminate at least one of the five multiple-choice options. Mark finished nearly all the questions. But, he finished in confusion, believing he had not mastered the questions and feeling as if he had just completed a game of chance. His scores improved over the previous two administrations, but not enough. Mark was rejected by each of the schools to which he applied. At the age of seventeen, he abandoned his hopes of studying biology or practicing medicine, shifted to an undefined field of study, and began looking for a college that would accept him.

The case of Rosita Ramo. Rosita Ramo, a sixteen-year-old from a working class home who made average grades at a parochial high school, didn't really know if she wanted to go to college. Studies had never been her main interest; she preferred to spend time with her friends when she wasn't putting in twenty to twenty-five hours per week as a waitress in a luncheonette. Outgoing, inquisitive, ambitious, and blessed with an excellent memory, she often wondered if she could be a nurse, community organizer, physical therapist, or stewardess. Rosita was considering junior college, maybe even a four-year school if her parents could afford it and a good opportunity came along. The schools about which she read were all considered to be "non-selective," but, since most of them required the SAT, her counselor suggested she take it. Rosita and several of her friends decided to give it a try. Although she didn't discuss academics much, Rosita had heard all about the SAT. "It's the test that measures how smart you are," she explained.

After she had sent in her registration form, the booklet explaining the test arrived from ETS and her parents urged her to study it carefully. They couldn't go out to buy cram books or spend a week's wages on a course, but they wanted her to do well, and Rosita had always buckled down and studied hard--usually successfully--for big tests and assignments. Yet, Rosita refused to look at the booklet. As the test date approached, she would clam up completely when the subject of the SATs came up. She knew exactly when the test was to be given, but she wouldn't study or discuss it, no matter what. The day before the test, she was visibly upset. Afterwards, when her parents and sisters asked how she did, Rosita shrugged it off, "Ah, I probably did lousy, I don't know, who cares?" She said she was not concerned about the results, "It doesn't really matter how I did. It's a test for smart people isn't it? It doesn't have anything to do with me."

When the envelope arrived from ETS, Rosita refused to open it. She gave it to her mother, saying, "You take it, I don't care." Her father was furious. He opened the envelope and told

Rosita her scores. She said nothing, and went to her room. She never talked to the family about her scores; in fact, for two months she wouldn't talk about her future at all--quite a switch from her previous speculations. Later on, when asked about her ETS scores, Rosita would quickly say that she hadn't paid any attention to them and couldn't even remember what they were, and that her scores were nothing to be surprised or upset about. After all, Rosita explained, "I always knew I was stupid."

The case of Sam Harrison. When Sam Harrison thinks about test scores it is in terms of correlation coefficients and analyses of variance. With his graduate training in statistics and his job as a data analyst for a large government testing agency, Sam has no illusions about what multiple-choice answers can tell about the quality and potential of his mind. Unlike the young people whose perceptions are shaped by ETS before they leave their teens, Sam encountered the test system at an age by which his confidence and aspirations had already been built on the foundation of performance.

Sam's experience and age shielded him from the kind of injury faced by most ETS consumers, the psychological kind which leaves no tangible traces. Instead, due to an unusual physical condition (a degenerative eye disease which attacks the retina) Sam became one of the millions whose life was altered by the power of ETS, but one of the few where the damage was recorded in the concreteness of physical pain.

Sam grew up in an Eastern Kentucky mining town where more than half of the teenagers left school to work before completing the 12th grade. Many of the teachers had never attended college. Books for the county's only library were screened and selected by the Daughters of the American Revolution. The nearest book store was sixty miles away.

At 17, Sam dropped out and joined the Army, where he completed his high school equivalency. He was honorably discharged when a childhood eye disease recurred. Within a few years, with his visual field cut to less than 20 percent of normal sight, he was declared legally blind.

Unable to find a job in his home county, Sam migrated to another state. After supporting himself and the family back home with a series of jobs whose wages never exceeded $60 per week, "I began to seek some way to improve my situation," Sam recalled. He enrolled in the state university. "My Eastern Kentucky education left me ill-prepared for academic competition," Sam later wrote. "My English grammar was atrocious, I wrote poorly, and had no study skills. Due to my decreased vision, I was rarely able to complete the reading assignments for a full time course load. In addition, I was working at a local factory forty-eight hours per week."[11]

Though unable to see more than a few feet in front of him, Sam read with the aid of a magnifying glass. Slowly, deliberately, pausing to rest his eyes after every few lines, he read the books and wrote out his assignments. Maintaining his factory job through all but the last three quarters, Sam put himself through college with a "C" average overall and a "B" in his major, sociology. He went on to a master's degree, with concentration in statistical techniques. After graduation, Sam joined a government agency where he analyzed the test scores of thousands of job applicants.

Gaining admission to college and graduate school, and completing the courses of study had been tough. But Sam's perseverance had impressed admissions officers, who made allowances for his blindness. While his two fields of study had been both physically and intellectually taxing--statistics requires manipulation of thousands of numbers and mathematical symbols, and sociology demands extensive reading--Sam felt that he could accomplish any reasonable task he undertook. Thus, in his early thirties and faced with still deteriorating vision, Sam decided on a bold career change.

Seeking a career where his hard-earned mental discipline could complement his concern for protecting the rights of others who suffered from physical handicaps, Sam decided to become a lawyer. "At present my visual condition seems to be in remission," Sam wrote in explaining his move, "but it could recur at any time and destroy my remaining visual field . . . This situation precludes my obtaining other employment, and . . . recent /vision/ losses threaten my future employability. The jobs for which I am presently qualified all require some visual acuity. I must therefore find a profession which requires the use of my mental abilities rather than my relative visual acuity. I also believe that the study of law would be a logical extension of my previous academic work. I have studied the surfaces of society, and, in my view, the legal system is one of the foundations of society."[12]

While preparing his application, Sam learned his first lesson about the foundations of the legal system: prospective lawyers are screened by the Educational Testing Service. The official law school admission directory, prepared for the Association of American Law Schools and the Law School Admission Council by ETS, informed him that every ABA accredited law school in the U.S. but one required applicants to submit scores from the ETS Law School Admission Test (LSAT). The directory noted that graduation from an accredited law school was required for admission to the bar in "almost all states," including his.[13] Sam learned that unlike the situation when he applied to college and graduate school, the local law schools had many more applicants than places and were not about to give him an exemption from the LSAT requirement. Sam knew that if he wanted to become a lawyer he would have to take the ETS test.

He also understood his doctor's reminder that the intense visual concentration involved in taking the LSAT would elongate his eyeball for extended periods. This pressure would stretch the vitreous strands which hold the retina in place--strands which his disease had eaten away at the root and, if broken, threatened a permanent loss of vision.

Sam was in a better position than most to know precisely what the ETS test meant. For Sam, this ETS test meant that his aspirations and plans had been brought to the razor's edge. At one end stood the sum total of Sam Harrison's past and ambitions: his experience, his education, his plans for himself and his community, and his personal qualities both intellectual and

18

physical. At the other end stood the people whose decisions about him would determine whether he would have a chance to become a lawyer. In between stretched the ETS test, the razor-thin link he had to cross in order to join his aspirations with the resources needed to make them possible.

Sam's experience was a dramatic example of the conditions created yearly for millions of individuals by the ETS test system. People whose decisions would have a big effect on Sam's life were going to believe the ETS claim that his test scores would measure something important about his mind. They were going to base a significant part of their evaluation of his thinking and potential on his ETS test score. Sam wasn't much impressed with ETS's claim, stated in the LSAT literature, that the test was a measure of his "mental capabilities";[14] he wasn't going to let the score change his estimate of his own potential. But, those law school decisions were important; they would determine if he ever got a chance to prove his potential in legal practice.

Sam called ETS and explained that, due to his eye disorder, he had to pause to rest his eyes after each passage he read using his magnifying glass. He told of the danger he faced if he failed to rest, mentioned the warning of his physician, and asked to have his time on the test extended.

Sam's request was not unfamiliar at ETS. Others like it had come up several times the previous year in meetings of the Law School Admission Council, the client organization convened by ETS to sponsor the LSAT. According to Council minutes, ETS executive Anthony Glockler had informed the Council's Test

Development and Research Committee that "his office receives a number of letters from blind candidates stating that they have been denied admission to law school because they cannot submit an LSAT score."[15] Minutes of another Council meeting noted that several Council members and ETS executives had been "contacted by a blind student who contended that blind and severely visually handicapped candidates should have the option of a test in braille or be provided with a reader and unlimited time."[16] Reaction to the grievances of the blind students was mixed. "This is another example of law schools using the test as a whipping boy," complained Council member Francis X. McDermott.[17]

Other members suggested the development of braille and larger type versions of the LSAT. Council officials Russell Simpson of Harvard and Emerson Spies of Virginia disagreed. "Messrs. Spies and Simpson both felt that the only need to offer the test to blind candidates is for public relations," the minutes noted. They argued that since a test given under such special conditions could not be fairly compared with the regular LSAT, there was no purpose to making the special tests in the first place.[18] A similar point was later made in an internal ETS operations manual which remarked that since there were so few handicapped students, "no meaningful statistical studies" could be conducted on the validity of the LSAT for the handicapped.[19]

Such doubts did not figure in the options of Sam Harrison. Administrators at the law schools requiring him to take the test informed Sam that a time extension was out of the question. "Everyone to whom I spoke stated emphatically that the time limit for the test could not be changed due to contractual arrangements with Educational Testing Service" Sam wrote. "The Law school cannot alter the time limit of the Law School Admission Test,"[20] one dean later explained.

When Sam called ETS he was told that time extensions would impair the validity of the LSAT.* When Sam pointed out that time extensions <u>were</u> available on the Graduate Record Examination (GRE), ETS responded that this was not the case for the LSAT. The rationale for this policy was explained in a February 12, 1974 statement from ETS executive Robert G. Wiltsey which was circulated to all accredited law schools. "Were we to allow more testing time for the physically handicapped," Wiltsey wrote, "those students would be treated and judged in an even less comparable way than they are at present. The results for the time, money and unsettling experience involved would be even more questionable. Giving more testing time would not mean that we would be providing better, more accurate, reliable and valid results. Such a procedure would not 'more adequately display the intelligence of these very capable and mentally alert persons' [as the president of the Kent State University Student Bar Association had contended in a letter to ETS]. <u>They would probably obtain higher scores, but so would anyone, given more time</u>. . .Because of these very real problems, some national testing programs do

---

*Braille and large type editions of the LSAT were first made available the year Sam applied. However, Sam did not read braille, and although the large type edition provided additional rest time <u>between</u> test sections, no rest time was allowed within sections, which was when Sam needed it. By 1978, the braille edition was no longer offered. The time limits remained in force.[21]

not provide any arrangements for the physically or visually handicapped."[22] (Emphasis added.)

Sam Harrison lost his appeal to the authorities at ETS. Though informed about the prospect of injury, they would not yield to ensure the safety of his eyesight. Weighing the danger to his sight and the future of his career, Sam felt that he had little choice. He decided to take the LSAT.

On the appointed day, Sam arrived at the test center and, like the hundreds of other candidates there with him, was finger-printed by the ETS proctors. He then took out his magnifying glass and when the proctor said "go," began to read through the LSAT. In order to prepare the answer sheets for the high-speed mark-sensitive scoring machines, each answer had to be marked in one of a row of bubbles, each less than a quarter of an inch in length. Even when Sam bent his magnifying glass close to the paper, the charts and graphs were just not legible. Moving as quickly as possible through the questions, pausing to rest occasionally, but trying to push on to the end of the test and the beginning of a legal career, Sam didn't come close to finishing.

Later that week, Sam started to suffer incidents of "simple vision loss"; all of a sudden, everything would go black. By the time he checked into the hospital, Sam's eyesight had begun to show new permutations. "All of a sudden I'm seeing all these fantastic light shows, it was indeed beautiful." Sam had suffered a retinal tear and two retinal detachments. The vitreous membranes had torn a hole in the retina, and then two had broken away themselves. In addition, "flotas," little bits of dislocated tissue, were floating freely in the liquid of his eye. Both Sam and his physician attributed the injury to the prolonged elongation of the eyeball caused by his taking the LSAT within the prescribed time limit. Sam explained what happened to his retina with a graphic analogy, "It's like taking a piece of paper and it gets wet and just gives there, the retina gave and broke." Sam underwent an operation and spent several days in the hospital.

For the next month, Sam suffered a number of other retinal tears associated with the disruption caused by the first one, and endured a partial freezing of his left eyeball known as "carotherapy." He was told by his physician that his vision might be permanently diminished. Later that spring, when his scores came back and law school admissions officers told him that the scores ruled him out of consideration, Sam wrote to ETS, asking that they invalidate the results of his test. He enclosed a statement from his ophthalmologist who reported that Sam had suffered "superior temporal retinal tear and local retinal detachment."[23] Sam received no response from ETS.

Sam Harrison's experience with ETS was unusual in that the pain and damage were both physical and exceptional. Detached retinas can be detected with medical instruments and are widely acknowledged as injuries--aberrations that are not supposed to happen.

Neither of these things can be said about the pain suffered by Gary Vladik, Frank Washington, Rosita Ramo and their fellow victims. Aborted careers and damaged self-images are not subject to easy measurement and are not recorded in injury statistics. In fact, rather than representing an injury that is not supposed to happen, the pain these students suffered is merely accepted as a normal result of the routine functioning of the ETS test system. Unlike most consumer products, the ETS test is not created to serve the person using it. Instead, the ETS test is created to empower those <u>above</u> the user--to help colleges and universities judge the minds of people who seek their favor, and make decisions that affect their futures. With such a function, it is to be expected that some test takers will be pained by the judgment the test hands down about them. But to the testing industry and its supporters in academe, the person who has been shown by the test to have less "aptitude" than they believed may be seen as deserving sympathy, but not the redress due a victim of an unjust injury.

Thus, within the logic of the ETS test system, the pain of people like Frank Washington and Rosita Ramo is perhaps sad, but certainly not an injustice. In an interview, ETS Executive Vice President Robert J. Solomon explained:

Q: What would you say to individuals who, because of their scores on ETS tests, have not been able to pursue the career options they wanted to? For example, we've gotten quite a few letters from people who apparently take their scores very seriously. One said, "My life has been sadly sidetracked, mainly as a result of very poor scores on ETS tests." Or another said of her scores, and the way they were used in terms of her career choice: "It crushed my soul." What would you say to those people?

A: (Solomon): Well, a number of things. First of all, I find it unfortunate that they think so. I hope it isn't so. I fully understand why people are upset by taking tests and test scores.

Q: Why is that?

A: (Solomon): None of us, I don't know anybody who likes taking a test, including me. There are very few people who do. It is a, it's a difficult experience . . . It's not just ETS tests, it's any kind of testing situation. And, I don't think we should pretend that people like necessarily having their egos challenged.[24]

Once ETS assumed that it had the ability and authority to judge people's minds scientifically, its belief that it could not be held responsible for pain caused by its verdicts followed logically. In their eyes, that pain grew either from an unfortunate but necessary adjustment to the hard facts of life (as reflected by the verdict), or from misunderstanding or "misuse" of the verdict, in President Turnbull's words, from "some students and some institutions /which/ have created an aura of importance around these test scores."[25]

The legitimacy of the test itself is assumed. Mr. Solomon resorts to medical analogy in an attempt to convey its integrity: "I don't think we could say in a blanket way that we are responsible directly for every test misuse any more than, for example, a manufacturer of a lifesaving vaccine can be responsible for misuse by a doctor. . . . If that doctor misuses it because he's ignorant or stupid I don't think you would say the manufacturer of the vaccine is responsible."[26]

By the logic of the authorities who run it, the ETS test system has no victims, only those misled by ignorance or those who simply have a painful time in accepting their proper role in life.

In a 1960 Columbia University speech to guidance counsellors, College Board President and ETS trustee Dr. Frank H. Bowles explored the lighter side of learning about the quality of one's mind. Bowles illustrated the impact of telling students their SAT scores (a policy begun at Bowles' initiative in 1958) by regaling his colleagues with an amusing domestic anecdote:

> It is curious now to realize that only two years ago there was very bitter opposition within the College Entrance Examination Board to the very idea of releasing scores to schools /high schools/ so that they could, in turn, release them to students. There was great fear that students would have their values warped by learning their own scores, but I have learned from hearing my own children's conversations that SAT scores have now become one of the peer group measuring devices. One unfortunate may be dismissed with the phrase, "That jerk--he only made 420!" The bright, steady student is appreciated with his high 600, and the unsuspected genius with his 700 is held in awe. This is not exactly the use of College Board scores we had in mind when we decided to authorize their distribution, but it's possible to think of many worse, so perhaps we had better not complain.[27]

More than ten years after Dr. Bowles' little joke, his successor at ETS and the College Board, Dr. Sidney P. Marland, noted with approval that ETS scores were routinely altering perceptions of the worth of individuals--not only by schools, but in the eyes of people's parents and friends as well.

> The College Entrance Examination Board, without necessarily meaning to, has become a universal symbol of academic quality and prestige in the eyes of high school students, parents and teachers. To be preoccupied with taking the College Board's tests is viewed as important, worthy, desirable and commendable. Not to be so preoccupied is viewed as something less important, less worthy.
>
> One may readily observe that this is as it should be. . . . In at least some parts of the country a student is viewed by his school, his peers, his parents and social institutions, first according to whether or not he even took the tests; then of course, if he enjoys this status he is viewed according to his scores. . . . Altogether, it is probably a good thing.[28]

As Henry Chauncey's vision of bounded hope implied--and a number of his successors have come close to making explicit--the delimiting of ambition is as much a part of the ETS test system as the sharpening of soft lead pencils. So, much as it would like, ETS cannot explain away the pain of people like Frank Washington and Rosita Ramo as self-inflicted: it is a direct reaction to the conditions imposed on students by ETS and the powerful institutions and interests it serves. Simply, ETS can change a person's opportunities and the way others think about that person's mind. This power translates into the power to inflict pain.

For most corporations such a power is only tolerated as an irregular accident, such as when one of their products or machines breaks down and unwittingly injures. Even then, the victim is given the right of redress. But, since 1948, the Educational Testing Service has routinely assumed the power to say "yes" to the hopes of some and a crushing "no" to the plans of others.

ETS executives, such as Robert Solomon, try to deny the significance of this power. In an interview, Mr. Solomon attempted to soften the human implications of Henry Chauncey's plan:

Q: Mr. Chauncey said in his '49-50 <u>Annual Report</u> that one of the effects of the use of ETS tests was that, in his words, "Hope will be kept within reasonable bounds." Do you think that's true? Do you think that's appropriate?

A: (Solomon): That hope will be kept within reasonable bounds? Well, I don't know, that's /chuckles/--I don't know what Henry Chauncey meant by that, so, and I don't,

A: (Solomon, continued) I don't, I didn't read that part, so it's, for the moment for me it's out of context. I'm not, but I'll try and answer the questions, just I can't quite answer it in terms of--

(1949-50 <u>Annual Report</u> is handed to Mr. Solomon)

--Where? I'm sorry.

Q: At the top of the page there, beginning paragraph.

A: (Solomon): Let me say I think in terms of what I think the intention of that statement is that, I, I guess, yeah, I would agree that to make one's way in the world, one should try to understand oneself as best one can and understand how one relates to the larger society and larger community of people in which one operates, and, within that, do one's darnedest to reach the goals that one elects for oneself to reach. I think we have to have hope. And I don't think Henry Chauncey was saying that we shouldn't have hope. I think we've gotta have hope. I think people should, should try their darnedest --if they want to try their darnedest. I think, incidentally, they have the option of not wanting to try their darnedest, if they want to, as well. But I think, again, I happen to be one who believes that, giving people information about themselves is useful and that all of us make better decisions about anything we're talking about, and better decisions either as individuals or groups if we have information. <u>I don't happen to believe</u> that a lack of information results in wiser decisions. That, that's uh, an article of personal faith.

Q: Uh huh.

A: (Solomon): So I want to know as much about myself, I want to know as much about the world in which I live, and I think you do too. I think in part that's why you're doing this study.[29]

Regardless of how it is viewed, the underlying fact is inescapable: the ETS test system causes many individuals painful upheavals. Whenever widespread pain is inflicted on people, it is essential to ask why. It is important to keep in the forefront of any such inquiry the experience of victims.

CHAPTER II

ROSEDALE: POWER AND PRIVILEGE AT ETS

"Hidden somewhere in the 400 acres of peace and quiet," wrote one observer, "the hum and whirl of computers go unheard, not unlike the 'unheard melodies' of the Grecian urn. Facts and data pour out in a ceaseless stream directed at the improvement of education and learning."[1]

On a secluded, landscaped retreat off Rosedale Road near Princeton, New Jersey, an IBM 3031 computer and a high-speed printer work 24 hours a day, every day of the year.[2] The computer, "The Wizard of OS" (Operating Systems) to intimates, coordinates the largest data bank of personal educational and psychological information in the world: it sorts files on more than thirty-two million persons from one hundred nations.[3] A bank of coded microfiche and a library of more than 40,000 computer tapes supplement the billion bytes of direct-access storage available to the machine's magnetic memory. Seventy technicians and a staff of IBM consultants work three shifts daily in the artificially lit, humidity-regulated room. Entry is controlled by pressure plates, and high-security keys activate sliding doors. "Most of the sounds are produced by a machine, and instructions come from a loudspeaker."[4]

This room occupies the center of a massive system which reaches from the central office outward to affect the thoughts and careers of millions. "Maybe only the C.I.A.," ETS executives concluded after a private December 13, 1972 meeting, "has greater and better capacities . . . for information collection, storage, and retrieval."[5]

This is the Educational Testing Service. ETS has more customers than new car buyers of Ford and General Motors combined.[6] ETS' claim is dramatically different than those made by corporate sellers of material goods. It will not only assess the quality of your mind, but also influence judgments about your potential in life.

On the morning of February 24, 1979, groups of people converged on an American embassy, an Army base, nine universities, a technical institute and an American cultural center. Acting on instructions from the ETS central office, they moved to their rendezvous points through the streets of Belgrade, Yugoslavia; Cape Town, South Africa; Natchez, Mississippi; Scranton, Pennsylvania; Moscow, Idaho; Kathmandu, Nepal; Morgantown, West Virginia; Stuttgart, Germany; Queens, New York; Benghazi, Libya; Malibu, California; Fort Wayne, Indiana; and Montivideo, Uruguay.[7] Each had a common destination: one of the more than 5,000 ETS test centers, each part of an international network with more outposts than the U.S. Department of Defense, and which extends, in the words of an ETS Annual Report, "from Antarctica to Zaire."[8]

Standardized test booklets and supervisors paid and directed by ETS were waiting as the test-takers arrived, each at the appointed hour in their own locality. The booklets were distributed in serial order so that ETS security forces could reconstruct the seating arrangement. After reading aloud from the ETS manual and, per instruction, synchronizing their watches at 8:59 a.m., the supervisors issued the command at precisely 9:00 a.m.--"Begin work!"--and aspirants worldwide had exactly 175 minutes to answer the multiple-choice questions prepared for them by ETS.[9]

Back at headquarters, operators and investigators from the ETS Office of Test Security were poised to answer emergency phone calls or cables from anywhere within the test center network. Assisted, when necessary, by private detectives, police handwriting analysts, and computers programmed to spot suspiciously high scores,[10] members of the Office--whose ranks have included veterans of Naval Intelligence, the FBI and the CIA--were responsible for preventing breaches of test question security.[11] Test center supervisors had been briefed with stern orders:

> You, as supervisor, are responsible for the security of all tests from the moment of their receipt until they are returned to ETS . . . ETS has developed the procedures . . . If you follow them carefully, you will protect yourself as well as ETS in those situations in which most breaches of security occur. Moreover, should there actually be a breach of security, you will be in a position to say when it occurred and . . . who was responsible . . .

> <u>Before the Test</u>

> Lock all materials in a safe, cabinet or closet to which only you, or you and a few specifically authorized personnel, have access . . .

> <u>During the Test</u>

> Generally, you should permit only one candidate at a time to go to the rest room. If two or more candidates leave the testing room at one time, a proctor should accompany them . . .

> (B)e sure to protect the test materials while the candidates are leaving the room . . .

> Lock up test books and answer sheets during the lunch period.

After the Test

Return the test materials to ETS as soon as possible. If you cannot do this immediately, lock them up until you can return them. Security must not be relaxed until you are certain that the sealed cartons of tests have been received by REA Express or other carriers . . .

Other Security Measures

Report any breach of security to ETS by telephone as soon as possible without interrupting the actual test administration. Furthermore, do not dismiss the candidates until telephone contact with ETS has been made . . .[12]

In February of 1973, ETS became the first organization, other than the military, courts, police or FBI, to begin mass fingerprinting of the public.[13] "It's an unhappy sight," wrote the legal periodical *Juris Doctor*, "young men and women, many just out of their teens, nervously being fingerprinted. With suspicious guards watching every move, their faces are solemn and drawn. A scene from a big city precinct house? Hardly. The scene is set at any one of the country's ubiquitous LSAT [ETS Law School Admission Test] testing centers . . ."[14] Responding to reports that candidates were hiring impersonators to boost their LSAT scores, the Law School Admission Council (the LSAT sponsor) and ETS began requiring all candidates to present a photo ID at the test center, give a handwriting sample, sign a pledge that they were, indeed, who they said they were, and submit to thumbprinting. According to private Council minutes, consideration was also given to photographing each candidate at the test center, taking a group photo of everyone in the room during the test, and offering "a bounty or reward for information concerning impersonation."[15] But the thumbprinting worked so well that, according to the director of Test Security, by the summer of 1975 ETS officials were talking about extending fingerprinting to other ETS programs.[16]

"In a country which is rather confused and not very well organized in almost all social fields," Nobel-prize winning economist and advocate of central social planning Dr. Gunnar Myrdal told a 1974 ETS conference, "this institution /ETS/ stands out as a complete success."[17] Thirty years after its founding, ETS could claim to influence, among other things, the chance to go to half of United States colleges, 75 per cent of the graduate programs and 100 per cent of the law schools; the opportunity to sell insurance in Illinois, fight fire or walk a police beat in Philadelphia, become an officer in the Liberian Merchant Marine, practice law in forty-two states, or receive a scholarship from the State of Georgia, Union Carbide, or the Brotherhood of Steamfitters.[18] Every year, seven to nine million people trying to advance through thousands of educational institutions and fifty different occupations[19] are judged by a multiple-choice test, written according to the directions of one looseleaf manual stored at ETS.[20]

From around the world, answer sheets are returned to headquarters in Princeton, New Jersey.[21] Propelled by jets of compressed air, these are passed single-file through the entry chute of an electronic scoring machine, the custom-built Westinghouse MRC mark-sensitive scanner. Scanning at the rate of over three sheets per second--24,000 answer sheet sides per hour--the MRC scores pencil marks representing the answers to millions of multiple-choice questions each year.[22] The scores are printed out and forwarded to the mail room where 230,000 letters are processed in an average day.[23] The scores are then sorted into outgoing envelopes embossed with the ETS monogram. On the outside is printed a message to open the letter immediately. On the inside is a quantitative evaluation of the recipient's mind on such qualities as "aptitude," "achievement," "mental capabilities," and "competence."[24]

By the early 1960s, roughly a quarter of U.S. teenagers were taking a single ETS test, the Scholastic Aptitude Test (SAT), used for college admission. By 1976-77 the number of SATs taken (which slightly overstates the number of individuals tested since some take it twice) was equivalent to 33 per cent of the U.S. 18 year-old population, 45 per cent of that year's high school graduates, and 70 per cent of that year's entering college students.[25]

The SAT was but a single layer of the ETS test system which a person could first encounter at age four (in the Preschool Inventory of Personal-Social Responsiveness) and then at all levels of education up through licensing and promotion on the job. Unlike many products, the ETS test entered people's experience not in the context of a routine transaction, but as a potentially decisive event in their life. Speaking only of the SATs, the College Board Commission on Tests wrote:

> One thing is clear: modern economy and modern society being what they are in the United States, anything—including obviously tests—that mediates college entry helps to determine in the process who will eventually get in which graduate schools, who will eventually (or immediately in the case of those who do not go to graduschool) get which or no jobs, who meets and eventually marries whom, and so forth.[26]

Former U.S. Commissioner of Education, College Board President, and ex officio ETS trustee, Dr. Sidney P. Marland described this influence in the College Board newspaper in June of 1974 under the heading, "CEEB President Sees Expanding Role for College Board in Society."

> "We are really the only voluntary association in the land that can offer an alternative to government prescription as to what shall be the way--the criteria through which our society offers upward mobility to its people."
>
> In most nations, Marland noted, the standard-setting function is performed by the government, by law, by regulations emanating from a central ministry which prescribes times, places, curricula, standards.
>
> "As a voluntary organization," he said, "we do this and together we must sustain this uniqueness--through a fraternity that embraces all relevant parts." (emphasis in original)[27]

The Big People

ETS dedicated the Henry Chauncey Conference Center on May 5, 1974 with champagne cocktails for selected friends.[28] The Reverend Paul C. Reinert, S.J., an ETS Trustee, delivered the benediction. "Heavenly Father . . . Thank you for Henry Chauncey. Thank you for all the big people without whom all this would never have happened. But thank you, too, for the little people who carried on so much of its complicated work."[29]

"We are just delighted at the fact that so many old friends and members of the 'family' could be here to join us," said President Turnbull.[30] ETS trustees, past and present, joined "prominent figures in education and government" to christen the $3 million hotel-conference center and celebrate ETS' twenty-fifth anniversary.[31]

Eighty-four individuals served on the ETS board of trustees from the organization's founding in 1948 through 1974. They included representatives from many levels of education and numbered among them such figures as the late James B. Conant, Harvard University president and U.S. High Commissioner to Germany; John A. Perkins, Dunn and Bradstreet president, undersecretary of the Department of Health, Education and Welfare, and consultant to the DuPont family; William J. McGill, Columbia University president, Texaco director, and member of the current National Academy of Sciences panel studying testing in the United States; J. William Fulbright, University of Arkansas president, U.S. Senator and Chairman of the Senate Foreign Relations Committee; Wallace McGregor, Kaiser Aluminum and Chemical Corporation vice president; Clark Kerr, Carnegie Commission on Higher Education chairman, University of California president, Rockefeller Foundation trustee; Caryl P. Haskins, Council on Foreign Relations and Rand Corporation trustee, and Yale Corporation fellow; John W. Gardner, Carnegie Corporation president, HEW secretary, and founder of Common Cause; Malcom Moos, University of Minnesota president, Ford Foundation director of policy and planning, and adviser on public affairs to the Messrs. Rockefeller; John Brademas, member of Congress, former chairman of the Select Education Subcommittee, legislative architect for the National Institute of Education, and House Majority Whip; and Juanita Kreps, Duke University vice president, director of Eastman Kodak, the New York Stock Exchange, Western Electric, R.J. Reynolds, and former Secretary of Commerce.[32]

A file of chauffeured ETS cars wound through the 400 acre Rosedale headquarters. The campus, formerly the site of the Stony Brook Hunt Club, had been personally selected by Henry Chauncey and his wife during a country hike in the winter of 1954.[33] "The gently rolling character of the land lends itself to a campus-like setting," reports the ETS grounds history. "The buildings, whose brick and fieldstone facades blend agreeably with the surrounding country-side, lie amid gracefully curving lawns and flagstone walks." Hedges of rose, autumn olive, and shrubs "selected for their ability to attract songbirds" provide food and cover for wildfowl and deer.[34] The staff of fulltime groundskeepers give form to what the house newspaper calls "Rosedale's arboreal wonderland." "Clusters of trees in seemingly careless arrangement belie the care with which they were placed. Small wooded sections, allowed to retain their natural characteristics, add pleasing contrast."[35]

The putting green, tennis courts, jogging trails, picnic areas and homegrown vegetable garden are barely visible amid the hundreds of trimmed and watered acres. In the summer, employees folkdance on the lawns. "The feeling," notes the grounds history, "is one of quiet charm and natural beauty."[36]

To the accompaniment of the Columbus Boychoir, the guests arrived and opened the Henry Chauncey Conference Center. A bronze plaque announced the Center motto: ". . . to serve education . . . ." "The central structure is a new, two-story complex of . . . striking contemporary design," the ETS brochure explained, "whose natural wood facades and stone accents blend with the rural landscape. . . .

The spacious lobby with vaulted ceiling, bluestone floor and corner fireplace opens on a terrace commanding a view of a picturesque pond and the rolling country-side. A spacious, three-level lounge serves as a center for hospitality."

Tastefully appointed guest rooms, furnished for elegance and comfort by designer Edith Queller of New York City featured alcoves "in which 2 or 3 people can gather to chat or lift a glass." For diversions beyond the library, the sauna, country walks, swimming pool, and putting green, reservations and limousine service for visits to nearby country clubs were available.[37]

Under the care of hotelier William Shearn (formerly of the Waldorf Astoria's Marco Polo Club, Laurence Rockefeller's Caneel Bay Plantation, New York's Hotel Pierre, and a Peruvian coastal resort),[38] the Conference Center has carried on the ETS tradition of entertaining visiting dignitaries. Three decades of hosting--including visits by Eleanor Roosevelt, the first Soviet delegation to study U.S. education, high officials from more than forty foreign countries, and scores of cabinet members, senators, corporation presidents, and eminent scholars--have accumulated important friends for ETS and a store of Rosedale legend.[39]

A glossy, twelve-page booklet for Rosedale visitors traces the "entire recorded history" of the ETS guest house ("The Farmhouse") from the earliest deed dated June 17, 1769. The ETS publication offers memorable glimpses of Rosedale family history. There was the time, for example, when ill-secured draperies fell from the curtain rod and buried a trustee's wife. Or that dinner party when a hard-of-hearing chairman of the board kept the servant's quarters buzzing all evening by resting his foot on the call button concealed under the table.[40]

Set apart from the body of the campus by a stretch of forest, the ETS President's residence, built in 1973 and valued at $250,000 in 1974, was featured along with the New Jersey Governor's mansion in a 1973 charity tour. "The curving interior walls and open floor plan are ideal for large-scale entertaining; the extravagant use of glass makes the most of five acres of woodland. . . ."[41]

The gracious accoutrements of Rosedale are not merely for the comfort of ETS professionals and guests; they are designed to advance the organization's larger purpose. An in-house memo on "The Henry Chauncey Conference Center (1972)" explains:

> While learning something about ETS, those who visit the Center will also come to recognize the wealth of human resources that is represented on the ETS staff and the extent of their devotion to the hallmarks of ETS: adherence to high professional standards and quality of performance, dedication to the educational community and all those it serves, and a deep and concerned interest in the individual.[42]

The ETS information services office explains that, while the Center's "primary purpose . . . is to provide meeting and living space for the hundreds of test development and program people who come to ETS each year from all over the world," it is also "used extensively by corporations, foundations and government agencies."[43] ETS runs periodic briefings for local, state, and federal legislators, staffers, and officials, such as the visit of Congressman Brademas' House Select Education Subcommittee where--after "an overview of ETS" and a tour of Rosedale featuring the Infant Lab*--President Turnbull, Executive Vice President Robert Solomon, and ten ETS professionals presented papers which, Chairman Brademas said, would be used "to help map the areas of Congressional intent in education."[44] A number of important convocations, such as the private 1977 Ford Foundation meeting on the Media and Business attended by Walter Wriston, William Colby, and others, or the summer-long 1975 retreat at which ATT executives gathered to plan a new marketing strategy, have found ETS facilities and staff congenial to their purposes.[45]

In April of 1978, a secret society of European nobility, world leaders and multinational executives known as the Bilderberg Conference called "100 world leaders from 22 Western European and North American Countries" to Rosedale for their annual meeting on global economic and military policy. Even in a community accustomed to gatherings of power, "a major stir was created," went the ETS account, when "limousines and embassy vehicles arrived for the conference carrying such notables as Henry Kissinger, Zbigniew Brzezinski and General Alexander Haig." Some thirty armed guards ringed the Conference Center, taking up positions according to their function. On the outer perimeter were the Mercer County Police--themselves barred from entering the meeting--who were instructed to keep press, public, and uninvited guests at bay. Inside, Secret Service agents, ETS security, and private bodyguards screened all entrants according to color-coded

---

*See Glossary

ID cards. According to members of the ETS serving staff (proceedings of the meeting were not made public), the meeting consisted of two sessions, one for mapping plans for increased economic cooperation between the Western and Soviet blocs, and the other for identifying world "hot spots" where the outbreak of strategically important wars might be imminent. The latter featured a discussion of the neutron bomb by a government specialist.

During breaks in the two-day session, the visitors toured the Rosedale facilities and renewed old acquaintances. David Rockefeller, Chairman of Chase Manhattan Bank, conducted business with a group of Northern European investors; Frank Cary, Chairman of IBM, mingled with the crowd, and Sir Alec Douglas Home, Chairman of the Conference and former Prime Minister of Britain asked for an introduction to President Turnbull to congratulate him on the fine work ETS was doing. The Bilderberg session closed with a banquet in the Conference Center's elevated, glass-enclosed dining room where President Turnbull dined with Fiat President and Italian political leader Giovanni Agnelli and an assortment of dukes, counts and statesmen. "It is also hoped," notes the ETS memo on the Center, "that by meeting on the ETS site, conferees will have the opportunity to learn something about ETS, even if only by osmosis."[46]

ETS has tax exempt, non-profit status. It is exempted from federal taxes by the same section of the Internal Revenue Code (Section 501 (c) 3) which exempts garden clubs, civic groups, cooperative nursery schools and burial societies. Despite its worldwide sales to millions of people and $94 million annual income, ETS is considered nonprofit because it pays no money to stockholders and plows its revenues back into the company.[47] Money from what Vice President Samuel Messick calls ETS' "non-profits" -- ranging from 10 per cent to 75 per cent of income from individual tests and services -- is reinvested in salaries, Rosedale maintenance, research and development and capital for corporate expansion.[48]

ETS sales, which doubled every five years from 1948 through the early 1970s[49] have "served to generate a sizable pool of retained earnings,"[50] which supports, among other things, a small blue chip portfolio featuring holdings of Bethlehem Steel, Monsanto, Pittsburgh Plate Glass and RCA.[51]

ETS is working from a long tradition of corporate support for the science of mental measurement. Between 1900 and 1947, Andrew Carnegie, John D. Rockefeller and their foundations gave more than $7 million to the testing organizations which later merged to form ETS.[52] Such leaders as the late Thomas J. Watson, Jr., President of IBM; Howard C. Sheperd, Chairman of the board of First National City Bank (now Citibank); as well as directors of Johnson and Johnson, Time, Inc., and the investment firms Lazard Freres, Kuhn, Loeb and Company, and Lehman Brothers have joined ETS trustee committees to lend their guidance.[53] These men of commerce sat on the advisory committees which "help ETS to define its special role in the educational community." They were serving not just in their roles as controllers of production but as, in the words of an ETS report, "'consumers' of the educational product, i.e. members of industry."[54]

In its 1967-77 master plan, ETS saw a bright future in providing "innovations to help handle the mounting load of students," ranging from tests which covered all levels of education to computer analysis of financial aid applications. "/I/t is clear that if ETS is to serve education effectively," the plan stated, "it must become intimately linked to all aspects of the educational enterprise both in the United States and abroad." While anticipating resistance to this undertaking, ETS counted on corporations as allies. "It is possible that by 1977 some of the innovations will be showing some genuine results," the plan concluded, "but this will probably depend to a considerable extent on how successful various external and internal influences, including those exerted by private industry, will be in breaking down the probable resistance of the forces of conservatism in education--the local school boards, the teachers' unions and professional groups, the administrators' organizations, and the bureaucracy in general."[55]

As a corporation backed by the nation's most powerful institutions and charged with a mission to measure people's minds, ETS was on its way to establishing a test system which bypassed traditional authorities and crossed national boundaries to enter the lives of millions.

Through the Balance of Life

"At the age of twenty-five," wrote ETS Vice President Henry Dyer in a 1974 company history, "ETS has had reasonable success in fulfilling the objectives set forth at its founding. . . . This record springs not only from the diligence of the officers and staff but from the foresight of those 'social inventors' who knew their idea's time had come." Though different in many particulars from Henry Chauncey's 1950 plan for a national census of human abilities, the vision of a centralized national test system had become reality by the time Dyer wrote. "To recognize that ETS was a social invention," Dyer concluded, "requires no more than an understanding of the importance testing has assumed in college admissions, student guidance, scholarship awards, professional certification, and occupational licensing."[56]

Four years later, in 1978, President Turnbull confidentially reflected in a corporate strategy memo, "We grew to be a large omnipresent organization . . . a powerful, little-known organization that many people had to deal with involuntarily in order to gain (or be denied) access to educational opportunities."[57] One internal staff study even claimed that "Educational Testing Service . . . singularly influences the educational pursuits of a vast majority of this country's students. ETS in its role as gatekeeper, is necessarily an impediment to the ideal that all individuals should have unfettered and continuous opportunity to pursue their educational interests and utilize their academic talents."[58] ETS dominance of higher education admissions testing had become so self-evident at Rosedale that one program director, reporting on plans for a new occupational guidance test, could note in passing that "ETS may become the gatekeeper for jobs in addition to being the gatekeeper for colleges it presently is."[59]

In only thirty years, ETS had assembled a test system which defied comparison with conventional corporate empires. In defining and centralizing the means by which many of the nation's most powerful institutions judged people's potential, ETS' direct influence on the deployment of human resources was vastly out of proportion to the dollar figures listed on its balance sheet. Thousands of institutions controlling tens of billions of dollars and millions of educational opportunities and jobs were linked by a single test system which ranked minds and to a significant extent allocated rewards and penalties on the basis of ETS scores. Perhaps more than any single American organization--business or governmental--ETS was in a position to determine what individuals would be permitted to attempt, and to influence their position in the educational and economic hierarchy. The reach of the ETS test system, noted a confidential 1972 study prepared for President Turnbull, extended to "the millions of adolescents whose course through school and into jobs and careers is now daily affected by what does or doesn't happen to them through testing, and the millions of adults who may increasingly be affected by testing that can extend through the balance of life."[60]

Even a brief survey of the ETS test system suggests the sweep of its range and the extent of its power.

Preschool and Elementary. The tests begin before the age of five with the Cooperative Preschool Inventory, advertised by ETS to measure within fifteen minutes "achievement in areas regarded as necessary for success in school," such as perception, thinking and verbal expression.[61] It is the first in a series of ETS instruments to follow students through their elementary and high school careers.

President Chauncey explained in the 1955-56 ETS Annual Report that these tests would purport to tell teachers and parents far more about their children than merely how well they performed classroom tasks of reading, writing and arithmetic. In describing the ETS Sequential Tests of Educational Progress (STEP), Chauncey invoked Alfred North Whitehead: "'Though knowledge is one chief aim of intellectual education there is another ingredient, vaguer but greater, and more dominating in its importance. The ancients called it "wisdom." You cannot be wise without some basis of knowledge; but you may easily acquire knowledge and remain bare of wisdom.' The STEP tests represent one of the first attempts to measure this 'wisdom' and to use tests to encourage its development."[62] Chauncey cited the example of STEP social studies tests, which would test students not just on knowledge but on their "understandings" of social and political values such as "the rights . . . and responsibilities of free men" and "the means by which society directs and regulates the behavior of its members."[63]

The 1978 ETS Annual Report announced that with STEP, the CIRCUS tests for young children and the School and College Ability Tests (SCAT) for older students, "ETS now has tests available--for the first time--that permit monitoring a student's progress in major areas of instruction from preschool through the twelfth grade."[64]

High School Admission, Graduation and Equivalency. At Andover, Groton, the Dhahran Aramco School, and more than 450 private secondary schools--including many of the world's most expensive prep schools--applicants are screened by the ETS Secondary School Admission Test (SSAT).[65] In some 200 U.S. school districts, public high school students are also screened by ETS tests, but for entirely different purposes. The rapidly growing ETS Basic Skills Assessment program tested 70,000 seniors in 1977, in many cases to determine if they would be permitted to graduate. In addition to developing the tests, ETS "staff . . . provided guidance to district personnel regarding methods of setting appropriate standards."[66]

In 1978, more than half a million people sought to advance their schooling and job prospects by seeking a high school equivalency diploma from the American Council on Education. The applicants included workers, homemakers, and military personnel. They were granted or denied the diploma on the basis of an ETS test score on the General Educational Development test (GED). When this test is offered to federal employees, they are allowed in many agencies not only to attend preparatory courses for the GED but also to take the test on government time, indicating its significance in personal advancement.[67]

College Admission, Financial Aid, and Placement. ETS screening of prospective college students begins in seventh grade with the Junior Scholastic Aptitude Test (JSAT), marketed by ETS' Educational Records Bureau (ERB). In addition to providing a scale enabling teachers to convert JSAT scores into "IQ" scores, the JSAT is advertised by ETS as a predictor of high school grades, which can be used to decide whether students should be directed to a college preparatory curriculum.[68]

The sorting continues each October, when three-quarters of all United States high schools (18,000 of 24,000) become direct extensions of the ETS test system by administering the ETS Preliminary Scholastic Aptitude Test (PSAT) to more than a million sophomores, juniors and seniors.[69] The PSAT scores are reported to school administrators and guidance counselors who call in students to inform them of, in ETS' words, "how your verbal and mathematical abilities rank when compared with those of students across the nation." The high schools distribute ETS literature advising students to use the scores to "plan for your education beyond high school." In addition to directing the student's choice of high school courses and college prospects, the test "can be used to estimate your probable performance on the SAT."[70]

For students seeking scholarships from such diverse philanthropists as the Lutheran Church, the International Union of Bricklayers, Getty Oil Company, Minnesota Mining and Manufacturing, Sunshine Biscuits, the Westinghouse Foundation; the States of California, Maryland, New Jersey and Kansas; or more than 400 others--churches, corporations, unions, foundations, professional associations, trusts and government agencies, the PSAT score takes on added significance. The test's full name, as noted earlier, is the Preliminary Scholastic Aptitude Test/National Merit Scholarship Qualifying Test (PSAT/NMSQT). It is used to pick the winners of $12,000,000 worth of National Merit and Achievement Scholarships each year; it is also required of candidates for hundreds of other scholarship programs. In more than forty major corporate scholarship competitions in addition to the National Merits, committees chosen by ETS select the winners. According to the ETS newspaper, "ETS /then/ determines the financial need of each of the winners and recommends the distribution of scholarships on that basis. . . ."[71]

The PSAT is only a preliminary hurdle. The college screening process culminates with what the ETS company newspaper calls "the good old SAT, a familiar fixture in the lives of millions of Americans." More than one thousand colleges require applicants to submit SATs, or comparable test scores, to be considered for admission. Sixty-eight percent of the more than 2,000 colleges listed in Petersen's Guide to the Colleges require applicants to take the SAT or ACT of the American College Board Testing Program. (In 1977-78, 1,416,400 individuals took the SAT.)[72] A 1976 College Board survey of member colleges found that "Test scores were identified more often than any other variable as being a major criterion used in the admissions process. Among both private and public institutions interviewed, four out of five institutions selected test scores as most important when compared to high school grades, rank in class and other variables."[73]

The SATs are designed to begin screening out applicants even before the colleges make their admissions decisions. Students are encouraged to use their scores for <u>self</u>-selection. ETS literature includes charts showing students how to calculate where their SAT scores would rank among other college applicants. Publications such as the <u>New York Times Guide to the Colleges</u>, a student's manual similar to Peterson's <u>Guide</u>, depict education as a hierarchy of schools in which ETS scores determine one's place. The <u>Times</u> <u>Guide</u> classifies schools not according to alphabetical order or the states in which they are located, but according to the average SAT scores of the entering class.[74]

The power of the SAT as an instrument of self-selection was illustrated by a 1969-70 pilot program in which 493 colleges attempted to pay the SAT fees of their applicants who came from poor families. The program failed because of a harsh reality. As an internal ETS study discovered, students are "reluctant to apply to [a] specific college until after SAT scores determine their eligibility."[75]

Once students are admitted to an institution of higher education, then ETS' twenty-two Achievement Tests, as well as its Advanced Placement Tests, College Level Examination Program [CLEP] tests, and its series of college-administered language placement tests can help determine where they will be placed in the curriculum and whether they will receive credit for learning completed outside of college. (More than 465,000 students were placed by such tests in 1977-78.)[76]

Students who seek financial aid from their school submit to ETS a detailed accounting of their family's income, assets and debts. The ETS College Scholarship Service (CSS) analyzes this information and reports to the college a judgment on the amount of money the family can be expected to contribute and the student's level of financial need. The ETS finding becomes the basis for college scholarship, loan and work-study awards. ETS requests that families supplement their CSS form--which requires more detailed disclosure than a standard mortgage application or a federal income tax return--with a copy of their IRS 1040 income tax return.[77]

Graduate School Admission and Financial Aid. As a student advances through higher education, institutions which do not allocate learning opportunities on the basis of ETS scores become increasingly hard to find. According to the Graduate Programs and Admissions Manual 1979-1981, a survey of over 12,000 graduate departments and programs, over 75% require or recommend that applicants take the ETS Graduate Record Examination (GRE). A smaller survey by ETS in 1971 produced similar results. At 45 percent of the schools surveyed by ETS, all departments required the GRE. Of 4,926 United States graduate departments surveyed, 3,600--or 74%--required the GRE. Students aspiring to advanced learning in Slavic studies, industrial education, Far Eastern literature, metalurgy, ceramic engineering, cell biology, oral surgery, aerospace management, accounting, politics, and more than 200 other fields, are screened by the ETS tests.[78] GREs are also required by hundreds of fellowship granting agencies--from the Malaysian American Commission to the

Institute of Electronics Engineers--and by the financial aid offices of graduate departments themselves.[79] According to an ETS survey, "almost half of the departments" which used a GRE cutoff score to determine who would gain admission set a <u>higher</u> cutoff for the admission of people who would need financial aid.[80]

As on the college level, ETS recommends to school the amount of aid applicants need through its Graduate and Professional School Financial Aid Service (GAPSFAS).[81]

<u>Business School Admission and Financial Aid</u>. Aspirants to the executive suites of General Motors and Citibank are screened by the same test used to select many of the future managers in the countries of Kenya, Australia and South Africa. More than 430 U.S. business schools (eighty per cent of the nation's total) depend on scores from the ETS Graduate Management Admissions Test (GMAT) to choose their students. Like the multinational corporations whose trainees it sorts, the GMAT spans international boundaries. Applicants to the Saudi Arabia University of Petroleum and Minerals and Switzerland's Institut pour l'Étude des Methodes de Direction de l'Entreprise, for example, must sit for examination at an ETS test center and have their scores forwarded from Rosedale. More than fifty foreign business schools in Nigeria, Israel, France, Japan, and some fifteen other countries require the GMAT.[82] Some corporations, such as Citibank, hire coaches to prepare their executives for the GMAT before sending them to business school for mid-career training.[83] One hundred sixty-six thousand applicants took the test in 1977-78.[84]

Law School Admission and Financial Aid: Admission to the Bar.
Lawyers occupy two out of three U.S. Senate seats and half of the nation's governors' mansions. They constitute one of the highest paid professions in the country, with an average income greater than that of ninety-three per cent of American earners.[85] ETS publications for prospective law students emphasize the profession's strategic position: "the lawyer can function . . . as social planner. In business, labor, personal, family, and governmental affairs, the lawyer will usually be the one who builds the institutional framework." ETS literature explains that the profession is looking for youth who "have . . . drunk rather freely of the best our culture can provide" and who have a grasp of "the democratic process in western societies /and/ awareness of the moral values inherent in these processes."[86] It finds them by means of ETS tests.

In most states, candidates for the bar must be graduates of an accredited law school, and every accredited law school requires the ETS Law School Admission Test (LSAT). With nearly two applicants for every law school opening in the United States, a low score on the LSAT can prohibit a person from entering not just a particular school but the profession itself. In the most recent year for which such figures are available (1976-77), astoundingly, half of the applicants who had earned an "A" average through four years of college but who scored below 500 on the 215 minute LSAT were rejected by every accredited law school to which they applied.[87]

In addition to providing test scores, ETS has for years recalculated college grade averages of applicants and made confidential predictions (not disclosed to the applicant) of the grades they would earn if admitted to the law school of their choice.[88]

Upon graduation from law school, prospective lawyers meet yet another ETS test. In forty-two states the multiple-choice ETS Multistate Bar Examination (MBE) is required for admission to the practice of law.[89]

Certification to Teach. In thousands of the nation's public schools, an ETS test helps determine who will be certified to teach. In 1974, thirty state departments of education, the Bureau of Indian Affairs (which runs the schools on reservations), and over 450 local school districts in forty-three states required applicants for teaching positions to submit the ETS National Teacher Examination scores. From the rural parishes of Louisiana to the school systems of New York, Chicago, Boston and Los Angeles, teachers were certified, and in some cases hired and promoted on the basis of the ETS National Teacher Examinations (NTE).[90]

The ETS test system extends far beyond education. Its tests are used for certification and advancement in occupations ranging from auto mechanics and beauticians to stockbrokers and gynecologists. ETS also does consulting and testing for governments around the world. In the Caribbean nation of Trinidad and Tobago, for example, where resources for secondary education are scarce and only some of those who want to attend high school are permitted to do so, an ETS test screens the applicants.[91]

In summary, the chances of people who seek to advance in their education and work may depend less on what they have done than on what an ETS multiple-choice test says they are capable of doing.

CHAPTER III

FIVE PERCENT OF NOTHING: APTITUDE TESTING, THE RESPECTABLE FRAUD

According to an ETS technical manual, "an aptitude test is . . . a device for measuring the capacity or potentiality of an individual for a particular kind of behavior."[1] Such a device, says ETS, is "used to predict success in some occupation or training course."[2]

Five of ETS' largest income sources are aptitude tests: the Preliminary Scholastic Aptitude Test/National Merit Scholarship Qualifying Test (PSAT/NMSQT), the Scholastic Aptitude Test (SAT), the Law School Admission Test (LSAT), the Graduate Record Examination (GRE) Aptitude Test, and the Graduate Management Admission Test (GMAT).[3] Aptitude tests constitute the largest of what ETS' 1966-77 corporate master plan called "the major operational programs that are the rock on which the ETS enterprise is founded."[4] (Original emphasis.)

In families where children aspire to higher education, some ETS aptitude tests have become household words. ETS aptitude tests influence decisions about which students will get higher education, where they will get it, and with how much financial aid. They influence the occupations people will pursue when they graduate. And, in perhaps their most penetrating consequence, ETS aptitude tests are used by young people, whose goals are still unformed, to decide how much and what kinds of potential they have and how it can be used.

ETS makes certain claims about its tests, claims which must be compared with the facts behind them. ETS claims that its aptitude tests can predict success by measuring potential for certain important kinds of thinking. The SAT student bulletin informs teenagers that the test can "measure /their/ ability to understand what /they/ read...the extent of /their/ vocabulary.../and other/ abilities /which/ have been shown to be related to college work."[5] The LSAT student bulletin asserts that the test is a reliable measure "of certain mental abilities related to academic performance in law schools."[6] In 1977 the GRE student bulletin announced that the GRE Aptitude Test had been reissued in a new, improved model which would "measure analytical ability as well as...verbal and quantitative ability."[7]

Behind these claims are the tests themselves: collections of multiple-choice questions administered under time limits. The February 2, 1974 SAT, for example, consisted of ninety questions on antonyms, analogies, sentence completion, and the themes and contents of paragraphs (for which students had an average of fifty seconds per question) and sixty questions on algebra, geometry, graph reading, data sufficiency and diagram games (for which students had an average of seventy-five seconds per question).[8] ETS does not present the results of these tests as mere records of performance on a given set of multiple-choice questions. Instead, it presents them as measurements of "aptitude," measurements which can be used to influence a person's belief in one's potential and one's opportunities for advancement.

From the objective information of the number of questions individuals got right and wrong, ETS makes the subjective claim that they therefore have been found to possess a particular quantity of aptitude. This is the claim which sets the ETS aptitude test apart from routine classroom exams--which merely purport to measure knowledge of a particular subject--and makes the test influential in people's lives. ETS claims that its aptitude test measures not just how well individuals performed, but how well they are capable of doing; and shows not just how they thought about some analogy and geometry questions in particular, but how they are capable of thinking about intellectual problems in general.

When ETS' claims about its aptitude tests are juxtaposed with evidence from scholarly studies and internal documents, it becomes difficult to conclude that they constitute an even minimally prudent construction of the facts. ETS' descriptions in candidate literature of the predictive accuracy of its tests are undermined by hundreds of its own studies.[9] ETS' claims that the tests are not biased against minority students were repudiated as "untenable" in an internal memorandum by an ETS vice president in 1971.[10] ETS' claims that its aptitude tests are impervious to short-term improvement by cramming or coaching were characterized in a confidential 1979 memo by the director of the Federal Trade Commission's Bureau of Consumer Protection as "unfair and deceptive trade practices."[11] The discrepancies between image and reality are not merely flaws in description. They suggest instead that, in a fundamental sense, the ETS aptitude test is not what it purports to be.

But in the world of psychometrics, the academic fraternity spawned by the creators of ETS-style aptitude testing, the manner in which ETS presents its tests to consumers is the height of intellectual respectability. One reviewer in the <u>Mental Measurement Yearbook</u> has called the SAT "highly perfected--possibly reaching the pinnacle of the current state of the art in psychometrics."[12] In the outside world, however, where the psychometrician's claims are taken at face value and used to shape people's minds and lives, ETS' claims about its aptitude tests can perhaps best be described as a specialized variety of fraud.

The ETS consumer is a victim of a false representation of a product. This kind of fraud is respectable because ETS follows the rules of the psychometric profession and of the powerful economic and political institutions that for close to eighty years have been so receptive to that profession's often unsubstantiated verdicts on the potential of people's minds (see Chapter IV). This respectable fraud is based on a benignly confident adherence to a system of psychometric belief. It is a system characterized by a tolerance for obfuscation and a bedrock assumption about the right and responsibility of the mental tester to use multiple-choice questions to define the potential for thinking, and then, regardless of the evidence, to draw broad conclusions about the extent to which a person possesses it.

Prediction: The Roll of the Dice

The ability to predict grades is the empirical basis of ETS' claim to measure aptitude. For psychometricians, a "valid" aptitude test is one that can predict a person's performance. "Aptitude tests like the SAT," writes William Angoff of ETS, "are properly thought of as <u>prospective</u> measures and should be evaluated in terms of their relevance to . . . future activities" (original emphasis).[13] ETS aptitude tests claim to predict performance in college, and in law, graduate and business schools, <u>as measured by the standard of first year grades.</u> In a 1974 speech at Columbia University, ETS President William W. Turnbull put the claim boldly:

> The evidence about college entrance tests as predictors of academic success is no longer a subject of legitimate dispute. The studies have been widespread, they number in the thousands, and the results are consistent. By and large, the higher the test scores, the more successful the students are in college. . . . Most educators are quite familiar with the fact that the scores work in more cases than <u>not</u>, popular belief to the contrary notwithstanding.[14]

President Turnbull's assurances notwithstanding, the evidence of those thousands of studies is that ETS aptitude tests on the average predict grades only eight to fifteen percent better than random prediction with a pair of dice.[15] This is not the way the tests are presented in ETS candidate literature.

ETS statements to students about the predictive accuracy of its tests are full of references to the word "perfect" and analogies to physical measuring tools. Alongside a diagram of the SAT score scale, drawn to resemble a thermometer, the bulletin for students receiving College Board scores states that "the chances are 2 out of 3" that one's score will "fall within a limited band around . . . the score you would earn if a test could measure your ability with perfect accuracy."[16]

ETS literature repeats the theme that although its tests are not <u>perfect</u> measuring instruments, even physical measurements are known to have some error. "Test scores," says the bulletin for counseling, admissions and placement personnel, "like all types of measurements, physical as well as psychological, are not <u>perfectly</u> precise." The LSAT bulletin assures that, "While the correlations between test scores and grades are not <u>perfect</u>, studies show that LSAT scores help to predict which students will do well in law school."[17] "Although test scores are good predictors of performance in college," writes William Angoff of ETS in an article explaining the SAT to counselors and teachers, "they are not <u>perfect</u> predictors."[18] (Emphases added.)

This, to say the least, is putting it mildly. A perfect prediction would be 100 percent accurate. A physical measurement, such as that provided by a thermometer or a scale or a ruler (all of which have been compared to ETS tests by company officials) generally delivers accuracy upwards of ninety-five per cent. The Scholastic Aptitude Test, according to figures compiled from 827 different ETS validity studies conducted between 1964 and 1974, delivers an average accuracy--what statisticians call "percentage of variance accounted for" or "percentage of perfect prediction"*--of 11.9 percent in the prediction of first year grades.[19]

---

*Other terms for the percentage of perfect prediction are "r squared" and "coefficient of determination." This percentage estimates an instrument's effectiveness in reducing predictive error. An instrument which provides, for example, eleven per cent of perfect prediction, causes roughly an eleven per cent reduction in the errors that would result from prediction by blind chance. The percentage of perfect prediction is derived by squaring the correlation coefficient (see footnote 15).

The median percentage of perfect prediction (in predicting first year grades) provided by the Verbal and Math sections of the SAT in each of the years studied is presented below:

Percentage of Perfect Prediction of First Year College Grades*

	Verbal SAT	Math SAT
1964	13.7%	10.2%
1965	13.0	8.4
1966	10.9	7.8
1967	13.0	7.8
1968	16.0	10.9
1969	15.2	10.9
1970	13.7	8.4
1971	11.6	7.8
1972	12.3	10.9
1973	14.4	13.0
1974	17.6	15.2

SOURCE: Derived from Ford and Campos[20]

According to validity figures which ETS presented in a 1977 report for the Carnegie Council on Policy Studies in Higher Education, other ETS aptitude tests provide similar or slightly lower

---

*The 11.9 per cent figure on page 60 is obtained by taking a weighted average of the original correlation coefficients (based on the number of studies each correlation is derived from), taking the average between the weighted averages of the SAT Math and Verbal columns and squaring it.

percentages of perfect prediction: thirteen percent for the LSAT, eleven percent for the GRE, and eight percent for the GMAT.[21]

Test professionals are fond of contrasting their scientific rigor with the purportedly vague and emotional thinking of their critics and the public. "The psychometrician often has rigidly precise, and perhaps too narrow definitions," writes ETS researcher Ronald Flaugher, "while the lay critic is operating from . . . gut-level knowledge."[22] But, although ETS candidate literature refers to the precision of physical measures and the concept of perfect prediction, it presents no numbers to illustrate just how far from perfect the predictions of their tests actually are.

Testmakers have not always been so ambiguous in their publications. In a 1927 report to the College Entrance Examination Board on development and use of the SAT, SAT inventor Carl C. Brigham published a table which could be used to find the percent of perfect prediction the SAT provides. Brigham used a different, less flattering, method of calculating the percentage than that which is used in this report. If the percentages of perfect prediction given above were recalculated according to Brigham's formula, the SAT would be interpreted as providing only seven per cent of perfect prediction, the GRE and LSAT would yield six per cent and the GMAT less than five per cent.[23]

These facts, of course, are not unknown to test professionals. Their implications are occasionally acknowledged in print, but in places consumers rarely see. In contrast to the LSAT student bulletin quoted earlier, the LSAT Handbook for deans and admissions officers states that "Judged against a standard of perfect prediction, the correlation for Law School Admission Test scores is very low, and anyone using the scores for prediction should be prepared for many disappointments."[24] The GMAT dean's handbook contains an identical disclaimer.[25]

An ETS handbook on testing statistics for teachers describes an extremely weak relationship between a predictor (such as a test) and what it is supposed to predict (such as grades) as a: "zero or near zero correlation /which/ . . . means that a student who stood high on one measure might stand anywhere at all on the other (for example, the correlation between height and I.Q.)."[26] ETS defines a "zero or near zero correlation" as "roughly from .25 to -.25."[27] These correlations* are equivalent to percentages of perfect prediction of 6.25 per cent and -6.25 per cent. By ETS' own definition, then, the correlations between some ETS tests and academic success are "near zero."

One major study found, for example, the percentage of perfect prediction provided by SAT scores in estimating the likelihood of dropping out of college to be between 2.9 per cent and 3.2 per cent.[28] This is within the "near zero" range of 6.25 per

---

*The meaning of the correlation coefficient--the statistic used by psychometricians to characterize test validity--is often misunderstood. Although a 0.0 correlation indicates a test has no ability to predict, and a 1.0 correlation indicates perfect ability to predict, the coefficients in between are not simply equal to percentages of perfect prediction. A correlation of .37 for the SAT Verbal, for example, does not mean that the SAT yields 37 percent of perfect prediction. Rather, it is the square of the correlation coefficient (multiplied by 100) which equals the percentage of perfect prediction. Thus, a .37 correlation indicates that the SAT predicts first year grades with 13.7 percent of perfect prediction. See footnote 15 for further discussion.

cent to -6.25 percent defined by ETS in its statistics handbook for teachers. Similarly, the percentages of perfect prediction provided by the GMAT (8.4 percent),[29] the Math section of the 1971 SAT (6.8 percent), or the Verbal section of the 1969 SAT (7.8 percent),[30] all approach the level which ETS has characterized as near zero. While these percentages are particularly low, the average percentage predictions of first year grades provided by ETS aptitude tests (noted on p.61) are somewhat above the "near zero" level--but not by much.

In light of these and similar figures, Professor Dale Tillery's comment in a College Board sponsored study of aptitude tests and student selection is not surprising:

> For a long time it has been known that for many individuals such ability tests are poor predictors of either achievement or persistence in college. . . . Because a correlation of .50 improves the betting odds over pure chance by 25 percent or less, some writers have suggested that such predictors should be put on the shelf along with the crystal ball and the Ouija board.[31]

These prediction statistics can be given perspective by comparing how well the test predicts grades* with how well grades would be predicted by chance. To see how often chance would predict grade ranking within a group as well as an ETS aptitude test, one subtracts the test's "percentage of perfect prediction" from 100 per cent. The comparison gives the following result:

---

*Prediction of grades refers to ranking of candidates by grades they are expected to earn.

<u>Percentage of Predictions in Which</u>

<u>Random Prediction With a Pair of Dice</u>

<u>is as Accurate as an ETS Test:</u>

SAT (college)	88%
LSAT (law school)	87
GRE (graduate school)	89
GMAT (business school)	92

SOURCE: Derived from Ford and Campos, Willingham and Breland[32]

This means that, on the average, for 88 percent of the applicants (though it is impossible to know which ones) an SAT score will predict their grade rank no more accurately than a pair of dice. In some schools the test will predict better than this, in others not as well. The best known record of prediction by the SAT, reported in a 1978 ETS survey of studies, was at a New Jersey college where the 1978 SAT Verbal would have been matched as a predictor by random chance only 59 per cent of the time. The worst result was reported at a university in Indiana where chance would have predicted grades as well as the 1972 SAT Verbal 99.96 per cent of the time.[33]

Because test scores are not the only factor in admissions decisions, the practical contribution which they make to grade prediction is actually less than the 12 per cent average stated earlier. Most admissions decisions are based significantly on both scores <u>and</u> previous grades. Previous grades alone are a better predictor of academic achievement than the College

Boards*: the 1964-1974 compilation of ETS validity studies found that high school grades were about twice as good as SAT scores in predicting college grades. They provided an average of twenty-five per cent of perfect prediction.[34] At some schools, such as the University of Southern California, grades have been found to be four times better than scores as predictors.[35]

Although the SAT is an inferior predictor relative to previous grades, it has been found to slightly increase the accuracy of prediction when used in combination with grades. This is the argument for requiring the tests. Data from the 1964-1974 validity studies, however, indicate that inclusion of SAT scores in the prediction process improves the prediction of college grades by an average of only five per cent or less. This thin margin, the extent to which ETS scores improve the prediction already offered by previous grades, is the single thread--the single rational function--from which the ETS aptitude testing empire hangs. The SAT improved grade prediction by 5.1 per cent in the best years (1964 and 1974) and by 2.6 per cent in the worst year (1966). Again, these are average figures which vary among institutions.

The ability to improve first year grade prediction by small amounts is by no means unique to the ETS aptitude test.

---

*For other aptitude tests, such as the LSAT, the relative predictive ability of grades and scores swings back and forth from one time period to another. See Chapter VI footnote 9.

TABLE

Average Improvement in Predictive Efficiency

Gained by Adding SAT Scores to

High School Grades

1964	5.1%
1965	3.6
1966	2.6
1967	3.3
1968	4.4
1969	4.1
1970	4.3
1971	2.9
1972	4.4
1973	3.8
1974	5.1

SOURCE: Derived from Ford and Campos.[36]

A number of other "predictors" of college success have been found to be as accurate as the SAT.

The American College Testing Program (ACT) tests, which do not claim to be measures of "aptitude" but merely batteries of exams in different high school level subjects, have grade prediction statistics virtually identical to those of the SAT.[37] An ACT study suggests that the ACT may even be slightly better than the SAT in predicting grades at selective colleges, the testing market traditionally dominated by ETS.[38]

Still further from the mold of the standardized multiple-choice ETS aptitude test, various kinds of biographical questionnaires and personal rating scales have been found to predict grades nearly as well as, or better than, test scores. These instruments base ratings not on multiple-choice test questions, but on reports of past accomplishments and on judgments about the individual by teachers, fellow students, and individuals themselves. In a series of studies, psychologist Gene Smith used student ratings of their classmates on such characteristics as work orientation and whether they were "conscientious," "responsible," "insistently orderly," "prone to daydream," "resourceful," "quitting," etc. in order to predict college grades.[39] Smith found that in several cases a composite "strength of character" score, made up of the ratings from nine such variables, was three times more successful in predicting post-high school academic performance than any combination of thirteen "academic aptitude measures" including SAT Verbal, SAT Mathematical, and high school class rank.[40]

A study at Fordham University by Professors Anne Anastasi (later winner of the ETS Award for Distinguished Service to Measurement), M.J. Meade, and A.A. Schneiders, contrasted the predictive ability of a student biographical inventory with the SAT. A broad criterion defined as "the extent to which the student fulfills the recognized objectives of the particular college and displays the traits the college has undertaken to foster and develop" was employed.[41] Students were then grouped into three categories within this criterion ("positive," meaning the student advanced the objectives of the college; "negative," or failing to adjust to the college environment; and "average"), using information from academic records, faculty ratings, extra-curricular activities, and several other sources. Correlations between the biographical inventory--which asked students about their experiences, preferences for reading material, aspirations, and objectives--and placement in each of the three categories, and between SAT scores and placement in each category, were then made. Anastasi and her colleagues found that "In each of the three possible comparisons, the two parts of the SAT, taken separately, had lower correlations with the criterion than the biographical inventory."[42]

There is also some evidence that the SAT has less predictive validity than even simpler means. A 1976 ETS study found that "college freshmen were far better at estimating their year-end grade point average than were college entrance exams," said one review of the report.[43] "After twelve years of being compared with peers and getting daily feedback on performance in class-work and tests, students are apparently expert at estimating their own ability."[44]

And for those who are _truly_ serious about wanting to predict academic success, there has been talk at ETS of measures more powerful than aptitude tests as predictors which go beyond the realm of paper and pencil altogether. At a November 29 and 30, 1967 ETS conference on academic and business personnel policy,

Dr. John R.P. French, Jr. of the University of Michigan presented a paper on a measuring instrument which, he claimed, could predict the likelihood of graduation from school, something which ETS aptitude tests predict even more poorly than grades. Dr. French and his colleagues noted that:

> . . . on the basis of serum uric acid, we are able to predict four and a half years in advance which high school students would go on to college and which would not. We were also able to predict which ones would drop out of college, and if we took into account IQ, how long before they dropped out.[45]

French and colleagues made these predictions by determining the levels of serum uric acid in samples of the students' blood. "To give you the lay meaning of serum uric acid," he told the ETS conference, "when we were describing these results to Jimmy Doolittle, the famed aviator, he said, 'You mean those men /who do well/ are full of piss and vinegar?' I said that was about right."[46]

Five Percent of Nothing: Prediction of What?

The SAT has been shown to improve the prediction of college grades by an average of three to five percent. This slim improvement in prediction is the basis for ETS' claim that the test measures aptitude. Yet, the SAT has been shown to be still poorer at predicting likelihood of persisting in college than it is at predicting first-year grades. And, first-year grades have been shown by the test industry's own research to bear little relationship to "success" by any standard, from a student's achievement outside the classroom to accomplishment on the job.

Marginal as they are, the predictions of first-year grades are the tests' most accurate forecasts. Correlations between scores and grades in later years, and overall college average, are lower still. In his study, "The Fleeting Nature of the Prediction of

College Academic Success," Lloyd Humphreys of the University of Illinois found that the ability of college admission tests to predict grades declined consistently from one semester to the next throughout eight semesters.[47] In a follow-up study of "postdictive validities" Humphreys compared GRE scores with candidates' eight previous semesters of undergraduate grades. He found that "postdictive validities" dropped over the course of eight semesters, again in a very similar pattern. The GRE provided a 12.3 per cent improvement over chance in estimating first semester freshman grades; by the final semester of senior year the prediction was four times weaker, providing a 3.2 per cent improvement over chance.[48] These results troubled Humphreys, a staunch believer in aptitude testing. "The tests measure intellectual abilities," he wrote in the <u>Journal of Educational Measurement</u>, "but are more highly correlated with freshman grades than with senior grades. The seeming conclusion that senior grades are less intellectual than freshman grades is, to say the least, bothersome."[49]

The virtual disappearance of the aptitude tests' ability to predict beyond the freshman year has been explained by some commentators as a result of the nature of advanced study. Multiple-choice testing predominates in introductory courses, they argue, but intermediate and advanced courses demand a broader range of performance. The qualities students need to succeed over the long haul were examined in a 1972 survey of over 300 professors by ETS psychologist Jonathan R. Warren. His findings, reported in <u>Intellect</u> magazine, were as follows:

> What does it take to succeed in college? Motivation was the quality most frequently cited by over 300 college teachers during a recent study of academic performance. The teachers mentioned students' academic commitment and interest even more often than intellectual ability as characteristics of their best students.[50]

These characteristics, which professors include in their working definitions of "scholastic aptitude," are beyond what ETS claims its aptitude tests can measure. In fact, ETS personality studies involving student self-ratings have found that at the college, law and graduate levels, such important traits as commitment to knowledge are insignificantly or negatively correlated with ETS scores.[51]

If scholastic aptitude is defined as the ability of students to improve their knowledge during their time in school, then this is another aptitude the SAT--despite its name--has not been found to measure. In 1968 Dr. Alexander Astin of the American Council on Education (ACE) compared students' SAT scores with their gains in achievement in various subjects during their college careers. "Presumably," Astin wrote, "educational institutions exist in order to educate students. Their mission . . . is to produce certain desirable changes in the student or, more simply, to make a difference in the student's life."[52] Astin noted that an argument often given to justify heavy reliance on aptitude test scores in admission is that only those who score high "are capable of 'profiting' from higher education."[53] Astin concluded that "recent evidence, however, fails to support this assumption, since students at all levels of ability /as measured by ETS scores and previous grades/ showed similar gains in achievement during their undergraduate years, regardless of the type of institution they attended."[54]

An even more clear-cut standard of scholastic success is staying in school. Astin suggested in an ACE study of the scores and school records of 36,581 students who entered 180 different colleges in 1966 that:

> In a very practical sense, the student's ability to stay
> in college is a more appropriate measure of his 'success'
> than is his freshman GPA. Although it is true that good
> grades will help him gain admission to graduate school,
> to win graduate fellowships, and even to secure certain
> types of jobs, they are irrelevant to any of these
> outcomes if the student drops out of college before
> completing his degree requirements.[55]

Astin found that using college grades to forecast who will actually continue in school resulted in 5.8 percent of perfect prediction for women and 10.2 percent for men. In contrast, SAT scores provided percentages of only 3.2 percent for men and 2.9 percent for women.[56] This means that for over 95 percent the cases, blind chance would predict chances of persisting as well as the SAT. "Whether or not the student will drop out of college after the freshman year," Astin noted mildly, "can be predicted with only a low degree of accuracy."[57]

The ability of other ETS aptitude tests to predict graduation from law and graduate school is slightly better than the SAT's prediction of college persistence although each of these tests is matched by chance as a predictor of graduation at least 88% of the time

Predicting Persistence: Percentage of Cases in Which Random Prediction
   With a Pair of Dice is as Accurate as an ETS Test:

SAT (staying in college)	97%
LSAT (graduate from law school)	95
GRE (attain the Ph.D.)	
GRE Verbal	97
GRE Quantitative	93
GRE Advanced	88
GRE Composite	90

SOURCE: Derived from Astin, Baird, and Willingham and Breland.[58]

A 1973 study by the American College Testing Program found similar results. ACT reported that "variables such as motivation and a student's background" discriminated between average students and those who dropped out of college, while academic data such as SATs and College Board Achievement Tests did not discriminate between these groups.[59]

Statistics on test scores and college success, however, can never reveal what *might* have been accomplished by those who were rejected due to their scores. In a rare practical experiment designed to address this problem, Williams College, over a ten year period, admitted 358 students (roughly ten per cent of each year's class) who would otherwise have been rejected by the school's normal test score and grade requirements. The identities of the "ten percenters" were kept secret from faculty and students; they were subjected to the same academic requirements as other students and received no special aid. In 1976 the results were announced: seventy-one percent had graduated from that highly competitive school, compared to the Williams' average of eighty-five percent; in one graduating class, the class president, president of the college council, and president of the honor society had all been admitted under the special program. Williams found the program so successful that it has been continued to this day.[60]

ETS' claim to measure scholastic aptitude and predict school grades is explicit. But their claims regarding the connection between scores and success beyond the classroom are far more ambiguous. Tests which purport to measure "reasoning" and "verbal and mathematical abilities" might be thought by some students to be making claims about the general quality of a person's mind. However, the ETS candidate booklet, Taking the SAT, includes an explicit disclaimer about the prediction of lifetime success:

> Tests can be a useful measure of knowledge or academic ability, but no test predicts with any certainty "success in life" or is in any way a measure of an individual's total worth.[61]

Whether the text of the disclaimer, or the fact that it is buried among 800 fine print words on the back cover, represent the impression ETS intends to convey on this matter remains uncertain. In the June, 1978 issue of the College Board News, which announced this new booklet, then-College Board President (and ETS Trustee) Sidney P. Marland did little to discourage those who thought that their mind's long-term potential was being tested. "I think that we will continue to have something like the Scholastic Aptitude Test to help millions of young people know something about where they stand in the universe of their peers in terms of intellectual aptitudes and readiness for continued learning," Marland said.[62]

Marland is not alone in his confidence. In a 1977 report for the Carnegie Council on Policy Studies in Higher Education, ETS researcher Warren Willingham contended that "the intellectual competence that is heavily represented in grades and ability tests. . . . is _one_ of the important determiners of life success"[63] (original emphasis). At a 1978 college recruitment fair at the New York Coliseum attended by thousands of students, College Board representative Shelly Martucci made a similar claim: "It's an indicator of how well you will do from now on," she said to the author in regard to the SAT. "College is really only the beginning, college is an indicator of how you'll do after college. The SAT is a general overall measure of your aptitude."[64]

As the authors of the SAT booklet disclaimer were no doubt aware, such claims are difficult to support with evidence. In a January, 1971 paper given at ETS, which was later published in the American Psychologist, Harvard psychology professor and former ETS researcher Dr. David McClelland reported that two statistical studies "have shown that no consistent relationships exist between scholastic aptitude scores in college students and their <u>actual accomplishments</u> in social leadership, the arts, science, music, writing, and speech and drama"[65] (original emphasis).

Similarly, McClelland noted that for non-ETS standardized tests, "Thorndike and Hagen . . . obtained 12,000 correlations between aptitude test scores and various measures of later occupational success on over 10,000 respondents and concluded that the number of significant correlations did not exceed what would be expected by chance."[66] According to Professor Michael Wallach of Duke University, former member of the ETS Standing Committee on Research and author of a pioneering statistical study of the college admissions process, "Students may score well on these standard tests, but there is very little predictability of creativity, or talent, or accomplishment. . . . The evidence we report . . . shows that these test-taking skills are minimally related to direct forms of accomplishment. . . ."67

A 1979 literature review by ETS researcher Leonard Baird reported one study which found that "the best predictor of accomplishment in college" was not tests but "accomplishment in the same area in high school, as measured by simple check lists of nonacademic achievements." He noted another study which discovered that among adults, "biographical information predicted rated scientific competence, rated creativity, and the number of patents within a group of research scientists." A study of NASA scientists reached similar conclusions. None of the studies Baird reviewed showed comparable predictive capacities for aptitude tests. Baird summarized the research by stating flatly that "information about past accomplishments is the best predictor of future accomplishments."68

Aptitude test scores have even been found to bear little relationship to accomplishment in the psychometrician's own discipline. In a study of the relationship between GRE scores and the subsequent scholarly output of students who had obtained a PhD in Psychology from the University of Southern California between 1952 and 1966, USC professor Albert Marston found that the GREs provided only three percent of perfect prediction in assessing successful publication of academic research by nonclinical PhDs and had a _negative_ correlation with scholarly publication by clinical PhDs. Noting that his own department and others across the country had adopted GRE cutoff scores for admission, Marston wrote in _American Psychologist_ that "psychologists, ironically, seem most reluctant to let go of a quantitative, objective predictor that apparently does not predict very well. . . . To use any fixed cutting score, . . . in light of the above data, seems at best unscientific."[69]

Warren Willingham of ETS, claiming in the 1977 Carnegie Council report that ETS scores can predict career success, relied on an unpublished 1951 undergraduate thesis which contends that people with higher SAT scores are more likely to be listed in Who's Who.[70] He does not mention a more recent study of the same topic by a senior ETS statistician which came to the opposite conclusion. ETS' William Coffman and M. Mahoney compiled career data on 1,218 Yale graduates from the classes of 1931 through 1950. "To those who are tempted to view high SAT scores as the be-all and end-all of existence," Coffman and Mahoney reported in the 1966-67 ETS Annual Report, "this study may provide food for thought. . . . In general, no significant relationship could be found between original /SAT/ scores and present status. This finding was further underlined by a second study in which Who's Who in America, American Men of Science, and the Dictionary of American Scholars were searched for listings of these Yale graduates."[71]

Even these more professional studies of Who's Who listings are methodologically flawed because they simply correlate test scores with the measure of accomplishment, without taking into account other factors such as the social class of the person being studied. Since test scores tend to correlate with social class (see Chapter V) and people from wealthier classes have more opportunities than others for reaching high status positions, it is to be expected that the scores of people in high status jobs will be higher than average, simply by virtue of their class and regardless of their "ability" measured by any other standard.

A later generation of more sophisticated studies which control for such factors has found--like the research cited by McClelland--little connection between the things measured by aptitude tests and actual lifetime accomplishment. A 1974 study of the personal characteristics and lifetime earnings of more than 10,000 people by Drs. Samuel Bowles and Valerie Nelson concluded that "IQ is not an important criterion for economic success."[72]* Their study, published in the Review of Economics and Statistics, cited eleven other studies covering thousands of test-takers from across the country which supported the conclusion that test scores themselves bear little significant relationship to lifetime earnings success.[73] In a later analysis of additional studies, Bowles and Herbert Gintis found that people's eventual earnings were explained not by their test scores but mainly by the social class they started from and by various personality characteristics.[74] A 1979 study by Richard DeLone for the Carnegie Council on Children reaffirmed this point, finding that a person's social class at birth is a substantially better predictor of their eventual economic standing than are their test scores.[75]

A 1979 analysis of educational and occupational surveys by Harvard sociologist Christopher Jencks looks at the role of test

---

*IQ scores tend to have the same correlations with variables such as grade point average, family income, etc. as ETS aptitude scores. See for example, Arthur and Linda Shaw Whimby, Intelligence Can Be Taught, (New York: E.P. Dutton, 1975).

scores somewhat differently. Jencks confirms the importance of family background, concluding that it accounts for fifty-five to eighty-five percent of eventual earnings advantage. But, he argues that scores can affect one's prospects as well. Taking note of the fact that "high-scoring individuals have greater educational opportunity in the United States than low scorers," Jencks finds that "test scores affect a man's occupational status primarily by influencing his educational attainment." He argues that when people from the same kind of family background receive different scores, it can make a significant difference in their educational and, thus, their economic opportunity.[76]

Although the claim that ETS aptitude tests predict life success is not made consistently, the claim of first-year grade prediction is the linchpin of the psychometrician's definition of test validity; it forms the basis for asserting that "aptitude" is being measured. Aside from the fact, noted above, that grade prediction declines dramatically after the first year, the validity of grades in general as predictors of later success has not been upheld by evidence. Forty-six studies conducted between 1902 and 1965 which correlated college grades with future achievement were analyzed by Dr. Donald P. Hoyt for the American College Testing Program. These studies, which defined and measured professional achievement by a multitude of standards, covered eight categories: "business, teaching, engineering, medicine, scientific research, miscellaneous occupations, studies of successful individuals, and non-vocational accomplishments." "Evidence strongly suggests," Hoyt concluded, "that college grades bear little or no relationship to any measures of adult accomplishment."[77]

Professor McClelland told the ETS seminar that the lack of connection between grades and accomplishment had been demonstrated across a wide variety of jobs. He noted that Professor Ivar Berg of Columbia "has summarized studies showing that neither the amount of education nor grades in school are related to vocational success as a factory worker, bank teller, or air traffic controller." Perhaps more surprisingly, McClelland continued, "even for highly intellectual jobs like scientific researcher, Taylor, Smith and Ghiselin . . . have shown that superior on-the-job performance is related in no way to better grades in college. The average college grade for the top third in research success was 2.73 (about B-) and for the bottom third, 2.69 (also B-)."[78] "Such facts have been known for some time," he concluded. "They make it abundantly clear that the testing movement is in grave danger of perpetuating a mythological meritocracy in which none of the measures of merit bears significant demonstrable validity with respect to any measures outside of the charmed circle."[79]*

The ETS claim to be measuring aptitude has its rational basis in the supposed prediction of first year grades. The decades of research which have failed to document a significant connection between such grades and career performance are not referred to in the literature ETS sends to candidates. But among ETS professionals who make their living from the sales of aptitude tests, the evidence is not unknown.

---

*The "charmed circle" refers to the relationship between test scores and first year grades, the basis on which ETS claims its tests are "valid."

In a May, 1974 report for the Graduate Record Examination Board, issued as ETS Research Memorandum RM 73-17, ETS researcher Dr. Ronald Flaugher assessed the significance of the criterion which ETS had made the basis of its power--by improving its prediction from three to five percent. His verdict was unequivocal:

> No one can be found who will seriously defend the freshman year grade-point average as an important gauge of anything very important in life's list of desirable values, and in fact, a case is often made for its perversity. Yet, primarily because it is so easily obtained, it is the most frequent criterion variable in use for validating college selection procedures.[80]

Tricks of the Test: Playing the Game

ETS does not disclose to test-takers the evidence which constitutes the empirical basis of its claim to measure aptitude. But the intuitive basis of that claim is plain and is frequently pointed out by ETS representatives. The tests are, after all, composed of problems in reading and math, the basics of academic work. ETS president William Turnbull draws the obvious implication:

> to my mind the test is a small work sample of what it is to confront a tough intellectual problem expressed in words or numerical or abstract symbols. And there's nothing magical about why it works. It's simply a matter of discovering whether or not a student is good at that kind of task, which is the kind of task that he or she is going to confront in the study situation.[81]

While it is certainly true that taking an ETS aptitude test involves reasoning with words and numbers, the same could be said of many tasks, from writing a term paper or taking a classroom algebra exam to solving crossword puzzles or calculating batting averages.

In determining advancement, however, a single paper or classroom test carries nowhere near the weight of an ETS aptitude test and is rarely taken as a measure of potential. To suggest that puzzles or baseball statistics be used as a basis for admission decisions and the ranking of minds would seem farfetched. Performance on such tasks is recognized as either too vulnerable to the idiosyncracies of the grader, or too subject to the mastery of a narrow and peculiar kind of behavior, to support broad and far-reaching conclusions about a person's ability.

ETS, however, asserts that this is not the case with its multiple-choice test questions. College Board publications state flatly that the SAT Verbal section, for example, is "impervious to coaching" on test-taking skills.[82]

ETS' internal reports and the research of independent scholars and government agencies present a somewhat different picture. "Testwiseness," the mastery of skills required by multiple-choice tests, has been shown by ETS' own research to be as strongly correlated to SAT scores as SAT scores are to grades. "Test anxiety," susceptibility to fear and tension in response to test conditions, has been shown to have a slightly stronger correlation with scores than future grades do. And "coaching," which combines short-term training in test wiseness with exercises to reduce anxiety, has been found capable of producing significant gains in SAT scores--in the words of an unreleased FTC memorandum, "contrary to explicit claims of ETS/CEEB."[83]

The evidence indicates that multiple-choice test-taking is a specialized kind of game which rewards certain kinds of people and penalizes others for reasons apart from their ability to handle words and numbers. The ETS aptitude test, in addition to its better-known discrimination on the basis of race and social class,* also systematically discriminates on the basis of age and personality.

Aptitude test scores tend to decline with age, as the test-taker moves out of the test-oriented school world and into the performance and skill-oriented job world.

The decline of test scores with age has been a feature of standardized aptitude and intelligence tests since the early days of mental measurement. If the claims about what these tests measure are taken at face value, they show that adults decline in "aptitude," "reasoning," and the ability to solve problems with words and numbers as soon as they pass their early twenties. Or if, as President Turnbull asserts, the aptitude test measures "developed ability . . . to handle . . . abstract material," then the longer adults develop, the less of this ability they have.[84] Professor Karl U. Smith of the University of Wisconsin, a pioneer in the field of cybernetics, has commented on this pattern in light of research on the creative productivity of scientists, authors and artists, and the psychomotor tasks important to learning:

> Common intelligence tests picture the American adult, whether male or female, genius or common person, executive or janitor, as deteriorating into relative ignorance between the age range 20-25 and age 60, so that beyond age 25 all ages are less competent intellectually than those at 25 while those beyond age 40

---

*See next section of this chapter and Chapter V for a discussion of these issues.

> are less competent intellectually than those of the age range 15-19. In contrast, undisputed research facts show that general skill, creative productivity, learning ability and practical knowledge all increase sharply and progressively in almost identical ways beyond age 20-25 to reach varying peaks in the age range of 30-40. Thereafter, all of these real-life performances are maintained at a high level with some slight decline between the ages of 40 and 60.[85]

Beyond its implications for the claim to be measuring aptitude, the tendency of aptitude tests to penalize people without recent practice in test-taking skills has its greatest impact on applicants who seek to enter law, graduate or business school after several years on the job. Workers and homemakers who, having missed the opportunity to attend college in their teens, try to return to school in pursuit of a degree may also be penalized.

On the ETS business school aptitude tests, for example--which include questions designed to measure practical business judgment--older applicants who have actually been applying their skills in the business world systematically score lower than their younger college-aged counterparts. A 1969 ETS study of applicants to twenty-six business schools found that applicants aged nineteen to twenty-one had a mean Admission Test for Graduate Study in Business (ATGSB, now called the Graduate Management Admission Test [GMAT]) score of 563 compared to a mean of 524 for applicants aged twenty-six to twenty-seven and 490 for those aged thirty-five to fifty-seven.[86] The study also found that older students tended to perform better in school than the conventional method of combining scores and grades predicted. "The combination of ATGSB scores and undergraduate grades seems to be less effective as a predictor for older students. Their first-year averages tend to be higher than those predicted on the basis of scores and grades."[87]

A 1976 ETS study of the GRE found more mixed results (some categories of older students scored higher) but concluded that "on the average the older groups scored lower on the verbal and quantitative GRE tests."[88] The American College Testing Program technical manual openly admits the age discrimination in its college admission tests: "Age groups are . . . combined for prediction [by ACT scores]; however, this procedure leads to consistent underprediction of the grades of older students, and thus to bias against them."[89]

The ability to do well on multiple-choice aptitude tests declines with age regardless of the kind of person involved. But, other aspects of the peculiar skill of test-taking penalize only those with certain personality characteristics. Anxiety is a routine part of test-taking. An ETS survey in 1961 found that more than eighty per cent of students taking the SAT experience some degree of anxiety.[90] But, for many otherwise capable students, severe test anxiety can become a debilitating disadvantage. As Dr. Marjorie Kirkland pointed out in a review of the testing research literature, "extreme degess of anxiety are likely to interfere with test performance."[91] A 1961 study of SAT candidates by Dr. John French of ETS found that "college admission was cited overwhelmingly as the most frequent cause for concern, with short time limits, family expectations, and scholarship requirements contributing to the development of feelings of anxiety."[92] And, Kirkland noted, "there is a positive correlation between level of anxiety and level of aspiration. Those who are least anxious when facing a test tend to be those who have the least need or desire to do well on it."[93]

A 1968 ETS study by Bruce Bloxom similarly found that SAT scores were quite susceptible to the effects of anxiety. For male students taking the SAT Verbal section, Bloxom reported a correlation between "debilitating anxiety" and lowered scores which was twice as strong as the typical correlation between scores and first-year grades. For females, the anxiety effect was slightly stronger than the typical score-grade relationship. On the Math section the impact of anxiety was somewhat lower but still statistically significant.[94] Bloxom's results suggest that for those who suffer from anxiety, the SAT score can be more an indication of how they felt when they took the test than how they will perform in college.

Rather than lowering the scores of all students, however, anxiety has been found to increase the gap between those who usually do well on aptitude tests and those who do not. While students with low or average scores are hurt by anxiety, there is a small but significant tendency for high-scoring candidates to score still higher in response to moderate feelings of anxiety.[95] Although such information is not known to be available for ETS tests, anxiety on other kinds of aptitude tests has been found to be related to social class (the lower the class, the higher the anxiety) and ethnic background (some ethnic minorities tend to have higher test anxiety than whites).[96]

Anxiety occurs on all kinds of tests--multiple-choice or not--and is probably unusually intense for the ETS aptitude test more because of the test's importance than its format. But for some kinds of personalities, the test's tendency to reward some and penalize others is directly linked to the idiosyncracies of the multiple-choice question. The tests reward those who learn the multiple-choice strategy of sacrificing thorough reasoning and mathematical precision for quick approximation and test-taking speed. Dr. Glenn Rowley concluded in his study on "Which Examinees are Most Favoured by the Use of Multiple Choice Tests" that, unlike students who were reluctant to guess on questions when they were uncertain of the answers, "the risktaker was able to benefit from informed guesses."[97]

Rowley's findings were consistent with a 1964 book by Nathan Kogan and Michael Wallach of ETS which concluded that, at least on the SAT Verbal, "risktaking dispositions /which/ are associated with a gambling response set on aptitude tests . . . /seem/ to have . . . pay-off value."[98] Wallach now contends that "test taking is a specialized skill."[99] Rowley, Kogan and Wallach found that willingness to guess had greater impact on verbal scores than math scores. But, a later study by Kogan and Samuel Messick, the ETS Vice President for Research, found that even in the seemingly objective domain of math problems, the multiple-choice format could favor certain kinds of personalities. Messick and Kogan studied two different kinds of multiple-choice math questions--one set containing large differences between the numbers listed as possible answers ("widely spaced alternatives") and one set in which possible answers differed only by small amounts ("narrowly spaced alternatives"). For example:

Widely-spaced Alternatives

A certain public library has two books classified for children to every eight books for adults. If they want to keep the same ratio, how many children's books should be among the next 2,200 books ordered?

1. 200
2. 440
3. 525
4. 760
5. 1,100

Narrowly-spaced Alternatives

A family drove 116 miles in four hours. At that rate, how many hours would it take them to travel 203 miles?

1. 5 1/2
2. 6
3. 6 1/2
4. 7
5. 7 1/2

Messick and Kogan found that among students who performed <u>equally</u> well on math questions in the "free response" format--where the correct answer had to be figured out and written down, instead of chosen from a list of alternatives--some were hurt and some were helped when presented with questions in a multiple-choice format. Whether they gained or lost had little to do with their actual ability to work out math problems. Instead, it depended on two factors: first, an aspect of personality known as "categorization style," and second, whether the multiple-choice answers were widely or narrowly spaced. On a free response question, performance was simply a matter of math--you worked the problem out and got it right or wrong. But on a multiple-choice question--especially one given as part of a test where you only had a limited amount of time to finish--another skill entered the picture: what Messick and Kogan called multiple-choice "strategy."[100] With multiple-choice, students no longer needed to fully formulate an answer in their own minds, but rather had to choose one that was already down on paper. As Dr. Rowley puts it, the multiple-choice format "require/s/ examinees to select rather than construct their responses."[101]

This strategy could be used to advantage. By scanning the problem and the possible answer, the test-taker might be able to pick out the correct answer by eliminating the alternatives without having to take the time to work the problem through to a precise solution. Some personalities--Messick and Kogan call them "broad categorizers"--adopt this strategy intuitively. But others, the "narrow categorizers," are inclined to work the problem out from start to finish, insisting on the same accuracy they would for a free response question. While they might end up getting the questions right, the narrow categorizers will have less time to work on other questions, and their scores may suffer as a consequence.

This is where the spacing of the alternatives comes in. When differences between the possible answers are small, it is harder to get a quick fix on the likely answer and broad and narrow categorizers are placed on a relatively equal footing. But when alternatives are widely spaced, Messick and Kogan report, "broad category preferences may have an advantage on such tests since they might quickly estimate an answer, find one of the multiple-choice alternatives close enough to be considered roughly equivalent, and quickly go on to the next item."[102] Messick and Kogan concluded that "the customary multiple-choice quantitative aptitude test employing moderately-to-widely spaced alternatives gives a special advantage to the 'approximation' strategy that the broad categorizer will likely use."[103]

One consequence of the tendency of multiple choice aptitude tests to penalize those who are reluctant to gamble was suggested by the results of a 1974 study of the math section of the ETS School and College Ability Test (SCAT) conducted at Merritt College in California. In analyzing the scores and test papers of candidates who failed to finish all the questions, the Merritt study found "a wide discrepancy between the percentages correct of the problems completed and the national percentile standings /in scores/."[104] In other words, many people who scored lower than others had actually achieved a _higher_ percentage of correct answers on the questions they attempted--their downfall had been in failing to take a shot at enough questions within the alloted time.

The 1970 report of the College Board Commission on Tests contended that the "SAT reflect/s/ at least four 'factors' of ability." Three of these were factors routinely claimed in the ETS literature to be measured by the test--knowledge of vocabulary, quantitative ability, and reasoning ability. But the fourth factor had not been so vigorously publicized: in the Commission's words, "speed in test-taking."[105] Commission member B. Alden

Thresher, a former MIT Admissions Director, ETS and College Board trustee and incorporator of the College Board, wrote in the Commission's final report that "the speed element in the current Board tests constitutes a more serious constraint on their usefulness than seems to be recognized in the ETS studies of the subject."[106] Thresher challenged the ETS assumption (which he quoted from a company research report) that "'a test may be regarded as essentially unspeeded if at least 80 percent of the candidates reach the last item, and if virtually everyone reaches three-quarters of the test.'"[107] Thresher pointed out the effect of speededness on the way students would learn to approach the test and the kind of thinking it would reward:

> It is unquestionably true that the great majority of the candidates are under the threat of not finishing, and this includes most of those who actually do succeed in reaching all the items. Under this threat, the student's entire approach to each item is of necessity based on snap judgment, not on considered and deliberate thought. He knows that speed is of the essence, and that a lack of it is quite likely to affect his score adversely. (Original emphasis).[108]

Thresher's recommendation that the speededness of the SAT be reduced was endorsed by fourteen of the Commission's twenty-one members.[109]

The extent to which multiple-choice test-taking is a specialized, learnable skill, has long been appreciated by test professionals. A body of literature on test-taking strategy has been accumulating in psychometric journals for decades. In an internal May 24, 1973 report, ETS Director of Guidance Programs Arthur M. Kroll proposed that ETS publish a guide which would "discuss candidly certain strategies for test-taking" in order "to eliminate the disadvantage experienced by those students who lack test wisdom."[110]

Quoting a study from the journal, <u>Educational and Psychological Measurement</u>, by Drs. Jason Millman, Carol Bishop, and former ETS Vice President Robert Ebel, Kroll defined test-wiseness as:

> a subject's capacity to utilize the characteristics and formats of the test and/or the test taking situation to receive a high score. Test-wiseness is logically independent of the examinee's knowledge of the subject matter for which the items are supposedly measures.[111]

Kroll reviewed test-wiseness research which showed, for example, that instruction in "guessing strategy" could produce statistically significant score gains. He noted that several commercial test-taking guides included advice to students on this subject which systematic research has shown to be erroneous.

> Students sometimes wonder whether or not they should change their answers after reconsidering a given question. Several test-taking guides suggest retention of the original answer, despite the fact that most published studies show that it is to the student's advantage to <u>change</u> his answers after review. . . . It is generally <u>true</u> at all grade levels that the percentage of wrong to right revisions tends to exceed the percentage of right to wrong. (Emphasis added.)[112]

Kroll proposed, in effect, that ETS go beyond the innocuous, common sense advice usually presented in its literature--get enough sleep the night before, read the directions carefully, etc.--to inform candidates of the "tricks" of the multiple-choice aptitude test. He presented an "Outline of Test-Wiseness Principles," taken from Millman, Bishop and Ebel, which corroborated Thresher's warning that in the world of the speeded multiple-choice test, an informed guess could sometimes earn you more "aptitude" than sustained and rigorous thought. Kroll wrote:

> Time-using strategy
> 1. Begin to work as rapidly as possible with reasonable assurance of accuracy.

2. Set up a schedule for progress through the test.

3. <u>Omit or guess at items</u> . . . which resist a quick response. . . .

Guessing strategy

1. <u>Always guess</u> if right answers only are scored.

2. <u>Always guess</u> if the correction for guessing is less severe than a "correction for guessing" formula that gives an expected score of zero for random responding.

3. <u>Always guess</u> even if the usual correction or a more severe penalty for guessing is employed, whenever elimination of options provides sufficient chance of profiting.

Deductive reasoning strategy

1. Eliminate options which are known to be incorrect and choose from among the remaining options.

2. Choose neither or both of two options which imply the correctness of each other.

3. Choose neither or one (but not both) of two statements, one of which, if correct would imply the incorrectness of the other.

4. Restrict choice to those options which encompass all of two or more given statements known to be correct. . . . (Emphasis added.)[113]

Kroll noted that these principles would apply to all speeded multiple-choice tests, regardless of how professionally they were constructed. But he also went on to list a second set of principles "which relate to the idiosyncracies of the test constructor or the test purposes."[114] "ETS would confront a policy issue if it were to present such principles in its own publication," Kroll pointed out, "particularly since careful test construction would supposedly eliminate the usefulness of such principles."[115] Some of this second group of principles, such as being on the lookout for a tendency in the testmaker to make the correct options longer than the incorrect ones, clearly would not apply, since ETS designed its question-writing procedures to guard against such lapses. But others had more universal relevance: "Answer items as the test constructor intended," the testers advised in their section on "Intent Consideration strategy," and "adopt the level of sophistication that is expected."[116] The message was clear: beyond the content of the questions, multiple-choice test-taking was a game in itself, a game where too much thinking could be hazardous to your score.

In a 1978 review of the test-wiseness literature, ETS researcher Dr. Lewis W. Pike noted that many students were either not aware of or not applying important rules of test-taking strategy. "Ironically," he wrote, "research has shown that even when there is a penalty for guessing, most examinees would do better if they did more guessing." Pike reported the suggestion of ETS researcher Dr. Frederic Lord who wrote in 1975 that "it may be time for children in school to be taught how to behave effectively when taking a test."[117]

Previous ETS research had already indicated that such instruction could be effective. A 1967 study by ETS researchers Henry Alker, Julia Carlson and Margaret Herman of students taking the SAT Verbal section concluded that "test-wiseness was positively and significantly correlated with multiple-choice performance. Consistent with the critic's position, test-wiseness was related to a higher score on the multiple-choice aptitude and achievement questions."[118]

Although ETS never implemented the recommendation for an open and thorough publication of test-taking strategies,[119] the demand for such information from students was welcomed in other quarters. By the early 1970s, commercial "coaching schools," which charged fees from $40 to $300 to prepare students for standardized tests with instruction in test-wiseness, drill on multiple-choice questions, and exercises to reduce anxiety, were enrolling an estimated 50,000 customers annually, according to the Boston Regional Office of the Federal Trade Commission.[120] The coaching schools' claim was explicit: for a fee, they would boost students' scores. "Don't let 4 years of college go by the boards," warned ads for a GMAT and LSAT review course. "Thousands have earned increases of a hundred points or more," advertised another coaching conglomerate which offered instruction in the PSAT, SAT, LSAT, GRE, and GMAT.[121]

Cram schools were not the only organizations convinced of the effectiveness of coaching. The FTC Boston office found that "a large number of undergraduate colleges and universities . . . offer preparation for admission tests to graduate schools," including such institutions as the University of Michigan, Cornell University, and Amherst College.[122] A 1978 ETS survey of 253 Northeastern secondary schools found that nearly one third of them offered some form of special preparation for the SAT.[123]

In contrast to the internal statements of Kroll and Pike on the importance of test-wiseness, ETS' public position on coaching was vigorous opposition. In the words of ETS' William Angoff: "Appalled by the subversive effect of these commercial enterprises on the goals of education, the /College/ Board prepared a special booklet . . . which show/s/ at best only small and insignificant gains on the SAT resulting from short-term intensive coaching. . . . /It/ urges students and their parents not to waste their time and money on this kind of coaching."[124] Robert Stoltz of the Law School Admission Council approached the Federal Trade Commission in 1974 to see "whether we could get the FTC to carry the ball for us" in the war against the coaching schools.[125] The previous year, the LSAC had considered whether to "secretly enroll a substantial number of people in several cram courses" or "have a Council representative purchase a /coaching/ franchise" in order to obtain data to discredit the schools."[126]

Much was at stake in the ETS campaign to refute the coachers' claims. For students, there was the question of equity. If a student could pay to boost their scores he or she could gain advantage in the competition for admission. In its crudest form, the edge offered by some schools to their customers was a respectable form of cheating; they got to see some of the questions, or near identical versions, before they took the test. Robert Scheller, proprietor of an SAT coaching school in Washington Township, New Jersey, explained to the Morris County Daily Record how the process worked: "There are about five of us who take the SAT on a frequent basis. We all have photographic memories and from this we make up our own version of these tests. Our exam is as close to the actual test as possible, without using the exact same questions."[127] The owner of one large national coaching school admitted to the FTC that his organization used the same method.[128] At a 1979 legislative hearing, New York State Senator Donald Halperin told of how he had taken a coaching course and been drilled in questions which later appeared verbatim on the SAT.[129]

Regardless of how the score gains were attained, the larger equity problem arose from the fact that they were being sold for a price. The FTC found that the test candidates who had taken advantage of coaching were heavily concentrated in the upper income brackets.

Comparison of Coached and Uncoached Students[130]

Parental Income	Coached	Uncoached
Less than $12,000 per year	15.7%	23.3%
Between $12,000 and $17,999	15.6	25.9
Between $18,000 and $23,999	16.2	20.5
Between $24,000 and $29,999	11.3	13.0
$30,000 or more	41.2	17.2
	100 %	100 %

As Lewis Pike remarked after leaving ETS in 1979, "I think there are certain social class biases in the tests to begin with, and then when on top of that some people can afford to receive coaching and some can't, . . . I think that compounds the problem."[131]

The coaching school's claim was not just of importance to consumers concerned about fairness. For ETS, it struck to the heart of scientific credibility. The test was advertised as a scientific measure of aptitude developed over the course of a lifetime. If coaching schools could significantly change the amount of this measured "aptitude" with a few dozen hours of instruction in test strategy, the ETS claim would be called into question. One coaching school proprietor defined the issue sharply: "If our claim that we can teach for parts of these tests is true, then the tests are not really measuring what they claim to measure."[132] "If the tests were changed to really test aptitude, we could not teach for them and we would be out of business."[133] In the November 9, 1974 meeting of its Legal Affairs and Finance Committees, the Law School Admission Council recognized this point as well. "The Council and ETS are injured by assertions that the test /LSAT/ is not one of aptitude," the minutes said, "and can therefore be coached."[134]

For years, ETS was careful to expunge evidence which supported such assertions from the literature it circulated to candidates. The 1965 ETS-College Board Booklet, Effects of Coaching on Scholastic Aptitude Test Scores, (designed to fight what Angoff called the "subversion" of the coachers) summarized seven studies of coaching programs which had failed to produce significant score gains. It did not mention a College Board sponsored study at the U.S. Military Academy which showed a coaching gain of 136 points.[135] The studies which the booklet did choose to report involved coaching programs substantially shorter and less intense than those offered by the large coaching schools. A 1972 evaluation by ETS researchers of the studies cited by the booklet on coaching for the SAT math section, for example, questioned their unequivocal denunciation of coaching:

> The instruction provided in these studies /cited in the booklet/ was, where its nature can be ascertained, rather scanty. There appeared to be little or no systematic attempt to identify the skills needed to perform well on the test and to develop materials to meet these needs. Since most previous research on this question involves subjects at the extremes of the ability range, generalization to the more heterogeneous population of candidates seeking admission to higher education becomes hazardous.[136]

Despite such internal professional criticism, ETS and the College Board continue in 1979 to circulate the booklet to college admissions directors and high school counselors.[137] This is not the first time that ETS had continued to publicly make claims about coaching which its professionals and clients had privately renounced. At the same 1974 LSAC meeting where coaching was described as harmful to the claim to measure aptitude, the Council received a report on "methods of attacking cram courses" which "noted that the 'Bulletin' statement that the LSAT is not coachable is of doubtful value, and we cannot prove that courses do not, at least in the case of certain individuals, help. The kind of research needed to test this would be elaborate, expensive and of no conclusive value either way."[138]

In March 1976, ETS was informed that its longstanding wish for a government investigation of coaching schools had been fulfilled.[139] Independent of the LSAC's solicitation of the FTC national office, the FTC Boston regional office had decided to investigate whether coaching schools were engaging in unfair and deceptive trade practices with their promises to raise scores. The FTC subpoened records from both ETS and the coaching schools, learning who had taken courses and how much their scores had improved. With these actions, the FTC accumulated an information base unprecedented in the history of coaching studies. The results were analyzed by computer and supplemented with a review of the coaching research literature.[140]

In September 1978, FTC attorney Arthur Levine, director of the Boston coaching study, submitted a 258-page staff memorandum to FTC headquarters reporting the study's findings. Levine reported that no coaching school had been able to provide adequate documentation in response to FTC subpoenas demanding substantiation for their advertising claims. For most of the courses, the substantiating materials consisted of letters from students and unsystematic survey results which, Levine wrote, "would not constitute a reasonable basis for supporting claims of specific score increases."[141] One course, John Sexton's LSAT Preparation Center, prepared a statistical report after receiving the subpoena which was deemed to be "statistically invalid" by a mathematical consulting firm employed by the FTC.[142] The Stanley H. Kaplan Educational Centers, the largest coaching firm, did not receive a subpoena for substantiation because, Levine explained, "at two investigational hearings SHK /Stanley H. Kaplan/ representatives admitted not having documentation for score increase claims made."[143]

The bold claims of the coaching schools were found to be based more on advertising enthusiasm than reliable scientific data. By itself, Levine pointed out, this could have been construed as a violation of the Federal Trade Commission Act which prohibits "mak/ing/ an affirmative product claim without a reasonable basis for making that claim."[144] Had the FTC moved against the coachers on these grounds, as the LSAC had asked it to, it would have been another routine case of marginal entrepreneurs caught cutting corners to make a buck. But the fact that the coaching schools had not bothered to document their claims did not mean that they could not be documented, at least to some extent.

The Boston report, through a statistical analysis of test scores, found that the SAT coaching course studied had raised scores by an average of more than 100 points; one of the two LSAT courses studied had raised scores by an average of sixty points.[145] As Levine's memorandum to FTC headquarters pointed out, this had serious ramifications for ETS.

THE REPRESENTATIONS OF ETS AND ITS CLIENTS CONSTITUTE DECEPTIVE ACTS AND PRACTICES WITHIN THE MEANING OF SECTION 5 OF THE FEDERAL TRADE COMMISSION ACT

> The representations of ETS and its clients regarding the susceptibility of their standardized admission examinations to coaching are false, misleading, deceptive, and perhaps are or have been made intentionally or with a reckless disregard for the truth. . . .
>
> Earlier statements by ETS and its clients regarding the coachability of their examinations were unequivocal. The more recent vintage representations in some instances indicate that a review of mathematical concepts may help individuals who have not recently enrolled in a formal mathematics course but that coaching is otherwise ineffective. The statements of course are misleading, and in most instances false. As our statistical analysis indicates both sections of the SAT are coachable and the LSAT is coachable although to a lesser degree than the SAT. . . .
>
> Many consumers of ETS' examinations (who are compelled to take the examinations) who could afford the tuition for coaching, have been dissuaded from enrolling in coaching courses as a result of the 20 years of misrepresentations by ETS and its clients. As a result they have likely obtained lower scores on the standardized admission examinations they have taken than they would have received had

> they been coached. This has resulted in a diminishing of their competitive position for admission vis-a-vis their coached counterparts. . . .
>
> The aforementioned set of circumstances of course gives rise to classic violations of Section 5. . . . Not only do ETS' and its clients' representations have a tendency or capacity to deceive but they actually deceive. The interest at stake as we have indicated may mean the difference between acceptance or rejection at an academic institution and all of the economic, social, and psychological ramifications attendant thereto. . . . (Emphasis in original.)[146]

The Boston report went on to point out that more was involved than just the veracity of ETS' claims on the limited subject of coaching.

> ETS and the College Board have recognized that if coaching is effective then the value of standardized examinations becomes suspect. /Quoting the ETS technical manual for the SAT/ "Indeed, the usefulness of the SAT as an indicator of a student's potential for college work depends in large measure on the fact that the SAT measures general ability developed over the full range of experiences in a person's life." False statements have been made to assure ETS' clients, undergraduate and graduate colleges and universities, and consumers, that scores can not be increased by any short-term mechanism thereby allowing ETS to maintain its position in the standardized admission testing market. These reasons are no different from those that exist in the traditional disparagement area. One competitor falsely disparages another's products or services to maintain or enhance its current market position and divert trade away from a competitor. (Emphasis added.)
>
> This is also . . . /an/ example of ETS placing its obligations to the public in an inferior position to its thirst for revenue, thereby weakening any argument that it is a not-for-profit corporation within the meaning of Section 4 of the Federal Trade Commission Act /which confines the FTC's jurisdiction to profit-making companies/.[147]

The Boston report, then an unreleased internal document, created a political dilemma for the FTC's Washington headquarters. Its finding that coaching could improve scores was sure to stimulate both widespread public interest and forceful attack from ETS. As FTC Chairman Michael Pertschuk explained in a

1979 interview, the Commission was in the position of "finding ETS in effect exposed as misleading students."[148]

Before a decision could be made on what to do with the Boston report, its results were leaked to the press. On November 17, 1978 the Harvard Crimson reported the Boston office finding (without actual score gain figures) that coaching helped.[149] The Wall Street Journal and the Washington Post followed suit.[150] But as pressure mounted for release of the report, FTC statistical analysts Drs. Ken Bernhardt and Michael Sesnowitz told Albert Kramer, Director of the Commission's Bureau of Consumer Protection, that the Boston report was vulnerable to attack on technical grounds. Although the average score gains of 100 and sixty points had in fact occurred, Bernhardt and Sesnowitz pointed out that the gains might have been influenced by differences between the educational and social backgrounds of students who took coaching courses and those who did not. While coaching had helped dramatically in these cases, there were not enough data available to conclude that it could be expected to help as much when the coached and uncoached students had similar background characteristics.[151]

In response to these criticisms, Pertschuck and Kramer ordered a reanalysis of the Boston data which would control for background factors. Pertschuk contends that the reasons for ordering the reanalysis were strictly technical. "The information in this report was so significant that the most important thing the Commission could do was make sure its data were impeccable and then release it."[152] But due regard was also paid to covering the Commission's flanks from ETS disapproval. The model suggested for reanalyzing the Boston data was, according to a May 15, 1979 memo from Kramer to the Commission, "reviewed by researchers from the Educational Testing Service." Kramer noted that while ETS offered some criticisms, "they did feel the basic methodology used to analyze the observational data was sound."[153] As its outside adviser on the reanalysis, the FTC chose Professor Gene V. Glass of the University of Colorado, a longtime ETS adviser.[154] When the Commissioners met in May of 1979 to make their final decision on how to portray the results of the coaching investigation to the public, they each received a black pasteboard folder containing, along with the staff analyses, a brief from ETS and CEEB explaining their view of the issue* (no comparable brief was presented on behalf of the coaching schools).[156]

The consultation with ETS, which had been identified as a target of investigation by the Boston report, was not the only remarkable feature of the FTC's reanalysis and release of the coaching study. According to Pertschuk, the Federal Trade Commissioners personally directed preparation of the press release which accompanied the reanalyzed report, a chore usually left to the agency's public information office.[157] Critics had already asserted that the Commission was holding back on the report for fear of entering into conflict with ETS: Arthur Levine, who began the coaching study had resigned from the FTC charging Washington with sitting on his report. The National Education Association (NEA) had filed a freedom of information suit to

---

*The brief had originally been prepared for a meeting ETS and CEEB requested with Kramer. As Kramer told the Commission, "I concluded that such a meeting would not have advanced our investigation and therefore declined it."[155]

compel FTC release of the Boston report and the accompanying data.[158]

The Commission's press release, dated May 29, 1978, did little to dispel these suspicions. The release made no mention of the ETS claims that its tests were invulnerable to coaching. Four paragraphs describing the results of the reanalysis were balanced by nine paragraphs of disclaimers, from the mild warning that "a variety of factors limit generalizations that can be drawn from the study," to a specific denial by the Commissioners of accountability for the findings of their staff: "The Federal Trade Commission itself has reached no final determination regarding the conclusions reached by the Bureau of Consumer Protection," the release stated.

> The Commission's unanimous decision to release the study and underlying data was made in order to permit review of the staff's work and in the hope that release would stimulate further research and debate on the effectiveness of coaching on standardized examination performance.[159]

The release was accompanied by a report of the reanalysis by Sesnowitz and Bernhardt, and an edited version of the Boston report with an additional disclaimer stapled on: "The attached 'Staff Memorandum'. . . has several major flaws in the data analysis, making the results unreliable."[160] (All of the material quoted earlier from the Boston report is from the legal and policy analysis section which was edited out and has never before been released to the public.)[161]

ETS immediately issued a release saying that the Boston report had been repudiated and the ETS position on coaching upheld.[162] The College Board issued a "backgrounder" for the press claiming that the FTC findings were consistent with their own studies purporting to show that coaching had little impact.[163] In a letter to Science magazine, ETS Executive Vice President Robert J. Solomon quoted the disclaimers from the Commission's release and told of how ETS had "encouraged the Commission to publish its study."[164]

Despite the FTC disclaimers, however, the final report was not the vindication for ETS which the corporation portrayed it to be. The Boston report finding that ETS was misleading candidates was omitted from the final FTC release not because the reanalyzed data failed to support that finding, but because of a political judgment by Pertschuk and Kramer that a direct attack on ETS would not be the most effective method of getting the company to alter its coaching claims. The Sesnowitz and Bernhardt reanalysis found that, after background factors were taken into account, the score gains to be expected due to coaching on the SAT were twenty-five points on both the verbal and math sections.[165] The implications of this finding were summed up in the May 15, 1979 memo to the Commission from Bureau of Consumer Protection head Albert Kramer: "Our conclusions are less dramatic than those of the Boston report, but nonetheless show that, contrary to explicit claims of ETS/CEEB, coaching can be effective, at least for the SAT."[166] (Original emphasis.)

In much the same manner as Levine's Boston report, Kramer went on to discuss the consequences which could be suffered by those who believed the ETS assurances that coaching would not help:

> The greatest consumer injury suffered by an applicant taking a standardized test comes not at the top or in the middle range, but as the student's score approaches

whatever arbitrary cut-off the college or university imposes.... If the school's cut-off is 500, the difference between 520 and 495 is critical. Therefore, perhaps even the small coaching-attributed score gains <u>acknowledged</u> by ETS/CEEB portend some degree of unfairness to test-takers and would render deceptive their admonition not to be coached... The score gains we have found are more clearly significant in view of the ETS/CEEB admonition.[167] (Emphasis added.)

After reviewing the Sesnowitz-Bernhardt findings, Kramer reached a conclusion about ETS' claims which paralleled that of Levine: "unfair or deceptive trade practices," Kramer wrote, "were indeed occurring."[168]

Yet, despite finding that ETS and the College Board were deceiving consumers, Kramer advised the Commission that the problem could best be remedied by cooperation, not confrontation, with the testing industry. "I do not recommend formal law enforcement action against ETS/CEEB at this time," Kramer wrote, "because of the excellent prospects for ETS to join with other interested persons in addressing the problems raised in our work."[169] Kramer had prepared the memo after consultation with Commission Chairman Pertschuk who said the memo reflected his thinking on the matter as well. Pertschuk explained that the findings of the reanalysis were clear: "What I drew out of the study," he said, "was that students could be helped by coaching and that ETS was not disclosing that information.... There is no question that the ETS statements were not accurate." Pertschuk said that Levine's recommendation for a deceptive trade practices suit against ETS "struck me as crazy." Pertschuk believed that given the FTC's limited resources, recent political criticism of the Commission's breadth of activity, and the problem of whether ETS, as a non-profit organization, even fell under the jurisdiction of the FTC (see Chapter VII), a suit was not the best strategy. Pertschuk thought that simply releasing the findings would give Congress "the means to go to ETS and force appropriate changes." "It was a problem that we felt should best be handled by exposure of the report."[170]

Eight months after release of the FTC report, the claims about coaching in the SAT candidate literature remain unchanged. The ETS-College Board pamphlet, Taking the SAT, states flatly: "The verbal and mathematical abilities measured by the SAT develop over years of study and practice. Drilling or last-minute cramming probably will not do much to prepare you for the test."[171]

When interviewed in September of 1979, Pertschuk conceded that if ETS' claims do not change, his strategy will have failed and Levine's recommendation for litigation will have to be reconsidered. Speaking of the current ETS claims Pertschuk commented, "If nothing happens, then . . . he [Levine] will be right, and I will be wrong."[172]

Random Prediction, Systematic Exclusion

ETS aptitude tests can penalize students for reasons quite apart from their reading and math skills. Scores on the tests can be influenced by a number of factors--age, anxiety, test-wiseness-- which contribute to the specialized skill of multiple-choice test-taking. Though some of these factors may be linked to social background (low-income students, for example, may have less access to coaching for test-wiseness than more affluent students) these external influences on aptitude test scores generally cut across ethnic and economic boundaries.

But some of the penalties meted out by aptitude tests are concentrated on people from particular ethnic and economic groups. ETS President William W. Turnbull stated in a 1974 speech that it is a "plain fact that the average test scores of many minority groups . . . fall below the average scores of people from the predominant white middle-class culture."*[173] When ETS aptitude tests are used for regulating access to higher education, the systematic distribution of low scores creates formidable barriers to minorities trying to go on to college, graduate or professional school. And when those scores bear an essentially random relationship to ability to succeed in one's chosen career (see Five Per Cent of Nothing: Prediction of What? section, p. 70,) members of low-scoring groups are excluded for a reason unrelated to their actual potential for accomplishment. President Turnbull came close to acknowledging how this aspect of the test system worked in his 1974 address: "Since there is no necessary relationship between the scores and what happens after graduation when a person enters a career," Turnbull said, "we see the phenomenon of gross underrepresentation of ethnic minorities in the jobs, notably the professions, for which a college education is a necessary card of entry."[174]

The systematic effect of aptitude test scores on minority opportunities is illustrated by the fact that, contrary to the

---

*While Turnbull limits his comparison to minorities and the white "middle class," the scores also penalize by class just as they do by ethnic background. Thus middle-class whites and working class whites tend to score lower than upper-class whites. The same division by class applies within minority groups. (See Chapter V.)

belief of some that minorities face lower standards due to special admissions programs, in many cases minority students must earn higher grades than whites in order to have an equal chance of admission. In a 1971 study of black and white students at integrated colleges, ETS researchers Junius A. Davis and George Temp found that, in the six schools for which the information was available, "while the SAT score means for (admitted) blacks were lower than those for their white counterparts, the mean high school ranks were higher."[175] (Emphasis added.)

An extensive ETS survey of the grades and test scores of all applicants to ABA accredited law schools in 1976, found that sixty-eight per cent of the white (and ethnically unidentified) applicants with college grade point averages of 2.75 or above were admitted to law school in 1976, compared to only fifty-eight per cent of the black applicants with the same averages.[176] Among applicants with averages above 2.50, sixty-four per cent of the whites and "unidentifieds" were admitted compared to only fifty-one per cent of the blacks.[177] The black applicants were placed at a disadvantage created not by their past performance--on grades they ranked just as high as the whites--but by the results of the ETS aptitude test.

ETS insists that the low scores of minorities do not reflect deficiencies in the tests, but rather deficiencies in the preparation and potential of the minority students themselves. In 1976 College Board President and ETS Trustee George Hanford reaffirmed the findings of an earlier College Board study which maintained, "It is simply not true, as far as we can tell, that the disadvantaged student is penalized by the SAT, if you mean that he makes a misleadingly low score."[178] In July 1979 ETS Executive Vice President Robert J. Solomon told a Congressional hearing: "The results have been quite consistent. Differences in test score averages across groups are consistent with differences in actual performance in college. Tests typically predict the same way with the same validity for whites as for minorities."[179]

The ETS claim that its tests are not biased against minorities is based on a definition of bias which has been repudiated by an internal company report as "untenable," a definition based strictly on the limited criterion of first year grades.[180] By the ETS definition, a test is unbiased if it predicts the first year grades of minorities about as accurately as they predict the first year grades of whites. This definition ignores the fact that since the validity of grade prediction is low for both whites and minorities, and minorities tend to receive lower scores, they can be excluded by a test score which has little connection to their actual ability to succeed.

As some psychometricians have only recently come to realize, the result of using a low-validity test which places one group at the bottom of its rankings is the admission of a smaller percentage of minorities than of whites who are capable of succeeding in school. An extensive study by Alexander Astin, for example, found that "dropout rates of black students attending white colleges . . . are slightly lower than is predicted from grades and test scores."[181] (Emphasis in original.) In 1979, for example, the American Bar Association issued a press release on the Council on

Legal Education Opportunity (CLEO) training and financial aid program (supported in part by ETS) for minority students which noted that "while most of their LSAT scores and undergraduate grade point averages showed them to be high risk students, 'CLEO students have performed at a level consistent with or better than their fellow law students.'"[182]

The lower average scores of minority applicants are primarily a reflection of what is perhaps the single most important characteristic of the test, its tendency to rank people by income. In a massive College Board statistical report on students taking the 1973-74 SAT, students with an average score of 750-800 (800 being the highest score), for example, were found to come from families with an average income of $24,124. Students with scores from 700-749 came from families with an average income of $21,980; students who scored slightly lower--from 650-699--came from families with a slightly lower average income--$21,292. This correlation held firm for not only rich versus poor students, but through every bracket of the income scale.[183] Students from families with higher incomes tend to receive higher scores; this pattern holds nearly constant across ethnic and geographical boundaries.[184]

The likelihood of a student being from a family in a given income bracket has been found to be directly linked to race. A survey of the parental income of 1978-79 SAT candidates laid this out graphically. White students taking the tests came from families with a mean annual income of $27,300; Puerto Rican students from families earning an average of $14,500; and black students from families earning an average of $13,700--<u>barely half</u> of the mean annual income for white families.[185] (See Chapter V for a discussion of social class and test scores.) Given such a distribution of income, a substantial correlation between aptitude test scores and ethnic group membership is to be expected.

It is sometimes argued that other forms of evaluation would discriminate among ethnic groups to the same degree as aptitude tests. This is simply not the case. College grades, for example, have less connection to ethnic background than do LSAT scores.[186] Baird's 1979 report on the use of biographical information to predict performance noted that "studies of the large samples of college freshmen obtained by the American Council on Education also show that Black students report just as many accomplishments . . . as do White students. . . . These results held in all types of institutions. In short, the evidence indicates that reports of accomplishments do not discriminate against disadvantaged or minority students."[187]

A number of explanations have been offered as to why aptitude tests, unlike other measures, discriminate so heavily against minorities. Some of the more basic theories are discussed below. Familiarity--or lack of it--with the language and vocabulary of a test can affect the scores of entire groups of people. For a study of questions used on the National Teacher Examinations (NTE), Donald M. Medley of the University of Virginia and Thomas J. Quirk, of ETS, developed an experimental test that included questions "intended to recognize the contribution to American culture of people who happened to be black (in the case of black items) or of people who happened to live in the last few decades (in the case of modern items)."[188] Medley and Quirk found that the shift to the modern and black item questions resulted in a dramatic increase in the scores of black test-takers. A complete shift from traditional to black items "would boost the score of the average black candidate relative to that of the average white candidate by almost 19 points, nearly 30%."[189] The researchers concluded that "these results leave little doubt that black candidates tend to possess a different set of knowledge than white candidates, and that these differences have to do with conventional subject-matter areas."[190]

Dr. Robert L. Williams of Washington University in 1972 developed an even more powerful example of the impact of language on standardized tests. Williams prepared a test which he called the BITCH--the "Black Intelligence Scale of Cultural Homogeneity." "For the BITCH," he wrote in a 1972 paper, "the content of all items was drawn exclusively from the Black experience domain."[191] The results of the test were striking. Williams gave the exam to a sample group of 100 white and 100 black high school students from St. Louis, and the traditional pattern of Saturday morning test-taking was reversed. "Virtually all Black subjects became intensely interested in the test," he wrote, ". . . Black S[ubject]s frequently came across items which were humorous and quite familiar to them. White S[ubject]s seemed to be quite challenged by the test and appeared tense. Many sighed and showed other signs of discomfort."[192] The changed circumstances showed up in the bottom line as well. Black students systematically scored higher than white students, receiving on the average, seventy-one per cent higher scores.[193]

With an eye toward this reversal of the usual aptitude test score distribution, Williams concluded, "The BITCH-100 is designed primarily for the Black experience. Whites are clearly penalized. Using the Black norm as a basis for determining the value of a white student's scores, it is clear that most white S[ubject]s would generally score at the lower end of the distribution."[194] Though ETS never stated it quite so frankly, the same could be said about the experience of many minority students on ETS aptitude tests.

Attorney David White, who is conducting a study of law school admissions for the National Conference of Black Lawyers, has demonstrated how more subtle but equally powerful biases can underlie verbal aptitude test questions. Using a sample SAT sentence completion question which concerns a confrontation between people of an island and an occupying power, White shows how the answer the test-taker chooses can depend on the group with which they unconsciously identify. On a still less obvious level, White argues that ETS "minority content" items, such as a sample LSAT question he analyzes concerning a black entrepreneur opening a community store, can be even _more_ biased against minority students than conventional questions because of hidden political assumptions of the testmakers (see appendix for text of White's question analyses).[195]

Other factors which may contribute to the lower average scores of minority students are levels of test anxiety sometimes higher than those found among whites and less exposure to coaching in multiple-choice test-taking techniques.[196] On a more fundamental level, the lower scores are often said to reflect poor educational background resulting from the lower average incomes of minority parents and racial discrimination in elementary and secondary schools.

In a speech delivered while he was serving as ETS Director of Minority Affairs, C. Sumner "Chuck" Stone--now a leading ETS critic--noted a way in which aptitude test scores could _serve_ the interests of minorities by dramatizing the gap which exists between the quality of schooling provided to blacks and whites.[197] A variation of this argument is frequently used by test professionals who criticize those who attack the discriminatory impact of aptitude tests as wanting to "kill the messenger" who brings the bad news of educational deprivation. But as Stone and Robert L. Williams have pointed out, the test is more than just a messenger; it is also a gatekeeper which can bar people from future opportunities because of past educational deficiencies which conceal their ability and will to learn. In Williams words, "the bad news is in the system and not in the victim."[198] Further, "the system that produced the damage must be closely examined and modified."[199] It is one thing to inform people that they have been victimized by inadequate education, which as Stone points out, scores can do when used in the aggregate for entire groups. But it is something else entirely to use those scores to <u>prevent individuals</u> from pursuing opportunities. This is where the ETS aptitude test can serve to perpetuate the educational inequality which it purports to merely illuminate.

Regardless of the reasons why minority students are penalized by aptitude test scores, the consequences of this systematic pattern are evident, and have been noted by many observers. As early as 1969, the Association of Black Psychologists called for a complete moratorium on standardized testing. "It is unfair to assume that Black and White cultures are so similar that the same tests can be properly used in psychological testing and placement." Dr. Williams wrote in a later paper," . . . Conventional intelligence and ability test scores are unfair to Black children and can endanger their futures." Noting the use of standardized tests on the elementary and secondary level, he continued:

> They have supported the phenomonon of the self-fulfilling prophecy. Black children are tracked by the schools on the basis of these inappropriate tests. Teachers develop expectations based on essentially meaningless test scores, which, in turn, influence their behavior toward Black children. A vicious circle is created in which the Black child is the victim.[200]

In their official statement, the Association saw the use of the tests as the beginning of a long, downward spiral that denied black students opportunities all along the way. The Association said it "fully supports those parents who have chosen to defend their rights by refusing to allow their children and themselves to be subjected to achievement, intelligence, aptitude, and performance tests."[201]

In a 1975 report published in the *American Psychologist*, Association of Black Psychologists Chairman George Jackson, charging that "psychological testing historically has been a quasi-scientific tool in the perpetuation of racism on all levels of social or economic intercourse," (see Chapter IV for an account of the history of psychological testing), called for a federal "truth-in-testing" law which would require disclosure of information about the tests' impact on minorities.[202]

At the January, 1976 meeting of the American Psychological Association Council of Representatives, members of the Clinical Psychology Division proposed that standardized tests used for the selection of minority students be labelled with a warning modeled after the one required on cigarette advertisements:

> Uses of this test on populations other than those for which it was standardized may be harmful to the individuals being tested, and such usage is deemed contrary to the ethical standards of the American Psychological Association.[203]

Responding swiftly to this challenge to their professional turf, the members of <u>another</u> APA division--the Evaluation and Measurement Division--introduced a resolution of their own. The psychometricians' measure, which complained that "The science and profession of psychology are damaged by the lopsided attacks which often go without correction, comment or rebuttal," and affirmed that "standardized testing . . . can be a valuable technique in psychological and educational decision-making," was carried by the APA Council; the clinical psychologists' warning label was set aside.[204]

Outside their own professional organizations, however, test industry representatives have not been as successful in quelling the growing realization of aptitude tests' impact on minority opportunities. When in 1975 the NAACP convened a panel of educators and psychologists to study this question, ETS and the College Board joined in with financial support and expert consultation. Six ETS or College Board executives, including now College Board president George Hanford and ETS Vice President E. Belvin Williams, aided the committees' deliberations. Yet much to the test company's displeasure, the NAACP committee, which included such testing authorities as Dr. William Brazziel of the University of Connecticut and Dr. A.J. Franklin of the City University of New York, issued its own call for a moratorium. In a 1976 report which began with a page of disclaimers by the ETS and College Board representatives, the NAACP concluded:

> It is abusive to misassess with an inadequate instrument. Equally important, it is abusive to continue, year after year, to use testing programs which have proved themselves to be tools which are either irrelevant to student progress or which actually, by predicting failure, induce

malevolent results. Current aptitude testing or other testing processes and practices which result in the misassessment of blacks and other minorities result in educational mistreatment.[205]

By 1979, over a dozen national organizations concerned with education had expressed their opposition to standardized testing or supported the concept of Truth-in-Testing legislation, with damage to minorities frequently cited as a reason.[206]

Inside ETS, though no support is known to have surfaced for the ultimate step of moratorium, a number of test professionals were beginning to question the role their product was playing in minority students' lives.

At a January 1971 ETS seminar, Dr. David McClelland noted that while aptitude tests were of questionable efficiency in the prediction of career success, their effect on the chances of minority students was considerably more consistent. His remarks were later reprinted in expanded form in the American Psychologist.

> Intelligence and aptitude tests are used nearly everywhere by schools, colleges, and employers. It is a sign of backwardness not to have test scores in the school records of children. . . . /ETS/ tests have tremendous power over the lives of young people by stamping some of them "qualified" and others "less qualified" for college work. Until recent "exceptions" were made (over the protest of some), the tests have served as a very efficient device for screening out black, Spanish-speaking, and other minority applicants to colleges.[207]

The following year, 1972, Dr. David Loye of ETS conducted a review of all prior ETS research on cultural bias. In January of 1973, he summarized his findings for President Turnbull in a confidential report entitled, "Cultural Bias in Testing: Challenge and Response":

> In a profound and basic sense, cultural bias still exists within testing because practically everyone involved with testing has lived within its "house" for so long that they take too much for granted. The house is familiar to them, comfortable, built to specifications based on a presumably sacrosanct model of man, and they tend to assume that their modular man is everybody and the house will fit all men. But in fact the model of man to which the bulk of ETS and College Board operational tests are linked generally takes into account a small portion of only two of at least six aspects an adequate model must account for. . . . The growth of both social and social scientific awareness over the past two decades has brought ETS and the College Board to a juncture where . . . it must align its programs as well as its research with this larger view of man.[208]

Concern about the use of narrowly based tests for decisions with broad implications for minority students' futures has been voiced by other ETS advisers as well. Dean Bernard W. Harleston of the Tufts University Graduate School of Arts and Sciences, who had been brought in by ETS as a consultant on the Graduate Record Examination (GRE) program, advised in a confidential memorandum to ETS program director (now vice president) Richard Burns that "the GRE in its present form is unfair to the Black student." Even within the very narrow range of thinking that, as Loye pointed out, aptitude tests attempted to challenge, Harleston found that the kinds of problems posed to test-takers were restricted to the detriment of minorities. ". . . The test has embraced very little of the Black experience," he wrote. "Its constructors appear to have overlooked the 300 odd years of subhuman treatment that Blacks have received in these United States."[209] He recommended that "until the test has undergone major surgical operation," the GRE literature should state explicitly that the tests are designed primarily for students from traditionally white schools.[210]

Harleston had raised what was for ETS a sensitive matter of internal politics. Since the 1960s, several ETS staff members had been proposing action against this most obvious aspect of cultural bias in aptitude testing--the lack of questions written by, for and about people other than affluent whites. While they did spur some changes, both in test content and the procedures for selecting question writers, they did so in spite of, not because of, ETS corporate policy. In a June 1970 report on ETS tests and minority students a committee of six ETS professionals, chaired by Dr. Thomas Donlon, then Director of Test Development, traced the history of their efforts:

> In coming to grips with minority problems a step has been /taken/ to search out and appoint black teachers from black colleges and universities to Committees of Examiners. Appointments from these colleges represent one of the recent innovations in the test development process. . . . It may be helpful to note how and why this change took place. The change reflects the initiative of a very small number of staff members who approached the problem individually. There was and is no organizational directive. There was and is no concerted ETS plan. In essence, several staff members (who fortunately held strategic positions in the organization) perceived, or were made to perceive as a result of confrontations at conferences of black educators, a glaring lack in ETS's representation of the black academic community on test development committees.[211]

If the political benefits of modifications in question content were not apparent to ETS executives when first proposed, the items which test professionals call "racial respect signals" have since become an integral part of ETS' publications and public relations efforts. The 1978 publication, Taking the SAT, for example, includes sample sentence correction questions which mention the names of tennis champion Althea Gibson, poet Gwendolyn Brooks, and politician Kwame Nkrumah.[212] Yet the insertion of such piecemeal changes into a test the structure of which is otherwise unaltered may well do more for the image of ETS than it does for the scores of minority applicants. In an article for <u>New York</u> magazine, writer Steven Brill explored this point with ETS test development official Marion Epstein:

Q: "If the tests weren't culturally biased in the first place, why did you make the change?"

A: "Because minorities feel at ease reading this kind of passage."

Q: "If they feel at ease reading this one, does that mean they <u>don't</u> feel at ease reading the six or seven other passages in the text?"

A: "No. It just means they feel more comfortable with this one."

Q: "Well, if they feel more comfortable, does that mean their scores will be higher?"

A: "No, I don't think there will be any differences in 'scores.'"

Q: "Well, if there won't be any difference, why would you make the change? Was it just so you could look like you were doing something?"

A: "No, it's because when people are more comfortable, they'll do better on the test. They feel less threatened."[213]

As the report of the Donlon committee recognized, however, the way people react to aptitude tests depends on things more fundamental than the wording of a particular passage. The power of these tests is a fact which is hard to avoid, a fact which minority students in particular have reason to appreciate. The committee wrote:

> Students who score high on selection tests may view them as a useful method of confirming their superiority and their right to continued superior education--or as a painful and tedious annoyance. To students who score low on such tests, however, the tests are seen as barriers to educational and employment opportunities and as a basis for labeling them as inferior. Typically, tests are not

perceived as contributing to self-understanding or as
helping to facilitate continuing education by supply-
ing information on relative strengths and weaknesses.
Nor is there much recognition among low-scoring
students (or those who evaluate them) of the esteem-
restoring fact that even a low score indicates a
certain level of attainment and competence by the
individual, a level which may represent strong success
for that individual and his education.[214]

Many members of minority/poverty groups view current
testing practices as being so many establishment
barriers to higher education and status, or as attempts
to perpetuate a stereotyped label of inferiority.[215]

In a 1972 speech before the Border College Consortium, Dr. George Schlekat, then the ETS Director of College Board Admission and Guidance Programs, went a step further, arguing in effect, that not only did minority people view ETS aptitude tests as exclusionary, but that, in fact, they were right. ". . . Test scores," Dr. Schlekat said, "serve as devices for selecting out minorities for exclusion."[216] Schlekat observed:

A student who learns to reason in Spanish, . . . to make
cerebral connections, to ponder relationships, to observe
human behavior, . . . If you have learned those skills in
non-standard languages that are not incorporated in the
standardized verbal aptitude tests, then you are out of
luck. You receive a low score on the test: you are certified stupid, and you must live with that opprobrium for
the rest of your life.[217]

Schlekat argued that such consequences could be traced directly to the power of the test system: "I maintain that testing, tests, are the admission and placement policies of countless colleges and universities throughout the United States, and I maintain accordingly that the testing community may not shrug off respon- sibility for all of those systems that determine admission to the economic and intellectual centers of American life."[218]

Schlekat's analysis, though similar to views occasionally expressed by other middle level ETS executives, differed considerably from the company line. In the official ETS view, as frequently stated by President Turnbull, "testing can and does facilitate rather than impede the evolution of a fairer society" and "has had a major influence on opening higher education opportunity to new groups of students."[219]

Yet, in August of 1969, as his first major policy proposal after assuming the ETS presidency, Turnbull circulated among ETS officials a paper which acknowledged the exclusion of minorities from educational opportunities and conceded that the prevailing system of aptitude testing was, though in a modest way, indeed part of the problem. The paper he drafted with George Hanford began with an epigraph from the comic strip "Pogo": "We have met the enemy, and they is us." "Education is the avenue for rapid and sustained progress of minority group children from poverty to an acceptable standard of living," Turnbull contended. "The trouble is that at present the number of minority group children who gain access to higher education is pitifully small. . . . The system is simply not designed to handle the ghetto child." Turnbull preferred to see the problem with the tests as being not so much that they <u>excluded</u> minority students, but that they often failed to reveal their potential. "The tests are . . . not [built] to uncover the depth and variety of skills and abilities possessed by the bright student who has come through a vocational program, or an academic program in a school where the college-going tradition is weak or non-existent."[220]

But, regardless of whether the tests were seen as actively excluding or simply failing to adequately facilitate advancement, the result was the same: elimination for entire groups of people of opportunities to learn and work. Turnbull sought to address the problem by proposing a major overhaul of the ETS test system. None of his major recommendations--for reasons that are discussed in Chapter VIII--were ever adopted.

While the consequences of low test scores for minorities are difficult to deny, assertions that this score pattern is in any part due to bias in the tests themselves are vigorously rejected by test industry representatives. The logic of the industry position has perhaps been stated most clearly by Thomas C. Oliver, a vice president of the American College Testing Program (ACT). In a December 1975 essay for the ACT newspaper, Oliver addressed the question: "What About Test Bias and Discrimination?":

> Are tests culturally biased? Sure they are! Do tests discriminate against certain students? Sure they do! . . . Good educational tests are designed to discriminate --against ignorance![221]

Though in more subtle and delicate tones, ETS President Turnbull has advanced the same argument.* The tests, the industry claims, merely reflect the culture of U.S. higher education; if minority students do not perform well on them, that says something about the students, not about the tests. This was the thesis of the

---

*Turnbull asserted in a 1974 speech: "If school and college work is culture-bound, and if tests are devised mainly to predict success in such work, then it follows that culture-bound tests will do the best job of prediction."[222] "Neither black nor brown students, as a group," he concluded, "do less well on the tests than in their academic work, relative to whites."[223]

first major scholarly publication of President Turnbull's psychometric career, a 1951 article in the Canadian Journal of Psychology.[224] It is an argument that in 1968 was fashioned into one of the industry's most widely used tools of defense against criticism from minorities: a theoretical definition of test bias which enabled psychometric researchers to claim that not only were aptitude tests not biased <u>against</u> minorities, but rather were biased in their favor.

The definition was proposed by T. Anne Cleary, an ETS researcher, in a 1968 edition of the Journal of Educational Measurement. Cleary argued that a test was biased against a particular group not if that group scored lower than another, but only if its success was predicted with less accuracy. She wrote:

> A test is biased for members of a subgroup of the population if, in the prediction of a criterion for which the test was designed, consistent nonzero errors of prediction are made for members of the subgroup. In other words, the test is biased if the criterion score predicted from the common regression line is consistently too high or too low for members of the subgroup. With this definition of bias, there may be a connotation of "unfair," particularly if the use of the test produces a prediction that is too low.[225]

Cleary, like other ETS researchers, defined the criterion for success as being first-year grades. Based on her definition, she exonerated the SAT from any charges of being unfair since it predicted first-year college grades for minority students about as well as it predicted them for whites.*[226] Later ETS research, employing this same definition, reaffirmed that the tests were not biased--and if anything were slightly biased in favor of minority

---

*Although minority students on the average get lower first-year grades, as predicted, some studies have found this gap to average only about one-half of a grade point.[227]

students.*[228] Using such research as the basis for its claims, ETS continued this line of defense through the decade. In 1974, ETS President Turnbull told the Conference of Academic Standards and Their Relationship to Minority Aspirations:

> Most educators are quite familiar with the fact that the scores work in more cases than not, popular belief to the contrary notwithstanding. What is less well-known is that they are about equally predictive for minority students. That is, the reversals that do occur, occur with the same frequency among minority and majority students. There is no ethnic monopoly on making it against the odds or on blowing an apparently fine set of chances.[230]

Reliance on the Cleary definition and the research based on it was undermined from the outset by several inconvenient facts. Since minorities on the average scored significantly lower, reliance on the test for selection would result in rejection of much larger percentages of minority than white applicants. And although the predictive validities for minorities and whites were about equal in relative terms, in _absolute_ terms both of those validities were so low that there would be significant numbers of both minorities

---

*The appearance of "overprediction," i.e. prediction that applicants from a certain group will perform better than they actually do, is simply a result of peculiarities in the statistical procedure used to predict grades; it has little substantive significance. Former ETS researcher Dr. Robert Linn has noted that "there appear to be technical phenomena that tend to result in overprediction for groups of individuals that score low on the predictor." A University of California task force which studied the issue concluded that "the phenomena of overprediction seems largely irrelevant to detecting bias in the tests as inherent statistical artifact." White provides the following explanation: "The statistical effect can be understood by analyzing the extreme example of a completely invalid test. Such a test would give no information about future academic performance. One would have to assume that the applicant with the highest test score will achieve only average academic grades; so too with an applicant scoring lowest on the test. If, however, one group of students achieved below average grades, their grades would have been 'overpredicted.'"[229]

and whites for whom the predictions were substantially inaccurate. For the admitted whites, this inaccuracy would be revealed when they performed differently than the test had predicted. But for the minority applicants, most of whom would have already been rejected on the basis of their score, the opportunity to prove the test wrong--as many could statistically be expected to do, given its low validity--would never come to pass.

The Cleary definition as applied by ETS was further weakened by its acceptance of first-year grades as the sole criterion for success. ETS' own manuals for colleges conceded that many minority students often improved their grades relative to whites beyond the first year.[231] Grades themselves had been shown to have little relationship to career success. And, as Dr. Astin found, not only was the correlation of scores to grades low to begin with, but the correlation of scores to staying in school was lower still.[232]

In sum, ETS scores were putting many minority students in peril of rejection because of a weak prediction that they would rank slightly lower on a fleeting criterion of questionable validity--a state of affairs for minority applicants which ETS characterized as free from unfavorable bias.

It was not until 1971 that the injustice which thousands of minority students had been experiencing for years was acknowledged as a theoretical possibility by professional psychometricians. That summer, the Journal of Educational Measurement published papers by Professors R.L. Thorndike and R.B. Darlington which proposed new definitions of test bias.[233] The papers sent waves of controversy through the profession. Not only were they considered to have broken new theoretical ground, but, unlike the model of

Cleary and ETS, they offered definitions of bias under which current aptitude tests could actually be considered unfair.

This intellectual breakthrough received immediate attention from executives at ETS. The papers were analyzed by a committee of senior ETS researchers and test development experts. Their reports were forwarded to eleven ETS executives, including Solomon and Turnbull, by the ETS Vice President for statistical analysis, Richard S. Levine. In his covering memo of September 24, 1971, Levine assessed the implications of Thorndike and Darlington's work for continued reliance on the Cleary definition of bias (which, one of the reports noted, might also be called "the ETS definition"[234]) in preparation for an upcoming meeting with corporate officials:

> The general topic for discussion is culture fairness and/or test bias. In particular, we will review statistical indices of the bias of a test as a predictor of success on an academic or job performance criterion. <u>The major conclusion is that the customary statistical criterion, sometimes attributed to Ann Cleary, is inadequate. The argument that bias does not exist if regression lines coincide for two groups appears to be untenable.</u>[235] (Emphasis added.)

This conclusion never appeared in ETS candidate literature and statements to the general public, which continued to use the Cleary definition to claim that the tests were not biased. Thorndike (as paraphrased by Ronald Flaugher of ETS) had defined a biased test as one which "is unfair to the lower scoring group of applicants, in the sense that the proportion of that group that qualifies on the test will turn out to be smaller than the proportion who would be qualified on the job /or in school/."[236] "What Thorndike has pointed out," wrote senior ETS researcher Dr. Frederick M. Lord in his report to Vice President Levine, "is that if the blacks score below the whites on a test satisfying Cleary's definition, then the lower the validity of the test for a given criterion, the lower the proportion of blacks selected in comparison to the number that should be selected."[237] Since this problem would apply with *any* test of less than perfect validity, it was of considerable significance for ETS aptitude tests, which typically offered only eight to fifteen per cent of perfect prediction.*

"It is neither necessary nor possible for ETS to build a 'fair' test. . . ." Lord wrote.[238]

> It is consistent with Cleary's definition that blacks and whites may differ sharply on selection test scores, in which case, the selected group will consist largely of whites. Even though it satisfies Cleary's criterion, such a selection procedure would almost surely be considered very unfair, since the blacks are almost as good on the criterion as the whites and should therefore be almost equally represented in the selected group.

Lord continued:

> A reasonable viewpoint is that the /Cleary definition/ is completely fair to the selecting institution in that it is the procedure that will maximize the average criterion score of the selected group. However, we cannot be fair in this sense to the institution and at the same time be fair to all cultural groups. If the test has low validity, the gain to the institution is negligible compared to the loss suffered by the blacks.[239]

As a formula for admissions decisions, the Thorndike model has been extensively criticized by test professionals on logical and legal grounds.[240] As a method of demonstrating the discriminatory impact of a test selection system on minority students capable of succeeding, however, its effectiveness has been considerable.

---

*See pps. 58-70.

In a May 1972 report, Nancy S. Cole of the American College Testing Program analyzed the admission potential of minority students under the selection models set up by the differing definitions of test bias. On tests with equal predictive validity for minority and non-minority students, with minority students receiving lower mean scores--essentially the situation in admissions today--Cole found that three times **more minority students** would be admitted under the Thorndike model than under the Cleary (ETS) definition of bias. Under Cleary's model 4.5 per cent of the minority applicants would be admitted; under the Thorndike model, 13.3 per cent. What is more, Cole found that the increased admission of minority students would have virtually no effect on overall rates of success for the entering class. Expected success rates for the minority students admitted under the Thorndike model (64 per cent) were very similar to those for the (fewer) students admitted under the Cleary model (70 percent).[241]

Research has confirmed that under Thorndike's definition, the use of aptitude tests in many actual admission practices discriminates against minority students. As Frank L. Schmidt and John E. Hunter of Michigan State University (who both differ with the Thorndike model on theoretical grounds) pointed out in a 1974 paper, "Most research on the question of test fairness has been based on the Cleary definition . . . these researchers have almost invariably concluded that the tests and regression equations investigated were either fair to both races or were biased significantly in favor of blacks."[242] But reanalyzing several of the studies under the Thorndike definition of bias, the researchers found that the tests were, in fact, biased against minority applicants.[243] Subjecting a 1971 study by ETS' **Junius Davis and George Temp** to the Thorndike definition, Schmidt and Hunter wrote, "In 12 of the 13 colleges he studied, the trend...was in the direction of unfair bias against black students, and in 8 of the colleges this effect reached statistical significance."[244] After reanalyzing Cleary's own 1978 data, they concluded that, under the Thorndike definition, the tests were being used unfairly at the schools studied by Cleary as well.[245]

The implications of this pattern of bias are particularly severe in a highly selective admissions arena such as law school. According to information presented in the Law School Admission Council's brief in the Bakke case, thirty-seven per cent of white students taking the LSAT in 1976, for example, received scores of 600 or above compared to only three per cent of the black students. Sixty-seven per cent of the white students scored 500 or above-- compared to nineteen per cent of the black applicants.[246] An ETS study by Franklin Evans later calculated that if 1976 law school admissions decisions had been based strictly on the numerical predictions derived from grades and scores, seventy-six to seventy-eight per cent fewer blacks and forty-five to forty-eight per cent fewer Chicanos than were actually chosen would have been admitted.[247] Thus, more than half of the minority students were admitted only because some schools chose to disregard the test score ranking to some extent. Even with such cases of flexibility, on the average minorities still had to present higher college grades than whites in order to have an equal chance of admission. And, as Vilma Martinez and Mario Lara of the Mexican American Legal Defense Fund pointed out in a 1978 article, at some law schools, such as Boalt Hall at Berkeley, the trend has been toward increased reliance on the LSAT. "Such a shift in admissions policy," they wrote, "could effectively discount even a superior academic performance by a minority in favor of the advantageous margin of achievement that Anglo-Americans enjoy on the test."[248]

Roy D. Goldman and Melvin H. Widawski of the University of California at Riverside reached similarly disturbing conclusions in a 1976 study of four institutions in the University of California system. "Blacks and Chicanos are clearly not benefited by use of the SAT in selection of college students--at least at the institutions we have investigated. In every instance, far fewer Black and Chicano students would be selected when the SAT is used than when it is not."[249] At two of the four schools investigated, the addition of the SAT to high school grades "produce/d/ virtually no increase in valid prediction of GPA /grade point average/."[250] But, "use of the SAT would eliminate more than half of the Chicano students who would have been admissible if HSGPA /high school grade point averages/ alone were used for screening." At the other two schools, the addition of the SAT would wipe out nearly one-third of the Chicano applicants who would have qualified for admission.[251]

The apparent increased selectivity obtained through the addition of the SAT did not, however, increase the number of students likely to succeed in the selected class, the researchers found. Although consideration of the SAT eliminated some students who would not have been predicted to succeed at the schools ("false-positive" admitees), it also eliminated a nearly equal number of students who would have been expected to succeed if admitted ("false-negative" rejectees): "It appears that the use of the SAT in the selection of Blacks and Chicano students simply 'shifts' false-positive selection errors into the false-negative category."[252] Use of the SAT," the researchers wrote, "produces increases in correct selections that range from modest to virtually nonexistent." The incremental increase in accuracy of prediction came at a heavy price to minority applicants. Using a definition of "success" as a student who would earn a 2.5 grade point average in college, Goldman and Widawski found that "use of the SAT at the four universities would make inadmissible 15 percent, 12 percent, 14 percent, and 14 percent of Chicano applicants who would have been admissible through the use of HSGPA alone."[253] For black students, "the use of the SAT would reduce Blacks' admissibility by 15 percent, 14 percent, 21 percent and 43 percent . . . at the four institutions."[254]

In concluding, Goldman and Widawski discussed the long-range impact of the ETS aptitude test on the lives of minority students:

> There may be a real dollar loss to individuals who are the victims of false-negative selection errors. . . . False-negative admission errors are probably more costly to minorities than to whites. It is paradoxical, therefore, that these errors are probably more prevalent for minorities than for whites. . . . A false-negative error deprives society of a college-educated individual. . . . This may not be a great loss when it is spread across the whole of society. Yet, this lost productivity may be rather costly when it must be borne by a small section of society. There are probably proportionately fewer college graduates among Mexican-Americans for example, than among Anglo-Americans. The loss of a Mexican-American college graduate is, therefore, a bigger burden for the Mexican-American community than for society as a whole.[255]

No studies have even attempted, however, to estimate how many college graduates, lawyers, doctors, and professional people have been lost to the Mexican-American and other ethnic communities as a whole by the reliance on ETS aptitude tests to serve, in the words of an ETS researcher, "as the gatekeepers for much of society's rewards."[256]

The Test: Manufacturing Multiple-Choice

The most important questions about ETS aptitude tests concern their effects on people's lives and the evidence behind ETS' claims about them. The sections of this chapter, thus far, have addressed these issues. This section and the next will deal with two aspects of ETS aptitude testing which, although of secondary importance, bear on the image of the tests which ETS tries to project to its customers: the cost of developing tests and the method of scoring them.

The arcane subject of test development cost is of interest to ETS consumers because it is on this issue that ETS has chosen to make its stand against efforts to open its tests to public scrutiny. In July of 1979 New York State enacted the nation's first Truth-in-Testing law, which requires higher education admission testing companies to disclose internal studies of their tests, give candidates factual information about what test scores mean, and disclose test questions and correct answers after scores have been reported.[257] The bill was enacted despite an intensive lobbying effort by ETS and the College Board. The law reverses a fundamental presumption of the ETS test system: the idea that candidates have no right, after they leave the test center, to inspect the questions and answers which will determine their score. It also reverses the ETS assumption that it may set the ground rules for determining which scholars will have access to studies and test forms often necessary for independent evaluation of ETS tests. (See Appendix V for a copy of the New York Truth-in-Testing law.)

To ETS, these prerogatives of secrecy are basic. In an unsigned 1979 memo circulated among federal agencies ETS went so far as to argue that disclosure of test questions was an unconstitutional taking of private property without just compensation and that disclosure of validity studies was a violation of the company's first amendment right to freedom of speech.[258]

Some observers have questioned the appropriateness of such claims from an organization which enjoys the image, and legal privileges, of an educational institution but which operates as a business corporation. In a letter to New York State Senator Kenneth P. LaValle, the prime sponsor of the Truth-in-Testing bill, an assistant professor at the State University of New York argued that the ETS secrecy was inconsistent with educational standards. T.J. Larkin wrote:

> Suppose, for one moment, I told my classes that I was not going to return their answer sheets to them; that I would not show them the test; that there was no method by which they could see that their exam was graded properly; that they would not be told their raw scores (number of correct answers) but only given a figure between zero and 800; that they would not be told how their score compared to others in the class. I can promise your committee that were I to behave in the above manner, I would be taken before a grievance committee and convicted of unfair testing practices, and the verdict would, of course, be a just one.[259]

In the report of the CEEB Commission on Tests, Vice-Chairman B. Alden Thresher found the ETS secrecy inconsistent with scientific principles as well.

> I recall being shown some years ago a file at ETS containing something of the order of 100,000 reserve items for the Scholastic Aptitude Test (SAT) . . . The policy has been to keep under lock and key a limited bank of test items carefully screened and pretested, and to economize by reusing them at subsequent test

administrations. This miserly and secretive policy
treats knowledge as if it were a closed and secret
matter, hidden from the public eye in the custody of
a hieratic group. Nothing could be farther from the
spirit of free inquiry and universal publication.[260]

The secrecy extends beyond questions to the statistics contained in test analyses and other internal documents which summarize patterns of test results. When challenged, ETS executives point out that some secure tests and internal data are released to professional reviewers (chosen by ETS). Perhaps the most frequent recipient of such preferential access was the late Oscar K. Buros, editor of the authoritative test review, the <u>Mental Measurement Yearbook</u>. In a 1977 speech looking back on his fifty years in testing, Dr. Buros, winner of the ETS Award for Distinguished Service to Measurement, thanked ETS for its "wholehearted cooperation" in giving the psychometrics yearbook copies of secure tests. Buros continued, however:

> I would like to point out that the information available to permit an adequate assessment to be made of these secure tests is quite unsatisfactory. Although our reviewers generally receive some in-house material, which is not available to other educators and psychologists, even this material is inadequate. . . . Since the tests themselves can be examined only under highly restricted conditions, if at all, it becomes of greatest importance that detailed information be provided for secure tests. The important role which these tests play in influencing the lives of the examinees is much greater than the role of the commercially available tests. Yet far less information is available on these secure tests and, to make matters worse, much of the information which the publisher does possess is considered to be confidential. . . .[261]

Speaking of the ETS College Level Examination Program (CLEP) tests, Buros said,

> Roadblocks have been placed between the test user and what the scores mean. Only confidential house papers present raw score distributions. . . . I find it discouraging that . . . /ETS and ACT/ have not provided test users with the hard data. . . .[262]

Buros then repeated a statement he had published years before:

> Today it is practically impossible for a competent test technician or test consumer to make a thorough appraisal of the construction, validation, and use of most standardized tests being published because of the limited amount of trustworthy information supplied by test publishers and authors.[263]

Despite the professional criticism it occasionally engenders, ETS has a very rational reason for wanting to run its test programs under a corporate standard of secrecy. Once the questions and answers themselves are open for inspection, the image of the test as a measure of an intangible quality, as opposed to a mere collection of multiple-choice questions, becomes increasingly difficult to maintain.

On February 23, 1972, aspiring lawyers in Pennsylvania, Georgia, New Jersey, Ohio, California, Florida, and thirteen other states took a test which would prove to be a landmark in ETS history. For what is thought to be the first (and last) time ever, the questions of a secure ETS test were released for public inspection following the exam.

In developing the multiple-choice Multistate Bar Exam, consultation with outside experts had been especially thorough. Along with "the technical assistance of testing experts provided by a contract with . . . /ETS/," lawyers on five committees of the National Conference of Bar Examiners (NCBE) had individually "drafted a quota of items"; later "each committee held a two-day meeting to review, redraft, and refine the items."264 States set MBE cutoff scores which determined who would be admitted to practice law.

After ETS had reported the scores and candidates had been accepted or rejected, the National Conference released the questions, and law professors teaching bar review courses began studying the questions and preparing answer keys for their students. The faculties of two such courses in the Washington, D.C. area differed on the answers to fifty-four of the 200 questions (some twenty-seven per cent of the MBE). When the answer sheets of four bar review faculties (including the two D.C. courses) were compared, the law professors were found to differ on the correct answers to sixty-nine questions, or nearly thirty-five per cent of the MBE.*265

The NCBE later announced that upon reexamination of the test they had determined that five of the questions had more than one correct answer; they would not, however, say which questions they were referring to.

Professor Sherman Cohn of Georgetown University Law School and the Bar Review Institute (BRI),

> submitted the Multi-State Examination of February, 1972 to several authorities in each of the fields to take as an examination, and then to ponder and research without time limit. /He/ found that they . . ./in/ many

---

*There were five questions on which the four faculties arrived at three different correct answers. On two questions, they chose four different answers, each faculty selecting a different multiple-choice option.

occasions, disagreed as to which of the two final choices was the most correct.[266]

At the 1973 American Bar Association Convention, Joan Claybrook, then a candidate for the Bar, now Administrator of the National Highway Traffic Safety Administration, asked MBE director of testing Joe Covington to release the official answers used by ETS to score the exam. As Claybrook later wrote, Covington explained that the answers had not yet been released because "he saw no reason to do so and it might cause controversy" (as indeed it would).[267] Two months later, Covington wrote Claybrook that the NCBE had decided to keep the answers confidential: "The Committee . . . thought it would not be particularly helpful to release the answers, but would only raise additional problems."[268]

Embarrassing incidents such as this did not occur again for the simple reason that questions were not released again. Secure national tests received their only public exposure when a select few were "retired" and chosen for inclusion as sample questions in ETS test booklets.

When the New York Truth-in Testing bill threatened to make such scrutiny of ETS tests routine, ETS argued that writing new questions to comply with the bill would necessitate heavy fee increases for New York test-takers.[269] ETS did not choose to mention in its initial memos and testimony opposing the bill that, in fact, only a small portion of the candidate's test fee actually went to the cost of test development (ETS was later compelled to acknowledge this when some of its internal financial documents were revealed to the legislature by NYPIRG).[270]

Although the Educational Testing Service has 2,300 full-time employees,[271] few spend their time writing educational tests. In 1949, an estimated ten of ETS' fifty-two professionals actually wrote tests.[272] In 1974, ETS test development professionals, known as "Examiners," numbered less than eighty and comprised less than four per cent of the ETS staff.[273] According to internal ETS organization charts, by May of 1978, the staff of examiners had shrunk to less than seventy people[274] who were turning out tests to measure the minds of perhaps seven to nine million test-takers a year.[275]

The SAT, ETS' most widely used and influential test, administered to some 1.5 million people yearly, is one of the largest test development projects. According to Dr. Marion Epstein, a test development veteran who is currently an ETS vice president, in 1975 three full-time and six part-time ETS staffers developed the Verbal portion of the SAT.[276]

The entire College Board ATP (Admissions Testing Program) series of tests, consisting of the SAT plus fourteen Achievement Tests, was developed by eighteen ETS examiners, according to Dr. Epstein. Those working on the Achievement Tests worked with advisory "Committees of Examiners"--educators chosen by the College Board who spent two-and-a-half to three day sessions at Rosedale planning the test and writing items. (The examiners writing the SAT did not work with such committees.) Dr. Epstein felt that this deployment of personnel was more than sufficient for question writing.

Q: How are you able to develop the SAT (and Achievements) with only eighteen staff members working in that area?

A: (Dr. Epstein): Well, it sounds like a lot of people to me. Why do you feel that's so few? . . . You have many fewer people working on your Achievement Tests, . . . I mean, if you have a Math Achievement committee that has five faculty members on it and we have two staff people working on it, that's seven people who will be working on that and nobody full-time. . . .

You know, <u>it probably takes somewhere in the neighborhood of half to three quarters of an hour--hour--you know, to write a question</u>, and less than that for each review. And if you have, . . . the SAT has, what is it? Maybe something like eighty-five questions in the Verbal portion, sixty in the Math, and you pretest probably each year one-and-a-half to two times as many questions as you're going to need for the five or six forms that you're going to develop in a year. It's still not a tremendous, it's still within two or three--<u>a couple of people could write all of the questions</u>.

We involve more people because you want a variety of input. But I think that number of people /who/ have some kind of contribution to it is certainly more than enough.[277] (Emphases added.)

When it comes to actually writing multiple-choice questions, according to Dr. Epstein, the amount of training needed depends on whether one has the knack. All new examiners are given an "item-writing workshop" which teaches the basic principles of multiple-choice.[278] ("Make sure that the item has one and only one correct answer. . . . Guard against giving clues in the correct answers."[279]) Some need the help more than others. "We find that some people pick it up very, very rapidly and write good items almost in the beginning," said Dr. Epstein. And, there are others "including some of the top committee members who are really expert in te field" who never demonstrate the appropriate aptitude. The actual question writing involves no formulas or statistics-- thee are only used to choose the mix of questions which puts the tets at the appropriate level of difficulty and maximizes its ablity to discriminate among candidates. "/Question writing/ is really an art as well as a skill," said Dr. Epstein.[280]

The technical refinement comes in the statistical theory ad techniques used to analyze aspects of question difficulty. he analysis is performed using mathematical procedures which are known to thousands of students, teachers, and researchers in statistics and psychology, and are routinely programmed into ETS computers and procedures.*

Although conceptually complex, the technical procedures can be applied with relatively few people and in little time-- requiring only someone who knows the rules and has access to computing equipment. As ETS' internal test development manual states:

> The bulk of the Test Development staff . . . started
> . . . with a subject-matter specialization and very
> little, if any, formal training in statistics and
> measurement. Through . . . experience most have
> reached the point where they have a great deal of
> working knowledge and skill in psychometrics, statistics,
> and testing. They may not be able to state the theoret-
> ical rationale for everything that is done or to derive

---

*Some of the values calculated include "r-biserial"-- "a measure of a question's usefulness in distinguishing among students of different levels of ability," "reliability"--"the extent to which a person taking alternate parallel versions of the test would obtain about the same score each time"; predictive "validity"--the connection between scores and some standard, such as first-year grades; "equating"--inflating or deflating scores to adjust for different levels of difficulty on different forms of the same test; "norming"--figuring out how the candidate scored in relation to all test-takers; and "scaling"--reporting scores in terms of 200-800 or other ETS scales.[281]

the formulas for the statistics that are employed,
. . . but . . . they know . . . whether the technique
in question will work in their particular situation.[282]

The writing of a test like the SAT Verbal has often been depicted by ETS and the education press as a monumental and expensive feat of psychometric technology. Professor Diane Ravitch wrote, incorrectly, in the New York Times Magazine that "the SAT . . . is developed almost entirely in-house by a staff of 58 test-developers. . . ."[283] (This was the size of the entire test development staff of the College Board and Higher Education and Career Programs which was responsible for dozens of major tests, including the GRE, LSAT and business school test).[284]

In addition to developing new questions, the staff could draw on a thirty-year ETS inventory of re-usable multiple-choice items.[285] As the ETS test development manual put it, "Much of the strength and versatility of ETS as a testing organization lies in its 'pool' of more than 300,000 test items, most of which are ETS-owned and therefore available, within the limits of certain overlap restrictions, for use in programs other than those for which they were originally developed."[286]

The items, all written according to carefully standardized ETS guidelines, were typed on green, white, orange, brown, yellow and blue cards categorized according to security level and ownership (whether owned by ETS or a client organization), and were further divided into subject areas ("Education, Verbal Aptitude," etc.).[287]

The test development manual laid out procedures and techniques designed for getting maximum mileage out of a single item. It gave the example of a single antonym question which had been inherited by ETS from its founding organization in 1948:

MITIGATE:

    (A) solidify

    (B) humiliate

    (C) deviate

    (D) intensify

Over the next twenty-five years, ETS used it to test, among other qualities, the "scholastic aptitude" of college applicants, the preparation of aspiring Merchant Marine sailors, and the proficiency of Peace Corps volunteers. "This single item," the manual pointed out, "has appeared in twelve different tests that cover eight different programs." After such arduous service, "the item has now been retired."[288]

The manual explained that before "pretesting" items on sample groups of candidates, ETS examiners would routinely write two to three times as many new questions as were needed for a test; a portion of each test would be drawn from the ready-made questions in the item files. "In the absence of appropriate rules of thumb, one should plan to pretest about twice as many items as will be needed."[289] An "ETS CONFIDENTIAL" set of overlap guidelines specified that five to twenty per cent of the questions on a test could be taken from another ETS test purporting to measure something different, depending on the security level of the items.[290] Thus, generally, the majority of items for each test would be newly written by the examiners. But once the questions had been written, they could be re-used many times, for other tests--even for tests where they had already been used before and seen by thousands of candidates. (The "Mitigate" item was used on four different SATs.)

ETS executives sometimes point out that more than a hundred steps are involved in test development and that the process is set up to span two years. An internal ETS "Checklist for Developing Tests" used by the occupational testing section gives perspective on the nature of this multiple-step process. The checklist is broken down into 150 different steps used both for preparing a new form of an established test like the SAT, and for building a whole new test from scratch. The large number of steps is due to the detailed specification of office paper-work procedures: (" /Step No./ 65. Prepare Official Key for Reproduction, 66. Proof Key and Release for Printing, 67. Key Sent to Printing, 68. Print Key, 69. Distribute Key to Appropriate Divisions. . . .").[291]

According to Dr. Epstein, the actual question-writing and review process is less complicated. After the initial half-hour to hour question-writing process, a typical SAT Verbal question will be reviewed, at various stages in the process, for several minutes by two to five ETS staff members or consultants. (ETS guidelines require at least two reviews for each Verbal question and three for each Math question.) The twenty-four months required for an item to pass from the question-writer's mind to a printed test results from the administrative delays involved in a question being pre-tested--either on students, a particular institution, or as an "experimental" question on a regular ETS test--then analyzed and, if necessary, revised before it is included in the final test. But, not all test questions are pretested, since finding people to give them to can be a considerable administrative chore. In an interview, Dr. Epstein outlined the problems:

Q: In selecting the sample for the pretests, do you attempt to include the same proportion of minority students in that sample as will be taking the final test?

A: (Dr. Epstein): No, it can't be done. It's difficult enough really, to get pretest populations at all.[292]

These test development activities do not absorb a large portion of candidate fees. A 1972 "Activity Analysis" prepared by ETS financial executive Herman F. Smith for ETS management indicated that test development generally accounts for less than ten per cent of the cost of producing an ETS test. The Activity Analysis, the result of an extensive study of all major ETS test programs for the year 1970-71, broke down the cost of each product into twenty-one functional categories (Planning, Tooling-up, Registration, etc.) figured to the penny. The analysis included three categories of test development: "Development of Measuring Instrument" (i.e., writing the questions), "Pretesting," and "Item and Test Analysis."[293]

Cost Per Candidate (Dollars)[294]

	CEEB*	PSAT	AP	LSAT	GRE	ATGSB
Development of Measuring Instrument /question writing/	.24	.01	4.10	.34	.77	.33
Pretesting	.05	---	.10	.05	.02	.05
Item Analysis	.04	---	.32	.10	.07	.06
Total Test Cost	$5.09	$ .54	$23.84	$10.83	$10.83	$9.22
Total Development Cost	$ .33	$ .01	$ 4.52	$ .49	$ .86	$ .44
Development As % of Test Cost	6.5%	1.9%	19.0%	4.5%	8.7%	4.8%

According to these figures, ETS spent an average of twenty-four cents per candidate writing the questions for an SAT test. Total test development costs came to thirty-three cents per candidate, or 6.5 percent of all costs involved in the test. (For the LSAT, test development was only 4.5 percent of cost, and for the PSAT, 1.9 per cent. In the Advanced Placement Program, one of the very few ETS tests involving essay questions, nineteen per cent of costs went for test development.) Most of the costs for each test line were attributed to physical production operations such as administering the tests, registering the candidates and scoring and reporting the results. It should be noted that test development constituted a still smaller share of SAT _fees_ paid by candidates than of SAT costs, since ETS and the College Board together typically take a profit margin of roughly twenty percent on each ATP test. (See Chapter VIII.)[295]

---

*This column refers to the SAT program.

The Activity Analysis indicates that, even for the Graduate School Foreign Language Tests (an especially complex series of advanced foreign language tests begun in 1968-69), test development averaged only twenty-four per cent of total costs during the first three years of operation.[296]

Even these comparatively small expenditures have been among the first to be sacrificed by ETS during times of financial austerity. In 1974, when ETS was experiencing a financial squeeze precipitated by inflation and rising wage costs, its solution was to cut the test development budget. At the same time, it increased expenditures for travel and consultant fees. In a confidential September 24, 1974 memo to the ETS Advisory Board, Financial Vice President David Brodsky described the company's financial comeback:

> As we all so painfully remember, last year began in the wake of several disappointments in 1972-73 and with an awareness of a number of fundamental problems that still had to be overcome. . . .
>
> Virtually all of these problems were met and successfully resolved by vigorous and imaginative staff effort. As one measure of success, ETS net income in 1973-74 was approximately $1,400,000--double the amount earned in 1972-73. This outcome was achieved almost entirely by getting and keeping expenses under tight control. . . .
>
> Expenses for consultants increased substantially in 1973-74 as one might expect from the extraordinary amount of outside assistance sought to help us with our cost problems. <u>This increase was virtually offset, however, by reductions in the use of test and testing committees, as test development activity declined.</u>[297] (Emphasis added)

The ETS financial statement, audited and approved for the 1977 Annual Report by Coopers and Lybrand, breaks down ETS expenditures into eight broad categories which convey little information on the priorities of corporate spending. The one category which makes a substantive statement about how ETS spends its money--"Test administrators, readers, item writers and other professional services,"--is listed at over seven million dollars.[298] But if Annual Report readers are impressed by such apparently substantial expenditures on test development, ETS vice presidents know better. The confidential 1977 ETS budget breakdown reveals that, in fact, only $390,000 (six per cent of the $6,367,600 originally budgeted for this category) was allocated for the testing committees and item writers. Within this category, more was allocated for consultants ($526,800); legal and accounting services ($437,500--consisting largely of fees to the Washington, D.C. law firm Wilmer, Cutler and Pickering in part to defend ETS from suits by consumers); and the "other outside services" ($542,600). The bulk of the category, some four million dollars, was budgeted for proctors who administer the test at centers around the world.[299]

Financial information elicited from ETS during the New York legislative battle indicates that the pattern of test development costs which prevailed at the time of the Activity Analysis is still intact. ETS told the New York Senate Higher Education Committee that in 1978-79, it spent only 6.9 per cent of the candidate's ATP fee on test development.[300] ETS also submitted to the committee an estimate of cost to the ATP program of compliance with Truth-in-Testing which amounted to about one-quarter of yearly ETS-College Board profit on the program[301] (see Chapter VIII, p.338)

The Test Score: Mystification at the Razor's Edge

As soon as the candidate completes the test and leaves the test center, all information about the questions themselves is placed beyond their reach. In place of objective information on how they performed on specific questions, the candidate receives from ETS a number on a scale from 200 to 800 (twenty to eighty in the case of the PSAT/NMSQT) which purports to measure the amount of aptitude they have.

The origins of this scale are explained in the ETS biography of SAT inventor Carl C. Brigham. Prior to 1934, the College Boards were scored on the simple percentage correct scale of 0-100%. But "the fluctuation in the percentage of candidates who made 60% (the unofficial passing mark) or higher had frequently embarrassed the College Board," notes the ETS biography [302] "In 1926, for example, 52.8 percent passed the physics examination; two years later the number increased to 81.9 percent. Such fluctuations were caused by the varying difficulty of the examinations."[303] In 1934, Brigham eliminated the percentage correct scale in favor of another 0-100% scale which, regardless of the variations among the test forms, would report a more consistent pattern of scores each year. In 1937, the 0-100 numbers were dropped and the unfamiliar and arbitrarily chosen range of 200 to 800 became the new SAT score scale. With that change, not only did it become impossible for candidates to know what percentage they had answered correctly, but all variations in the difficulty of the exams were rendered undetectable to the test-taking students. "The new scale is designed to give a more exact picture of the candidate's ability than was possible under the old percentage system," the College Board reported.[304] The ETS biographer was more blunt: "Brigham's statistical tables had solved one of the College Board's oldest and most embarrassing problems."[305]

The College Board exams of 1937 relied heavily on essay questions, which are more subject to uncontrolled variations in grading and difficulty than the multiple-choice items which replaced them after World War II. Current ETS test-development procedures are designed to minimize differences in difficulty between various forms of the same test. But Brigham's scoring technique persists and has been adapted by the other ETS aptitude tests.

The announced purpose of the 200 to 800 scale is to put all candidates on an equal footing, regardless of the difficulty of particular test forms. Students taking an "easy" form of the SAT, for example, will have their scores adjusted downward relative to those who take a "hard" form. A student will have to get more questions correct on an easy SAT to earn a reported score equal to that of a student taking a more difficult version. But when this readjustment for reasons of equity is accompanied by a policy under which actual percentages of correct and incorrect answers are never disclosed, the 200 to 800 scale comes to serve another purpose as well. By concealing the direct connection between reported scores and the questions they are derived from, it enables ETS to invest the scores with a significance beyond their objective meaning.

This practice also means that discrepancies among test forms or questionable practices by ETS in transforming the multiple-choice answers into final scores can only come to light through happenstance, or through a breach of corporate secrecy.

One such incident, during the winter of 1977-78, revealed the disruptive effect of ETS scoring procedures on the careers of an undetermined number of applicants to the law school class of 1981. The law schools of Yale, Columbia, and the University of Chicago began noticing that ETS was reporting an unusually large number of high scores for people who had taken the Law School Admission Test (LSAT) in October and December. At Yale, which had 3,700 applicants, the number of scores above 750 doubled over the previous year.

The admissions officers became curious about the rush of high scores and asked ETS for an explanation. ETS admitted that the LSAT had been changed prior to the October, 1977 administration of the test, and that scores on the "new" LSAT, "vary from the experience of the past three years."[306] The test had been made more difficult, and ETS had failed to adjust its equating procedure to account for the changeover equitably.

ETS ended up giving higher scores to applicants who took the test in October and December than those same individuals would have received had they turned in an equivalent performance on the "old" LSAT in July.[307] Similarly, students who decided to assemble their credentials early and take the test in July received scores <u>lower</u> than they would have earned with the same performance in October or December. ETS advised institutions to treat all scores as comparable, regardless of the time of the year the test was taken.[308]

The score discrepancy came to light only after hundreds of places at schools with "rolling admissions" had been filled on the assumption that all the scores meant the same thing, which meant July students, by and large, came up short. "We had admitted quite a few people before figuring out that scores were higher on the October and December tests," Harvard Admissions Dean Patricia Lydon told the <u>Yale Daily News</u>.[309] Even after the discrepancy became known, ETS did not provide statistical tables for comparing the two sets of scores. Some law schools said they would encourage application readers to make a "mental adjustment" in reviewing the applicant's scores. Other schools told applicants that they did not have the time to search their files to distinguish the summer and winter test-takers.[310]

During the summer of 1977, a UCLA Law School interviewer informed Gary Hirsch that he was a "shoo-in" for admission. When his July LSAT was swamped by waves of high-scoring October-December competitors and UCLA put him on the waiting list, Hirsh called the admission office. He was informed that the admissions committee could neither "add nor take away points" due to fear of legal action by winter candidates who had scored higher and might sue if rejected. When Hirsch asked how two equally qualified applicants, one with a July 650 score and the other with an October 670 score, would be treated, he was told "Of course, we would accept the student with the higher score."[311]

Although the score changes which occur due to such errors are small, their impact on people's admissions prospects helps to illustrate the importance of ETS scores in the admissions process. At schools which use cutoff scores for example, a single point can be the difference between acceptance and rejection. A 1976 College Board study of admission practices looked at 144 schools and found that forty per cent of public institutions surveyed, as well as twenty percent of the private institutions used absolute cutoffs.[312] Further, "Test scores were identified more often than any other variable as being a major criterion used in the admissions process," according to an article in the summer 1976 <u>College Board Review</u>. "Among both private and public institutions interviewed, four of five institutions selected <u>test scores as most important</u> when compared to high school grades, rank in class, and other variables."[313] (Emphasis added.)

In 1971, Professors Clifford Wing and Michael Wallach, formerly of the ETS Standing Committee on Research, published the first and, thus far, only systematic statistical study of college reliance on the SAT. After analyzing data from 224 colleges of varying degrees of student selectivity, Wing and Wallach discovered that in marked contrast "with the descriptions often given by colleges themselves," the test was exceedingly important in admissions decisions.[314] Wing and Wallach documented "a highly systematic positive relationship between the magnitude of SAT-V[erbal] scores and the proportion of the applicant population accepted for admission."[315]

Relatively small differences in SAT scores were found to alter the applicant's chances significantly.[316] This pattern prevailed at virtually all the schools studied, regardless of whether they were of low, high, or moderate selectivity. According to ETS' psychometric theory, the "error of measurement" of an SAT score is a range extending from thirty points above to thirty points below the score a person actually receives. This means that if individuals were to take the test an infinite number of times, this "true score"--the average of all their scores-- would likely fall somewhere within this sixty point range. (A third of the time their score would be expected to fall outside this sixty point range.)[317] Yet, at **many of the schools studied** by Wing and Wallach, a score difference of _less_ than sixty points could alter chances for admission by more than 100 percent. For an applicant to a school of moderate to high selectivity, a score increase from 350 to 400 could double the chances for admission. An increase from 425 to 475 could boost the chances by seventy percent. On the other hand, a drop of fifty points* would lower the chances by the same amount.[318]

---

*These figures may be somewhat inflated since they do not control for possible differences in high school grades among people at different score levels; nevertheless, they suggest the substantial effect of test scores on admissions prospects.

Such is the meaning lent to ETS points by test professionals and institutions. Where do those fifty SAT points that can so alter the odds of your educational future come from? As we have seen, they are derived from statistical formulas that transform the answers to a few multiple-choice questions into an elaborate three-digit report of "aptitude." For the 99,784 candidates who took the SAT on February 2, 1974, for example, fifty Verbal SAT points were gained or lost depending on their answers to six multiple-choice questions--the equivalent (if you spent an equal amount of time on each question in a given section of the test)--of five minutes of work. On the math section, six questions--or seven-and-a-half minutes of work--could have cost you sixty points.[319]

For institutions which use the ETS Validity Study Service, the transformation of the score, rather than the score the candidate sees, ultimately shapes the admissions decision. In addition to sending the scores of their applicants on print-outs, punch cards, and magnetic computer tapes, ETS will help schools devise a formula combining grades and ETS scores into a single index number which can be used to rank all applicants from top to bottom. The ETS manual on how colleges can order such formulas gives the example of "Clifford College, Myth City, Any State, USA" where ETS recommends that the SAT Verbal score be weighted four times greater than the math score.[320] Tracing the implications of such a formula back to the test center (using the February, 1974 example), one finds that candidates who have a bad five minutes and answer six verbal questions wrong instead of right not only lower their score fifty points, from, for example, 550 to 500, but also have this score difference in turn multiplied four more times by a formula (often not disclosed to the applicant) which may largely determine their chances for admission.[321]

When such large decisions about a person's future can turn on such small samples of their performance, it is evidence of an impressive concentration of power. The implications of the mission which ETS had created for itself were evident to some within the corporation. In a September, 1972 "Five Year Plan for College Board Programs" one ETS executive describing the SAT as "a national test of human intelligence," wrote:

> . . . We have to question the propriety of continuing with the sorting of people according to theoretical definitions of intelligence. It would surely be better to rest the SAT on empirical observations.
>
> . . . The whole test structure is vulnerable to . . . /attack/, in fact, because the test structure is closed to influence from actual student performance.
>
> . . . We are saying . . . that we have defined for ourselves what human intelligence is and have developed a test reflecting what we say human intelligence is.[322]

Others at ETS may have chosen different words to describe what the company was claiming to measure about people's minds. But, however it was described, ETS' claim to be measuring basic mental qualities gave the tests and decisions based on them a significance which was beyond dispute. As ETS public relations director Robert Moulthrop and John Fremer pointed out in an internal 1978 briefing paper on "Criticism of Testing," "Tests do play a significant and important role in the lives of students and others. Test results often determine whether students will receive credit, gain admission, win scholarships, achieve licensing or certification. Test results can and do determine access to jobs and careers."[323] (Emphasis in original.)

For ETS, the attainment of such power meant the fulfillment of a mission. But for millions of people it meant the alteration of their lives by an aptitude test which told them less about what they were capable of doing than about what they would be permitted to attempt.

CHAPTER IV

"THE WORTH OF OTHER MEN": THE SCIENCE OF MENTAL MEASUREMENT AND THE TEST OF TIME

When test-takers open a letter from Rosedale to discover how much "aptitude" ETS says they have, they probably do not question how the test system judging them came to be. If they did, they would discover they are not the first to have been told by professionals about the quality of their thinking and how much they are capable of doing.

Test professionals have been using multiple-choice questions to draw conclusions about people's minds since the early 1900s. The importance of this history for understanding ETS today is acknowledged in many quarters. ETS Executive Vice-President Robert J. Solomon says:

> I think one has to consider the context of American education and . . . the nature of American society . . . in order to better understand why (ETS) exists and why a great many people use its services and why it has grown . . . /The role of ETS testing has grown from the/ recognition that it's the individual's educational development that's significant.[1]

For Carl Campbell Brigham, the inventor of the SAT, the function of the tests was to "estimate the worth of other men . . . to reckon their potential possibilities." Brigham did not shrink from this task.[2] But he cautioned that, since the tests "d/īd/ not warrant any certainty of prediction," the estimates were to be made with discretion.[3] For Brigham, as for his successors at ETS, the authority to judge minds with a test score was not itself a problem--so long as it was entrusted to responsible professionals trained in the science of mental measurement.

In *Testing: Its Place in Education Today*, Henry Chauncey
traces the roots of testing to the ancient Greeks:

> The Spartans . . . had an elaborately graduated series of tests through which every boy had to pass in demonstrating his growing mastery of the required skills of manhood. In Athens a more intellectual kind of testing was refined by Socrates to extend and enrich the learning of his pupils.[4]

Chauncey does not mention a later generation of Greeks, those who were prevented from entering the United States by the Immigration Act of 1924. This law was passed in large part on the strength of claims by testing experts who affirmed that Greeks, Poles, Italians, others of the "Mediterranean and Slavic races," as well as the Irish, constituted a threat to America's intellectual capacity due to their low scores on standardized tests.[5]

The story of the Immigration Act of 1924, as with the history of mental measurement in America, is the history of the theory that a few professionals can define and place a value on people's capacity for thinking. It is a history occurring simultaneously at two different levels: at the level of theory, in the interplay among professionals--those who think about where people should be placed in society and develop the techniques for placing them; and at the level of experience, in the lives of millions of people who feel the consequences of the professional's words--those whose thinking capacity is constantly measured but whose thoughts are rarely heard.

Although the basic mental measurement technique (the mass administration of multiple-choice tests and the application of correlation statistics to the results) has remained intact for eighty years, the claims about what the tests measure have gone through several phases of dramatic fluctuation. Yet, throughout the odyssey of the testing profession's scientific verdicts, there have been at least two constants. First, there is the consistent finding that the working class, the poor, and the most oppressed minorities of a particular historical era have relatively little "intelligence", "aptitude", or whatever the profession is purporting to measure at the time. And, second, one consistently finds an institutional arrangement whereby the professionals who construct these tests and report these findings are backed and employed by the nation's richest and most powerful institutions; they persistently report and interpret their findings with confidence in their authority to direct the course of people's lives and thoughts.

English biologist Sir Francis Galton launched the mental testing movement. In the 1880s Galton began a program of measuring the intellects of English school children by testing their hearing, coordination and reaction time. He pioneered the statistical technique of correlation analysis which ETS uses today to determine the validity of its tests. Galton's achievements made him, in Chauncey's words, "a major figure in the early attempts at measuring individual differences and in the development of formal testing methods."[6]

In one of his pioneering scientific studies, published in 1901 in the scholarly journal Nature, Galton defined and measured those intangible qualities "that go toward the making of civic worth in man." Galton illustrated his point with statistical tables, classifying the people of London into eight categories of "civic worth," complete with population breakdowns. Class A consisted of "criminals, semi-criminals, loafers and some others"; Class B of "very poor persons who subsist on annual earnings, many of whom are inevitably poor from shiftlessness, idleness or drink"; Class C of "hardworking people, but /with/ a very bad character or improvidence and shiftlessness;" and so forth through "the mediocre class" and "the honourable class" to H, where "the brains of the nation lie."[7]

Working from this hierarchy, Galton developed a technique for figuring the proper placement of people in society by calculating the "Worth of Children." Citing the data of an "eminent statistician" who had "endeavored to estimate the monetary worth of an average baby born to the wife of an Essex labourer," Galton noted that, "On balancing both sides of the account the value of the baby was found to be five pounds." Similar measurements estimated the worth of upper-class babies to be considerably greater, since they became the citizens who "found great industries, establish vast undertakings, increase the wealth of the multitudes and amass large fortunes for themselves."[8]

Francis Galton's measurement techniques were designed to do more than advance the frontiers of knowledge. Galton had a theory that measurement of personal qualities could be used to change the character of human life itself. Through the practice of eugenics (the identification of the degree of desirable or undesirable qualities in individuals and the control of their reproduction through planned marriages and sterilization to maximize the desirable), Galton and his successors sought to improve the quality of the world's gene-pool. "The practice of eugenics," Galton wrote in the American Journal of Sociology, "should hereafter raise the average quality of our nation. . . . The race as a whole would be less foolish, less frivolous, less excitable and politically more provident than now."[9]

Galton's eugenic program would rely partly upon tests for college students aimed at guiding their careers and reproductive energies. Noting the need for research on "correlations between promise in youth and subsequent performance," Galton predicted:

> No serious difficulty seems to stand in the way of classifying and. . . granting diplomas to a select class of young men and women. . . encouraging their intermarriage, /and/ hastening the time of marriage of women of that high class . . . It is no absurd idea that outside influences should hasten the age of marrying and make it customary for the best to marry the best.[10]

Backing for this enterprise would come from men of means who would sponsor the most meritorious young candidates. "It might well become a point of honour," Galton conjectured, "and as much an avowed object, for noble families to gather fine specimens of humanity around them, as it is to procure and maintain fine breeds of cattle and so forth, which are costly, but repay in satisfaction."[11]

The opportunities available to eugenics, Galton concluded, were almost limitless.

> It must be introduced into the national conscience, like a new religion. It has, indeed, strong claims to become an orthodox religious tenet of the future, for eugenics co-operate with the workings of nature by securing that humanity shall be represented by the fittest races. What nature does blindly, slowly, and ruthlessly, man may do providently, quickly, and kindly.[12]

The boldness of this vision may have shocked some, but Galton was confident it was one to which future generations would become accustomed.

In 1904, the French Minister of Public Instruction had asked psychologist Alfred Binet to develop a test which would identify public school children who needed special instruction.[13] Binet responded by assembling the first easy-to-administer standardized intelligence test--a test whose descendent is still used around the world.[14] In Henry Chauncey's description:

> The problems [Binet] posed for youngsters were both complex and sensible: Younger children (ages 3-6) were asked to give their family name, to identify familiar objects, to copy figures, to point to their right and left ear, to obey commands. Ten- and eleven-year olds were asked to name the months of the year in correct order, to recognize and name various coins, to make up sentences in which various key words were provided, to define abstract words, and to arrange scrambled words into a meaningful sentence. . . . Binet proposed that the degree of brightness in children could be judged by observing their ability to perform correctly tasks similar in nature to those faced in their daily lives.[15]

Many of the leading psychologists who first used Binet's test believed that it measured an "intelligence" inherited from one's ancestors and unlikely to change throughout life. (For Binet himself, this was a view of "brutal pessimism.")[16] Later testers, including Chauncey and the current professionals of ETS, strongly disagreed with this interpretation. They argued that test score data indicated "intelligence" was not inherited, and not fixed.[17] Nonetheless, Chauncey and colleagues left little doubt of their confidence that the test was, in fact, a scientific instrument that measured something of profound importance. The schoolyard questions of Alfred Binet, Henry Chauncey wrote more than fifty years later, would enable professionals to measure and calibrate the mind just as physical scientists mapped the material universe:

> His method was truly scientific and remarkably like the method used by physicists forty years later to detect and

> measure the forces released by the atom. The cloud chamber does not permit the physicist to see the atom or its electrically charged components, but it does reveal the tracks of ionizing particles and thus permits the scientist to deduce the nature of the atom from which the particles emanate. . . .
>
> The measures that Binet and his co-workers developed for estimating mental ability marked the real beginning of modern psychological testing. These measures demonstrated that complex mental processes, processes generally associated with intelligent behavior, could be called forth and evaluated in a systematic way.[18]

It didn't take long for the Binet tests to cross the Atlantic. In 1908, Dr. Henry Goddard of the Vineland, New Jersey Training School for the Feeble-Minded, translated and introduced the Binet test to the United States.[19] This test had already attracted the attention of psychologists worldwide; it quickly had a decisive impact on the theoretical disputes of America's leading psychologists and on the genitals of its least esteemed public wards. At the urging of Goddard and other professionals, the test became a leading justification for the eugenic sterilization of people with low scores. As Professor Leon Kamin has pointed out, "The rise of the mental testing movement coincided precisely in time with the passage of such /sterilization/ laws by a large number of states."[20]

Although proper application of psychometrics was seen as a matter of urgent national necessity, Goddard and his colleagues emphasized that such crucial matters as directing the educations and careers (and sex lives) of other people was a task for trained professionals only. They contended that any inappropriate interpretations of test scores could be attributed to outsiders, whose claims were not up to the standards of the field's leading professionals. As Henry Chauncey later lamented:

> Most of the tests put together by eager amateurs and hawked among their colleagues were not very good, and they soured a lot of teachers on the whole idea of testing. Almost without exception the amateur-made tests measured only recall of specific subject matter content, asking only for regurgitation of the text . . . Many people grew to think that all objective tests were true-false tests (as many of the slapped-together instruments of the period were).[21]

This unfortunate trend, Chauncey concluded, undermined early public acceptance of the burgeoning science of mental measurement.

Amateurism was not a characteristic one would have dared to attribute to Dr. Lewis M. Terman of Stanford University. President of the American Psychological Association and personnel consultant to the U.S. military, Terman produced in 1916 one of the most widely used tests in the history of mental measurement, the definitive U.S. version of Alfred Binet's intelligence test. According to Chauncey's account, Terman introduced new questions and gave guidance for administering and scoring the tests and interpreting the results. The Stanford-Binet Test became the standard American "intelligence test." As a responsible professional, Chauncey points out, Terman's directions for the proper use of his test included an appropriate "word of caution." Unlike less judicious interpreters of test scores, Terman did not overemphasize the significance of the "intelligence quotient" (or "IQ") used to score the test. Rather, Chauncey writes, "Terman used this score device for the interpretation of performance on the <u>Stanford-Binet</u>, carefully describing it as a convenient 'index of brightness' that had a comparison built into it."[22]

Despite such efforts to keep IQ interpretation on an objective, professional level, Chauncey complains, "the IQ of a child was erroneously assumed to be a permanent and immutable characteristic, like blue eyes or big ears, rather than a score in a particular test at a particular time." Nevertheless, he asserts, "The shortcomings of the IQ in school test score interpretation were the fault of the users far more often than of the index itself."[23]

Thus, it was Dr. Lewis M. Terman who was presented as a paragon of the professional principles that remain fundamental to the science of psychometrics. "For two decades," Chauncey reports, "the 1916 edition of the <u>Stanford-Binet</u> held a position of outstanding prestige and usefulness." During that time Terman and his associates produced a complete revision of the test, as experience and research had dictated. In its present version, the <u>Stanford-Binet</u> remains "the most widely used individual test of the mental ability of children in America."[24]

Terman's scientific explanation of the usefulness of psychometrics is found in his detailed book of instructions on the 1916 <u>Stanford-Binet</u>. In his opening chapter, which discussed the people who score low on the test (but not low enough to be classified as "imbeciles" or "morons"), Terman predicted:

> . . . in the near future intelligence tests will bring tens of thousands of these high-grade defectives under the surveillance and protection of society. This will ultimately result in curtailing the reproduction of feeblemindedness and in the elimination of an enormous amount of crime, pauperism and industrial inefficiency.[25]

An IQ in the seventy to eighty range, which purportedly places one on the borderline of deficiency, Terman continued:

> . . . is very, very common among Spanish children and Mexican families of the Southwest and also among negroes . . . Children of this group should be segregated in special classes. . . They cannot master abstractions but they can often be made efficient workers . . . There is no possibility at present of convincing society that they should not be allowed to reproduce, although from a eugenic point of view they constitute a grave problem because of their unusually prolific breeding.[26]

Psychometrics, Terman found, was useful for directing the lives of more than just the people who got the lowest scores. Standardized testing was also designed to guide the selection and placement of people at all levels and functions of society. As Terman wrote in his 1923 book, Intelligence Tests and School Reorganization:

> Preliminary investigations indicate that an I.Q. below 70 rarely permits anything better than unskilled labor; that the range from 70 to 80 is preeminently that of semi-skilled labor, from 80 to 100 that of skilled or ordinary clerical labor, from 100 to 110 or 115, that of semi-professional pursuits; and that above all these are the grades of intelligence which permit one to enter the professions or the larger fields of business. . . [The test score] information will be of great value in planning the education of a particular child and also in planning the differentiated curriculum here recommended.[27]

Thus, the work of Terman and his colleagues on mental measurement had more than scientific significance. Millions of school children were having their educations directed by scores from standardized intelligence tests. Moreover, according to Professor Clarence Karier of the University of Illinois, "Between 1907 and 1928, twenty-one states practiced eugenical sterilization involving over 8,500 people."[28] California's sterilization law, which neutered at least 6,200 of the "morally and sexually depraved," was designed with the help of the Human Betterment Foundation, a group which included Dr. Terman among its many leading professionals.

Changing people's bodies because of what scientists thought was in their minds was not an idea promoted by amateurs or crackpots. The nation's leading professional social thinkers, from writers in the Harvard Law Review to the officers of the American Psychological Association, committed their authority to the cause of improving the human breed.[29] Eugenic planning was carried beyond mere words of social theory by the generous support of some of America's wealthiest families. The Carnegie group of foundations was pouring thousands of dollars into research projects and professional organizations designed to promote the twin sciences of eugenics and psychometrics. As Clarence Karier points out:

> While America has had a long history of eugenics advocacy, some of the key leaders of the testing movement were the strongest advocates for eugenics control. In the twentieth century the two movements often came together in the same people under the name of 'scientific' testing and, for one cause or the other, received foundation support.[30]

Mrs. E. H. Harriman, wife of the New York railroad magnate, became a generous patron of the Eugenics Records Office, a research and debating organization founded in 1910 which was to serve for thirty years as a meeting place for the leading lights of the science of mental testing.[31] In addition to practical activities such as helping the state of Indiana identify "mental defectives" for sterilization,[32] the Office published research on such matters as ridding the U.S. gene pool of "defective germ-plasm."[33] In 1916, the National Council on Education and the National Education Association, two groups which had earlier launched "the movement which resulted in the organization of the College Entrance Examination Board" established the "Committee for Racial Well Being," a eugenic strategy group which included testing pioneers Henry Goddard and Robert M. Yerkes.[34]

According to Chauncey's account, when the United States entered World War I in 1917, "The Army asked the American Psychological Association to help devise a method for classifying recruits rapidly according to their mental ability."[35] A committee headed by Robert Yerkes, then president of the APA:

> . . . develop[ed] the group test soon to be known to millions of doughboys--the Army Alpha Test. They also devised a group test for illiterates, using drawings and other non-verbal materials, called the Army Beta Test. Nearly two million soldiers took the Army Alpha in the training camps.[36]

Created by the cream of the nation's mental testers, the Army tests were scientifically devised to reveal the intangible traits crucial to success in modern warfare. The "Practical Judgment" of raw recruits was assessed by a battery of questions headed by the instruction: "This is a test of common sense." Some of the items included:

3. Why do soldiers wear wrist watches rather than pocket watches?

 ___ they keep better time

 ___ they are harder to break

 ___ they are handier

13. Why should a married man have his life insured?
    Because

    ___ death may come at any time

    ___ insurance companies are usually honest

    ___ his family will not then suffer if he dies

16. Why should we have Congressmen?
    Because

    ___ the people must be ruled

    ___ it insures truly representative government

    ___ the people are too many to meet and make the laws

The Army Alpha "Information" test probed the soldier's knowledge of the world around him.

8. Revolvers are made by

    ___ Swift and Co.   ___ W.L. Douglas

    ___ Smith and Wesson   ___ B.J. Babbitt

10. "There's a reason" is an "ad" for a

    ___ drink   ___ flour

    ___ revolver   ___ cleanser

16. Alfred Noyes is famous as a

    ___ painter   ___ musician

    ___ poet   ___ sculptor

17. The armadillo is a kind of

    ___ ornamental shrub   ___ musical instrument

    ___ animal   ___ dagger

19. Crisco is a

    ___ patent medicine   ___ tooth-paste

    ___ disinfectant   ___ food product

38. The Pierce Arrow car is made in

    ___ Buffalo   ___ Toledo

    ___ Detroit   ___ Flint[37]

The Army Alpha was a high point in the professional development of mental science. In Chauncey's view: "This test turned out to be a remarkably good instrument for assigning recruits to jobs with different intellectual demands, for picking out promising officer candidates, and for rejecting those who lacked sufficient mental ability to complete military training successfully."[38]

Meanwhile, a growing fraternity of eugenics professionals was considering an expanded domestic role for the science of psychometrics. By 1916, the Eugenics Research Association was publishing its own professional journal--Eugenical News, edited by Harry H. Laughlin, a frequent consultant to foundations and a leading advocate of eugenic planning. Eugenical News editorialized that mental test scores should be used to screen people who wanted to immigrate to the United States.[39] Control of immigration, though given a high priority, was only one of many subjects under study by the ERA and associated groups. The mental traits of Oriental laborers,[40] a model eugenics and sterilization law for state legislatures,[41] and a Harvard professor's discourse on the assessment of ballroom dancing ability[42] for selecting a eugenically appropriate mate were among the many subjects pondered by the readers of Eugenical News.

With such a diverse and vigorous program of work, the eugenics organizations had little trouble enlisting the nation's leading foundations and social and behavioral scientists. The Carnegie Institution of Washington, which first became associated with the ERA in 1916, assumed control of the Eugenics Record Office in 1918.[43] The July 8, 1920 ERA annual meeting, for example, saw the induction of prominent psychologists from Columbia, Stanford, Johns Hopkins and, from Princeton, Carl Brigham, a former Yerkes aide who had that year been commissioned by the prestigious National Research Council to analyze the World War I Army test results.[44]

Within the distinguished but large membership of the ERA, there existed an organization reserved for only the most formidable eugenic scholars. The Galton Society, convened in April, 1918 by nine "students of man,"[45] was the creation of Madison Grant, the author of The Passing of the Great Race, an influential book, published in 1916, which attributed the decline of western civilization to the dilution of pristine Nordic bloodlines by Mediterraneans, Jews, and other lesser "races."[46] The Galton Society, Grant announced, would be

> . . . an anthropological society. . . here in New York City with a central governing body, self elected and self perpetuating, and very limited in members, and also confined to native Americans, who are anthropologically, socially and politically sound, no Bolsheviki need apply."[47]

Taking part in Madison Grant's select society of eugenic planners were Henry H. Goddard, noted test pioneer, Carl Campbell Brigham of Princeton University, and Edward L. Thorndike of Columbia University.[48] Thorndike, Chauncey reports, was

> A giant of the early years of testing. . ./who/ in 1904 published the first textbook in educational measurement, An Introduction to the Theory of Mental and Social Measurement, which is taken by many to mark the beginning of modern times in testing.[49]

While learned men in Park Avenue drawing rooms laid plans for measuring minds, subjects for their social experiments arrived at Ellis Island at the rate of 5,000 a day.[50] By May, 1920, immigration to the U.S. was booming following the World War I period of net loss in U.S. residents.[51] Harry Laughlin of the Eugenical News had been appointed "Expert Eugenics Agent" to the U.S. House Committee on Immigration and Naturalization.[52] House Committee Chairman Albert Johnson of Illinois, a member of the ERA, was elected its chairman in 1923.[53] Citing the fact that most immigrants were from southern and eastern Europe and that people from these countries tended to be "defective and unfit," Eugenical News called in 1921 for a one year suspension of all immigration.[54] That same year, as a temporary measure, Congress for the first time limited the number of immigrants.[55]

In 1923, the Princeton University Press published a scholarly book which would excite the academic interest of the few who read it and change the lives of millions who had not. Carl Campbell Brigham's, A Study of American Intelligence, applied the science of psychometrics to the question of who should be admitted to the United States. "The book is a landmark of sorts," contends

Leon Kamin. "Though it has disappeared from contemporary reference lists, it can be argued that few works in the history of American psychology have had so significant an impact."[56]

Sponsored by the wealthy eugenicist Charles W. Gould, Brigham re-analyzed the World War I Army test results. Edward G. Boring of Harvard and Edwin G. Conklin of Princeton, two lions of American psychology, carefully reviewed the manuscript. The U.S. Army Surgeon General's Office provided statisticians for Brigham's calculations. Robert Yerkes monitored the research and launched the book with a preface in which he noted that the author presents "not theories or opinions but facts."[57] Brigham heralded "the army mental tests . . . [as] an opportunity for a national inventory of our own mental capacity, and the mental capacity of those we have invited to live with us."[58] The scores of 81,000 native-born whites, 12,000 foreign-born individuals, and 23,000 blacks were the raw material for Brigham's study of who in the United States held the important commodity of scientifically measured "intelligence." "These army data constitute the first really significant contribution to the study of race differences in mental traits," he wrote. "They give us a scientific basis for our conclusions."[59]

Brigham acknowledged that the army tests had been criticized. Of those who quibbled over the content of particular test questions, he said:

> After weighing all the evidence, it would seem that we are justified in ignoring most of the arm-chair criticisms of this test and in accepting the experimental evidence tending to show that the test was a fairly good one.[60]

He defended his use of the scores of 116,000 men to draw conclusions about the whole population of the U.S. and other countries. "The tea taster <u>samples</u> the tea to be graded. He does not need to brew a whole bale of tea to find its worth. . . In the same way, no one could seriously question the reliability of our sampling. . . ."[61]

The army test scores showed a clear pattern: the foreign-born people who had lived longest in the U.S. scored highest and recent arrivals scored lowest. Some critics suggested that new immigrants scored lower because they were less familiar with the peculiarly American topics included in the test. Other critics claimed that immigrants' lower scores merely reflected their poor command of the English language. These criticisms challenged the notion that the test measured something basic to the person--his "intelligence." Brigham dismissed such criticisms as the fruit of unprofessional thought and denied that the language factor distorts the scores. Brigham addressed his critics boldly:

> . . . if one wishes to deny, in the teeth of the facts, the superiority of the Nordic race on the ground that the language factor mysteriously aids this group when tested, he may cut out of the Nordic distribution the English speaking Nordics, and still find a marked superiority of the non-English speaking Nordics over the Alpine and Mediterranean groups.[62]

According to the nation's leading testing scientists, the mental measurement of soldiers, randomly drafted for World War I had shown that Americans who were born in some countries were, in fact, more "intelligent" than Americans who were born in other countries. These tests, advised Carl Campbell Brigham--professor, Galton Society fellow, and inventor of ETS testing--showed that people who got too many questions wrong were representatives of an inferior race, an inferior lot of people who ought to be kept from America to save its politics, society, and sexual integrity.

Brigham's A Study of American Intelligence includes a diagram in the form of a ruler on which is ranked, from top to bottom, the "average intelligence" of seventeen nationalities--including separate rankings of "U.S. (Officers)," "U.S. (White)," and U.S. (colored)."[63] The score differences among these "nativity groups," Brigham explains, are due to "the race factor."[64] Considering the fact that the recent immigrants were mainly from southern and eastern Europe, Brigham announced: "The decline in intelligence is due to two factors, the change in the races migrating to this country and the additional factor of the sending of lower and lower representatives of each race."[65] After correlating racial composition with the test scores of people from different nations, Brigham was ready to tell people, in straight-forward scientific terms, whether they were intelligent enough to be allowed to mingle with the descendants of America's founders:

> The intellectual superiority of our Nordic group over the Alpine, Mediterranean, and negro groups has been demonstrated[66] . . . This superiority is confirmed by observations of this race in history. . . .[67]

Quoting Madison Grant, Brigham noted that: "The Nordics are, all over the world, a race of soldiers, sailors, adventurers and explorers, but above all of rulers, organizers, and aristocrats in sharp contrast to the essentially peasant and democratic character of the Alpines."[68]

Brigham's exposition was not limited to demonstrating Nordic superiority. Lesser peoples were also assigned their appropriate place in the hierarchy of scientifically measured intelligence:

> Our results showing the marked intellectual inferiority of the negro are corrobated [sic] by practically all of the investigators who have used psychological tests on white and negro groups. . . . Our figures [also] tend to disprove the popular belief that the Jew is highly intelligent.[69]

Yet, despite the apparent power of his method and the clarity of his data, Professor Brigham scrupulously abided by the limits of testing science; he conceded freely:

> At the present stage of development of psychological tests, we cannot measure the actual amount of difference in intelligence due to race or nativity. We can only prove that differences do exist, and we can interpret these differences in terms that have great social and economic significance.[70]

The situation, as seen by Brigham and his followers, was clear; lacking a selective admissions policy, the U.S. was hurting present and future generations. Wrote Brigham:

> We may consider that the population of the United States is made up of four racial elements, the Nordic, Alpine, and Mediterranean races of Europe, and the negro. If these four types blend in the future into one general American type, then it is a foregone conclusion that this future blended American will be less intelligent than the present native born American, for the general result of the admixture of higher and lower orders of intelligence must inevitably be a mean between the two. . . .[71]

"We must face a possibility of racial admixture here that is infinitely worse than that faced by any European country today," Brigham further warned, "for we are incorporating the negro into our racial stock, while all of Europe is comparatively free from this taint."[72]

If psychometrics and social theory could diagnose the problem, only political institutions had the power to do something about it:

> The deterioration of American intelligence is not inevitable, however, if public action can be aroused to prevent it. There is no reason why legal steps should not be taken which would insure a continuously progressive upward evolution. . . . Immigration should not only be restrictive but highly selective. And the revision of the immigration and naturalization laws will only afford a slight relief from our present difficulty. The really important steps are those looking toward the prevention of the continued propagation of defective strains in the present population. If all immigration were stopped now, the decline of American intelligence would still be inevitable. This is the problem which must be met, and our manner of meeting it will determine the future course of our national life.[73]

Brigham's findings, though not without political implications, were intended to be used in only the most objective manner. "The steps that should be taken to preserve or increase our present intellectual capacity must of course be dictated by science and not by political expediency," he wrote.[74]

A Study of American Intelligence, according to the ETS biography of Brigham, "received several adverse reviews in the press, especially in the liberal journals."[75] But, among those professionally trained in the science of mental measurement, Dr. Brigham's test scores were more fully appreciated. The respected Journal of Educational Psychology reported:

> The thesis is carefully worked up to by a logical and careful analysis of the results of the army tests. . . . We shall certainly be in hearty agreement with him when he demands a more selective policy for future immigration and a more vigorous method of dealing with the defective strains already in this country.[76]

"The book. . . received favorable comment /from/ many of Brigham's colleagues," noted the ETS biography, "and was considered by many people as the last word on the subject of racial differences. . . The book rendered a useful service as a digest of the data from the Army tests. . . it added considerably to Brigham's reputation."[77]

The effect of Brigham's landmark work did not depend on how it fared in the polite debates of academic journals. The science of mental measurement had come to the attention of people with institutional power, and its ranking of individual mental worth fit their purposes nicely. On January 10, 1924, Brigham's fellow eugenicist, Congressman Albert Johnson, chairman of the ERA, convened his House Committee on Immigration and Naturalization. The topic was Rep. Johnson's H.R. 101, "A bill to limit the immigration of aliens into the United States, and to provide a system of selection in connection therewith." The immigration bill, written in consultation with the ERA, set up a quota system to limit immigration to two per cent of the number of people of a nationality who lived in the U.S. in 1890.[78] The 1890 "grandfather clause" was the heart of the bill, since in 1890 there were few people born in southern and eastern Europe living in the U.S. The Eugenical News editorialized that Chairman Johnson's immigration bill "seems to us to be, in most respects, admirable and demands the support of all eugenicists."[79]

In 1923, 3,333 people from Greece, 46,674 from Italy, 17,507 from Russia, 48,277 from Germany, and 26,538 from Poland, had immigrated to the U.S.[80] In the same year, Dr. Brigham's test scores marked them as inferior, and the following year this massive influx of largely poor Europeans was curtailed by federal law. The connection between these two events is made explicit in the records of the House Committee. A report from an ERA study group, chaired by Madison Grant, and including Harry Laughlin and Representative Johnson, lays out the implications of the findings of mental testing:

> The country at large has been greatly impressed by the results of the Army intelligence tests as carefully analyzed by Lieut. Col. R.M. Yerkes, Dr. C.C. Brigham, and others. . . . With the shift in the tide of immigration. . . to southern and eastern Europe, there has gone a decrease in intelligence test scores . . . . The experts. . . believe that. . . the tests give as accurate a measure of intelligence as possible. . . . Had mental tests been in operation. . . over 6,000,000 aliens now living in this country would never have been admitted.[81]

The chairman of the Allied Patriotic Societies of New York testified that "Professor Brigham's tables bring out certain very startling facts. . . . Professor Brigham figures out, moreover, that as many as 2,000,000 persons have been admitted. . . whose intelligence was nearer the intelligence of the average negro than to the average intelligence of the American white."[82]

Francis Kinnicutt of the Immigration Restriction League drew the obvious conclusion in testimony before the Senate Committee on Immigration. The solution was "to further restrict immigration from southern and eastern Europe."[83] Kinnicutt had sent Senator Colt, the chairman of the committee, a copy of Brigham's book and had brought with him an additional copy. Colt thanked him and urged that "every member of the committee read /the/ book and then arrive at his own judgment in regard to it."[84]

The Johnson-Lodge Immigration Act of 1924 was passed on May 26, 1924. Its eugenically designed quotas remained in force until 1968.[85]

Although America's most accomplished mental testers generally lent their support to eugenic sterilization and immigration restriction, they recognized that conscientious eugenic planning required a more thorough program of mental measurement. By 1926, the ERA membership included such testing leaders as Brigham, Thorndike, Goddard, Yerkes, James McKeen Cattell (in Chauncey's words, a "major figure" in testing),[86] and Dr. Charles W. Eliot, president of Harvard and key member of a young testing organization called the College Entrance Examination Board.[87] With men of such broad experience, the eugenics movement began to look beyond restrictive measures to more positive, active means of guiding people to appropriate life choices. In 1923, for example, the "Ultimate Program of the Eugenics Committee of the U.S.A." called for national "systematic mental testing" of people in many walks of life.[88]

Two essential elements that would later help form a centralized testing system--a measurement technique and a national organization to apply it--were only beginning to converge in the mid-1920s. Both had their origins in the previous century with influential social theorists. While Francis Galton was measuring the worth of English children, some distinguished educators intent on forming a new organization were gathering, as Columbia University's Nicholas Murray Butler wrote, "at my dinner table in New York in the early autumn of 1892."[89] This was the Committee of Ten, chaired by President Eliot of Harvard (later of the ERA), its members selected with "scrupulous care" by the National Education Association; in Butler's words, they were "the real leaders of educational thought and practice in the United States." [90] The Ten were planning the organization which would be convened in 1900 as the College Entrance Examination Board. This act of organization, College Board associate Julius Sachs would later remark, was an event "of no mean significance, the definite triumph in our educational situation, of order over chaos."[91]

The Committee of Ten was out to establish a central authority--in President Eliot's phrase, "a uniform standard of enforcement" to govern American education.[92] Julius Sachs explained the need for establishing such a central authority for directing the future of the educational system:

> Our Anglo-Saxon heritage accentuates the significance of unified expert thought, "the give and take" of a number of conscientious counselors, each one open to conviction and ready to modify his own opinion in a frank interchange of thought, that is accepted as the American method of advancement.[93]

Some 973 applicants took the first College Board exam in June of 1901 at sixty-seven locations in the U.S. and two in Europe.[94] According to the official account, the College Board's importance was established at two key points in its early history:

> The first was in 1916, when Harvard, Yale and Princeton simultaneously gave up their own examination and turned all their candidates for admission over to the Board. The second was in 1919, when Vassar, Smith, Mount Holyoke and Wellesley, by mutual agreement,.... sent their hundreds of candidates to join the already swollen ranks.[95]

It was not until around 1920, according to ETS, that colleges--mainly the elite Eastern schools--began a policy of selective admissions.[96] Previously, anyone who met certain minimum standards of schooling or who won the dean's approval was admitted. As more people began to apply than some colleges could physically handle, choices had to be made. As Carl Brigham's ETS biographer put it: "Admissions committees adopted for their motto the dictum--many are called, but few are chosen. In the process of selection they relied heavily upon the scores of the College Board Examinations."[97]

The job of choosing the chosen did not intimidate the College Board. At a banquet for the Board's twenty-fifth anniversary, Dr. Henry S. Pritchett pondered the examiner's role in the chain of educational survival.

> When one considers the swarm of untrained and immature youths admitted to the high school without any discriminating test, he realizes how convenient it is to have a goodly number of elective rivulets in which these little fishes can swim and from which through another certification they may float safely into college,--sometimes to the slaughter, sometimes to other brooks in which little fishes may find safe water. Whatever may be said in favor of admission by certificate no one can doubt that the certificate system sadly needs the tonic of a sharp but firm test free from the pressure that rests upon teacher and principal. The College Entrance Examinations have served this great purpose. . . .[98]

Although the professional examiners had already defined their mission of separating those who have it from those who don't, they did not yet control an institution which could make their ideas a national reality. In 1925, the College Board was only testing five per cent of all entering freshmen, and these were all at rich, elite schools.[99] Even more important, the College Board had yet to grasp the possibilities of the science of mental measurement. The College Board exams were all essay tests, not too different from college classroom exams. In 1920, however, some of the more progressive officials organized the first Board committee to study the use of standardized multiple-choice intelligence tests.[100]

Meanwhile, Brigham was dividing his time between his massive study of the World War I Army test results, and the development of multiple-choice intelligence tests for the admissions committees of Princeton and Cooper Union. In 1923, Brigham completed both his Study of American Intelligence and his first "verbal intelligence test," the forerunner of the SAT.[101] In October, 1924, with his reputation firmly established, Brigham met the officers of the College Board and was shortly appointed chairman of a committee to make recommendations on the future of the Board's tests.[102]

Events moved quickly to a conclusion. The Brigham committee's plan for a new test was submitted in February 1925 and approved by the Board in April of that year.[103] By the spring of 1926, after drafting sessions with psychologists from Princeton, Dartmouth, Smith, and Yale, forms A and B of the new Scholastic Aptitude Test (SAT) were ready for America's youth.[104]

Brigham's effective use of psychometrics was attracting considerable attention. The U.S. War Department had retained him to test its officers after he volunteered his services in a 1924 letter: "In case of a national emergency, when it would be necessary to select commissioned personnel, it would be most important to have available the best tests yet developed."[105] Two years later, Brigham began testing West Point students. And, as ETS notes,

> the first validity and reliability studies on the Scholastic Aptitude Test were based on West Point scores. . . . The Academic Board and the faculty of West Point made extensive use of test results, and it was said that the Army football coach used the Scholastic Aptitude Test in selecting his quarterbacks.[106]

At Princeton, Brigham had been named to the Committee on Admissions where he developed the procedure for using SAT scores to help predict college grades[107]--a technique used by nearly sixty per cent of American colleges today.[108] This formula, which uses an equation to sort out test scores and high school grades, produced the "Princeton bogie grade,. . . the predicted freshman average grade of an applicant for admission to Princeton."[109] According to the ETS biography, the bogie was too potent a commodity to remain a Princeton monopoly. By 1930, its use had spread to Cambridge after a meeting between Brigham and an assistant dean from Harvard by the name of Henry Chauncey.[110]

Carl Brigham did more than change the College Boards into a scientific, standardized multiple-choice format. In the years immediately following the release of his claim of Nordic superiority and the development of his verbal intelligence test, he developed most of the methods of question-writing, question-selection, test scoring and statistical analysis used by the ETS test of the 1970s. As an ETS Annual Report later pointed out, "One man--Professor Carl Brigham of Princeton University--had more to do with the shaping of the first Scholastic Aptitude Test and its early history than any other individual."[111] In 1926, Brigham set up his psychometric laboratory at 20 Nassau Street in Princeton, the same building from which, two decades later, Henry Chauncey would administer the ETS test system.[112]

In the midst of Brigham's prodigious effort, he made a remarkable admission with an unpretentious footnote. Writing in the Psychological Review in 1930 Carl Brigham stated that after reassessing his methods, he had determined that his conclusions published seven years earlier in A Study of American Intelligence, were erroneous.[113] Unfortunately, it was too late for millions of poor families in southern and eastern Europe. Though passed partly on the weight of Brigham's (false) conclusions, the Immigration Act of 1924 still stood, obstructing their immigration to America.

Brigham's quiet admission--which, in the words of the ETS biography, "effectively scrapped . . . his major scholarly publication"[114]--was courageous by any standard; but it did not damage his flourishing career. At the time, he was in the midst of a three-year term as secretary of the American Psychological Association. That same year, Brigham was appointed associate secretary of the College Board.[115] The footnote resolved the question of Brigham's racial intelligence hypothesis, but only in the realm of scholarly journals and abstract theory. The effect of his erroneous conclusions would still reverberate painfully in the lives of many individuals for years to come. One interpreter, Princeton psychologist Leon Kamin, in his book on The Science and Politics of I.Q., goes so far as to say this of the 1924 Immigration Act:

> The law, for which the science of mental testing may claim substantial credit, resulted in the deaths of literally hundreds of thousands of victims of the Nazi biological theorists. The victims were denied admission to the United States because the "German quota" was filled, although the quotas of many other Nordic countries were vastly undersubscribed. The Nazi theoreticians ultimately concurred with biologist Laughlin's assessment that, in the case of D- and E /low-scoring/ people, "Cost of supervision greater than value of labor."[116]

Eugenicists often wrote that their motives were humanitarian. They professed merely to be following their testing method to its logical conclusion. The method, the science of psychometrics, gave them reason to believe that they could measure other people's thinking, place a value on it, and recommend how these people should be dealt with.

Two priority projects of the eugenics movement, immigration restriction and mass standardized testing, met no decisive resistance. But one of their central endeavors had a losing encounter with history. In its September-October 1933 issue, <u>Eugenical News</u>, the organ of the Galton Society, the Eugenics Research Association (ERA), and two other eugenic organizations, carried an article on the implementation of a policy which their organization had been pushing in the U.S.--with some success--since 1905.

EUGENICAL STERILIZATION IN GERMANY

Germany is the first of the world's major nations to enact a modern eugenical sterilization law . . .Doubtless the. . . experimental sterilization laws in 27 /American/ states provided the experience which Germany used in writing her . . .statute. To one versed in the history of eugenical sterilization in America . . . the German statute reads almost like the "American model sterilization law." /Written by Laughlin of the ERA/. . . In its /Germany's/ compulsory phase. . . the superintendent of a custodial institution for any one of the several types of the socially inadequate classes may "request" the application of the law. Following such a "petition or request," each case is decided, according to its eugenical merits, by a specialized court and procedure, in which the eugenical facts and the rights of the subject . . . are duly represented.

. . . if the final court approves of the operation it shall be carried through, regardless of consent or dissent by the subject. Full privacy, under severe penalty, is provided. Also provision is made for adequate surgical skill.

It is further understood that the German Reich proposes to refuse marriage licenses to all individuals who do not

> measure up to the new eugenical standards of the nation in reference to inborn physical and mental quality.
>
> . . . the Reich will secure data on prospective sterilization cases . . . /and/ will, in fact, in accordance with "the American model sterilization law," work out a census of its socially inadequate human stocks.
>
> The new law is clean-cut, direct and "model." . . . From a legal point of view nothing more could be desired.
>
> It is probable that the sterilization statutes of the several American states and the national sterilization statute of Germany will, in legal history, constitute a milestone which marks the control by the most advanced nations of the world of a major aspect of controlling human reproduction, comparable in importance only with the state's legal control of marriage.[117]

The second part of the article was, in full, a "Text of the German Sterilization Statute," signed by Adolf Hitler.[118]

The lead item in the March-April 1934 Eugenical News was a six-page speech by the Nazi Minister for the Interior on "German Population and Race Politics" in which he warned his countrymen that "we must carefully watch the progressing race-degeneration of our people." The same issue reported on "German Sterilization Progress": "The Hitler Government in Germany is proceeding with its eugenics program. . . . The Bavarian Government has examined 100,000 persons with a view to establishing which should be subject to sterilization under the Hitlerian campaign for better babies. . . ." Eugenical News followed with a detailed four-page digest of eugenical organizations, laws and activities in Germany and a letter from France, from one Count de Lapouge to Madison Grant:

> Next door, the Germans give a splendid example of an attempt at a solution. . . . All the laws which they have just applied are the literal application of my writings

>   . . . They are doing what could have been done in
> France fifty years ago. . . .[119]

The Nazi's defeat in World War II and the exposure of their extermination policies effectively destroyed the movement for eugenic planning. The eugenic organizations which had harbored and supported the nation's leading mental testers quietly disintegrated, and the testers were kept busy designing tests to meet the growing demand on their science by scores of influential institutions. Many test specialists continued to plan for a reorganization of America in accord with the scientific lessons of mental measurement--but by the forties, the sexual-genetic aspect of their blueprints had been abandoned by most testers.

One of the more ambitious descriptions of the task of mental testing came from E.L. Thorndike, a universally acknowledged giant in psychometrics and the author of more than 450 scholarly articles, 50 books and numerous tests, as well as the Thorndike-Barnhart dictionary.[120] In a post-World War I address on "Psychology: What Is It?," Thorndike made America an offer: "Psychology will undertake to do its share in an inventory of the human assets and liabilities of the United States, whenever it is asked to do so."[121] Though no organization yet existed to carry out this inventory, Thorndike persisted with the proposal that a national testing system identify those with the abilities needed for leadership. "To him that a superior intellect is given," he wrote, "also on the average ⎣is given⎦ a superior character."[122] The implications of his calculation, and of the existence of scientific tools to measure ability, were seen as inescapable. Thorndike's monumental 1940s book, Human Nature and the Social Order, described a society where the information derived from testing helped direct people's lives:

> The able and good should acquire power. In order to support the truth, defend justice and restrain folly, superior men should acquire power. They should acquire pecuniary, political and persuasive power as well as that personal power which they wield by their reputation for ability and good will. . . . It is unjust that the able and good cannot be left in peace to advance science, practice the fine and useful arts and professions, conduct industry and trade honestly and efficiently, and serve in government. . . .[123]

While some test specialists were not so confident of the beneficence of people with high test scores, many test-makers saw the need for using psychometrics to organize post-war America. A committee of distinguished psychologists, including Edwin G. Boring and Robert Yerkes, reported to the National Research Council in 1942 on "The Status of Psychology":

> As science, psychology has progressed rapidly in the last hundred years, and its present rate of advance is unequaled . . . . Despite its false moves and setbacks, psychology stands forth as a field of inquiry and constructive intellectual endeavor which is of profound significance for individual welfare and for civilization.[124]

The scientific tools which had been developing for years were now ready for application on a massive scale. Individuals and civilization, the psychologists believed, would not have long to wait: "It is reasonable to predict that in the post-war world the services of mental engineering, whose primary scientific basis psychology must supply, will become varied, widely accepted, and highly prized. . . ."[125]

Among those responsible for higher education, acceptance of mental engineering had been growing fast. By 1933, Carl Brigham was writing in the College Board's annual report that the Board had gone beyond its original function concerned with college admissions requirements and the maintenance of school standards:

> An organization set up for the sole purpose of collecting tickets at the gate is now asked to show people to their seats. The notion of a general admissions ticket is yielding to the notion of a more exact description of the individual which will make possible his proper placement in definable universes of knowledge.[126]

The rise of scientific testing in higher education created not only a class of students whose educational future depended significantly on their test scores, but a corps of professionals whose economic future depended on growing sales of their scientific instruments. As Brigham's ETS biography notes:

> The problem of finance, of meeting expenses without charging exorbitant fees, was a persistent one for the College Board. . . . By the mid-1930's there was serious question whether the College Board would survive. That the Board did survive was in considerable part, the result of the growing popularity of the Scholastic Aptitude Test. The test had become a major source of the College Board's income.[127]

In 1937, while Brigham shaped the SAT into final form, the people who would create the organization envisioned by testing specialists for decades were moving into place. The year before, Henry Chauncey had proposed to Brigham that the College Board supplement the SAT with a series of subject matter achievement tests.[128] At an October 28, 1937 meeting of measurement professionals, President James B. Conant of Harvard had proposed the consolidation of the nation's leading testing organizations, including the College Board, into one comprehensive national testing service.[129] After ten years of consultation and planning by prominent educational, business, and governmental authorities, the Educational Testing Service--ETS--was finally chartered in December, 1947.[130] In the meantime, the College Board had dropped the essay section of its tests in 1942--as a temporary measure due to the shortage of essay readers caused by World War II--and decided in 1946 not to revive them.[131] Before his death in 1943, Carl Brigham issued a stern warning that the new national testing organization must adhere to the most rigorous scientific principles; moreover, it must be guided only by men of the broadest learning and culture:

> A new organization solely for the dissemination of present knowledge concerning tests and the promotion of testing programs would be difficult to justify. . . . It is the writer's belief that the present testing movement carries the germs of its own destruction. . . . The cure is found in research and more research. . . . The provision for an extensive research program will prevent degeneration into a sales and propaganda group. . . . We are today approaching the ultimate state in which the /testing/ movement may take on the aspects of a religious crusade. . . . The governors should not be administrators but representatives of learning. . . . As it is probably simpler to teach cultured men testing than to give testers culture, the research wing should act as a training school for promising young men drafted from the major fields of learning. . . . It is easy for a powerful organization to set up false ideals. The new organization must be so contrived that it will always remain the servant of education and never become its master. It should inquire into the nature of values but it must not determine those values. At the present time there are men of learning who see these values intuitively yet are unable to put them on canvas with pigments that will stand reproduction. Testing situations, when properly formulated, and with responses fully analyzed, constitute the most searching system of lenses yet contrived for photographing the canvas and making it generally available to mankind.[132]

The ETS mission, as enunciated by Henry Chauncey and carried on by the Rosedale professionals, took full account of Brigham's challenge. With Rosedale's Carl Campbell Brigham Memorial Library, dedicated in 1964, and the periodic exhibits on Brigham's work in the ETS main lobby, ETS commemorates the creator of its measurement technique. However, the Brigham legacy is strongest in the organization's daily work, as the ETS biography points out:

> The new organization was greatly indebted to Brigham's earlier work. He created the nucleus of a testing and research organization in Princeton, and developed the basic techniques of analysis. In carrying on the work of item analysis and basic research for new types of tests, the Educational Testing Service acknowledged its debt to Carl Brigham. The new organization also incurred the responsibility of measuring up to Carl Brigham's principles and of demonstrating that his fear of consolidation /of the Carnegie Foundation, the College Board, and the American Council on Education into ETS/ was unfounded. In acknowledging this responsibility the Educational Testing Service accepted an exacting and unending task. By this acknowledgement, Carl Brigham, once the critic of the testing movement, has now become its conscience.[133]

The number of people tested by ETS in 1948 was less than one-tenth of the test system's current reach.[134] But, at the founding of ETS in 1947, the science of mental measurement (which ETS had been created to centralize and lead) was already a shaping force in society. The January 1947 issue of The American Psychologist surveyed the extent of scientific testing:

> The totals are large. During 1944 approximately 60,000,000 standardized tests were administered to approximately 20,000,000 people in this country. . . . This is big business. When one adds the uncounted unstandardized tests which were influenced in their construction by standardized tests, a total is reached which any pioneer of the testing movement must find a satisfactory reward for his early enthusiasm and labor.[135]

Thus, what began as social theory invented by the original test professionals was already a tangible experience in the lives of millions.

CHAPTER V

CLASS IN THE GUISE OF MERIT

In 1950, Frank Ashburn, headmaster of a Massachusetts prep school, chairman of a College Board committee on achievement tests, and later an ETS trustee, put the message bluntly: "the present College Board system is strictly cutthroat competition and . . . emphasizes scholastic aptitude, which it is able to identify with embarrassing accuracy."[1] Three decades later, ETS Information Services Director Robert Moulthrop, repeated the theme in more diplomatic language: "Tests such as the SAT . . . allow students regardless of race, religion or sex to 'run the same race.'"[2] According to ETS researcher Ronald Flaugher, "the psychometric model is based /on/ the meritocratic principle . . . those who are predicted to do best . . . are the ones who are given top priority."[3]

After their College Boards, Professor Michael Schudson wrote in the Harvard Educational Review, students "are more finely differentiated than they were before." On the basis of their "scholastic aptitude," students have "differential access to higher education and, hence, to economic, social and political rewards. This is stratification. . . . /Wherein/ the scores, and education generally, act as a social sorting device. . . . A society where stratification" results from "achievement or merit," Schudson observed, "can be called a 'meritocracy.' . . . The College Board has helped to organize an American meritocracy."[4]

In the United States today, institutions with the power to decide who gets what usually claim to base their decisions on merit. When given a ranking of people from top to bottom according to some definition of merit--such as ETS score points--institutions tend to reward people at the top and reject people at the bottom.

Many individuals who run powerful institutions and many academics who write about them contend that American society, and higher education in particular, used to be something of an aristocracy where wealth and privilege ruled and the future of individuals was shaped largely by their economic background. This system, they argue, has been replaced by selection according to merit. Economic class is said to have given way to "the democracy of multiple-choice tests," in Henry Chauncey's words.[5]

"We believe that justice should be done each individual according to his merit," Chauncey wrote in the 1960-61 ETS Annual Report. Describing testing on a large scale as "a necessity," he went even further. "If it did not exist, it would have to be invented." For, the objective test provided "a common touchstone /giving/ all students who take it the same chance . . . even though they have had different economic backgrounds, different educational, cultural and social opportunities."[6]

Former ETS Trustee John Gardner made the same point. In his influential book, Excellence, he noted that before the general use of objective tests, American teachers were subjective in their interpretations of their students' abilities, a propensity which systematically favored students from higher income groups. "Against this background," Gardner said, "modern methods of mental measurement hit the educational system like a fresh breeze. The tests couldn't see whether the youngster was in rags or in tweeds, and couldn't hear the accents of the slum."[7]

This view--that the science of mental measurement was impartial and that it avoided subjective, and thus potentially class-biased interpretations by authorities--has persisted to the present. ETS President William W. Turnbull summarized it:

> The ability to perform well on tasks sampled by examinations, along with other common indices of accomplishment, has come largely to replace considerations of family or wealth or religion or ethnicity as a basis for acceptance into selective colleges and professional schools.[8]

The implication by the test professionals that standardized aptitude testing replaced ranking based on class with ranking based on merit is misleading. A ranking of people by SAT scores remains by and large a ranking of people by family income. This point is not mentioned in the literature ETS sends to the millions of Americans who take the tests, and is rarely studied in the scholarly articles of psychometricians.[9] Nonetheless, such tests produce rankings parallel to those produced by the early tests of Galton, Terman, Yerkes, Thorndike, and Brigham which they used to "scientifically demonstrate" the intellectual inferiority of the working class.*

The pattern is consistent over time, geographic region, and fine gradations of income. The SAT does not just discriminate between rich and poor, or--as ETS representatives frequently

---

*See Chapter IV for a discussion of this topic.

describe the situation--"the affluent" and "the disadvantaged." It is not simply a matter of penthouse versus tenement. The ETS score discriminates not only between the rich and a minority of Americans (the very poor) but also between the rich and a majority of Americans (the members of the working and middle classes). The SAT discriminates among virtually all levels of the country's class structure--across both income and occupation. The more money a person's family makes, the higher that person tends to score; people from homes with $21,000 incomes tend to score higher than people from homes with $18,000 incomes; people from white collar homes tend to score higher than people from blue collar homes.[10]

A College Board statistical report illustrates this point: the ranking by ETS scores of 647,031 students* who took the 1973-74 SAT (the most recent such figures available) was systematically related to parental income. (See Table I.)

This pattern is consistent for applicants across the country. For some regions, such as the Middle Atlantic States (New York, Pennsylvania, New Jersey, Delaware, Maryland, Washington, D.C.) and the South, the ranking by income is still stronger. (See Table II.)

---

*These are the students who estimated their parents' income on the ETS "Student Descriptive Questionnaire."

TABLE I

(1973-74)

SAT Average	Parent's Mean Income
750-800	$24,124
700-749	21,980
650-699	21,292
600-649	20,330
550-599	19,481
500-549	18,824
450-499	18,122
400-449	17,387
350-399	16,182
300-349	14,355
250-299	11,428
200-249	8,639

SOURCE: <u>College Bound Seniors</u>, 1973-74, Table 21, p. 27.[11]

TABLE II

(1973-74)

SAT AVERAGE	Southern	Middle States	New England	Midwestern	Western
750-800	$23,648	$25,536	$22,556	$21,171	$25,823
700-749	22,066	22,765	21,565	21,439	21,798
650-699	21,210	22,002	20,415	20,862	21,239
600-649	21,083	20,128	18,680	20,607	20,656
550-599	20,242	18,811	17,900	20,130	20,008
500-549	19,557	18,144	16,908	19,889	19,098
450-499	18,598	17,359	16,491	19,209	18,554
400-449	17,604	16,761	15,826	18,555	17,880
350-399	15,986	15,554	15,103	17,558	16,584
300-349	13,534	14,017	14,083	15,887	14,639
250-299	9,872	11,747	12,570	12,954	11,711
200-249	7,565	9,150	8,844	10,035	10,024

PARENT'S MEAN INCOME

SOURCE: College Bound Seniors, 1973-74, Southern, Middle States, New England, Midwestern and Western Editions.[12]

The ranking by class prevails not just when large groups are averaged together; it also prevails among applicants to individual institutions. Colleges receive from ETS score-income breakdowns of their applicants. "Your table will most likely show this relationship," says a footnote to the accompanying manual: "Every time you move from one income group to the next higher, the mean SAT-verbal and -mathematical scores increase."[13]

Less detailed data on the scores and incomes of 1978-79 test-takers indicate that the ranking still holds firm. Applicants averaging below 350, for example, had a mean family income of $18,400 while those averaging 650 or over had a mean of $33,400; as before, income and scores increased together every step of the way.[14]

According to figures compiled by Dr. Humphrey Doermann for a College Board colloquium, a student from a family earning less than $4,600 (1969-70 income) had a ten per cent chance of scoring above 450; in the $7,500 to $10,699 range, the chances had doubled to twenty-one per cent, and above $16,200, they quadrupled to forty per cent.[15]

For the years Doermann presents national figures (1964-65), he estimates a score-income correlation (.4),[16] which is higher than the correlation which ETS claims to have found between scores and the first-year grades the SAT is supposed to predict (1964: SAT Verbal .37, SAT Math .32; 1965 SAT Verbal .36, SAT Math .29).[17] Doermann notes that among lower income students the score-income correlation may be significantly stronger.[18]

A table from an appendix to a 1977 College Board study indicates that SAT scores differentiate people not only by income but also by their parents' role in the system of production: the children of professionals and managers receive mean scores significantly higher than the children of white collar workers, who, in turn, receive higher scores than the children of blue collar workers.[19]

Average score differences among ethnic groups have received national publicity. At the same time, the primary basis of those score differences--social class--has been given less attention.

Although the score differences, in part, reflect the strictly racial biases of the U.S. education and test system (see Chapter III), they mainly reflect the role of income level in the ETS scores of *all* American workers: blacks—like whites, Chicanos, Puerto Ricans, Asians, and native Americans—tend to score in accordance with their economic class. "The test scores . . . are characteristic of the class," wrote Dr. Samuel Kendrick of the College Board, "and not of race." ETS researcher Ronald Flaugher noted the pattern in his review of an ETS high school testing program: "the level of performance was lower in each of the ethnic groups for those children from the lower class."[20]

In the United States, the chances of being at a given income level are directly related to ethnic background. This relationship holds among SAT candidates' parents as well. Table III illustrates the extent to which members of various ethnic groups (parents of SAT candidates) are concentrated at lower income levels than the population as a whole.

If ETS scores really measure an important aspect of a person's "merit" or, as ETS specifically calls it, "scholastic aptitude," then merit in the United States is distributed according to parental income.

The belief that ETS tests rank people by individual "merit" does not stand up to the hard facts of performance, even by prevailing educational standards. As discussed in Chapter III, there is only a marginal relationship between ETS scores and the test industry's chosen standard of first year grades. When used as a supplement to previous grades, the SAT has, on the average improved the prediction by only three to five percent. And, the

TABLE III

Annual Parental Income by Ethnic Group of 1978-79 SAT Candidates

Income	American Indian %	Black %	Mexican-American %	Oriental %	Puerto Rican %	White %	Other %	No Ethnic Response %	All Students %
Under $3,000	4.0	6.7	3.1	2.5	5.0	0.8	4.1	2.1	1.5
$3,000-5,999	8.6	15.4	9.0	5.4	16.8	2.0	7.7	5.0	3.8
6,000-8,999	12.1	20.1	14.4	10.4	20.1	4.5	12.5	8.2	6.7
9,000-11,999	11.8	16.0	15.4	11.7	15.4	7.2	11.9	9.6	8.5
12,000-14,999	9.6	10.7	13.0	10.6	10.4	9.1	10.8	9.6	9.4
15,000-19,999	17.0	12.6	18.7	14.8	11.6	17.9	15.3	17.1	17.2
20,000-29,999	21.8	11.8	18.4	23.2	11.9	29.4	19.9	25.4	27.1
30,000 or over	15.0	6.6	8.1	21.4	8.7	29.1	17.8	23.0	26.0
Total	100.0	100.0	100.0	100.0	100.0	100.0	100.0	100.0	100.0
Number Responding	3,453	71,771	13,570	22,475	8,053	668,445	18,443	16,939	823,149
Mean Income	$19,600	$13,700	$16,500	$22,600	$14,500	$27,300	$20,400	$23,800	$25,400

SOURCE: National Report, College Bound Seniors, 1978, Table 10, p.16.21

first year grades themselves have been shown to bear little significant relationship to a person's future success. One ETS researcher characterized this as a standard which "no one can be found /to/ seriously defend . . . as a gauge of anything very important."[22]

Even if one were to accept first year grades as the standard of merit, the belief that a ranking by merit is the same as a ranking by class has been directly challenged. Alexander Astin's American Council on Education study (1971) of 36,581 students in 55 colleges concluded flatly:

> The income of the student's parents has no relationship to freshman GPA /grade point average/, either before or after controlling for high school grades, academic aptitude, and college selectivity.[23]

An ETS study of 15,535 college bound students (1969) found that actual accomplishments outside the classroom did not correlate with income either: "Although educational ambitions were significantly related to accomplishments in several areas, family income was not. <u>That is, students from families with different incomes did not significantly differ in the number or level of accomplishments they reported.</u>"[24] (Emphasis added.)

"This lack of relationship between accomplishments and family background," noted a 1979 ETS summary of research in the field, "is supported by the National Merit studies which reported no significant correlation between these two types of variables in their samples. These results suggest that the accomplishment measures do not discriminate against disadvantaged students, although disadvantaged students do score lower on academic ability tests /i.e., ETS aptitude tests/."[25]

When test professionals extol the tough, practical glory of "cutthroat competition" or "running the same race," they are talking about a system of purportedly impartial tests which, in effect, ranks people more by their class than by their potential for actual accomplishment. Some exceptional people overcome the odds against their class and beat the ETS test system on its own terms. But, the vast majority, including many with drive and potential, continue to suffer the consequences of a now indirect and hidden ranking by class.

In earlier times, this kind of ranking by class was open and explicit. In 1919, a Princeton University lecture hall was the forum for Dr. Henry H. Goddard who informed his audience, first, that:

> Testing intelligence . . . is fast becoming an exact science?[26] . . . Over one million, seven hundred thousand men in the army have been tested by these methods, their mental level determined and recorded.[27]
>
> . . . With this army experience it is no longer possible for anyone to deny the validity of mental tests.[28]

A natural position, then, for Goddard was to advocate the systematic use of these tests in "a conscious effort to fit every man to his work in accordance with his intelligence level."[29] By testing, he would discover the "special abilities of various students with an idea to guiding them in their choice of work or profession."[30]

Second, noting the distribution of test scores by social class, Goddard asserted that to demand for a workman "with a ten year intelligence" such a home as someone with a "twenty year intelligence" enjoys "is as absurd as it would be to insist that every laborer should receive a graduate fellowship. How can there be such a thing as social equality with this wide range of mental capacity?"[31]

In addition to identifying a proper place for individuals, a national system of psychometric testing would, for Goddard, be humanitarian, as well. He would save individuals from " a serious humiliation" by telling them early that they lacked "sufficient intelligence to undertake a given line of work." Whatever momentary humiliation they suffered, Goddard argued, "can never compare with the humiliation of failure that is sure to come later."[32]

Goddard believed "there are enough people of high intelligence to guide the Ship of State, if they are put in command . . . the disturbing fear is that the masses--the seventy million or even the eighty-six million--will take matters into their own hands."[33] The testing techniques were ready, Goddard said: "We only await the Human Engineer who will undertake the work."[34]

In many of its particulars, ETS and its psychometric colleagues have created the national test system Goddard projected; but descriptions of that system's purpose by test professionals have undergone deep and subtle changes. While early generations of testers openly linked test scores and social class--inferring that working people were therefore intellectually inferior--ETS avoided mention of the class relationship, instead telling people that the scores measure them as _individuals_.

"Never was Socrates' injunction 'know thyself' more significant than it is today," wrote Henry Chauncey in the ETS 1956-57 Annual Report. "Modern tests can help the individual understand himself in relation to the vast array of educational and occupational opportunities that confront him. . . . The more thoroughly an individual understands himself, the better he will be able to make the crossroads decisions . . . and ultimately to find the field of greatest satisfaction to himself and society."[35]

ETS today is still uncomfortable with reminding individuals of the extent to which their scores actually reflect their class. "Even if it were the case that the correlation between the scores on the test and income equalled the correlation between test scores and college grades," ETS Senior Vice President E. Belvin Williams told the journal Politics and Education, "the implication that one can draw from that is not much [of] anything."[36] In a 1977 interview, President Turnbull continued the company practice of describing the score-income correlation strictly in terms of the poor (as distinct from the working and middle class majority) and asserting that the scores measure the test-taker's individual potential-- not their class. He said:

> I think it is certainly true that students from backgrounds of poverty do less well on the test than students from affluent families. That doesn't mean that the test score is a measure of parental affluence. . . . The reason for giving those tests is that the tasks that they ask the student to perform have proved to be reasonably similar to the exercises that a student is given to perform in college or in law school. . . . Students who are from poverty backgrounds typically do not do as well on those tasks. . . . The test, however, mirrors the readiness of the student to tackle the academic job at the point in time at which the student is tested. The score doesn't tell you anything about how the student got there.[37]

President Turnbull explained why test-takers were not told about the score-income facts:

> The reason, or one reason, why one would, I think . . . be quite wrong to emphasize that /the score-income correlation/ in the literature is that it would suggest to students that if you are poor you don't have a chance, whereas we know there are a great many students who come from poor backgrounds, poor in the sense of financial poverty, who do superbly on the test.38

While President Turnbull's concern for such exceptions to the rule is admirable, suppression of the score-income correlation only serves to mislead the vast majority of students from the poor, working, and middle classes. ETS does not tell them that the assessment of their "aptitude" is more a reflection of socio-economic status than their actual potential for future accomplishment.

In contrast to this ETS position, the old affirmation that these test scores place people where they deserve to be in the class structure remains a central assumption of some test theorists. One of the more extreme advocates of this interpretation, psychologist Richard Herrnstein of Harvard, looks at the correlation of scores and family income and puts the point bluntly: "Depending on whether one is for or against testing, one will see the class difference as a weakness either in the intellect of the underprivileged or in the tester's definition of intelligence."39 Herrnstein chooses the former.

Others, such as psychometrician Lloyd Humphreys of the University of Illinois, warn against the purported costs of "instant egalitarianism." "Insistence on racial and sexual balance throughout our society," predicts Humphreys, "could, even in the time span of several generations, result in a reduction in the productivity of our economy, in the quality of our research and development, and in the quality of students graduating from our schools."[40] More subtly, standard testing textbooks for teachers and psychologists (such as those of Cronbach and Thorndike, both one-time ETS consultants) offer charts ranking occupational groups according to their "IQ's"; an ETS guide[41] helps teenagers anticipate their futures by presenting an occupation-IQ chart with the explanation that "(IQ's) do not change very much" so "high school students can be quite confident that their scores have some meaning."[42]

    The current claim by ETS that it can determine the potential of *individuals*, distinct from their class, is a relatively new development in the history of psychometrics. From Francis Galton's eugenics through Carl Brigham's ranking of nationalities by intelligence, psychometricians believed that their tests revealed something about the intellectual merit of a person's race, ethnic group, nationality, or social class. Hundreds of pages of psychometric literature purported to document the mental characteristics of various social groups as measured by standardized tests.

    The test results showed that people with lower incomes from socially oppressed races and ethnic groups, and newly arrived immigrant nationalities consistently scored lower. Comparing the scores of the paper-and-pencil tests with the real-world social experiences of the test-takers, the most prestigious test professionals in the nation decided that the tests revealed the thinking potential of social groups. Some social groups scored low on tests designed to measure ability; therefore, testers reasoned, some social groups had less ability. (See Chapter IV.)

Fifty years later, in the 1970s, millions of testing sessions had produced the same results. ETS test scores were still directly connected to social class. The ethnic groups with low incomes still scored low. However, test professionals were no longer associating test performance with genes or ethnic background, nor claiming that scores indicated different social groups had different levels of ability. Rather, they now claimed that tests showed the characteristics of the _individual_. The link between test scores and social class--once the heart of how they interpreted their own tests--was, accordingly, omitted from the millions of booklets and score reports which informed people where they stood. As the ETS public relations office put it, ETS tests were designed "to allow students . . . to 'run the same race.'"[43] In short, the test-takers had run their own race and, since the test was a measure of personal potential, those with low scores had learned an important lesson about themselves as individuals.

The process of persuading people that ETS test scores reflect their personal potential began years ago and was aimed at students of an age most susceptible to the assurances of friendly authority. _YOU: Today and Tomorrow_, first issued in 1959, is an ETS text for classroom instructors which helps ten-year-olds understand the importance of the qualities measured by the ETS test: "So in making their decisions, the first questions that John, Andy, Betsy and Bill have to ask themselves are these: How much general scholastic ability have I? What special abilities have I?"[44] "General scholastic ability," ETS explains, "is especially important in <u>all</u> 8th- or 9th-grade pupils' decisions" (original emphasis).[45] Such ability, ETS continues, should be measured to help the student decide on "different occupational goals . . . different educational plans . . . /and/ different school subjects to be chosen for next year."[46]

"Can you measure scholastic ability?" asks ETS. "This is where you can use your 'magic mirror!' Take a good look at the facts about your scholastic ability <u>now</u>."[47] The ETS test, like any mirror--magic or not--shows that some people are big and others are little.

> Would you call the tallest boy in a class of pygmies "tall" or "short"? It all depends on the group you're comparing him with. . . . The percentage of people <u>shorter</u> than you is your "percentile rank" in height. . . . If you are between the 75th and 99th percentile ranks, you are in the tallest quarter. . . . In the same way you can see where you rank in scholastic ability by taking a test. . . . There are many tests of this sort. . . . Your test scores . . . will tell you something about yourself and about your chances of success--"strong" and "weak" scores, "high" and "low" marks can tell you your chances of success or failure.[48]

<u>YOU: Today and Tomorrow</u> likens the ETS score to a source of power: "Your scholastic ability is like the engine. It is the source of your power and speed in school: it tells you how fast and how far you <u>can</u> go. But are you getting as much mileage out of it as you should?"[49]

ETS executive Robert Moulthrop elaborated some years later, in 1976: "Questions in tests such as the SAT are selected because they represent certain aspects of competence. . . . The competencies tested are some of those deemed important for success in the culture we all share. . . . If you want to be on the football team or in the school orchestra, you'd better be able to play reasonably well."[50] A 1961 ETS description of how the tests are constructed made a similar point in different terms.

> A valid test item is one which consistently distinguishes the bright person from the less intelligent. If an item is valid, the intelligent people will consistently choose the correct answer, and the less intelligent will be misled by one or another of the incorrect alternatives.[51]

Such proclamations by ETS and its testing colleagues over the decades have been effective; scores of psychological and polling studies show that American students, parents and teachers believe that standardized tests measure personal potential. According to a summary of 235 studies prepared by Dr. Marjorie Kirkland for the Review of Educational Research:

> People generally view all tests as accurate and are quite willing to accept test results as lawful. . . . A similar readiness to uncritically accept test interpretations was seen in college students (Forer, 1949). . . . The Russell Sage study (Goslin, 1967) found that teachers tended to view standardized tests as fairly accurate measures of a student's intellectual potential and achievement. The kinds of ability measured by such tests were seen as important determinants of the subsequent academic success of children and, to a lesser degree, a determinant of their success in later life.[52]

A 1969 Russell Sage Foundation study of <u>American Beliefs and Attitudes About Intelligence</u> (which included SATs in their definition of "intelligence" tests) noted that in that year some 250 million standardized aptitude tests had been administered:

> It signifies the extent of a fundamental, important social process: that of making standardized appraisals of intelligence of the members of society and then using this information as the basis for decisions, whether by social institutions about people, or individuals about themselves, which influence the life course of the humans who are tested. . . . We seem to be moving toward a society that is organized on the basis of standardized intelligence test scores.[53]

The 1969 survey found that "52% of the respondents felt that tested intelligence is of considerable importance to success in school, while 45% felt it is of considerable importance for success in life after school."[54] The use of standardized tests for decisions far beyond the classroom won the support of significant numbers of those surveyed. Thirty-nine per cent supported the use of tests to help "select leaders in the government," and thirty-six per cent to help "select leaders for large corporations." In a lingering tribute to the public education efforts of the eugenics movement, eight per cent of those surveyed approved the use of standardized tests to "decide who should be allowed to mate" and five per cent to "decide whom one should marry."[55]

The Sage study noted that "Most people, or certainly most students, think about how they compare with others in intelligence, and are able to rank themselves in these comparisons." Although five per cent of the respondents said they never thought about their intelligence, ninety-five per cent did. Of these, only eight per cent were unable to rank themselves relative to others.[56] Sixty-eight per cent said they were "very" interested in finding out how they had done on standardized tests; twenty-four per cent were "moderately" interested.[57]

Several studies have noted the effect of test scores on the aspirations of students. Professor Dale Tillery of Berkeley, in his massive six-year College Board sponsored study of 80,083 students, noted that while some had criticized the SATs for having a predictive value comparable to "the Ouija board" (see Chapter III), "these predictions continue to be used because they are quite successful in channeling groups in ways that many colleges highly approve of, and they continue to influence students' self-estimates which, of course, contributes toward fulfillment of the prediction which they purport to make."[58] Tillery found that: "While in high school, students learn to judge themselves by these same measures /scores and high school grades/ and, when they do not measure up, they either abandon certain educational and career goals or try circuitous routes to achieve them." Moreover, he wrote, SAT scores have influenced decisions concerning placement of students in state colleges and universities.[59]

In a study of the class of 1969 at forty-seven Boston area high schools and their success in fulfilling their educational aspirations, Dr. Dennis Dugan also found that the student's Scholastic Aptitude Test (SAT) score was a critical variable in the decision about higher education.[60] The SAT, wrote Dugan, "has its greatest impact upon the decision /of high school students/

to . . . enter the labor market . . . instead of pursuing more education."[61]

Writing in Christopher Jencks' study of <u>Who Gets Ahead?</u>, James Crouse of the University of Delaware summarized how aspirations may be shaped by testing which begins early in the school career.

> Higher-scoring individuals are treated differently than lower-scoring individuals especially in school. Adolescents with high scores are more likely to be in a college curriculum, more likely to receive high grades, more likely to report that their parents want them to attend college, more likely to say that their friends plan to attend college, more likely to discuss college with teachers, and more likely to have ambitious educational and occupational plans.[62]

Test scores can change thinking in ways which cut deeper than decisions about the direction of one's career. One study Kirkland noted, "found that test scores can contribute to a positive self-concept or can result in emotional disturbance engendered by a sense of failure." She also reports a study of 2,433 students at sixteen colleges and universities which concluded that "Self-concept can also act as a sensitive barometer of emotional health." And, in reference to standardized tests, Kirkland indicated that "failure experiences" have produced "a disrupted pattern of attitudes. . . . An individual may raise his own self-concept while lowering his concept of close friends, or he may lower his own self-concept while rating his close friends higher."[63]

Of the many serious human consequences resulting from the science of mental measurement, perhaps the most socially important has been in convincing the classes of people whose opportunities are reduced most by standardized test scores that it is all for their own good. The Sage study found that "a majority of those who had taken tests reported that their lives had been influenced by the results." It also discussed a remarkable public belief: "tests were seen as helpful for college admissions but not blamed for failure to be admitted; they were seen as determining placement in special advanced classes, but not placement in special slow groups."[64]

The groups which systematically scored lowest on the tests were found to have the <u>highest</u> confidence in the tests' validity. Karier reports a 1965 Sage survey which found that while "the upper class respondent is more likely to favor the use of tests than the lower class respondent," the "lower class respondent is more likely to see intelligence tests measuring inborn intelligence."[65] The 1969 survey found that public school students were more likely than prep school students, and blacks more likely than whites, to believe that "intelligence" as measured by the tests was important for success in life.[66]

The belief in the ETS test as a measure of personal potential was prominently noted in the September 1978 issue of the <u>College Board News</u>. The College Board, which had commissioned a survey of 2,024 students who had taken the SAT, announced the results:

> High school students believe the tests to be fair and accept the role of the SAT in the college admissions process. . . . The margin favoring the SAT was about two to one. . . . The main reason given by students who felt the SAT should be continued was that it is a fair and objective measure of students' abilities. Another benefit of the SAT, according to the students, is that it lets them know where they stand.[67]

Long since submerged were the observations of a report by the Commission on Financing Higher Education on "Who Should Go to College," which was published in 1952. Recognizing the disproportionately low number of working class students who apply to and are accepted by colleges and the tendency of the test to rank students by their socio-economic class, the Commission stated that:

> This group should not be overlooked in the search for ability, because the current scholastic aptitude or intelligence tests are not 100 percent accurate. <u>These tests systematically penalize working class youth</u>, because the problems of the tests are more familiar to middle-class than to working class experience. . . . When better tests are made and used, and when better means of motivating working class youth are employed, a significant number of /such/ youth . . . will prove themselves worthy of post-high-school education.[68] (Emphasis added.)

This report was issued under the imprimatur of the presidents of Brown, Stanford, Johns Hopkins, California Institute of Technology and the University of Missouri. Also sitting on the Commission were two men who would serve on the ETS Board of Trustees, Harvard Provost Paul H. Buck and Commission Director John D. Millett.[69]

By continuing to promote a class-determined test, ETS reduces both the aspirations and opportunities of millions of people. Its literature describes **ranking by scores** in terms of "aptitude" and "reasoning"; college catalogues describe decisions made using these scores in terms of merit. But, ETS' own statistics are the most telling; they document **ranking by SAT scores**, in effect, as a ranking by social class—class in the guise of merit.

CHAPTER VI

ETS: BARRIER TO THE BAR

In both technical sophistication and client control, the ETS law school program stands out. It could be argued that in this program the ETS test system has reached its most advanced stage. As a kind of best-possible-case example of the application of selective aptitude testing, and as an influence on the selection of an entire professional community, the program is of particular interest.

By 1977, six law schools were tied to a direct computer hook-up with the Rosedale data bank. Admission officials at these schools were not limited to ETS printouts on their applicants. They could--by typing instructions into computer terminals located in their offices--summon an instant analysis of ETS data on individual candidates.[1] The terminals were an extension of data analysis services available to other law schools, services offering more information and more advanced equations for the prediction of first-year grades than were available to colleges, graduate schools, or other ETS clients. Overseeing this arrangement was the Law School Admission Council (LSAC). Though created by ETS, this Council enjoyed a reputation as the most independent and probing of the ETS client organizations.

By the early 1970s, shrewd corporate strategy had combined with demographic trends and bar association policies to place ETS in a position of power with little precedent in U.S. educational history: a single corporation, ETS, had become the primary arbiter of who would be permitted to enter the American legal profession. As any aspiring lawyer would soon discover, the facts were inescapable:

-- Recently, the number of applicants to U.S. law schools has regularly exceeded the number of available places by a ratio of two to one. By 1973, the Association of American Law Schools noted, "for the first time in the history of United States legal education every accredited law school denied admission to applicants who it considered qualified for the study of law."[2]

-- Rejection from law school could therefore mean not just exclusion from a particular institution, but from the legal profession itself. "Law school admission officers, rather than bar examiners," ABA President-Elect Chesterfield Smith observed in 1973, "are in large measure picking our future lawyers."[3]

-- ABA accreditation rules required law schools to screen their applicants with "an acceptable test."[4]

-- The only national law school test available was the one that was recommended by name in the ABA Accreditation rules: the ETS Law School Admission Test (LSAT).[5]

-- Thus, by 1979, each of the 168 ABA accredited law schools used the LSAT to screen their applicants.[6]

-- Also by 1979, the ETS Multistate Bar Examination (MBE) had diminished the importance of the traditional state-prepared essay question bar exam as the requirement for legal practice in forty-two states (and some territories),[7] strengthening ETS' role as the gatekeeper for the legal profession. Many states give the 200-question MBE equal or greater weight than the written portion of the exam. In some states, such as Pennsylvania and New Jersey, the applicant could, by exceeding a cut-off score on the MBE, flunk the written exam and still gain admission to the bar. For candidates who got enough multiple-choice questions right, the bar examiners would not even grade the handwritten essay.[8]

The influence of these ETS tests can hardly be overstated. The prediction formulas ETS devises for law schools often make the LSAT the single most important factor in ranking a pool of applicants.[9] At some law schools, such as the University of California at Berkeley, the LSAT was reportedly weighted twice as much as four years of college grades.[10] A number of law schools, such as the Universities of Illinois and Wisconsin, had admitted no applicants with scores under 500.[11]

Reliance on the LSAT was systematic, and its effects could be seen across the entire applicant population. Data compiled on all 1976 applicants to accredited law schools show that among applicants with "B" to "B+" college averages, for example, a score increase of only fifty points from 425 to 475 would increase their chances of getting into (any) law school by fifty per cent; an increase of 100 points would _more than double_ their chances. Fifty points on the LSAT can be the equivalent of less than thirty minutes of work.[12]

The 1976 admission results document clearly that, regardless of how well individuals had performed in school, a poor score on the 190-question LSAT could exclude them from the legal profession. Of the 1,728 applicants who had earned "A" averages in college but scored below 500 on the LSAT, 872 of them, or slightly more than half, were rejected by every accredited law school to which they applied.[13]

This exclusion of "A" students from the legal profession simply because their LSAT score was below 500 should be put in historical perspective. "In 1961," notes ETS research fellow Dr. Barbara Lerner, "the median LSAT score of students at 81 percent of the nation's law schools was below 485."[14] Lerner, the former staff director of the National Academy of Sciences Committee on Ability Testing, pointed out the implications of this fact in a paper delivered in 1977 before she joined the ETS staff. "What this means in comparative terms," she said, "is that <u>most American lawyers and judges practicing today would never have gotten into law school at all if they had had to compete against the inflated standards which now govern admission</u>."[15] (Emphasis added.)

For millions of qualified people, the opportunity to enter the legal profession had come to depend less upon academic accomplishment or promise of professional competence than upon a multiple-choice ETS aptitude test. As will be discussed below, it was a test that, while never shown to bear a relationship to the successful practice of law, distributed its scores systematically according to factors of class, ethnicity and test anxiety. But most of all, it was a test that had created a new and unusual application of the science of mental measurement: the task of choosing the members of one of the nation's most powerful professions. "The LSAT represents a filtering device through which all must pass to become a lawyer," writes ETS researcher Dr. Hunter Breland. "There are, of course, other paths to law practice--but probably not many."[16]

The LSAT: Exclusion Without Cause

The LSAT systematically rewards and penalizes certain kinds of people in patterns similar to those of other ETS aptitude tests. Like the SAT, it tends to rank according to economic and social class.

The law school applicant pool tends to be wealthy to begin with. One researcher found in studying eight American law schools:

> Each school drew a majority of its 1970 and 1972 classes from relatively high economic groups. . . . Only 2.9 percent of the students in our sample came from the lowest parental income group, even though this group represented 10.3 percent of the general population. At the same time, there was a much closer correspondence in the highest income group: while only 14.7 percent of all families had incomes exceeding $15,000, over 14 percent of the students sampled came from families earning over $40,000.[17]

Even within this predominantly elite group, the LSAT allocates scores--and thereby odds against entering the profession--roughly by class. A 1973 ETS study by Franklin Evans and Donald Rock, for example, analyzed the scores and backgrounds of incoming students at eight law schools. The LSAT distinguished not only rich and poor, but also rich and middle class. Students of "high" socioeconomic status had a mean LSAT score about forty points higher than those of "average" background who in turn ranked higher than the "low" status students by about thirty points.[18]

Evans and Rock also found scores to be related to an aspect of the candidate's personality, their test anxiety. Among students from the same socioeconomic backgrounds, anxiety made a significant difference in scores. For the upper-class students, high or low anxiety accounted for a gap of thirty points; among middle-class and poor students it made a difference of forty to fifty points. When the effects of social class and anxiety were combined, the impact was considerable: low-income people with high test anxiety received an average LSAT of 505; high income people with low anxiety averaged 622.[19]

As with other ETS aptitude tests, LSAT scores are also systematically related to racial and ethnic background (see Chapter III, section beginning on p.109 for a detailed discussion). The lower LSAT scores generally received by black and Chicano students, for example, put them in the position of having to earn higher college grades than their white counterparts for an equal chance of admission. This effect is illustrated by the 1976 law school admissions data; these show that at each descending level of college grades, smaller percentages of blacks and Chicanos than of whites were admitted.

<u>Percentage of Applicants From Various Ethnic Groups
Accepted by an Accredited Law School</u>[20]

	White and Unidentified	Chicano	Black
GPA 3.25 or Above:	80%	77%	74%
GPA 2.75 or Above:	68	64	58
GPA 2.50 or Above:	64	56	51
All Grade Averages:	59	47	39

While LSAT scores can determine who will be allowed to become a lawyer, and while they *are* systematically related to class, personality and race, these scores have not been found to be associated with the ability to practice law.

"There is no empirical evidence," noted a study in the legal journal Law and the Social Order, "of a significant correlation between LSAT scores and probable 'success in the practice of law'; indeed, such evidence would be difficult to come by in light of the inherent difficulty of empirically measuring success as a practitioner."[21]

Furthermore, the Rutgers University Board of Governors in their *amicus* brief to the U.S. Supreme Court in the landmark case Defunis v. Odegaard contended: "The LSAT has not been validated as a criterion reasonably related to legal job performance."[22] Justice Douglas in his opinion, took the same position, quoting Professor Sanford Jay Rosen of the University of Maryland that "there is no clear evidence that the LSAT or GPA provide particularly good evaluators of the intrinsic or enriched ability of an individual to perform as a law student or lawyer in a functioning society undergoing change."[23]

Though empirical studies are not available, when lawyers have been asked to evaluate the relationship between LSAT scores and "success" by their own varying standards, opinion has been decisive. A 1977 survey by the legal journal Juris Doctor found that "One thing most of the respondents agree on is that the Law School Admission Test . . . is not a valid predictor of who will be a good lawyer and who won't. Only 16 percent say that it is (62% say it isn't); and 22 percent say they don't know."[24]

In a 1973 address to the Law School Admission Council, ABA president Chesterfield Smith echoed this theme. "Certainly there is strong reason to doubt the reliability of the Law School Test as a predictor of future law success, and I do not believe that any responsible authority suggests to the contrary." Smith went on to point out that the LSAT did not even purport to measure many qualities important to success in law:

> While we all admit that the so-called "predictors" are sometimes deficient in forecasting academic success, I believe that we all suspect that they are even less reliable in predicting success in actual law practice. We do know that they fail to tell us about such critical factors as motivation, maturity, energy, client relations, business sense, and the like.[25]

Dr. Lerner goes still further, arguing that many such desirable characteristics may be negatively related to LSAT scores. Lerner contends that "while a certain level of verbal facility and reasoning ability may be necessary for competent performance as a lawyer or anything else, above that level the differences between superior and inferior workers are a function of other characteristics."[26] She points out that given the oversupply of law school applicants who have already demonstrated that they are intellectually qualified, attempts to make fine distinctions among these high-quality applicants may result in rankings that "bear no meaningful relationship to intellectual merit and may be inversely related to important nonintellectual traits which are also necessary for competent performance in the law as in other fields."[27]

Though Lerner cited no evidence on this point, the relationship between LSAT scores and personal attitudes had been studied. In a 1976 paper in Educational and Psychological Measurement, Dr. Leonard Baird of ETS found that LSAT scores were positively related to people's estimates of their own abilities. The LSAT, however, did not correlate significantly with people's ratings of how much sympathy they would have for others in trouble. Moreover, significant negative correlations were found between LSAT scores and self-ratings on such values as "making a contribution to knowledge important in vocational choice," or "working with people important in vocational choice."[28]

Rejected applicants and groups whose members were penalized disproportionately felt the direct consequences of reliance on the LSAT. This reliance also had implications for the legal profession as a whole. The ETS selection system was difficult to square with the bar's stated objective of improving the distribution of legal services by admitting more working class and minority lawyers likely to serve the underrepresented.[29] The ETS tests penalized precisely those groups for whom the bar claimed it wanted to improve access. Conceding that "clearly an unmet need for legal services exists in the poor and disadvantaged community," the members of the American Bar Association and of the Law School Admission Council argued in the Defunis case that schools should be permitted to place minority applicants in special admissions categories where their scores would be deemphasized.*[30]

---

*Such attempts to compensate for the test's discriminatory impact highlighted the inequitites created by its being used in the first place. By establishing special categories, institutions acknowledged the inequity but continued their overall reliance on the test which produced it.

Special categories were by definition limited and, in practical terms, could never encompass all of the ethnic, social class, personality and personal aspiration groups which were systematically ranked low by the LSAT.[31] Even for black and Chicano students, as the grade figures cited earlier indicate, special categories failed to compensate for the admissions disadvantage the LSAT created for them. Most fundamental of all, such categories fed the damaging myth that those admitted through them were somehow less competent. In fact they had merely been penalized by a test which bore no relationship to legal competence.

Although there is less information available on the LSAT and social class than there is on the test's effect on different ethnic groups, increasing emphasis on the LSAT--which correlates significantly with family income--can logically be expected to decrease the admission opportunities of working-class and low-income applicants in favor of those from wealthier backgrounds. While undoubtedly due to several factors, law school student bodies are increasingly dominated by upper-class students. According to surveys reported in the Virginia Law Review, from 1960 to 1970 the percentage of low-income students in law schools declined while the percentage of high income students rose significantly. At one law school, the University of Southern California, "the percentage of students from families with incomes of at least $40,000 increased from three percent in 1960 to 23 percent in 1970."[32]

Thus, the ETS legal selection system does little to encourage the admission of potential advocates for working class and minority people. It is, however, congenial to the philosophy and priorities of the corporate bar. ETS legal tests available for public inspection show a tendency to stress corporate topics and perspectives in their questions. The only publicly released edition of the MBE (the test of February 23, 1972) reveals questions dealing mostly with commercial, property, negligence and traditional criminal law. There is little mention of environmental, civil rights, consumer or tenant issues. Candidates were asked repeatedly to elucidate the rights of large property owners in simulated cases involving "Royal Oaks," a 500-acre estate; "Dee Railroad Company," the owner of "a family heirloom, a Picasso original," and "Motorco," a manufacturer of motor vehicles.[33] Sample questions for the LSAT, which includes an entire section dealing with business situations, indicate a similar pattern.[34]

Even if the ETS selection system was working against the profession's stated objective of drawing lawyers from broader segments of society, this situation did not seem to provide grounds for legal action against law schools. By the early 1970s, however, another aspect of law school admission practices had some administrators worrying about their vulnerability to challenge from rejected applicants. At a November 12 and 13, 1971 conference on "The Future of the LSAT Program," LSAC member Millard H. Ruud, who also served as Consultant on Legal Education to the American Bar Association, raised a pertinent question. According to a summary of the meeting (prepared by Ruud himself):

> Professor Ruud asked whether the LSAT might be challenged upon the basis of Griggs v. Duke Power Co., 401 U.S. 424

> (1971). Admission to law school is the primary gateway to membership in the profession, and a satisfactory LSAT score is essential to admission to law school. If there is no connection between LSAT score [sic] and "success" in the profession, is the LSAT vulnerable?[35]

The LSAT was threatened by <u>Griggs</u> not just because it denied opportunities to minorities--other ETS tests, such as the SAT, did this as well--but because it could arguably be considered an <u>employment</u> test. While discriminatory tests were legally permissible in educational selection, in the <u>Griggs</u> case the Supreme Court had barred their use by employers.

On March 8, 1971, Chief Justice Warren Burger presented the Court's unanimous decision in this landmark case. The Court held that employment screening tests on which blacks tended to score lower could only be justified if they tested ability to succeed on the job. Discriminatory employment tests that were not job-related violated Title VII of the Civil Rights Act of 1964. The fact that blacks and whites were given the same objective, professionally developed test was immaterial, the Court found.[36]

The central question was whether the test mainly discriminated among classes of people--in this case, blacks and whites--or reflected genuine differences in merit between the two groups as measured by performance on the job. Burger wrote:

> The Act proscribes not only overt discrimination but also practices that are fair in form, but discriminatory in operation. The touchstone is business necessity. If an employment practice which operates to exclude Negroes cannot be shown to be related to job performance, the practice is prohibited. . . . Good intent or absence of discriminatory intent does not redeem employment procedures or testing mechanisms that operate as "built-in

headwinds" for minority groups and are unrelated to measuring job capability.[37]

The standardized "intelligence" test used by the Duke Power Company to accept and reject job applicants was ruled illegal, since the test had not been "shown to bear a demonstrable relationship to successful performance of the jobs for which it was used."[38] If a plaintiff could argue --as did Professor Millard Ruud of the Law School Admission Council (LSAC)--that the LSAT, ostensibly a school admission test, was in substance a test for potential employment as a lawyer, then the LSAT could have to meet the Griggs standard of a test of job performance.[39] This worried the Law School Admission Council.

Eight years after Griggs, no such case is known to have been brought. It is not only rejected law school applicants who have been unable to connect the LSAT's lack of demonstrated relationship to legal competence with the implications of the Griggs decision. Up until about two years ago, the U.S. Department of Justice used the LSAT in the manner the Supreme Court decision specifically prohibited.[40] Unlike the case of law schools where the link to job opportunity is second hand, the LSAT was used directly as a factor in who got hired. Until 1979, this practice was followed by the Federal Trade Commission as well. The FTC dropped the LSAT requirement as part of a settlement in an employment discrimination suit by a Commission attorney.[41]

According to a 1974 report presented to the LSAC Legal Affairs and Finance Committees by Patricia Lydon (who later served as admissions director at Harvard Law School) use of the LSAT for hiring is common among private law firms and other employers as well. Lydon noted that "There is an unfortunate tendency among admissions people, employers, etc. to reach for whatever 'objective' criteria are available. The goal could easily become--'let's get the highest average LSAT.'"[42]

The extraordinary leverage which the United States bar has granted to ETS multiple-choice tests--using them for regulating advancement at no less than three key points: law school admission, bar admission, and employment--may derive in part from a belief among some lawyers that the tests can reveal mental qualities essential to success in their profession. In 1947, the committee on teaching and examination methods of the Association of American Law Schools identified five such qualities involved in "thinking like a lawyer" ("ability to determine the holding of a case . . . ability to form principles from the study of separate cases" etc.) and set out to find a test which could measure this kind of thinking.[43] According to one participant, psychometricians had ready advice on where such an instrment could be devised:

> When it was proposed to institute a nationwide test, the statistical testing experts at Yale assured us that the College Entrance Examination Board, soon to be the Educational Testing Service, could by virtue of its great experience and large technical staff produce from the beginning a test equal to if not superior to the then current Yale Legal Aptitude Test. With this assurance we went ahead enthusiastically.[44]

The first LSAT was administered in 1948.[45] ETS devised this test of "thinking like a lawyer" by pulling together "test questions already included in the files of ETS from tests for other occupations."[46] Thirty years later the LSAT was being constructed with somewhat more attention to the specific characteristics of legal work (of the six question types on the 1979-80 LSAT, one dealt with "Principles and Cases," two with grammar, one with math, one with "practical judgment" and one with "logical reasoning").[47] Nonetheless, in all important respects it was still poured from the same mold as the other ETS "aptitude" tests.

This point is best illustrated by the fact that LSAT scores have been found to correlate more closely with the ability to score high on <u>other</u> ETS aptitude tests than with any aspect of legal performance or study. In 1963, ETS examined the relationship between SAT and LSAT scores with the intention of giving college students an idea of how well they might do on the LSAT. However, the study, conducted by senior ETS statistician William B. Schrader, found SAT-LSAT correlations so high that ETS and the LSAC became concerned about how they would be interpreted, explaining that: "<u>the feeling in the Council was that undergraduate advisors were not generally equipped to make appropriate use of such information.</u>"[48] (Emphasis added.) Appropriate handling of this ETS study would have required advisors to explain to aspiring lawyers that they would be sorted by LSAT scores related more directly to their proficiency at taking ETS tests than to their likelihood of success in law. For people who have not mastered the skill of taking ETS aptitude tests, such closely related tests can present a recurring obstacle, confronting them again and again as they try to work up through the academic and professional system.

The clear finding that ETS tests correlate better with each other than with what they supposedly measure could be cause for embarrassment. However, the implications of this finding were small by comparison to those of an unpublicized 1970 ETS study. In a study of the Advanced Tests of the Graduate Record Examinations, W.B. Schrader and Barbara Pitcher found that the GRE, an ETS test ostensibly unrelated to law, was a better predictor of law school grades than the LSAT, which is advertised by ETS as an instrument that can "measure certain mental abilities important in the study of law."[49] In addition to casting doubt on the idea that the test is somehow designed to probe legal thinking abilities, this finding suggests the question of how lawyers would react to selecting their colleagues with the Graduate Record Examination. In empirical terms, using the GRE, which is devoid of legal trappings, would be at least as rational as the current practice.

Buttressed by their faith in the LSAT, law school admission officials have come to rely on the test a great deal. This was not always the case. Less than fifteen years ago, the admission process placed comparatively little emphasis on the ETS ranking. As Patricia Lunneborg and Donna Radford noted in their 1966 survey of 125 law schools which required the LSAT,

> The typical admissions procedure described by these schools was of a faculty committee of about three members, each of whom evaluated the complete dossier

of every candidate and agreed with the others which
students to accept. . . . As the respondents' comments
indicate, there is widespread distrust of formulae and
a visible shrinking away from the spectre of automated
admissions.[50]

By 1975, however, a survey of law school admission practices showed that formula admissions had become the rule for more than seventy-two per cent of schools.[51] And, in these formulae (which were justified as tools for predicting first-year average), the LSAT had replaced GPA as the most heavily weighted variable.

A three-year LSAC-sponsored study, "prepared for confidential circulation to Law School Admission Council members," by professors Albert R. Turnbull, William S. McKee, and Dr. L. Thomas Galloway, summarized the role of ETS index number and predicted first-year average ranking systems in law school admissions:

> It is clear that the simultaneous surge of application
> volume, readily available admission indices from LSDAS,
> and severe understaffing of law school admissions offices
> have created pressures toward a highly mechanical,
> computerized admission procedure. Most law school admis-
> sions officers realize the shortcomings of making decisions
> solely by choosing in descending unadjusted admissions
> index-order, but when confronting thousands of applications
> without adequate staff help or access to sophisticated adjust-
> ment formulae, the temptations in that direction are great.[52]

By 1979-80, all of the country's 168 accredited law schools required applicants to take the LSAT, and 193 schools in all required them to forward their applications via ETS' Law School Data Assembly Service.[53] One hundred forty-nine law schools were using an ETS-devised formula for ranking their applicants by admissions indices.[54]

According to a 1974 study presented to the LSAC, recommendations are "seldom given substantial weight" in admissions decisions, and "few schools rely on personal interviews for evaluating applicants."[55] "Some law schools," notes the report, "use the LSDAS or similarly organized information to place all applicants into one of three groups based on a numerical index developed from the LSAT score and undergraduate grades. These groups are sometimes labelled as (1) Presumptive Admit, (2) Presumptive Deny, and (3) Hold."[56]

Some institutions assign such a pivotal role to the LSAT that their practices are questionable even by ETS' own standards. At least twenty law schools have indicated anonymously in ETS surveys that they reject applicants whose scores fall below an LSAT cutoff.[57] Even ETS President William Turnbull, with equity in mind, has expressed disapproval of the cutoff practice:

> I think cutoff scores are usually a very bad idea. Certainly an absolute cutoff such that you would not look at a student who made a score below any "X" point, I think there's almost always a better procedure than that. Anybody who can indicate that a student who scored below that cutoff has extenuating circumstances or special reasons for bringing that score to the attention of an admissions group I think they /admissions officials/ ought to give the student that chance to do it.[58]

The rationale most frequently used for justifying reliance on the LSAT, as well as the elaborate system of admission formulas which ETS devised for law schools, is the prediction of first-year law school grades. An ETS report issued in book form by the Carnegie Council on Policy Studies in Higher Education contends that a major reason for the growing reliance on the LSAT is the test's "demonstrated predictive capabilities."[59] However, the study by Turnbull, McKee and Galloway gives another perspective.

After reviewing the results of fifty-seven different validity studies, they concluded that:

> Not surprisingly, admissions directors at many schools have found that, for the great majority of their students, grades and LSAT scores are not very closely related to actual first year performance.[60]

A more recent compilation of validity studies indicates a mean percentage of perfect prediction of thirteen per cent for the LSAT and twenty per cent for grades and LSAT combined.[61] Turnbull, McKee and Galloway say that:

> One can easily understand why numerous admissions directors are rather disturbed by these low correlations, but when directors complain of this low correlation, ETS points out that, according to the predictor, all students who were admitted were of high quality and all could be expected to do well.[62]

ETS fails to add that precisely the same could be expected of literally tens of thousands of applicants who are also of "high quality" (the AALS estimated in 1973 that every law school rejected applicants that it considered qualified)[63] who had been _rejected_ because of slightly lower LSAT scores.

Dr. Lerner made this point forcefully in her 1977 paper presented at ETS. Noting that law schools were differentiating "not only between qualified and unqualified applicants but also between the qualified ones, selecting only those with the highest scores and rejecting those with lower, but still quite adequate, scores,"[64] Lerner contended that many schools based their selection and rejection decisions on artificial distinctions cr by the LSAT scores. "Test score differences above a certain level," she argued, "become, in essence, differences between Tweedledum and Tweedledee. In this realm, the maximum is not necessarily the optimum."[65] Lerner suggested that given such a selection system, the usual depiction of law school admissions are based on standards of significant and distinguishable merit had little basis in fact.

> Screening on this basis produces unjustified feelings of inferiority in hundreds of thousands of people whose abilities are fully adequate for the positions they aspire to but who are led to believe that they have been rejected because their abilities are not good enough. Telling them that the standards by which they have been judged and found wanting have become so arbitrary as to verge on meaninglessness would be more candid but is unlikely to mollify them.[66]

Lerner found support for her argument about artificial distinctions in some little-noticed statements by the Law School Admission Council, the Association of American Law Schools, and the Council on Legal Education Opportunity. A "Statement of Interest in Behalf of the Law School Admission Council," submitted in a 1973 brief to the Washington State Supreme Court in the <u>Defunis</u> case decried the very practices which the LSAC's ranking system had helped create and foster. The statement expressed concern about making mathematical calculations the dominant consideration in admissions decisions and excluding "other critically important factors which cannot readily be reduced to or expressed in a numerical formula."[67] To the authors--unlike the ETS specialists who rank applicants according to infinitesimal gradations in test scores, and law school officials who use those rankings in admissions--the advantages of directing careers with miniscule increments of predictive validity were not persuasive. The statement concluded, "<u>the probability that one student will</u>

<u>receive law school grades slightly better than another fully qualified applicant is not of decisive importance.</u>"[68] (Emphasis added.)

In a Bakke case brief, the LSAC in effect acknowledged that the practice of rejecting people due to small score differences was difficult to justify:

> Well above the range of probable failure, however, lies a much larger volume of applicants than the schools' total capacity. All are fully qualified to perform well on law school grades, and many are nearly indistinguishable on these measures. In this range, where most of the admissions work must be done, predictions of relative law school ranks are less accurate. But at the same time, they are less significant. Whether an applicant is predicted for the 40th or 50th percentile of the class is a matter of no real consequence.[69]

For applicants rejected on the basis of such predictions, such words offered little solace.

As ETS' and the LSAC's own data and analyses are drawn together, a rational explanation for heavy reliance on the LSAT becomes increasingly difficult to construct. Determining entry to legal education and entry to the profession with the LSAT-- a test which has been shown to discriminate systematically against certain groups, but which has not been shown to be job related, and which admittedly fails to do much more than make insignificant distinctions among qualified applicants--are hardly practices based on logic or social justice.

Even two of the more modest arguments in defense of the LSAT, while perhaps having some basis in fact, are considerably less substantial than institutions sometimes suppose. One point often made is that law school failure and drop-out rates fell significantly in the 1960s (from 29.8 per cent in 1960 to 12.7 per cent in 1970),[70] a trend ascribed to increased reliance on the LSAT. This assumption neglects the fact that during this period the ratio of applicants to places grew by more than sixty per cent,[71] meaning that law schools had far more qualified applicants to choose from than before and therefore could be expected to obtain academically better classes regardless of how they were selected.

Another rationale for use of the LSAT, the theory that it serves to compensate for differences in grading practices among different colleges, owes more to speculation than to hard data. One study found that even after recalculating college grades by inflating or deflating them according to a common standard*, prediction was not improved:

> Results make it unlikely that substantial gains in validity would be obtained . . . by using these College Means as added predictors. Only six out of 27 school groups showed increases in validity of .05 or more. . . . Although results varied from one law school to another. . . . None of the college means . . . contributed substantially to prediction . . .[72]

In other words, differing college standards did <u>not</u> affect the predictive usefulness of grades.

ETS: Sentry for the Legal Profession

Though the conventional rationale for the dominance of the LSAT is difficult to defend, the phenomenon can be plausibly explained in terms of institutional politics. ETS long ago

---

*The LSAT College Mean (LCM), which is the mean LSAT score earned by graduates of each college, is discussed in this Chapter. See p. 246.

recognized that law school admission officers would be receptive to the creation of a national admission system to enhance their prestige within their own schools and provide them with scientific authority for defending their admission decisions. Working in consultation with law schools, ETS began the LSAT program in 1948.[73]

Twenty-two law schools had representatives on a policy committee which advised ETS.[74] By 1961 ETS had convened the Law School Admission Test Council.[75] But by early 1962, according to a series of confidential ETS memos, LSATC chairman Louis Toepfer, had become "quite unhappy" with, among other things, consistent ETS mistakes in scoring the LSAT. Toepfer, Chauncey wrote, had gotten the "impression that we (ETS) tried to minimize the errors and, if possible, sweep them under the rug."[76] Although the LSATC had no formal power over ETS or the LSAT program, Chauncey noted that their participation was essential to ETS' credibility in the law school world.

In addition to a new policy of disclosing ETS mistakes to the Council, ETS executives decided to reorganize the LSATC to give the law schools, according to a confidential memo from Vice President Robert Ebel, "a sense of direct involvement in the determination of ETS policies."[77] President Chauncey wrote that ETS could help secure the support of the law school community by enhancing the prestige of one segment of that community: law school _admissions_ officers. "Unless we fulfill effectively the functions of the secretariat of the LSATC Council," he warned, "the time may well come when these functions will be transferred to the AALS /Association of American Law Schools/. . . . The AALS . . . is an association of the <u>deans</u> of law schools. Consequently, the admissions officers would not have the same prestigious position in the AALS that they do in the LSAT."[78] (Emphasis added.)

Immediate steps to improve the image of the LSATC included the scheduling of frequent meetings and conferences at resorts and fine hotels, the assignment of ETS staff members to produce reports on the LSATC letterhead, and the creation of more advisory committees and titles for admissions officers.[79] In 1968 the LSATC became an incorporated legal entity.[80] Instead of being mere advisers to ETS, the admissions officers became contractors who chose ETS as the agency which would administer their LSAT program. Though ETS retained ownership of the test and the LSATC had no staff beyond what ETS provided, Council members expressed pleasure with ETS management of their affairs.[81] In 1972, as LSATC meetings and reports had begun to address a broad range of issues regarding access to law beyond just testing, the LSATC became the Law School Admission Council (LSAC).[82]

With the strategic assistance of ETS, the LSAC had come a long way from the unincorporated advisory board of a decade before. By 1974, the Council had standing committees which held dozens of meetings yearly. The annual Council meeting had become a three-day affair where ABA presidents came to speak and admissions officers could hear presentations ranging from ETS staff seminars on the statistics of mental measurement to a training session (with a psychologist) concerning how to word rejection letters entitled, "ON SAYING NO!"[83] (Emphasis in original.)

As the ratio of applicants to places rose sharply in the 1960s, the LSAT system provided the added benefit of an administratively convenient method for sorting out the crunch of candidates. In the early 1970s, ETS began developing what one program director called a "central pre-admissions office" which would concentrate in ETS many of the functions then handled by individual law schools. The program evolved over three years of intensive ETS staff work and LSAC-sponsored meetings in Florida, Newport Beach, California, and the Virgin Islands.[84] A comprehensive series of ETS application-analysis programs resulted. For a nominal fee, ETS would give law schools:

--A Law School Data Assembly Service (LSDAS) profile on each candidate. Included were identifying information, social security number, grades at all previous colleges and graduate schools attended and LSAT scores[85]

--A listing of the candidate's previous grades standardized according to an ETS formula. School transcripts, which recorded grades in several different systems (A, B, C; 1.00 to 4.00; 3.00 to 1.00; etc.) were analyzed and the candidate's previous grades reported according to ETS' 1.00 to 4.00 scale.[86]

--A formula, using variables chosen by the law school (grades, LSAT, LCM, writing ability scores as the options) calculated by ETS to yield an "index number" for each applicant; a number designed to predict how well the candidate would do in his or her first year, if admitted to that law school.[87]

--A computer print-out ranking all applicants by their index numbers. Supplementary print-outs, ranking the members of certain groups of applicants, such as an index-number ranking of female or black applicants, were available upon request.[88]

--A computer print-out ranking all applicants by their Predicted First Year Average (PFYA). The PFYA is ETS' prediction--spelled out to two decimal places--of the grade average each candidate will earn if he or she is admitted to a particular law school. ETS computers can calculate the PFYA from previous candidate grades, the overall distribution of grades at the candidate's college, LCM, the average LSAT of the law school he or she is applying to, the overall distribution of grades at the law school he or she is applying to, and, most importantly, the LSAT score.[89]

Such administrative convenience had many attractions for institutional authorities. The Supreme Court had noted this propensity in a landmark decision in the intelligence testing case Castro v. Beecher, 1971, "No doubt, among the reasons that intelligence tests, particularly of the multiple-choice type, continue to be so popular is that not only do they appear to be so objective, but it is so easy to grade them quickly."[90] Even some ETS employees were surprised by how enthusiastically the law schools adopted ETS as their central pre-admissions office. While the convenience of the LSDAS for law schools committed to reliance on the LSAT was evident, this new concentration of power at ETS created problems for some undergraduate colleges. Some felt that ETS' recalculation of their students' grades put them at a disadvantage in the game of inches which law school admission had become. Harold N. Moorman, Director of Student Services at Dartmouth College, wrote to ETS President William Turnbull:

> In effect ETS is saying Dartmouth College does not grade on a 5.0 basis, but rather that we grade on a four-point scale . . . I have no knowledge of what information could have led to this conclusion. . . . We grade on a five-point scale, that is, we give five equally spaced passing grades labeled A, B, C+, C-, and D weighted, respectively, 5, 4, 3, 2, 1. If you can accept that fact (and I certainly urge that you do),

> then I ask how you would convert our grades if there
> were no letters involved but only numerical grades
> from five down to one? Is it not just as reasonable
> (or unreasonable) to compress our A (5) and B (4)
> into a single-point span as to compress our C+ (3)
> and C- (2) grades as has been done this year?[91]

Similarly, a 1976 LSAC study of the admissions process reported that other undergraduate colleges:

> believe that the ETS conversions penalize their
> students. The University of Rochester, for example,
> has complained that ETS unfairly converts its grade
> of B+ to a 3.33, when it should in fact become a
> 3.50. Bryn Mawr treats a grade between 87 and 100
> as a 4.0, yet ETS, following its standard formula,
> only equates grades of 90 and above with a 4.0 . . .
> /still/ ETS refuses to make school-by-school judg-
> ments in such cases, believing that its service
> should be purely a clerical one, reporting grades
> without interpreting them.[92]

ETS maintained the public position that its adjustments of college grades were only minor and clerical. In a 1972 LSAT newsletter article on "Common Questions and Answers About /the/ LSDAS /and/ LSAT" it put the claim bluntly: "Does ETS rank schools according to quality? No".[93]

As law school admission officers knew, this was not quite the case. In calculating "index numbers" from test scores and college grades, ETS used a factor known as the "LCM" (LSAT College Mean) for inflating or deflating the value of grades from different schools. A school's LCM was based on how well previous students from that school performed on the LSAT. Drawing on its computerized files of old LSAT scores, ETS arrived at LCM figures by calculating the mean score of students from a particular college who had taken the LSAT in the previous few years. ETS compiled a two-inch thick directory listing the LCMs and undergraduate grade distributions of more than 1,000 colleges, and, on request of the law school, inserted the LCM into the predictive formulas used by admissions officers.[94] All LSAC member law schools were told of this service and by 1975, at least forty-eight were using it.[95] The applicants were not so informed.

The ETS LCM directory, the "Guide to the Interpretation of Undergraduate Transcripts," carried the boldface warning: "CONFIDENTIAL"; circulation of the directory was carefully controlled, and admissions directors of LSAC member schools were among the few authorized to have a copy.[96]

As with other ETS test scores, the LCM created a hierarchy dominated by social class; only this time, entire institutions were being ranked. The grades from each college were given a different value based on their graduates' LSAT scores.[97] Students, who worked hard for four years to earn an A average at the best school they could afford, could find their grades devalued relative to those of mediocre students at an elite institution. The LCM put a ceiling on the value of grades earned at each school, and no amount of individual effort could pierce this predetermined ceiling. The schools whose students systematically scored lowest on the LCM were the ones where students had the lowest incomes. Some entire classes of schools--such as the predominantly black colleges--had their grades systematically valued as inferior by the LCM.[98]

While ETS computers were reevaluating the grades of thousands of students, ETS researchers were studying whether the practice was improving the prediction of law school success. From the researchers' point of view, the results were not encouraging. In March, 1975, the LSAC discussed the progress of research being conducted on the LCM by ETS' Robert Boldt and noted tersely, "It was generally agreed that results...would probably not lead to any improvement in prediction."[99]

A little over one year later, more firm results were available for the LSAC. And they confirmed the earlier doubts. At a May 7 and 8, 1976 committee meeting, researchers reported:

> A close review of validity studies conducted for law schools by VSS /Validity Study Service/ demonstrated that use of LCM as an additional predictor does not significantly enhance the prediction of law school performance...Cross-validation of prediction equations developed for 41 law schools that furnished LCM data to VSS in the summer of 1974 showed that apparent gains resulting from including LCM in prediction equations were not "real" or lasting gains. [100]

Finally, in August, 1976, Boldt's study was completed. Though Boldt did not dispute the right of ETS to decide for itself and America's law schools how much grades were worth at colleges across the country he did note that: "Though it is eminently plausible that grade adjustments be made, we do not know how to make them effective."[101]

The schools whose students were judged by an LCM which ETS had individually calculated for them were not those receiving the most inequitable or irrational treatment. At schools where fewer than twenty-five people had previously taken the LSAT, ETS arbitrarily assigned them a "default" LCM, consisting of the most recent national mean score on the test.[102] At a June, 1974 LSAC committee meeting, ETS researcher Barbara Pitcher suggested that another way to develop LCMs for these students "would be to lump all such individuals from small colleges and use their mean...."[103]

Such insensitivity to individual aspirations and careers characterized the use of the LCM, which based significant decisions about a students' future on factors over which they had no control. At the March, 1975 meeting of the Programs Operation Research Committee, member George Dawson remarked on the discouraging data on LCM and asked that its use be stopped "until such time as it is determined how LCM operates." Mr. Dawson's motion, the minutes continue, "failed for lack of a second."[104]

Use of the LCM meant a second-generation of systematic discrimination for low-income students hoping to attend law school. First, they were likely to score lower on the LSAT than wealthier students. And, with the addition of the LCM, their undergraduate grades--the only other credentials they could present to law schools-- would be devalued if they attended a school whose previous graduates had not scored well on the LSAT. Those schools, in turn, tended to be the schools where students had the lowest incomes.

Eight months after this report became available to LSAC officials, Dean Orin Slagle, Chairman of the LSAC Legal Affairs Committee, appeared before the Federal Privacy Commission to offer justification for ETS' continued use of the LCM and to explain to the Commission why the LCM, Index Numbers, and Predicted First Year Averages (PFYA) should not be disclosed to applicants.

> The service extends to a law school the opportunity to have the undergraduate average manipulated in such a way as to equate it to some standard established by the law school....Now, if I understand this--and I hope I certainly do, or I shouldn't be here--what we are dealing with here is a more sophisticated way of saying that grades from X college mean one thing to us and grades from Y college mean another thing to us; and I

don't think that you can go anywhere in this country and talk to an educational officer in higher education that doesn't have some preconceived notions about the value of undergraduate averages from one institution vis-a-vis yet, another institution. Many of us unhappily have not had enough experience with persons from those various institutions so we don't know what to do about it and probably don't do anything about it except that many of us do have these hunches, these notions, these preconceptions about this particular matter. . . .

The index number is a number that is achieved as the result of the application of a multiple regression equation. . . . What we are attempting to do in the index number is to generate a number which says to the law school admission officer: This is our best prediction of the academic potential in the first year of that law school's academic program; and we do not report that to the candidate. . . .

I think I believe fully in fairness; I think I believe fully in the need for accuracy; and I think I believe fully in the right of privacy. Even with those beliefs, I would suggest that it is not appropriate for the candidate to have this information. . . .

No doubt a great number of persons will have to be disappointed by nonadmission to a law school. We want those people who have the greatest potential for success in the academic environment and in the profession to be admitted.

We do not want a false self-selection system operating within that potential applicant population denying persons the opportunity to go to law school. . . . I am afraid that when we announce publicly that school X's grades were being reduced in this particular system by a school here, a school there, wherever it may be, we will discourage a number of people who should not in fact be discouraged.[105]

Dean Slagle's fears were never realized. Neither the individual LCMs nor the index numbers calculated with them were ever released to the applicants concerned. When asked about the LCM in an interview in May 1977, ETS President William Turnbull and his associate, ETS Vice President Robert E. Smith, could not recall having heard of such a thing, and were skeptical of the very idea of such a practice.[106]

More than a month later, President Turnbull sent a four-page, single-spaced letter concerning "a few topics on which some amplification or clarification might be helpful." One of them was the LCM:

> During our discussion of the Law School Admission Test College Means (LCM), I believe I made a statement that could be misleading. Use of the LCM in prediction formulae was discontinued last year by the Law School Admission Council. Prior to that time, however, such formulae including the LCM were used as part of the admission process of some law schools.[107]

As the experience of the LCM illustrates, from the answers to ETS questions to the formulas of law school admission committees, aspiring lawyers often are not allowed to examine the evidence--or even know the rules--which may exclude them from the legal profession. At the 1974 LSAC annual meeting, a seminar on due process in admissions focused on a Virginia Law Review article by Professors Ernest Gellhorn and D. Brock Hornby, which examined the law schools' legal obligations to their applicants. Gellhorn and Hornby found that, with the sole exception of a prohibition on severe racial discrimination, law school applicants did _not_ have clear legal rights of procedural or substantive due process, or equal protection.[108] Gellhorn and Hornby noted that not only were applicants denied the chance to present their case in person and explain their background and aspirations to the deciding officials, but even their paper applications were screened first by ETS computers and received a minimum of human evaluation:

This /typical law school/ procedure means that only a small percentage of the applications are considered by the entire committee. Even then the files are seldom considered in committee sessions, though committee members do consult with each other and frequently discuss individual cases. In other words, even the extraordinary or difficult application receives limited attention, and most consume less than half an hour of administrative or committee time.[109]

Though ETS devises individually tailored multiple regression equations for subscribing law schools, it never discloses the formulas used to rank and reject applicants, and institutions rarely reveal them. Applicants are offered an often effusive general description of the kind of meritorious individual the school is seeking. But, as Gellhorn and Hornby point out, "No formal appeal process exists for those rejected or placed on the waiting list, nor is an applicant advised of the specific basis for a decision."[110]

Gellhorn and Hornby recommended that although law schools were not legally obligated to give applicants due process, in light of the importance of admissions decisions to careers and society, institutions should offer applicants five minimal rights modeled on fair treatment standards which an individual can demand from a government agency:

1. Tell applicants what the real standards for admission are.

2. Demonstrate that the standards are relevant to the objectives of the school (such as producing competent or creative lawyers).

3. Give applicants a chance to show that these standards do not do them justice. (Pointing out that at state schools students are allowed to talk to admission officials to show that they are in fact state residents, Gellhorn and Hornby conclude: "Therefore, just as a student is entitled to show that she is now a Connecticut resident despite her Wisconsin address at the time she applied, law schools

> should afford applicants the opportunity to show that
> they will be good performers despite their scores.")

4. Tell rejected applicants, on request, specifically why they were rejected.

5. When applicants are rejected because of information not submitted by them, let them see and explain or contest it.[111]

Gellhorn said in a 1979 interview that he believed that the opportunities for due process had improved at many law schools since the time of his paper, a progression which he attributed in part to attempts to avoid pressure from rejected applicants and which he thought would be accelerated by legislative efforts such as New York's Truth-in-Testing Law (which Gellhorn opposes).[112]

However, an important element of due process in law school admissions -- the disclosure of information on which decisions were based--was not entirely under the control of individual law schools. As with the process of test-making, it had been delegated to ETS and its organ in the law school world--the LSAC. At a February 6 and 7, 1970 Sun Valley ski weekend for law school officials organized by ETS, the LSAC agreed not to show candidates the ETS forms which listed "index numbers" calculated by ETS for each candidate and used by admissions committees to rank and reject applicants.[113] Like the LCM, this information was to be withheld not only from applicants but also from their college pre-law advisers.

The official, private minutes explained the rationale: factors against reporting include "the complexity of explaining and justifying to each candidate how the evaluations were made and computed. . . ." The Sun Valley conferees did acknowledge that "The primary reason for reporting is to give the candidate an opportunity to see that no miscalculation has been made thereby causing him prejudice at numerous law schools . . . but concluded that the candidate should not receive a copy of his analysis."[114]

This was reaffirmed at a 1973 meeting of the LSAC where, "It was decided that if a candidate requests copies of LSDAS reports in the candidate's LSDAS file, the reports would be sent with information unique to each law school such as admissions indices, adjusted UGPA's, LCM's and percentiles--supressed."[115]

Beyond considerations of convenience and prestige, ETS realized that a large part of its service to law school administrators consisted of the provision of political defense. In line with this commitment, ETS established the Higher Education Admission Law Service (HEALS), a sophisticated legal briefing service which informed thousands of subscribing institutions of their legal position with regard to their applicants.

> Trustees, presidents, deans--all who are involved in the process . . . are increasingly exposed to the threat of litigation. Students and parents are more inclined than ever before to turn to the courts to obtain redress of real or fancied ills.[116]

At about the same time, ETS began a program of what the LSAC's internal reports called "Defensive Research."[117] ETS researchers identified issues and constituencies--such as women and blacks--that might prove threatening to the LSAC; they then designed research studies to be used in response to criticism.[118] On September 29, 1976, for example, the New York Times reported the release of an ETS study by Alfred Carlson and Charles Werts under the headline "Law School Aptitude Tests Backed." Not surprisingly, Werts and Carlson found a high correlation between scores on ETS' multiple-choice LSAT and ETS' multiple-choice Multistate Bar Examination (MBE); higher in fact than the LSAT's correlation with law school grades, undergraduate grades or any other non-ETS performance measure.[119] The *Times* story did not mention that no research supports a connection between MBE scores and legal success.[120] "Thus," the *Times* concluded, "the Educational Testing Service ostensibly has offered scientific documentation in defense of an examination that is one of the obstacles that must be hurdled by men and women aspiring to enter one of the country's most prestigious, best-paying professions."[121]

This public relations coup for the LSAT had its genesis in the February 1973 proposal prepared by ETS researchers Alfred B. Carlson and Charles Werts, for one of the most strategically crucial pieces of ETS "Defensive Research."[122]

Carlson and Werts noted that the National Council of Bar Examiners, which sponsors the ETS Multistate Bar Exam, "needs objective evidence that the MBE is positively related to . . . competency in the practice of law" and that "the determinative function of the LSAT, law school grades, and the MBE in the progress of students toward legal practice could be much better understood and justified," if such evidence were available. Carlson and Werts pointed out that although data linking the LSAT and MBE to professional success could be hard to come by, the tests could to some extent be defended by showing that they correlated with each other. They argued that, "The need for such a study becomes urgent as the gatekeeping function of law schools and bar examinations is increasingly challenged."[123]

An item currently at the top of ETS' "Defensive Research" agenda is an ongoing study on "Becoming a Competent Lawyer." This study will attempt to discover relationships between LSAT scores and success in actual legal practice.[124] ETS and the LSAC had long been familiar with the political problems caused by their inability to demonstrate such a connection. At a September 15, 1972 LSAC committee meeting, ETS researcher William Schrader discussed this point. According to the minutes:

> There has also been growing interest in doing a research project which would correlate LSAT scores with "success" in practice. Mr. Schrader stated that the present feeling is that such long range studies are not fruitful. However, in light of the public's growing interest in testing, and as the LSAT and MBE come under attack, we may well want to initiate such research.[125]

Within a few years, technical misgivings had been overcome, and the study, directed by Alfred Carlson, was on its way to a release which is sure to have appropriate publicity.[126]

ETS' vigor as guardian of LSAC's political interests has outstripped its performance as a provider of day-to-day test and data processing services. Though President Chauncey was able to mollify law school officials about the scoring errors of the early 1960s, a series of publicly exposed service breakdowns and privately discussed cost-overruns in the early 1970s caused considerable consternation among LSAC officials. Massive mishandling of LSDAS applications in 1970-71 (see Chapter VII for discussion), budget overruns in 1973 and 1974 (see Chapter VIII), and LSAT equating errors in 1978 (see Chapter III) brought embarrassment and financial inconvenience to the LSAC. The Council began negotiating with ETS to have more and more rights to the programs on which it put its name placed under its control. It even considered going to ACT for testing services.[127]

Though ETS owned the stock of questions and the LSAT name, and thus could administer the tests with or without LSAC endorsement, it recognized that continuing political support from the Council was important to ETS' prestige in the higher education community. ETS, thus, ceded to the LSAC program control rights more extensive than those enjoyed by other ETS client groups (see Chapter VIII for discussion of client groups). By 1979, the LSAC had obtained ownership of both the test questions and the LSAT name,[128] and even became the first ETS-established client board to hire a full-time professional administrator who was not on the ETS payroll.[129] In July, 1979, in the wake of ETS' LSAT equating error--which was reported in the New York Times and other publications--the LSAC established its own corporation which, according to Council administrator Bruce Zimmer, is expected to begin assuming, in the summer of 1980, some of the LSDAS duties now performed by ETS.[130] While Council chairman Orin Slagle denies that there was any connection between the 1978 errors and the founding of the new corporation,[131] Zimmer says that the Council believes it can do some of the LSDAS work more cheaply and with more accountability to individual law schools than it has under contract to ETS.[132]

As significant as the recent LSAC challenge to ETS' authority is in terms of corporate and institutional politics (it is the first ETS-created client group in company history to assert such independence), it has little apparent bearing on the future of how entry to the legal profession will be decided in the United States. The LSAC's reasons for now distancing itself from ETS resemble those which first helped bring many law schools into the ETS test system: public image and administrative and economic convenience. No aspect of the LSAC's recent actions challenges the fundamental premise that the LSAT, and index numbers calculated with it, should form the basis of the law school admissions process. They are simply trying to insure that the LSAT selection system operates more smoothly; they are not trying to change the system itself.

The idea that the LSAT admissions process should itself be called into question however, is not unknown in legal circles. In 1971, the Law Students Division of the American Bar Association called on law schools to stop using the LSAT[133]--a call echoed two years later in a Supreme Court opinion by Justice William O. Douglas.[133] At the 1973 LSAC Annual Council Meeting, the widely respected attorney Chesterfield Smith, then President-Elect of the American Bar Association, gave his views concerning the effect of the LSAT on the American bar. Smith remarked that "It just strikes against the grain of reason to predicate a life's work on performance on a one-day exam." He offered a modest recommendation: "all law schools should seriously consider reserving, at least for a while, a certain number of seats in each beginning class for random, subjective or other non-quantitative selection processes."[134]

Lawyers of Chesterfield Smith's persuasion were reluctant to reduce their profession to ETS multiple-choice tests. Nonetheless, among many lawyers (or at least law school admissions officers), ETS had found that the science of mental measurement had already proved its case.

How deep an inroad had actually been made was illustrated during the LSAC "Conference on the Future of the LSAT Program." Professor Walter B. Raushenbush, an official of the Law School Admission Council, asked

> whether a catalog of the characteristics of the "compleat lawyer" could not be developed with the assistance of the bar, such as a committee of the American Bar Association. In this way it could be decided that a lawyer should have courage, patience, listening ability, and compassion, for example.[135]

"Then," Raushenbush concluded, "we could go to the psychologists and have tests developed to measure these qualities."[136] Such is the faith which underpins ETS' power as the gatekeeper of the American legal profession.

CHAPTER VII

THE ETS WAY OF DOING BUSINESS:
STUDENT CONSUMERS IN CAPTIVITY

The Educational Testing Service has created a marketplace for its services. But, it is not a marketplace characterized by traditional checks and balances between sellers and consumers. It is a marketplace without adequate information, choice, competition or public safeguards (rights and remedies) for the consumers of the tests. Above all, these tests are sold through brokers who make the choice for the consumers. But, in an interview ETS Executive Vice President Robert J. Solomon saw it differently. He believes that consumers are not compelled to use ETS tests:

> (Solomon): ETS as an organization itself compels no one to use its services. . . . If the use of our services is voluntary, then the ultimate weapon the users have is not to make use of it, and there's nothing that ETS can do to compel the colleges' or the graduate schools' or government agencies' or professional societies' . . . use of the services. . . .

Q: . . . How can individual students use that ultimate weapon?

A: (Solomon): Well, I think that has to be answered more in terms of the place of students in American society and in the educational system, and to the extent that students can influence . . . the decisions of their schools and colleges and other organizations that are involved in the educational system . . . then there can be an impact. . . . To understand ETS you have to understand that in context. Because otherwise one could start from the misconception that somehow ETS _imposes_ its will on students. . . . ETS has no _power_ to impose its will on students, directly and per se.[1]

ETS consumers know better. ETS has an absolute monopoly in eight of its top ten testing markets; in the others, it dominates the field.[2] When an institution requires applicants to submit

ETS scores, the applicants have little choice. In most major ETS testing markets, consumers either patronize ETS or abandon their plans.

The business relationship between ETS and its consumers has few parallels in the U.S. economy today; involuntary consumption is only the beginning. Traditional business concepts--such as the idea that the party that receives the benefits bears the costs, or that contracts are based on bargaining between sellers and consumers, or that the conduct of interstate business is ultimately subject to federal oversight--do not apply to the ETS test system. In their dealings with a corporation that can change the course of their careers, ETS consumers lack enforceable legal rights.

The Costless Decision

Contrary to the belief of some, it generally costs institutions nothing to require an ETS test. For a college to require the SAT, for example, it does not have to be a member of the College Board and does not have to pay a fee to ETS. It simply states in its catalog that applicants must submit SAT scores. Applicants then pay the fees, sending their money directly to ETS. The ETS staff analysis of the report of the College Board Commission on Tests recognized this situation:

> It is a plain fact that higher educational institutions represent the primary clients of the College Board and ETS, not the students. This unpallatable /sic/ but clear observation means that the College Board and ETS may help students and colleges only as long as member colleges and universities continue to grant the Board and ETS a taxing privilege by requiring their students to write College Board tests.[3] (Original emphasis.)

In short, test takers are captives; they have no say as to whether they will pay and take the test. Moreover, as one parent pointed out, the ETS arrangement also obligates "the individual to pay to generate evidence which may, and very often is, eventually used against him. . . ."[4]

On the other side of the transaction, though institutions receive the benefits of the test, they bear none of the costs and, thus, do not have to weigh them against each other in deciding whether to require the test. Placing the burden of fees on applicants can have disruptive consequences for students from low-income families. The fees for ETS tests and services are not insignificant. In 1979, a student taking the SAT and an Achievement Test and reporting the results to four colleges, for example, would have had to pay $24.75.[5] A 1976 College Board report found that, "test fees themselves constitute a barrier to higher education for the very poor."[6] The College Board and ETS have adopted the solution of individual fee waivers which guidance counselors and social service agencies allocate to needy students on a case-by-case basis.[7] As in applying for welfare, this system may require a student to present proof of poverty and be judged by the issuing officer. Those reluctant to endure this rite, or those who never learn of the waivers or who get to the counselor or agency after their stock of waivers has run out, must pay the fee or lose the opportunity to take the test.

A case study from an internal ETS report on how the test-taking environment affects minority students illustrates the haphazard factors which can obstruct an applicant:

> Susan, a Puerto Rican student, a graduating senior at Waller High School in Chicago, Illinois, discovered to her amazement that she must take the Scholastic Aptitude Test before her application could be considered for entrance into college. She went to make an appointment with her guidance counsellor to obtain the necessary information. . . . When asked if it was possible to obtain fee waiver information (which, by the way, she learned about from a friend) she was told that it was too late and that the counsellor did not have time to check out the necessary information to see if she qualified for the fee waiver. She was also told that fee waivers were not an important concern for the counsellor and it was just an unnecessary waste of time. After obtaining the application, she found out that she might be able to get a fee waiver from ASPIRA, a community agency for Puerto Ricans. She obtained the waiver (a stroke of luck, for it was the last one they had) and then sent the application in.[8]

Thousands of others have not been so lucky. A 1971 study of ETS fee waiver programs found that in 1969-70 the College Board programs spent only $40,500 of the $150,000 budgeted for fee waivers. (In 1970-71 they spent only $155,400 of the $265,000 allocated.)[9] A 1971 internal ETS report concluded that:

> In essence, the various fee waiver programs, as they are now administered, are little more than token efforts to elevate public opinion and have no identifiable impact on perpetuating education for minority and poverty students.[10]

Even with improved administration and spending ratios in more recent years, the individual waiver system necessarily misses many needy students. A 1977 survey by the Philadelphia public schools, for example, found that of the 2,222 students who "could have used" waivers, only 851 had received them. Only two of thirty-one schools were found to have given out a sufficient number of waivers.[11]

In 1980, the ETS fee system may cut still deeper into the budgets of poor people in the State of New York. In response to New York's newly enacted "Truth-in-Testing" law, the College Board has announced retaliation by increasing SAT fees for New York students.[12] ETS' own cost estimates show that no fee increase is necessary since the SAT program can comply with the law for a cost equal to about one-fourth the current SAT profit margin. In contrast, New Yorkers who want to go to college will be forced to comply with the fee increase, if initiated. (See Chapter VIII for discussion of SAT profits and the concluding chapter for discussion of Truth-in-Testing and the fee increase.)

The Contract of Adhesion: Take it or Leave it

According to ETS counsel John Kramer, the consumer enters a contract with ETS when "he tenders a fee to ETS and signs an application form."[13] Yet, the ETS application forms list no conditions--such as scoring the tests accurately, getting the information out on time, or protecting confidentiality--that the consumer can legally compel ETS to honor. The registration forms fail to acknowledge that ETS has contractual responsibilities or that consumers have contractual rights. The only way an ETS consumer can claim such rights is to argue in court that ETS obligations exist where none are written.

The peculiar nature of the contract between ETS and its consumers was described by the New York State Supreme Court in a July 28, 1976 decision upholding ETS' right to cancel the scores of a candidate it suspected of cheating.

> The contract at issue here would appear to fit within
> the definition of a <u>contract of adhesion</u>.* . . .
> [A]pplicants have no alternative but to accept the
> standard conditions fixed by the testing service for
> all test takers. If he [the plaintiff] refused to
> accept the terms he would not have been permitted to
> take the examination, and would not have been admitted
> to . . . school.[14] (Emphasis added.)

A possible consequence of this absence of consumer leverage over the seller was noted by Professor Friedrich Kessler in his 1943 Columbia Law Review article, "Contracts of Adhesion":

> Standard contracts are typically used by enterprises
> with strong bargaining power. The weaker party, in
> need of the goods or services, is frequently not in
> a position to shop around for better terms either
> because the author of the contract has a monopoly
> (natural or artificial) or because all competitors
> use the same clauses. The contractual intention is
> but a subjection more or less voluntary to terms
> dictated by the stronger party, terms whose con-
> sequences are often understood only in a vague way
> if at all.[16]

Though candidates are not informed of ETS contractual obligations, they are given a stiff list of their own obligations when they sit down for a test. LSAT candidates, for example, are required to copy in their own handwriting a pledge of allegiance to ETS

---

*According to a 1974 study in the <u>Louisiana Law Review</u>: "contracts of adhesion . . . are characterized by a lack of bargaining power in one of the parties to the agreement and by the fact that they are written entirely by one party and offered on a 'take it or leave it' basis to the other. Adhesion contracts are a by-product of the growth of big business into monopolistic enterprises focusing on mass distribution and mass sales in the most effective way possible. The contracts are drafted and presented to the public rather than to individuals. Thus, the drafter may write the contract to his best advantage and the adhering party has no chance to bargain. If the enterprise offering the contract has little or no competition in the field or if the location of the buyer does not present the opportunity for comparative shopping, there may in fact be no choice at all for the buyer."[15]

rules: "I certify that I am the candidate whose name appears on this registration form. I certify that I have read the Law School Admission Bulletin and agree to be bound by the conditions stated therein."[17] A printed statement must also be endorsed: "If I take the LSAT, I further agree that, because of the limited purpose for which the contents of the LSAT are to be made known to me, I have no right to diffuse, reproduce, distribute, or sell any part of that test." These promises to ETS are sealed with a dated signature ("Sign your full first name, middle name and last name") and a compulsory thumbprint.[18]

The terms laid out in the registration materials require the candidate to pay ETS before the test is taken and before additional services--such as reporting scores to more than three schools--are received. In the case of the LSAT, they also state that the candidate can be liable to prosecution for breach of ETS rules:

> If a person engages in an act of dishonesty with respect to the test or the admission process, such information will be transmitted to the law schools receiving the person's LSAT or LSDAS reports (or to the law school in which the person is enrolled). In addition, the person may be subject to criminal prosecution and civil liability for damages. As a consequence, any hope of practicing law may be destroyed by participating in such dishonest acts.[19]

According to attorney C. Boyden Grey of Wilmer, Cutler and Pickering,* ETS' law firm, the contractual rights of ETS consumers have not been enumerated in internal memoranda by ETS or its advisors.[20] Within the ETS legal network--which includes at least two law firms other than Wilmer, Cutler and Pickering

---

*In 1979 Lloyd N. Cutler was appointed by President Carter as White House Counsel and the firm dropped his name from their masthead.

and ETS' internal law office[21]--public definition of the contractual rights of ETS consumers has been judiciously avoided. ETS counsel Thomas Robinson discussed why in an interview:

Q: Has ETS ever considered informing candidates what their legal rights are, regarding their contract with ETS?

A: (Robinson): Oh, I think a real effort is made on a continuing basis here to make sure that the candidate is apprised of their responsibilities and what they can expect from ETS, largely through the registration form for a particular test and the bulletin of information.

Q: If ETS says in a bulletin of information given to the candidate that data identifiable with an individual will not be used by ETS without that individual's prior consent, can the individual understand that to mean that that is part of ETS' contractual obligation to that individual?

A: (Robinson): (Shrugs.)

Q: Haven't you ever considered these questions before? As an attorney at ETS?

A: (Robinson): No.

Q: Why not?

A: (Robinson): I've had other things to do.[22]

ETS does not just fail to enumerate its contractual obligations. It also assumes certain unstated contractual *privileges*, such as the right to alter a student's previous grades and scores in ways that are reported to the schools but not to the applicant. It does this without the consumer's knowledge.

Though not covered by the "Buckley Amendment,"[23] which gives students the right to inspect the records a school keeps on them, ETS told the Federal Privacy Protection Study Commission in 1976 that it was voluntarily in compliance.[24] ETS' widely publicized "Principles, Policies and Procedural Guidelines" state that

". . . an individual should be able to obtain information about himself or herself in ETS-held data files, in order to ascertain the accuracy . . . of test scores or other processed information based on tests, questionnaires, or school records."[25] Yet, despite these public pronouncements, ETS routinely transforms the grades and test scores of law school applicants into "index numbers" and predicted first year averages. These are then sent to law schools but kept from the candidate (see Chapter VI).[26] In an internal report, the Boston regional office of the Federal Trade Commission has gone so far as to argue that:

> The non-disclosures of the existence of, and the unavailability of, the "index" score to students are deceptive and unfair practices in violation of section 5 /of the Federal Trade Commission Act/ in that ETS is failing to disclose material information to students. Furthermore, and perhaps most importantly, the creation of "index" scores by ETS is in direct conflict with its own definition of proper test use and therefore results in a breach of its confidential-fiduciary relationship with test examinees in violation of section 5.[27]

Judge and Jury: ETS Decides

Perhaps the most potent aspect of ETS' take-it-or-leave-it contract with the consumer is its assumption of quasi-judicial powers to make judgments about a person's integrity and report them to institutions. Through 1976-77, ETS used a code on LSAT reports to law schools designed to identify "unacknowledged repeaters." A question on the LSAT candidate's form asked if one had previously taken the LSAT. If the candidate had taken the test before but failed to fill in the answer to this question, an asterisk on their score report designated them an "unacknowledged repeater." As Professor Ralph Smith of the University of

Pennsylvania Law School told Kim Masters of the New Republic, though the candidate was not so informed, and though no investigation had been conducted, law schools often interpreted asterisks to indicate dishonesty, to the detriment of applicants who received them.[28] The injustice was compounded by an ETS computer error in 1975-76, which caused uncounted numbers of asterisks to be mistakenly affixed to the score reports of students who, by ETS' own admission, should not have received them.[29]

Institutions are accustomed to receiving from ETS reports bearing on an applicant's character. A test security office investigates possible cheating and a "Board of Review," consisting of senior executives, hears cases and decides whether or not to report the questioned scores or, if already reported, to notify the institution of their cancellation. ETS not only devises the procedures governing these inquiries but also holds the power of decision. As the candidate literature notes, "Educational Testing Service reserves the right to cancel any test score if, in the sole opinion of ETS, there is adequate reason to question its validity."[30] ETS knows full well what this action may mean. As ETS Vice President Robert E. Smith, then chairman of the Board of Review, wrote in a 1975 memo, "Notification of a score cancellation when made to an institution may raise questions concerning a candidate's character."[31]

In the resolution of cases of suspected cheating, cases which can affect a person's future at least as much as many kinds of legal trials, ETS acts as both judge and jury. Judicial standards of due process--such as the right to be present at the hearing on one's case, to have an advocate and to inspect all the evidence being used against one--do not apply to ETS test security inquiries.

Investigations may be initiated for several reasons, such as reports from test center supervisors of irregular behavior or reports from institutions of receipt of suspiciously high scores. Most cases, however, are initiated when ETS computers flag the files of candidates whose scores change by more than 250 points on SAT Math or Verbal (or 350 combined), 200 on GRE Verbal or Quantitative (or 300 combined), or 150 points on the Graduate Management Admission Test (GMAT), National Teacher Examination (NTE), or Law School Admission Test (LSAT).[32] Answer sheets of those who sat near the suspect are inspected for evidence of copying, and registration form signatures are scrutinized by in-house and outside handwriting analysts for evidence of impersonation.[33] According to former ETS director of test security Paul D. Williams, ETS has called high schools and colleges to obtain handwriting samples of the suspect, such as old school essays, test papers or forms, from the institution's files.[34] Williams stated in an interview that institutional officials sometimes provide derogatory information on the person under investigation along with the handwriting sample. He further stated that a call from ETS requesting access to a file usually brings results:

> Generally they /school officials/ say 'Well, it's not very, it's not exactly acceptable practice but I guess I can. . . .' And other times they'll say 'Sorry, the

policy of the president is not to give you a damn thing.' Fortunately, this doesn't happen often enough so that you really worry too much about it.[35]

This investigation takes place <u>before</u> ETS has decided that there may be grounds for score cancellation and before it has informed the candidate that they are the subject of inquiry.[36] Williams pointed out that most people who have their records scrutinized in this way are never charged, and never learn that it has happened.[37] When ETS determines that action is warranted, candidates get the news from ETS in a sternly worded letter[38] which, in the words of one former ETS attorney who helped develop the format, has been carefully drafted to "minimize the problems of libel accountability."[39] Suspects are offered the option of canceling their scores voluntarily and taking a free retest or submitting exonerating evidence to ETS.[40] It is up to ETS alone to determine whether the evidence is satisfactory; outside agencies have no role. In all programs except the LSAT--where the Law School Admission Council has requested special procedures--ETS rejects the involvement of arbitrators. According to Robert Smith, speaking for the Board of Review, "In the Board's view arbitration adds considerably to expenses but seems unlikely to improve the decisions made since the arbitrators are necessarily less acquainted with the information concerned."[41] In addition in the LSAT program, unlike the other major national programs, candidates may see the report prepared about them by the Board of Review and make comments on it which then are forwarded to institutions.[42]

In most ETS programs, after a score has been sent out and ETS decides to cancel it, the institution is informed of the cancellation without being told the reason why.[43] Since scores are sometimes cancelled due to an ETS scoring error--also without explanation as to why--this can create interesting problems of interpretation for institutions which must distinguish people who have been judged by ETS to have cheated and those who are victims of a clerical error. Williams explained this situation:

Q: When institutions are informed of a cancellation, you just tell them that the score is being canceled? You don't make any allusions to what the cause might be?

A: (Williams): That's right.

Q: What do those institutions generally think when they get a letter like that?

A: (Williams): If they've been doing business with us. . . . They would probably guess that was it.

Q: Guess that what was it?

A: (Williams): That there was some misconduct involved.[44]

The effect of the unappealable ETS security verdict can be devastating, indeed. It can go beyond the routine case of rejection due to a canceled score. One New England law student was expelled after successfully completing a year of studies when the school was notified that ETS had canceled the scores that had won him admission.[45] Another student, a Radcliffe graduate who had matriculated at the University of California at Berkeley Law School, had her future thrown into doubt when ETS told Berkeley that her score had been canceled. Berkeley put its own handwriting expert on the case. When he failed to reach a conclusive decision, she was permitted to stay.[46]

This student had had a long and arduous experience with the ETS security system. Although a superior academic performer, she suffered from severe test anxiety. She had taken the LSAT twice and scored very low, when she went to a psychology professor for coaching. After extensive work on test-taking technique and a strong dose of tranquilizers, she took the LSAT again and improved her score considerably. She believes that it may have been the tranquilizers which altered her handwriting enough for ETS to raise the charge of impersonation. Unlike most subjects of ETS security investigations, however, this one fought back. She brought suit against ETS to have her score reinstated. In the course of the case, it came out that one of the handwriting experts ETS had used to charge her with impersonation was the same individual who had attested to the authenticity of the forged Howard Hughes signature on the celebrated Clifford Irving check. She won her case, and filed a damage suit against ETS which is still pending.[47]

For most of those ETS investigates, however, such dramatic challenges are hardly practical. Placed in a position of maximum vulnerability without due process, they must rely ultimately on the discretion and sense of justice of their accusers at ETS. "They make or break you when you're applying to schools," reflected one student who had his scores delayed several months (causing automatic rejection by his first-choice school) before ETS cleared him, "I don't know why the government allows them to act with such a free hand."[48]

In ETS We Trust: The Corporation that Makes No Mistakes

The principle which underlies the ETS test security system is the same which determines the form of every aspect of the consumer's dealings with ETS: the individual is not to be given enforceable rights but is, instead, to trust in the beneficence of ETS. One result of this principle is ETS' presumption of its right, despite its non-profit educational status, to withhold from consumers, whose fees support its existence, a whole range of important information, from internal studies of information processing to their own corrected test papers. In an interview, ETS executive L. Lynwood Aris, now an Assistant Vice President, suggested that ETS had no obligation to provide such information.

Q: Well, if an individual feels that the services he purchased from ETS were not provided as the booklet stipulated they would be, what should they conclude about the manner in which ETS provides these services?

A: (Aris): Well, I guess if I were in such a situation as the purchaser of a service, I would be inclined to really ask whether this is an individual situation, or is it fairly widespread.

Q: How can they find out if it's fairly widespread?

A: (Aris): How can they find out? Why, I think in most of the testing programs which are our major activity, they would normally know other people who were taking the same test, have gone through the same procedure . . . did they also experience that kind of problem, or not? I think there is a fair amount of communications on individual campuses, and high schools and this sort of thing. . . . What experience are individuals having. I would not judge, I think, an organization on the basis of one instance.

Q: Yet these individuals should not be given access to materials which the organization itself compiles to see whether these problems are widespread?

A: (Aris): Well, I guess my judgment would be no, that there is adequate information available to individuals to make a judgment about how widespread. . . .

Q: What is that information?

A: (Aris): Communication with other people who are also buying the same service.[49]

This position has found one of its more curious expressions in the vigorous assertion of several ETS executives that consumers need not worry because ETS does not make mistakes. Bernard Tchorni, the ETS Vice President in charge of operations, gave the following responses to questions about error:

Q: What percentage of the reports that you send out are free of error?

A: (Tchorni): Free of error? One hundred per cent. We have this separate quality control system.

Q: You would estimate that one hundred per cent of these forms are error-free--in terms of the information ETS was given?

A: (Tchorni): You're saying in terms of the information ETS was given?

Q: Yeah.

A: (Tchorni): I would say, well, I don't say every one hundred per cent--I'm saying _practically_ one hundred per cent.[50]

Jean Kerr, the director of testing services, expanded on this claim:

Q: In your tenure in testing services, have you not been aware of any instances where the candidate has provided all the correct information on time, and for some reason ETS has not provided the service correctly. . . . Even in _one_ case?

A: (Jean Kerr): Well, I think that in terms of our reporting and our processing we have been virtually one hundred per cent correct. . . . I would say over the past few years, at least in my association with this division of operations, and that's really what I speak to, there have been virtually no errors.

Q: "Virtually no errors." Does that mean that to your knowledge there have been zero errors?

A: (Kerr): To my knowledge, yes.

Q: To what do you attribute this remarkable record?

A: (Kerr): Our ability to do things right.[51]

ETS finds ingenious ways to promote its desired image of near infallibility. In July of 1979, ETS public relations director Robert Moulthrop announced that ETS had informed an MBE candidate that his test had been incorrectly scored due to a "crinkle in the corner" of his answer sheet which disrupted the ETS scoring machine. The story had a notable twist. According to Newsday, Moulthrop asserted that "to his knowledge it was the first time a mechanical error interfered with the accuracy of computer corrections at the 31-year old testing service, which processes 12 million pieces of paper a year."[52]

In the internal discussions at ETS, however, the discrepancy between the company's public claims and its actual performance has long been a matter of concern. "Some serious public relations problems were generated this past year," noted the minutes of one 1972 meeting, "as a result of difficulties in processing LSDAS and SDQ."[53] At another meeting it was noted that "[A] task force to investigate various aspects of telephone service promises to introduce radical changes in the phone system in respect to written candidate inquiries. The existing machinery for responding to these inquiries is not adequate. As a result each failure to respond generates new inquiries."[54] Such problems have persisted. An ETS survey of LSAT consumers, for example, found that more than twenty per cent of those who had contacted ETS about their tests and application materials experience an "excessively slow or grossly inefficient" response or no response at all from ETS.[55] In the past, ETS anticipated such problems in dealing with candidates. Its operations manual even warned against hiring parents with college-age children or recent college graduates themselves to deal with complaints because "they may tend to be overly sympathetic."[56] Mechanical problems have occurred as well. In 1978, for example, a major ETS scoring error on the Graduate Management Admission Test came to light.[57] In 1979, thousands of candidates were turned away from test centers due to a foul-up in the distribution of LSAT test center admissions tickets.[58]

The overriding problem with ETS' information processing system is not so much that errors occur--this is to be expected in the delivery of any complex service--but that consumers have no way of discovering their occurrence and correcting them other than what ETS voluntarily decides to provide. Making scored answer sheets available to candidates (as provided for in New York's 1979 Truth-in-Testing Law) would facilitate systematic discovery of scoring mistakes. But, ETS has vigorously opposed such disclosure. This position is especially unfortunate in light of the federal Privacy Protection Study Commission's finding that test companies "sometimes have difficulty detecting the errors they do make."[59] The Privacy Commission summarized the test consumer's powerless position by noting that:

> [T]he oversight post-secondary institutions excercise over the operations of testing and data-assembly service organization tends to serve their own interests somewhat better than it does the interests of applicants. Thus, although such organizations deal directly with individual applicants, and collect and process mountains of information about them, they are less accountable to the individuals on whom they keep records than any other type of record-keeping institution in higher education.[60]

Beyond the Reach of Redress

Few of the usual avenues of redress are available to test consumers. For ETS' Robert Solomon, however, the means of justice open to ETS consumers are so many and self-evident that they hardly bear repeating. He developed this theme in an interview:

Q: What kind of redress can students seek if they are dissatisfied in some way with either the fact that they--

A: (Solomon): I would say they would have the right of redress that every citizen has--whatever those are.

Q: Specifically, how would they affect ETS? Are there any other agencies that the student can appeal to if they are somehow dissatisfied with the treatment they've received from ETS?

A: (Solomon): Well, I think there are, I think there are many. I'm not sure this a good use of our time because you know them as well as I do. First of all, once again, a student is, by definition, a member of an academic community. . . . So the first right of redress as a student is, is, is the channel, is the context in which the student is. Beyond that, a student may take suit, he may take legal action. He may, I,-- use all the other channels. He may appeal to consumer advocacy groups. He may write to all the various public interest groups who are interested, including the Congress and government agencies. . . .

Q: What government agencies?

A: (Solomon): Well, I don't, I, I'm afraid I don't, I mean I could repeat them but I think we are wasting our time because you know them and I know them.

Q: Well, for example. . . .

A: (Solomon): I'm not going to spend the next five minutes telling you that there are Congressional committees and the Federal Trade Commission and there is the Department of Health, Education and Welfare and various agencies in that and there is the Department of Justice, and I would think with some other activities we may do there may be other government agencies.[61]

Few citizens were in a better position to test the rights of ETS consumers—and the credibility of Mr. Solomon's assurances—than the Massachusetts constituents of Congressman Robert Drinan. Not only was Father Drinan a member of the House Judiciary Committee (which oversees the Justice Department) and the Government Operations Subcommittee on Commerce, Consumer and Monetary Affairs (which oversees the FTC and handles consumer rights for the House); he was also the former Dean of Boston College Law School. Drinan had acquired an insider's knowledge of the ETS test system during his tenure as a trustee of ETS' LSAT client group. In response to constituent complaints about ETS prices and treatment of consumers, Congressman Drinan wrote the Justice Department on March 4, 1976:

> It is clear that E.T.S. holds a monopoly position in a number of educational testing and data assembly markets.
>
> I would very much appreciate it if you would advise me whether E.T.S., in view of its monopoly power, behavior toward applicants to educational institutions, behavior toward educational institutions, and behavior toward potential competitors, may be in violation of the Sherman Act or other Federal Antitrust statutes.[62]

On April 15, 1976 Assistant Attorney General Thomas E. Kauper, head of the Antitrust Division replied for the Justice Department. Acknowledging ETS' monopoly power, Kauper asserted that: "ETS has a monopoly's special duty to treat its customers in a fair and equitable manner." The Justice Department also found that, in the case of a constituent complaint which Drinan forwarded, "The ETS personnel adopted a doctrinaire interpretation of their rules." Yet, Kauper concluded, the Justice Department could not take action against ETS on either count.[63]

The ETS monopoly was beyond his department's reach, said Kauper, because:

> It appears there can be only a limited number of testing services. While there is at least one other prominent college testing service (ACT), we agree that ETS is dominant in the field. However, since the market appears necessarily limited, an investigation into the possible acquisition or maintenance of monopoly power by ETS does not seem to be warranted.[64]

The ETS monopoly is not regulated by any public agency; the Office of Education has no authority over ETS testing practices,[65] and as a non-profit corporation, ETS is also exempt from the scrutiny of the Federal Trade Commission.[66] Daniel C. Schwartz, Assistant Director for Evaluation in the FTC Bureau of Competition, wrote to Congressman Drinan on February 25, 1976:

> [ETS] has been free to independently determine most of the details concerning its day to day operations. It is alleged that such decisions are sometimes made in an arbitrary and unfair manner.
>
> <u>It appears that the Federal Trade Commission lacks jurisdiction to deal with this issue, even if the alleged conduct might otherwise constitute a violation of the laws we administer.</u>[67] (Emphasis added.)

Schwartz continued:

> ... [I]t appears that [ETS] is a non-profit organization. The courts have held that the Federal Trade Commission does not have jurisdiction over alleged unfair and monopolistic methods of competition by non-profit associations on the basis that they are not a "person" within the meaning of the FTC Act.[68]

Although the Justice Department contends that ETS is exempt from antitrust law because the process of testing is somehow "naturally" conducive to monopoly, immunity from antitrust and consumer law has been applied solely to ETS, not to the testing industry in general. In 1957, for example, the FTC ordered the four largest profit-making companies--Psychological Corporation, Science Research Associates, World Book Company, and the California Test Bureau, all of which were and are several times smaller than ETS--to cease and desist from certain collusive and anticompetitive practices.[69]

Immunity for non-profit organizations was established by the courts in the matter of Community Blood Bank of Kansas City Area, Inc. vs. the F.T.C. This 1969 case concerned a Kansas City cooperative blood bank which allegedly used deceptive advertising to sign up members. The practices of the blood bank, like those of ETS, were found to be outside the jurisdiction of the FTC and federal law, since the organization did not have stockholders who received dividends from profits.[70] Thus, Congressman Drinan's efforts to secure redress for his constituents ended at the wall of ETS legal immunity.

Below the federal level, the situation is even more difficult for consumers. When the researchers of this report first approached ETS in the summer of 1974, ETS attorney Thomas Robinson advised that it would be "corporate suicide" for ETS to grant us access to employees; the study should be dropped, he said, and any "complaints" sent to the Attorney General of New York State. Since ETS was a corporation chartered in New York, the house counsel continued, the Attorney General had oversight responsibility for ETS activities.[71]

This came as a surprise to New York State Attorney General Louis Lefkowitz. On August 27, 1974 Lefkowitz and Assistant Attorney General Irwin Leibowitz wrote:

> . . . please be advised that the Educational Testing Service of Princeton, N.J. is under the jurisdiction of the N.Y. Department of Education. This office has no jurisdiction over the same, it being specifically exempted by statute from our supervision.[72]

When asked about ETS, the New York Board of Regents official who monitors non-profit corporations said that he did not know what ETS was. From the name, however, "I gather they're in educational testing of some sort." The Regents' files on ETS consisted of papers relating to ETS' 1947 incorporation, three letters from ETS announcing amendments to the corporate bylaws, and six letters from attorneys seeking confirmation of ETS' corporate status. Regents' counsel Michael Edre reported that, according to its records, the New York Board of Regents had not sent any letters to, made any inspection of, nor required any submissions from ETS in its twenty-seven year existence. The file did not contain any clippings or ETS annual reports. "From the information provided in the file you are looking at, can you tell anything about the size or activities of ETS?" Edre was asked. "No," he replied.[73]

Edre explained that the Board of Regents was mainly concerned with monitoring colleges, usually for financial solvency. Edre said that given the unique nature of ETS activities:

> we don't have any minimum requirements or guidelines that we have to meet. . . . They don't get involved with the kinds of programs we have bureaus to

supervise. . . . We don't keep an update on the financial status or who the trustees are. These are the kinds of things we could legally require them to submit, but in terms of the payments that would be involved it wouldn't be justified. We wouldn't have anything to do with the information once we got it.[74]

Edre concluded that if his office had ever supervised ETS, the actions would have been "negligible." "After all," he pointed out, "they're not running a college." "ETS, I guess, just sells their wares. The quality is not as important because the buyers can determine what they want."[75]

In New Jersey, home of ETS' Rosedale headquarters, the Secretary of State monitors non-profit corporations. ETS fulfills its public obligation by filing an "annual report," an 3" x 6" IBM card listing business address, trustees, date of next trustees' meeting, and an affirmation from the corporate secretary that ETS is in compliance with state corporation laws.[76]

According to the Secretary of State's files, which the office supervisor said nobody had ever read before, ETS did not file the required annual report between 1949 and 1959. When asked about this, the supervisor was not impressed; he stated:

It makes no difference. . . . We have thousands of non-profit corporations that haven't filed a report in twenty years and they're still good and active. All this doesn't prove anything. We don't chase nonprofit corporations. . . . The other day we had one that hadn't filed since 1898 and its still good and active. . . . They're nonprofit, we never try to catch them. . . . Why does this matter so much to you?[77]

With no channels of redress available to them in the public agencies that generally handle consumer grievances, ETS consumers are left with little alternative other than challenging in court ETS and its one-sided contract of adhesion. Consumers who attempt suit may have their grievances scrutinized by Washington, D.C.'s powerful corporate law firm, Wilmer, Cutler and Pickering, whose clients include General Motors, IBM, the pharmaceutical industry, and ETS.[78] In 1973, a Wilmer, Cutler legal team, led by full partner Howard Willens, responded to such a suit with a full-scale legal offensive. In nearly a year of litigation before the D.C. Superior Court, the Wilmer, Cutler attorneys, acting in defense of ETS, filed a docket of legal papers eight inches thick.[79] The adversary was Bruce C. French, age 23, a second-year law student handling his own case against ETS.[80] French had lost a semester from school when his attempted law school transfer from the University of Connecticut to Rutgers was aborted by an ETS records foul-up. He sued ETS for $8,000. Using techniques perfected in the service of their giant corporate clients, the Cutler firm inundated French with paper: interrogatories, challenges to his evidence, motions for summary judgment.[81]

After thousands of pages of legal micro-surgery, photocopy costs alone had drained French's modest budget. ETS, via the Cutler firm, settled out of court and compensated French for his lost time and legal costs with $250.[82]

ETS remains almost immune to public oversight. It has effectively moved beyond the reach of consumers whose lives may have been damaged by ETS errors or policies. This is what thousands of applicants to law school discovered in 1970-71 when ETS, after mishandling their applications, gave them a memorable post-graduate course in the definition of "unaccountability."

In the winter of 1970, a total of 82,481 law school applications from 52,759 students applying to over 150 law schools were delayed at ETS.[83] While they sat, the immediate prospects of thousands of American law school applicants were thrown into doubt.

The applications were at ETS because the Law School Admission Council (a group of ABA-accredited law schools organized by ETS) required it. Instead of applying directly to law school, candidates were now to send their grades and other applicant information to ETS. The ETS Law School Data Assembly Service (LSDAS) was supposed to standardize, analyze and send out the information to meet law school application deadlines.

According to an ETS program director involved with the program, ETS undertook the LSDAS on a crash basis and developed many of the procedures and systems as an unexpectedly large number of applications came pouring in.[84] LSDAS forms were piling up; ETS was not able to analyze and report them within the deadlines stated on ETS candidate brochures. Some forms never left ETS. Public relations executives say that their offices were "deluged" with calls from worried applicants, their parents, and their lawyers. At one point, an ETS investigation found a backlog of over 20,000 LSDAS forms an average of six weeks behind schedule.[85]

A confidential study of ETS law school programs by the consulting firm Peat, Marwick and Mitchell noted quietly: "The LSDAS programs were developed on a crash basis and may not be as efficient as they might have been with proper program planning."[86]

Six years later Executive Vice President Solomon became the first ETS official questioned under oath about an ETS mistake in processing consumer information. On November 12, 1976, members of the Federal Privacy Protection Study Commission asked Solomon to tell them what ETS had told the applicants back in 1970-71:

Q: (Senator Tennessen): One of the assertions yesterday dealt with the foul-up in 1970-71.

A: (Solomon): Yes.

Q: (Senator Tennessen): That does, I think, raise a serious problem dealing with those 15,000 phone calls from law students--hopeful law students. I guess the question dealing specifically with that foul-up was--or is, did ETS--or was ETS--able to straighten out the problem so that no students were denied the ability really to apply to a school or be considered by a school because you didn't supply the test in adequate time?

A: (Solomon): I think this does deserve some discussion. .../N/ either we nor the law schools were quite prepared for the volume of applications that flooded in. What we did was to try to notify the law schools as we began to get mired down in volume. We notified the law schools that, in fact, this system was not working adequately; and we advised them to accept directly, as they had in the past, student transcripts and student records so as to permit students another means of entry and consideration. <u>We also, when students called--and there were thousands of calls, we advised the students of the same thing. So we made every effort to make sure that despite the fact that the system wasn't working as well as it was supposed to, that students would not be denied an opportunity to have their credentials considered by the law schools to which they applied.</u>[87] (Emphasis added.)

There were, to be precise, 15,515 applicant calls and letters to the ETS Candidate Services office.[88]

The people responsible for dealing with upset candidates had been carefully trained. A training manual gave candidate service operators meticulous instructions "to ensure that the

Service Representatives handle each inquiry with tact and courtesy so that the caller will retain a high opinion of Educational Testing Service."[89] According to ETS correspondence and current and former ETS officials, ETS management reacted to the LSDAS foul-up by issuing a set of instructions which Mr. Solomon did not choose to share with the Privacy Commission.

Mrs. Beverly Lipps, who supervised the switchboard and passed the orders on to the operators, said:

> The training we received was not to make any definite statement that could be thrown back at you. . . . Anything that would have been a p.r. type answer. . . . At no time were we ever allowed to mention anything about the problems. We weren't even told about the problems, but we knew, because everything was so fouled up. . . . The biggest thing we claimed was that we hadn't received the transcripts.[90]

Operators accustomed to handling all test programs were moved to a special LSDAS switchboard set up to handle the unprecedented wave of calls.[91] "The girls hated the LSDAS calls," Mrs. Lipps remembers. "That was like punishment. The girls didn't like to always disappoint people. They always had to say, no we couldn't help. The response of the caller was constant abuse. Nobody likes to take that."[92]

Regardless of their instructions, operators often had no choice but to tell adamant candidates that ETS had not received their transcripts. The microfilm files they used to answer candidate questions, usually updated several times daily in heavy call periods,[93] were weeks behind, according to the operators involved. Transcripts sat in an ETS office while operators had to tell callers that ETS had not received their transcripts.

Sometimes the film would indicate that a transcript had been sent out while it was still sitting in the mailroom, often for weeks.

"Oh, you have no idea," Mrs. Lipps says. "I had fights with the upper echelons. I had kids on that phone who literally were crying, boys, grown boys who literally were crying. Oh, the real terror, they were in terror--it's hard enough to get into law school anyway. And we did absolutely nothing. . . . Their attitude was to cover it up."[94]

Routine denials of ETS error were established policy for answering candidates by phone or letter. "You stated in the March 7 letter that I should contact Holy Cross College in Worcester, Mass. a <u>third time</u> to make absolutely certain that my undergraduate transcript was sent to your office," wrote applicant Richard Terry in a letter to the ETS Candidate Relations head. But, Terry complained:

> I have a written statement from Eileen M. Tosney, Registrar at Holy Cross that such a transcript was forwarded to you in February. . . . I have communicated by telephone several times to Miss Tosney's office to make certain that her written communication was factual. Would you suggest that I obtain a sworn statement under the penalties of perjury from Miss Tosney at this juncture to satisfy your request that I recheck with Holy Cross again?[95]

Solomon testified in 1976 that ETS does not know how many applicants the LSDAS breakdown caused to be rejected out of hand: "I would honestly say that neither we nor anyone else knows whether there were any students that were literally denied an opportunity because of this. Honestly, I don't think we knew."[96]

A former ETS executive involved in the LSDAS incident estimates that up to 30,000 applications were endangered of the ETS foul-up.[97] One ETS program director commented, "Conservatively speaking, I'd have to say over 1,000 didn't get into law school in 1970-71, due to the problems ETS had in handling and processing the information and getting it mailed out. . . . I personally handled over a thousand complaints."[98] Current ETS Law School Program director John Winterbottom expressed skepticism about such estimates when confronted with the results of a Trenton Times investigation of LSDAS, but did not offer a different figure. "As far as the students that fell through the cracks they were just so botched up that we never heard about it," Dr. Winterbottom said. "That was just a bad scene, no question about it."[99]

Well after the LSDAS foul-up, ETS was still discussing the affair with considerable restraint. "There were some processing bottlenecks and delays last spring," the 1972 Annual Report noted in passing.[100] ETS flatly denied an October, 1974 report in New York magazine by Steven Brill that ETS had started the LSDAS prematurely. The denial, in point #49 of a fifty-five point rebuttal from Director of Information Services Jenne K. Britell, did not mention that program directors responsible for the program had privately affirmed precisely what Brill had reported.[101]

In his 1976 appearance before the Privacy Commission, Mr. Solomon reported that ETS disclosed the LSDAS foul-up to candidates who called and wrote.[102] When interviewed in the summer of 1975, Donald Schiariti of ETS' Candidate Services was not so certain:

Q: Were you head of candidate services when the LSDAS problems occurred?

A: (Schiariti): At one point. At one point.

Q: And, reportedly there were quite a few cases where ETS made a mistake in processing candidate applications. Did ETS tell each candidate who called up that it was an ETS mistake that was hindering their applications?

A: (Schiariti): I'm sorry, I can't remember.

Q: Were you the supervisor of the service representatives then? Were they under your jurisdiction?

A: (Schiariti): Well, the telephone people. Yes.

Q: And what kind of instructions did you give the telephone people regarding candidate inquiries about the LSDAS?

A: (Schiariti): I can't remember at this point in time.[103]

Like other ETS officials interviewed for this report, Mr. Schiariti was guided by the company's seventeen-point memo of instructions which noted, "Our lawyers have advised us that there are a number of possibilities for litigation arising out of any study of this kind. You should bear in mind that should there be a lawsuit, you could be called as a witness."[104] His corporate superior, Executive Director for General Programs Robert E. Smith, monitored his words. Corporate Counsel had briefed the interview subjects on prohibited topics and waited for a debriefing and analysis of the tape. Schiariti had this to say about the LSDAS problem:

Q: What do you remember about the LSDAS problems?

A: (Schiariti): Not much at this point in time. As I say, it's going back quite a few years.

Q: Do you remember getting calls from, do you remember speaking to any of the candidates involved personally?

A: (Schiariti): No, I don't.

Q: Were people upset?

A: (Schiariti): (thirty-five second pause) I would have to answer that yes and no. Let me explain. Were people upset? People are upset if they think something is wrong, if they think possibly ETS made an error. . . . Of course they're upset because they think something went wrong. I'd have to state it in the same context as, you know, in the other programs.

Q: To the best of your knowledge did ETS make an error regarding processing of the '70-'71 LSDAS forms?

A: (Schiariti): I don't know.

Q: Did ETS candidate services give candidates who were inquiring about the LSDAS problems a full and accurate account of what was happening?

A: (Schiariti): I can't remember at this point in time.

Q: You can't, you can't recall?

A: (Schiariti): No.[105]

Despite ETS' long-standing reluctance to release information on the debacle, some college officials found, from the beginning, a pattern in ETS explanations of LSDAS foul-ups: "We have had several situations such as yours during the past few months," wrote Donovan Parker, Associate Registrar of Minnesota's St. Olaf College, to one LSDAS consumer.

> The demands for service from LSDAS have apparently been beyond anything they could foresee and I understand they are sorely pressed. Although I can understand some of their problems in handling so many different files, I do not appreciate the way they inform their customers that "a transcript has not been received from St. Olaf College." We are immediately accused of not having fulfilled our function of sending transcripts promptly. Apparently it occurs to few students that the fault could be on the other end.[106]

College officials were not alone in doubting ETS' public explanations. Commenting on Mr. Solomon's assertion under oath that ETS told candidates about the LSDAS errors, Mrs. Lipps contended:

> It's not true. I could swear . . . they did not tell students there were problems. The reason I know is that I did have total control and total knowledge as to what the answers were to phone inquiries. And we did not, and I did not instruct the girls to answer candidates in that way. That is not what I was instructed by my supervisor . . . and that is not what I instructed the girls. . . . Nobody ever said there was a problem here, never. That I could swear to.[107]

Thus, when its policies, practices and methods are questioned, ETS uses tactical defenses, secrecy, manipulation of the facts and even deceptions. The case made is long on assertions and short on evidence to support ETS' claims of accountable behavior. While product failures and the urge to conceal them may be routine in many large corporations, what sets ETS apart is that there is no recourse for test consumers damaged by ETS errors or corporate strategies. And, ETS pays no price for its actions. The only major damage that can be done to ETS by its failure to provide adequate service is the harm which exposure of such incidents could do to the corporate image. In those circumstances, even given the best of intentions on the part of company executives, attention gravitates more toward concealing information to safeguard ETS' power and prestige than toward insuring the satisfaction of those who take its tests.

As the gatekeeper to educational and career opportunities, the credibility of ETS is essential for its survival; even a suggestion of doubt must be erased. As long as the credibility is maintained, educational and other institutions continue to use the ETS testing service, in effect creating ready-made customers for ETS tests. These consumers pay the highest price, for without access to the facts, without due process, and without the means to hold ETS accountable, the test-takers remain the captives of ETS.

CHAPTER VIII

INSIDE ETS: THE SOFT INSTITUTION

Many corporations plan for emergencies, but ETS does more. ETS has plans for carrying on the science of mental measurement in the event that America, or most of it, is annihilated in an atomic holocaust. Article I, Section 11 of the ETS bylaws states explicitly:

> During any emergency period following a national catastrophe due to enemy attack, a majority of the surviving members of the Board who have not been rendered incapable of acting, or prevented from attending the meeting of the Board either due to physical or mental injury or incapacity or due to the difficulty of transportation to the place of meeting, shall constitute a quorum for the transaction of all business of the Corporation.[1] . . .

The image of a hardy band of industrialists and educators making their way to Rosedale through the rubble of a dying civilization is more than sobering. It suggests an organization which was created to endure.

The founders of ETS believed that national testing was too important to be left to the uncertainties of politics and competition. Two years before the merger which formed ETS, one of the consolidation planners, William S. Learned of the Carnegie Foundation staff, envisioned a new corporation whose interests would be defined from the start as identical to those of society as a whole:

> The chief advantage to be foreseen and striven for is not mere economy of organization, great as this would be. Nor is it financial gain, although this might also be substantial. The all-important aspect of such unification /of testing organizations/ is intellectual, as should be the case when we are seeking the best

294

> interests of our national educational establishment. For us in the United States the true focal point of an examining body in education is identical with the need of the country as a whole.[2]

Mr. Learned cautioned that such an organization could not be created or sustained by the free play of the market, asserting that among uncoordinated agencies, "the ensuing scramble for business is likely completely to distort the long view of service that is needed."[3]

He further argued that the corporation should avoid becoming "the handmaid of any other organization to whose 'larger' policies it might from time to time be subordinated. . . . Its trustees, few at best, should naturally be drawn from no special group or area."[4]

In 1947, noting that "an era of competition loomed at the very time when, for the best interests of testing, it was important that the activities of . . . /the/ agencies be coordinated and integrated,"[5] the Carnegie Foundation, the College Board and the American Council on Education consolidated their separate testing programs to form ETS. They had made a decision in Henry Chauncey's words, to "subordinate self-interest and prestige in the furtherance of an ideal."[6] They had conceived a mission--that of measuring the minds of a nation--which they said transcended economic and political interests. And, to pursue this mission, they created a corporation designed to transcend such interests as well.

The Educational Testing Service was a new species of corporate organization, a "soft institution" which combined the techniques and wealth of industry with the privileges and immunities of non-profit education, all beneath the mantle of serving the public good. Insulated from many of the legal and economic obligations which constrain most corporate managers, and shielded politically by a mission under which each act of expansion is by definition an act of benevolence, ETS has become one of the nation's fastest-growing and most profitable corporations. To an extent unmatched by other forms of large-scale organization--private corporation, college, foundation, union, government agency--the soft institution operates beyond the reach of economic choice or political will. As an organization endowed by its creators with the right to perform a function central to millions of lives, the ETS test system has been built to absorb shocks from below and outlive the people it serves.

"This exceptional anointed organization," is how one Rosedale visitor, Rutgers University business administration professor Richard Marshall, characterized ETS' unique position of corporate privilege. In a seminar for ETS program direction staff entitled, "ETS--Free Agent or UFO," Marshall argued that ETS defied description in conventional business terms. "In the regular business world," said the ETS Examiner in its account of Marshall's presentation, "a stockholder who doesn't like the way management operates can sell his stock. ETS is different . . . /Marshall/ said, 'because the power lies entirely on the inside. I wonder what you can do if you don't like ETS.'" Marshall's observation hit home with some ETS professionals. According to the Examiner:

> Tony Glockler of LSAT pointed out that in actuality, for many programs ETS is paid by a client group which in turn collects a fee from students.

> [Senior researcher Ronald] Flaugher drew an analogy between ETS and the Krupp dynasty. "They made war machines and said 'we're not responsible for how they're used--we just make the best possible.'"
>
> . . . Joe Williams of General Programs cited ETS' unique responsibility as "gatekeeper" along the road of educational, and consequently, economic opportunity.
>
> Picking up on the gatekeeper reference, [Professor] Marshall said "the harshness of the results is the important thing when you affect a person's chance to enter the economic mainstream."[7]

ETS, Marshall pointed out, was operating outside the usual system of checks and balances "where the mere pressure and force of competition paints the white line of behavior." Instead, he said ETS was an "organization . . . created on the trust principle."[8]

Even if the idea was never stated explicitly, ETS bore all the characteristics of an organization built on the assumption that the desirability of sorting millions of careers with aptitude tests was no longer an open question. The appropriateness of the ETS mission was not a matter to be decided by consumer choice or public participation; the corporation was structured to operate beyond the reach of both.

It was a corporation designed to shape people's lives not with the hard imperatives of economic pull or legal coercion --the familiar tools of corporations and the state --but with the soft, firm persuasion of benevolent authority. It would operate on a massive scale, much as the College Board did according to Sidney Marland's description, "in the public interest as a large and powerful socio-educational force, 'doing good without gain.'"[9]

Non-Profit Privileges

As the dominant firm in an industry of about 300 testing companies--most of them profit-making[10]--ETS bears little economic resemblance to the schools, hospitals, churches and civic groups comprising the bulk of non-profit enterprises. Unlike the local garden club, ETS is in the business of selling consumer products on a national scale. It moves aggressively into interstate commerce to fulfill the obligation under its bylaws to "promote . . . the use of testing at all levels."[11]

But unlike a profit-making business, ETS does not have to contend with the demands and legal rights of stockholders, the prospect of outside takeover, state or federal income taxation, federal antitrust or consumer protection enforcement or public oversight of its primary line of business. Its freedom from antitrust jurisdiction facilitates the establishment of client relationships which help insulate ETS from the marketplace of consumer choice.

These privileges and immunities derive from ETS' non-profit, non-stock legal status. For although it controls more than $45 million in assets,[12] ETS is a corporation nobody owns. According to corporate counsel John Kramer, ETS "has no shareholders or other persons with any ownership interest in it."[13] Under its bylaws, ETS trustees and officers are merely agents retained to manage "the property, business and affairs of the Corporation."[14] They are custodians; "the Corporation" is the owner. And as Article I, Section I of the bylaws makes clear, "The Corporation shall not have members."[15]

With no shareholders, ETS is immune from accountabilities and risks of public ownership--from stockholder resolutions to dissident candidates for the board of directors to public disclosure under Securities and Exchange Commission regulations. Since there are no stockholders to conduct elections, the ETS Board elects its own successors, freeing the Board from outside influence.[16]

In addition, as a corporation nobody owns, ETS has been a corporation which nobody can buy. In the late 1960s and early 1970s, a wave of mergers swept the American economy as conglomerates such as ITT and diversifying giants such as Textron bought controlling shares of the stock of cash-rich growth companies, sometimes over heated objections from the executives of the firms being absorbed. In ETS' own industry, two of the eight major testing firms were swallowed up by larger competitors: the Psychological Corporation by Harcourt Brace Jovanovich, and the California Test Bureau by McGraw Hill.[17] In such a climate, ETS--amassing such yearly sales growth rates as 30.3 per cent (1965-66), 14.3 per cent (1969-70), and 20.4 per cent (1971-72)--could have been an especially inviting target.[18] "If Princeton N.J.'s Educational Testing Service were a public /stock issuing/ company and not a self-contained tax-exempt nonprofit organization," Forbes magazine wrote, "it would probably have long since emerged as one of the darlings of Wall Street."[19]

In addition to its non-profit charter from the New York State Board of Regents, ETS has been granted exemption from federal income tax under section 501 (c) (3) of the Internal

Revenue Code. ETS is still permitted, however, to engage in a limited amount of "non-exempt" business unrelated to its educational and test mission.[20] ETS may also join forces with profit making companies to market its products, as it did in 1976 with Addison-Wesley for promotion of ETS' Cooperative Tests for elementary school children.[21]

Besides augmenting its revenues with profit-making businesses, ETS has sought to protect that revenue with imaginative devices for limiting tax liability. Because ETS is chartered in New York but operates in New Jersey, New Jersey law has required it to pay property taxes despite its non-profit status. The 400-acre Rosedale campus makes ETS the second largest taxpayer in Lawrence Township, New Jersey.[22] While some might think of Rosedale as a place of testing and education, during the early 1970s, ETS tax lawyers successfully portrayed the legal fiction of a Rosedale where staff members roamed the forests and tilled the soil. New Jersey had passed a Farmland Assessment Act which lowered assessments on farms and woodlands in order to lighten the tax burden on farmers and protect rural lands from hasty development. ETS seized the opportunity by claiming that Rosedale, which was in no danger of being turned into a shopping center, was in fact a farm, entitled to tax relief. ETS sold the grass cut from its frequently-manicured lawns to a local sod company at a cost slightly above the legal minimum needed to qualify as being engaged in agriculture.[23] It also cut several cords of wood each year and sold them to Rosedale employees, thereby legally adding forestry to ETS' other lines of business. Thus, in 1973, by meeting the legal minimum of $500 worth of grass and wood, ETS reduced the assessment on its land by more than $400,000 and its property tax bill by $25,000.[24]

This disturbed local resident Len DiDonato who suspected that, as a Lawrence Ledger editorial had coolly noted, "It is doubtful that ETS needs the $500 to keep afloat in the corporate world."[25] ETS financial vice president David Brodsky had long maintained the Township was fortunate that ETS was paying any property taxes, since, as "a nonprofit educational organization concerned with the 'mental improvement' of citizens," ETS was not obligated to do so.[26]

DiDonato was not impressed. He challenged the ETS farmland assessment before the Mercer County Tax Board. Lawrence Township assessor Robert Immordino supported DiDonato's case and testified that ETS was not engaged in bonafide agriculture. The Board agreed, and raised the ETS assessment by $479,100.[27] The ETS Examiner responded with a front page picture captioned, "Who Says Its Not a Farm?" which showed a bucolic harvest scene "on Rosedale acerage as the 1973 crop of hay was being baled for sale."[28]

No such fencing is necessary in ETS' dealings with the federal government. Its testing and service programs are beyond federal regulatory jurisdiction. When ETS Corporate Counsel John Kramer was asked about an ETS Office of Information Services release which claimed that "ETS activities are audited extensively and continually by . . . the federal government,"[29] Kramer conceded that this oversight was limited to ETS' role as an employer and federal contractor (the IRS monitors ETS' compliance with unemployment compensation rules, the Equal Employment Opportunity Commission with affirmative action policies, the Defense Contract Audit Agency with spending guidelines on ETS' defense contracts, and the Department of Health, Education and Welfare--now the Department of Education--with rules on the privacy of research subjects), as opposed to the testing activities which generate ninety per cent of ETS income.[30] These programs, and the income they generated, were, from the government's point of view, a private matter between ETS and its accountants.

As discussed in Chapter VII, ETS' privileged position extended to antitrust and consumer protection enforcement. As Congressman Drinan learned in 1976, the Justice Department[31] and the Federal Trade Commission[32] both felt that ETS' status as an educational, non-profit organization put the corporation outside of their reach.

ETS and the Client Organizations

With its freedom from antitrust scrutiny, ETS has been able to construct a system of client groups connected to ETS. This arrangement helps insulate the company from public criticism and the rigors of competitive bidding. For most of its major programs, ETS is ostensibly an agent which merely carries out the policies of its clients. The clients are styled as representing entire levels of education, such as colleges or graduate schools. According to the 1975 report "Educational Testing Service: Students, Institutions, and Programs":

> The /client/ boards, their process of election, and their governance are independent of ETS. Each of the policy groups is representative of and elected by the educational

constituency it serves. The decision to use ETS services
rests, in each instance, with the educational institutions
and their representatives. Moreover, ultimate review of
these programs rests with the educational community that
uses them.[33]

"ETS is accountable to its client groups such as the College Board and the Law School Admission Council," the corporation wrote in a 1979 memo opposing federal "Truth-in-Testing" legislation, "and ultimately to their constituencies--the thousands of colleges, graduate and professional schools that opt to use the tests."[34]

Contrary to ETS claims, however, the client groups are not independent organizations which have chosen ETS from a field of competitors. In contrast to the usual client-agent relationship, for major ETS programs the clients, with the exception of the College Board, were <u>created</u> by ETS to sponsor programs ETS already owned. In 1949-50 complete ownership of the National Teacher Examinations program was transferred to ETS by the American Council on Education, one of ETS' founders; ETS then established an NTE advisory committee to oversee the program.[35] In 1953-54, ETS created the client boards for both the LSAT and the Admissions Test for Graduate Study in Business (ATGSB; now called the Graduate Management Admissions Test, or GMAT), two programs which it already owned.[36] In 1966, ETS convened the Graduate Record Examinations Board to sponsor the GRE.[37] ETS has organized similar boards for the Secondary School Admissions Test (SSAT), the Graduate and Professional School Financial Aid Service (GAPSFAS), the Test of English as a Foreign Language (TOEFL), and even for its national auto mechanic's certification exam.[38]

One former ETS official explained the strategy to the Trenton Times:

> Bob Solomon . . . had a brilliant managerial stroke in 1966, . . . He had the foresight to see that ETS might be coming under the gun for different accountability contingencies and cries for closer scrutiny in the future. So, Bob went ahead and initiated the idea of setting up the various councils and boards with very elaborate internal checks and balances which would hinder them from coming out and challenging ETS. Then, if someone said to ETS, "say, you monolithic testing Goliath you, who do you answer to?," he could point to the boards and councils and say, "We answer to them."[39]

As ETS Vice President Henry Dyer wrote in the 1974 Annual Report, "ETS has adhered to its original policy of seeking the sponsorship of user-organizations. . . . In 1949-50, ETS sponsored 41 percent of its own programs. That figure dropped to 33 percent by 1960-61 and, since then, has plummeted to approximately 13 percent."[40] A former ETS attorney who incorporated one of the client boards recalled during an interview for this report that when interest in forming a client group didn't surface from the educators requiring the test, ETS "drummed together a group of users" and set up a sponsoring organization.[41]

Although the client groups enjoy varying degrees of autonomy, whatever authority they hold is granted under terms set by ETS as the owner of the test questions. The ETS program directors manual stresses the importance of retaining this ultimate source of control:

> Although all of our clients may not share the same spirit of willingness exhibited by ETS's founding organizations to pool for the common good such resources as test items, a brief explanation to a prospective client of this philosophy behind the forming of ETS may go a long way toward a better understanding of why ETS seeks to retain ownership of materials. . . . [W]hy does he [the client]

think he needs to hold copyright? . . . There are other ways, short of giving away copyright ownership, of dealing with a client's concerns. . .[42]

The Graduate Record Examinations Board is one example of ETS client group structure. The seventeen member Board is elected by members of the Association of American Universities and the Council of Graduate Schools. The Board meets twice a year for about two days each time. It has subcommittees which meet with similar frequency. Though it makes policy recommendations, and, according to Board Secretary Maryann Lear, has been known to reject the advice of ETS staff, it does not have the option of taking the GRE program to another company, since it belongs to ETS. "Should the Board, for example, be dissolved," Lear says, "ETS would then get the tests back . . . the tests are the property of ETS."

The Board is not incorporated and therefore has no formal contract with ETS. Its powers are set out in a "compact" drafted in 1968 in cooperation with ETS. Since the Board is not an incorporated entity, it files no separate IRS return; all GRE program income legally belongs to ETS. The Board has no professional staff of its own aside from its Secretary, Lear, who is hired and paid by ETS. ETS has custody of the GRE Board files. Information on GRE operations and policy options is provided to the Board by ETS staff. When the Board sponsors research on the GRE or other topics in graduate admissions, it is conducted by ETS research staff; according to Lear, outside researchers participate "only in collaboration with ETS." On legal matters, the Board is advised by ETS counsel.[43]

Although GRE Board members may hold some influence at ETS--through simple protocol if not legal standing--the same cannot be said for individual schools. Their rights to scrutinize the inner working of the programs they ostensibly sponsor are not essentially different from those of student consumers: non-existent, except insofar as ETS decides to grant them. When interviewed for this report, ETS Vice President for Higher Education, Career Programs and Law Programs Richard Burns explained the ETS obligation to individual schools:

Q: If an individual graduate institution which uses the GRE and other graduate services, if they ask for various internal ETS documents relating to the services which they use, will they receive those documents?

A: (Burns): You're talking about individual institutions?

Q: Yes.

A: (Burns): I would doubt it.

Q: Why is that?

A: (Burns): Because in order to operate any kind of organization, you have to retain a certain proprietary . . . rights to the documents that are involved in the operation of that activity. . . .

Q: Would you care to comment on the degree of disclosure of information about how ETS operates the College and University Programs?

A: (Burns): No, I wouldn't.[44]

ETS and the College Board

The one major client board which has not been convened, organized or incorporated by ETS is the College Board (formerly known as the College Entrance Examination Board). Though the Board, unlike the other client groups, has its own substantial staff, it is bound to ETS by a series of interlocks and, until recently, restrictive contract clauses. The College Board existed long before ETS, having been "founded in 1900 as a voluntary organization to provide direction, coordination and research in helping students move from school to college."[45] "The Board's traditional role between 1900 and 1948," then College Board president and ETS trustee Frank Bowles wrote, "had been the administration of college entrance examinations on behalf of its members."[46] But that changed in 1948 when ETS opened its doors. "This was . . . the time," Bowles wrote, "when the Board's chief raison d'etre had just been transferred to the newly organized Educational Testing Service."[47]

In turning its chief "raison d'etre" over to the new organization, the College Board maintained close ties. The College Board President is an ex officio trustee of ETS, and the ETS president is an ex officio trustee of the College Board;[48] College Board membership requires a college to use one of the Board's test and service programs,[49] which are run by ETS.

In an agreement between the Board and ETS dated December 31, 1964, which was still in force as late as February, 1975, their binding mutual relationship was spelled out explicitly:

9. So long as this Agreement is in effect, ETS will not, except with the approval of CEEB, undertake either for its own account or for any other agency any other supervised testing service for the selection of secondary school students for admission to institutions of higher education.

10. So long as this Agreement is in effect CEEB will not, except with the approval of ETS engage in testing services either directly or through any organization or agency other than ETS.

> 11. This Agreement shall continue in effect unless
> and until terminated in accordance with the
> following: This Agreement may be terminated by
> either party hereto as of December 31 in any
> year by delivery of written notice to that
> effect to the other party on or before December 31
> of the third preceeding year. . . .[50]

Among profit-making firms such agreements between two companies to restrict their business options are known as "tying agreements" and are often struck down as being anti-competitive practices in violation of Section 1 of the Sherman Anti-Trust Act.[51] For the College Board and ETS, however, these have long been routine aspects of daily business.

On July 1, 1975, a revised basic agreement between ETS and the College Board went into effect. As with other client groups, ETS retained ownership of the tests.[52] A summary dated July 17, 1975 outlined the other terms of their relationship:

> 1-. . . CEEB has primary responsibility for planning, setting program policy and performance objectives, and for dissemination of programs and field support activities. ETS's primary responsibilities include program design, prototype development, and operation of the programs. ETS is also obliged to fulfill CEEB's needs for program research and development (R & D) services. CEEB has the exclusive right to set examination dates and program fees, but agrees not to change fees without consulting with ETS.[53]

The financial dealings of the two corporations were entwined another step, with a guarantee that the College Board would take two per cent of its annual income from ETS programs and spend it on College Board research--<u>to be performed by ETS</u>. Continued the summary:

> . . . To help insure that adequate resources will be available for CEEB R&D work during the three years ending June 30, 1979, CEEB agrees to budget for R&D work at ETS in each of those years an amount equal to 2% of the

prior year's income from the programs ETS conducts in CEEB's behalf. These budgetary commitments are subject to control of CEEB trustees, however, "having in mind their overall responsibilities for CEEB finances." ETS in turn, accepts the obligation to provide the staff and supporting services necessary to fulfilling its responsibility as the principal agency for CEEB R&D during this period.[54]

By 1979, however, with growing press and legislative interest in the power of ETS and its relationship with the College Board, attorneys for the two organizations had become more cautious about what they put down on paper. The College Board-ETS Agreement, which became effective on January 1, 1979, dropped the tying agreement and two per cent research clauses.[55] Instead, it included pointedly worded passages on the Board's right "to find alternate sources of services" and "to use sources other than ETS for R&D work."[56] Beneath the disclaimers, however, the contracts for administration of all Board national testing and service programs remained with ETS. The Board agreed "not to change fees without consulting with ETS," and, most importantly, "proprietary ownership of various materials used by ETS in the conduct of Board programs (e.g., tests and test items, answer sheets, supervisor manuals, computer systems, etc.) /remained/ vested in ETS."[57]

The ETS-College Board contract derives from a long relationship which began with CEEB contributing $300,000, its Princeton office facilities, and the rights to its testing programs as part of the founding assets of ETS.[58] It continued with the College Board contributing $7,600,000 in "capital gifts" to ETS from 1957 through 1970.[59] The capital was accumulated from profits on SAT, Achievement Tests, and other test fees, and was used to build up and expand ETS' Rosedale facilities. Today, the College Board receives ninety per cent of its income from ETS programs--compared to less than one per cent from dues from its institutional members--and has a staff roughly one-tenth the size of the ETS staff.[60]

During the past ten years, at least three College Board Vice Presidents have moved over to ETS, although none have moved in the other direction.[61] The two organizations are joined by a telephone tie line and daily messenger service (the College Board occupies a suite in a skyscraper on 7th Avenue in New York City, about two hours from ETS headquarters). College Board professionals, whose salaries are equivalent to those of ETS executives and who enjoy similar travel, benefit, and expense-account perquisites, owe their standard of living to the money-making operations of ETS;[62] but some are still wistful about the relationship with the organization forty-eight years its junior. It's "like the Greek myth of the parent consumed by the child," reflects one College Board professional.[63]

As one of the only ETS client groups with a large staff, the College Board has the ability to independently scrutinize the existing testing system. In practice, however, the interests, policies, and even planning committees of the two organizations are often one and the same.[64]

In 1978, then College Board President and ETS Trustee Sidney P. Marland, discussed the relations between ETS and the College Board. Marland told the Wall Street Journal that his two corporations, "are careful to . . . /remain/ at arms length, friendly though we are."[65] This was not the position taken by the companies' internal policy statements. In a "Joint Statement to Staff From the Presidents of ETS and CEEB," on December 15, 1972, following renegotiation of the ETS-CEEB contract, William Turnbull and Marland's predecessor, Arland F. Christ-Janer, announced the formation of a high-level Joint Administrative Committee*, a new "incentive fee" contract, and the beginning of a new era of "interdependence."

> We . . . have agreed to financial arrangements in the CEEB/ETS contract under which ETS and CEEB will share the risks and the rewards of their common enterprise.
>
> . . . The two organizations, as never before, stand to prosper or suffer according to the success of their joint venture. /Original emphasis./
>
> . . . The JAC /Joint Administrative Committee/ will be composed of the two presidents, the two executive vice presidents, the CEEB administrative vice president, and the ETS vice president for CEEB programs. The latter will be designated as executive officer for the Committee. . . .

---

* In a new basic agreement, effective July 1, 1975, a formal Joint Planning Committee "composed of senior officers of the two organizations" was established. Its responsibilities were to "facilitate communication between CEEB and ETS, to achieve increased economy and efficiency through joint planning and collaboration, and to coordinate the development of new CEEB services. Of particular interest to JPC is research and development. . . ."[66]

> . . . Consensus on questions of joint concern will always be the goal. If, however, consensus cannot be achieved the two presidents will decide.
>
> Establishment of the JAC expresses our conviction that new working relationships between CEEB and ETS are imperative. <u>Instead of dealing with each other like contractors at arm's length we shall collaborate like joint venturers</u> who, while retaining independent status, work in the closest cooperation possible. . . . /Emphasis added.7
>
> We hope this forthright acknowledgement of interdependence, the open discussion, and the spirit of mutual trust which enabled us to reach these new agreements will now characterize relationships between our two organizations. . . .[67]

A few months later, under a plan reviewed by the Joint Administrative Committee, ETS and the College Board decided to "join forces administratively" in five of their regional offices. "President William Turnbull reported that one ETS vice president and two College Board vice presidents will be put in charge of newly coordinated ETS-CB operations in three areas of the country," the ETS <u>Examiner</u> stated.[68] For two organizations that were "careful to . . . /remain/ at arms length" the new program promised an unusual degree of centralization. "'For instance,' he /Turnbull/ explained, 'the new arrangement will relieve schools and colleges of the inevitable confusion as to which of the two offices they should approach with a particular problem. To date, each office has had part of the whole picture. This should help put the whole picture together.'"[69]

The tax exemption, the freedom from stockholder and public oversight, the tight relationships with the College Board and the other client groups are only the most tangible privileges. Less specific but perhaps more important benefits derive from the political cover provided by ETS' avowed mission. Profit-making companies can be accused of making deceptive claims or of cheating workers and consumers to make a few extra dollars. But ETS is above such reproach. Its techniques might be controversial, but the institutional purpose beneath them is seemingly invulnerable to political attack. "As a nonprofit organization serving education," wrote President Turnbull in the 1973-74 ETS Annual Report, "ETS is concerned with everyone involved in the learning-teaching process. . . . Put more simply, our professional and technical services are intended to help people grow and learn throughout their lives."[70]

What reasonable person could quarrel with such a goal? Unlike a profit-making firm whose first responsibility is to make money for its owners, ETS is, ostensibly, an organization devoted not to profit but to service--its interests are simply to serve the interests of the individual. ETS, after all, has no owners and issues no stock; it is "operated exclusively for educational purposes."[71] Declaring itself open to all suggestions on how to serve the individual better, ETS assures that there is always room for discussion of ways to do this--a discussion in which ETS, as an impartial benefactor committed to the general good, reserves the final right of decision. By framing all questions in this manner, ETS can transform even the hardest political challenges into leisurely debates among colleagues.

The Business of Mental Measurement

Unlike many prominent educational institutions, ETS is not having financial difficulties at the turn of the decade.

With colleges and universities granting what the ETS staff has called "a taxing privilege"[72] to ETS over captive consumers, the corporation has grown into the IBM of the testing industry. Although it is an extremely profitable company[73]--as shall be seen shortly--ETS' exceptional power does not derive from the control of vast sums of money. In fiscal 1979, ETS grossed $94 million.[74] --an amount grossed by General Motors twice a day.[75] For most profit-making companies, generating income is the end; for ETS, it is only the means to its larger objectives as theorist and gatekeeper for the educational and career opportunities of millions of people. Distinct from most corporations, ETS' income figures greatly understate its influence. Few companies in history have had so much effect with so small a cash flow.

In eight of its top ten testing markets, ETS has no competition. In the other two top markets it controls well over half of each market.[76] ETS' largest direct competitor is the American College Testing Program (ACT) of Iowa City, a non-profit organization which administers forty per cent of college admissions tests--mainly for guidance purposes at nonselective schools.[77] The ACT does not actually score and report its own tests but contracts with Westinghouse Datascore Systems[78] for these purposes. With 2,300 employees and activity at all levels of educational and professional testing, ETS dwarfs both the ACT and its profit-making competitors.[79] These include Harcourt Brace Jovanovich, Inc., which markets "somewhat over 100 titles" through its subsidiary, Psychological Corporation, and other, smaller, firms such as Houghton Mifflin Company, which has about thirty-five major tests.[80]

The growth of ETS and its counterparts in the testing industry has not been based on major breakthroughs in psychometric technique. On October 28, 1977, Dr. Oscar K. Buros, the dean of American psychometricians, told a gathering of his colleagues that standardized testing had made few scientific advances in the course of his fifty-year career: ". . . We don't have a great deal to show for fifty years of work," said the founder and editor of the authoritative Mental Measurement Yearbook and winner of the ETS Award for Distinguished Service to Measurement. Moreover, he continued, ". . . The improvements--except for the revolutionary electronic scoring machines and computers-- have not been of enough consequence to permit us to have pride in what we have accomplished. . . . In fact, some of today's tests may even be poorer /than those of 1927/. . . ."[81]

If, as Buros believed, the science of his profession had failed to make advances in the fifty years since he began reviewing tests systematically, the same could not be said of the promotion of those tests. For, while the science of mental measurement has stagnated since the era of Calvin Coolidge and C.C. Brigham, the business of standardized testing has flourished.

B. Alden Thresher, the former MIT admissions director, who was an incorporator of the College Board and an ETS trustee, wrote in a report to the College Board:

> The automobile has been characterized as an engineering success but a scientific failure. Something of the same dichotomy of attributes is manifest in the standardized test. . . . Both devices owe their luxuriant growth more

to the American genius for mass production and marketing than to any notable originality exhibited in their development since they reached these shores.[82]

ETS mastered the technique of mass producing and processing large numbers of tests early in its history. Due to automation and careful study of paper processing techniques, it has been able to handle increasing candidate volumes with proportionately smaller and smaller shares of its staff devoted to test development and processing, and has thus been able to shift its resources toward management and promotional activities. In 1949 non-professionals comprised more than eighty percent of the ETS staff.[83] By 1972, they made up only about half of the workforce.[84] With the exception of the examiners who write test questions and the statisticians who analyze them, test production is primarily the job of non-professionals. By 1978, even the group of professional examiners writing and reviewing ETS tests comprised less than 4.0 percent of the ETS staff.[85] In place of many of these test-production-oriented staff members was placed a corps of professional public relations specialists, program directors, authors of corporate literature and field representatives, who never actually touched a test. Instead, they represented ETS and its products to institutions that required the tests and individuals who took them.[86]

ETS has long been aware of the importance of creating demand for its products. As early as 1949, Henry Chauncey had begun a program of promotional mailings to tens of thousands of influential individuals and institutions around the world.[87] In its promotional efforts, ETS has been aided by certain intangible factors. As an internal ETS report on the College Board programs acknowledged, "The SAT program flourished as much as anything because it gave institutions a public respectability."[88] Such prestige cannot be purchased at any price by a profit-making, tax paying firm. ETS' non-profit status gives it "an unfair advantage at times," complains Roger Lennon of Psychological Corporation. "Academic types tend to feel more at home dealing with something that isn't perceived as a commercial enterprise."[89]

The corporation's promotional efforts have also been guided in the 1970s by a strata of top executives increasingly sensitive, despite their academic image, to the techniques of Madison Avenue. As the minutes of the October 14, 1971 Programs and Services Planning Committee meeting pointed out:

> MARKETING - has become a "respectable" word around ETS only recently. Not long ago to some ETSers at least, the word smacked of Madison Avenue commercialism, and no one was much interested in it. Now, with new kinds of programs and services aimed at audiences not as familiar to us as our usual ones, we have come to realize the necessity for finding out what our target audiences /institutions/ want and will accept.[90]

A few months earlier, the Development Planning Committee made the point even more succinctly: ". . . discussion emphasized the point that marketing considerations may influence a product's impact as strongly as product quality."[91]

The official ETS "Criteria for the Evaluation of Developmental Plans" developed in 1970 by Turnbull, Solomon and Controller Herman F. Smith, required that all projects be evaluated in terms of "their potential impact" on ETS' "(1) reputation; (2) other ETS activities . . .; (3) finances; /and/ (4) potential for fostering additional new developments."[92]

In contrast to other corporations which resort to glossy brochures, traveling salesmen and other hard sells, the ETS marketing strategy is more intellectually respectable. Information tailored to the characteristics of several hundred categories of ETS target groups comes pouring out in streams of daily mailings. The Spring 1971 issue of the glossy magazine ETS Developments, for example, was mailed free of charge to over 32,000 recipients (almost 4,000 overseas) from thirty-one categories including: college presidents and directors of admission; U.S. junior and senior colleges; law school deans; graduate business school officers; school districts that receive NTE score reports; superintendents of school districts using the NTE; newspapers, magazines, journals and periodicals; major U.S. private foundations; state commissioners of education; over 5,000 past attendees at ETS invitational conferences on testing problems; state departments of education; elementary school district superintendents; catholic school superintendents; junior high schools; and county superintendents.[93]

In addition to the mailings, ETS representatives are flown at company expense to association meetings and conventions around the world when an officer determines that such attendance is justified for professional or business reasons. ETS staff are encouraged to publish papers or books in their fields and hold office in their professional societies.[94] The company also is not averse to using the facilities at Rosedale to woo potential customers.

The January 1976 issue of the ETS internal newsletter "Brief Reports" summed up a typical month's activities. ETS representatives gave twenty-one speeches and ten workshops in fourteen states, did four TV interviews, and issued six articles and two books. On the international front, while Rosedale hosted visitors from Australia, Colombia, and Japan, President Turnbull chaired a Paris meeting of the ETS-run International Association of Educational Assessment; Albert Beaton visited Dublin on behalf of the National Institute of Education and the Carnegie, Russell Sage, and Spencer Foundations to study "the effects of introducing objective testing in a society previously without such testing;" and Michael Zieky (after stopping off in Manila for consultations with the Philippine Ministry of Education) returned from Singapore where he and three other ETS professionals were helping the country to "restructur[e] its national education system," in large measure by engineering "a changeover from essay-type examinations to standardized tests."[95]

The use of all aspects of ETS' institutional prestige as an economic asset is well illustrated in the promotional campaign for one of ETS' most controversial tests, the National Teacher Examinations (NTE), which are used in the certification and hiring of teachers. After several law suits in the early 1970s charged some school districts that used the NTE with racial discrimination,[96] the Justice Department, intervening on behalf of teacher plaintifs in a North Carolina case, investigated the test. Justice discovered a PhD dissertation by an ETS staff member who had worked with the NTE. Based on a statistical analysis of NTE questions, this work "concluded that the allegation of cultural bias in the NTE Common Examinations had merit."[97] The Justice Department brief in the case quoted a study which found "no significant relationships between the selected criteria of teacher effectiveness and scores achieved on the Common Examinations of the National Teacher Examinations."[98] Furthermore, it cited an ETS report which noted "the low correlations between the National Teacher Examinations and ratings of on-the-job performance by principals and supervisors."[99]

These Justice Department findings were not well-publicized and the results of the court cases were mixed (in some cases use of the NTE was upheld, in others it was struck down, depending on how heavily it was relied upon and for what kind of personnel decisions). Nonetheless, the suits attained considerable public visibility. A number of school districts dropped their NTE requirement, and NTE candidate volume and ETS income from NTE fell.[100] But ETS' marketing experts were ready with a comeback plan.

In two lengthy memos ("Plans for NTE Promotion and Development," and "Concept Paper: The Revision of the NTE Common Examinations,") for ETS Vice President for Development Winton H. Manning, NTE Program Director George Elford laid out the problem and the ETS objective:

The Setting for Developmental and Promotional Efforts

> For a number of reasons, the number of candidates taking the NTE has declined steadily in the past three years from 119,619 in 1971-72 to 94,314 last year. . . . Publicity from court cases, changes in

> state NTE requirements for certification and a substantial effort to reduce repeaters can account for most of this decline. It should be noted that during this period, for reasons that are understandable, <u>no promotional efforts</u> of any large scale were undertaken. . . . /Emphasis in original./
>
> It does seem essential that for NTE to maintain its present net income level, promotional efforts should be directed at increasing the percentage of the teacher graduates taking the NTE. This promotional effort should first of all be directed at school district offices, taking into account the shift from a "seller's" to a "buyer's" market in teacher selection which especially affects suburban districts.[101]

Elford acknowledged that part of the problem was the ETS product itself. Although the NTE was used as an employment test, ETS had been unable to demonstrate that the test was related to actual performance as a teacher. As Elford mildly noted, "the main justification for the NTE contents is conceptual and not empirical."[102] He went on:

> [A] series of court decisions following the <u>Griggs v. Duke Power Company</u> decision have made it clear that for an employer to justify the use of test scores, these scores must be shown to be "job related" . . . .[103]

The difficulties this presented for ETS were succinctly stated in Elford's chart: "A Force-Field Analysis of Present and Possibly Increased Use of the NTE." The ETS "Force-Field" listed the "Driving Forces toward present or increased use" as well as the "Restraining forces" under the headings of "Forces Related to the NTE Itself" and "Forces Related to the Educational and Political Context." The foremost "restraining force," Elford wrote, was presented not by politics but by the NTE itself: ". . . lack of data showing test validity in predicting job performance."[104]

However, by acknowledging the test's lack of predictive validity--Elford did not mean to suggest that ETS could not sell the NTE. For, as ETS market analysts had long since discovered, demand for ETS tests did not necessarily depend on the function which those tests purported to serve. Elford's memo asked:

<u>IN THIS CONTEXT, WHAT IS THE FUTURE OF THE
NATIONAL TEACHER EXAMINATIONS?</u>

Three alternative futures logically present themselves: growth in NTE use, continued decline in NTE use, and a leveling off in the use of NTE in a sort of "plateau period."

Considering the balance of forces at work, the prospects for growth in the next five years are not promising in this present climate.

Continued decline might seem the safest prediction, representing, as it does, a simple linear projection based on present trends. <u>Such a prediction would, however, discount the impact of the promotion/development efforts presently being planned.</u> /Emphasis added./

Assuming an optimistic posture, we contend that with this presently planned investment in development and promotion, the volume of the NTE use could be maintained at present levels, with an added possibility of a gradual increase in use over time. . . . At present, ETS has a unique kind of experience and hence an advantage in the field of knowledge testing for teachers. This advantaged position should be maintained.[105]

Elford's proposals involved three techniques, all used to advantage by other ETS test programs, for increasing the use of the NTE: promotion of the test in scholarly meetings and publications; collection of ETS market intelligence in the guise of academic research; and use of the tax-exempt Henry Chauncey Conference Center for entertainment of officials from institutions which could require the tests.[106]

In accord with Elford's plan, NTE promotion helped overcome the test's inability to predict competence in teaching. Between 1975 (the time of the Elford memos) and 1977, NTE annual candidate volume reversed its previous decline and grew from 73,000 to 82,465.[107] By feting educators at luncheons and scholarly meetings to reinforce the prestige associated with the NTE, polling these school districts to establish that they preferred (though did not require) applicants to submit NTE scores and, in turn, informing prospective teachers of this carefully elicited preference, ETS attempted to shift the basis for NTE demand from decision-making by districts as to whether they wanted to require the test to general public belief in the test's necessity. According to Elford's plan, these strategies "would provide a reliable basis for demand since it does appear that for some years to come the supply of teachers will exceed the demand."[108]

Although it faces little head-to-head competition in its national testing programs, ETS is capable of tough strategic planning when competition looms for state and federal agency contracts. Several years ago, for example, ETS' Office of State Program Development prepared a thorough plan assessing the opportunity for expansion of the corporation's Illinois markets, either through creating new programs, or cutting into the American College Testing Program's business. In a memo entitled, "STRATEGY FOR ILLINOIS," the OSPD wrote, "In a recent issue of ACTivity, the American College Testing Program noted that the State of Illinois had the highest volume of ACT business again this year."[109]

But, as the OSPD pointed out, [d]eficiencies in the State's educational effort should indicate program development possibilities."[110] The OSPD proposed sending ETS representatives to interview eighteen political and legislative officials in the state "to collect . . . intelligence."[111] The questions to the Illinois officials would be phrased to reflect ETS' public position of "doing good without gain": "Where does education currently rank in the State's list of public goods and services? . . . What new concepts, such as non-traditional studies, external degrees, year-round calendar, shortened degree time, etc., are being considered as alternatives to the standard academic programs? . . . Please identify specific needs of the educational system for which CEEB/ETS could provide appropriate service to the State."[112]

The points considered in the OSPD's report back to ETS would have a slightly different focus. With the information in hand, the memo continued, the OSPD would gauge the chances of corporate expansion against ACT in Illinois, and the resulting potential for financial gain:

1-Does Illinois have <u>realistic</u> potential for program development that would impinge on ACT?

2-If not, is there any realistic program development area for CEEB/ETS in Illinois? . . .

5-What cost/benefit will result for CEEB/ETS as a result of program development?[113]

ETS' marketing efforts grow from a corporate philosophy which assumes that the company's mission requires expansion of ETS test volume and income. Throughout its history, whenever ETS and the College Board have been faced with declining or leveling demand in one test market, it has cultivated another. "It is . . . necessary," wrote a College Board task force considering expansion into the guidance testing market, "to generate new income to compensate for likely declines in traditional programs."[114]

In recent years, for example, as the number of college applicants has leveled off after the growth of the 1960s, volume on the SAT has declined from 1,605,900 in 1969-70, to about 1.5 million today.[115] To compensate, ETS has shifted an increasing amount of its promotional effort to the lucrative occupational testing field. Over the same period that SAT volume has declined, ETS revenues from occupational testing have grown fivefold from $2.1 million (in 1969) to $11.2 million.[116]

ETS has even moved aggressively into non-testing markets. In the early 1970s, for example, company officials decided to enter the field of computer scheduling of school bus routes. ETS sought to compete for a New Jersey contract for this purpose. According to a confidential memorandum from an ETS computer division executive, it was "necessary to have on staff at the earliest possible time a person who has excellent qualifications in the field of school bus scheduling and knowledge of the IBM Vehicle Scheduling Program. To the best of our knowledge (IBM's and mine), there are only two persons in the State of New Jersey possessing such qualifications." Acting quickly and circumventing the normal personnel procedures*, non-profit ETS outbid IBM and hired one of them.[117]

---

*ETS requires that job openings be posted so that people already on staff will have the first chance to apply.

Although the College Board tests remain its largest program, ETS has diversified to the point where it is not dependent on any single market for most of its income. Of its total $94.2 million income in 1978-79, $45.5 million came from College Board programs, $15.7 million from graduate and professional school programs, $11.2 million from the Professional and Occupational Programs, and $21.8 million from other programs, including elementary and secondary school testing programs.[118]

This well balanced assortment of tests is the result of a constant quest for growth. In the early 1950s, ETS compensated for the loss of its biggest program--the Selective Service College Qualification Test used to help determine who would get educational deferments from the Korean War--by stepping up its promotional efforts in college admission testing when the SSCQT program declined in volume and ultimately was awarded to another testing company. In 1950-51, the SSCQT was given to more than four times as many applicants as the SAT; forty-two times as many applicants as the GRE and fifty times as many applicants as the LSAT.[119] Elementary and high school tests in the Cooperative test division had greater volume that the SAT as well.[120]

In the late fifties, the SAT--and ETS itself--took off. From 1951-1955 the annual candidate growth rate for ETS tests stagnated: in 1951-52 ETS test volume dropped by 49.5 per cent from the previous year; in 1954-55 it grew only 6.3 per cent.[121] But, in 1955-56 the explosive growth began: candidate volume grew by 39.9 per cent.[122] This was followed by a growth rate of 30 per cent the following year.[123] In the four year period from

1955-56 to 1959-60, the annual growth rate for the number of candidates tested never fell below 26 per cent.[124] Volume increased more than fourfold over a five year period, with the number of candidates growing from 496,552 in 1955-56 to over 2.1 million in 1960-61.[125] SAT volume alone grew from 237,060 in 1955-56 to 732,843 only five years later.[126]

This growth was fueled not only by the increasing number of college applicants but also by the increasing numbers of colleges requiring the SAT of their applicants. In 1955-56, the number of SATs taken was roughly equivalent to twenty-nine per cent of entering freshmen.[127] Five years later, the numbers of SATs taken--some students, of course, took the test more than once--equaled seventy per cent of the entering class.[128] During the largest SAT volume years, the percentage remained at about ninety-five per cent or more, hitting 100 per cent in 1965-66.[129] Over the past fifteen years, the percentage has settled back into the seventy per cent range, the figure which prevails today.[130] While compiling these impressive statistics, the SAT has soared by comparison to its counterparts such as the elementary and secondary school programs which today make up only seven per cent of ETS operations, bringing in just $6.3 million.[131]

The rapid growth of test volume continued into the early 1970s with ETS income following apace. In the twenty year period from 1952-53 to 1972-73, ETS income doubled in size every five years. In 1952-53 the corporation took in $2.5 million dollars; in 1957-58 the figure was six million. Five years after that, income was $13 million and in 1967-68 it had grown to $27 million.

By 1972-73 it had doubled again to $53 million, and in 1978-79 stood at $94 million.[132] Though the income growth rate dropped to only 1.8 per cent in 1973-74 after five years of regular double digit growth, since that time the corporation has enjoyed a steady seven to eighteen per cent annual growth rate.[133]

Such tremendous and steady expansion of income is not routine for a non-profit corporation. "Growth requires capital," then-President Henry Chauncey wrote in the 1955-56 *Annual Report*, "and a non-profit organization does not ordinarily accumulate capital from net income on its activities, at least not to the extent necessary when expansion is rapid and steady."[134] ETS profit margins, however, have made it the exception to its founder's rule. At first, the large capital gifts from the College Board (drawn from profits on programs administered for the Board by ETS) aided ETS expansion.

Since then, however, it has expanded into new markets-- even new continents--primarily through the reinvestment of its own considerable profits.

A key factor in this expansion has been the client group structure discussed earlier. This structure has enabled ETS to generate capital for expansion by minimizing competition within each testing market, and insulating ETS from economic risk. Once ETS has convened a client group which represents all of the major institutions in a particular market--such as the GRE Board, on which ETS has reserved seats for the two national organizations of graduate school administrators--the opportunities for other testing firms are diminished considerably. Instead of dealing in a wide open market with hundreds of individual institutions, ETS can deal with a single client group--which it created and for which it provides the staff.

Once the client group has "chosen" ETS to administer the test program for their level of education, the only option for companies which might want to compete with ETS is to persuade individual institutions, one by one, to require their tests. This strategy has been tried by marketers of the graduate level Miller Analogies Test. However, most ETS client groups have met no such challenge.[135] This gives the groups, such as the Law School Admission Council and the Graduate Management Admission Test Board, effective monopoly power to <u>set</u> test prices, as opposed to taking the price set by the market, which a seller in a competitive situation must do.

Most client groups have been more than willing to set prices and establish payment systems which guaranteed large profits for ETS--even at their own expense. A confidential memo from ETS financial vice president David Brodsky points out that "[A]s recently as 1971-72, nearly three-fourths of our activities were operated on a cost-plus contract basis in which our clients took the complete financial risk."[136] Under the cost-plus percentage fee system, the contractor (ETS) receives a fee from the client board which is equal to the contractor's cost of providing the service plus a profit which is calculated as a percentage of the costs. The larger the costs, the larger the profit.

This lucrative contract arrangement meant that in theory ETS was guaranteed that its programs would turn a profit, regardless of how much it spent to produce them. Ideally, ETS would never absorb the costs. These would either be passed on to the consumer or, if the fees had not been set high enough, absorbed by the client organization. For some programs, there were years in which ETS would recover all of its costs plus a percentage profit but the books of the client organization would show a net loss. In 1972-73, for example, the Law School Admission Council suffered a loss of more than $500,000. At the same time, ETS recovered all of its costs plus a thirteen per cent fee for its work on behalf of the Council.[137] Even for organizations which owed their prestige--not to mention their existence--to ETS, such lopsided arrangements proved irksome. The client groups had their own reserve funds, accumulated from past test profits which they were able to spend for research, conferences, publications, and other purposes apart from test administration. When ETS spending forced the clients into deficits, they had to dip into their reserves. This limited their discretion and annoyed some Board members. A 1974 LSAC report complained that "LSAC now bears virtually all of the financial risk,"[138] and noted that even after receiving pledges from ETS that the risk would be shared more equitably, the Council Board "was still unpersuaded that the services rendered by ETS for the Council were priced at a reasonable level."[139] The contract arrangement was causing more than mere political friction. The reserves of some clients were being depleted to the point where, one ETS report noted, they were "encountering serious financial problems."[140]

ETS management recognized quickly that the client group financial shell game--where inefficiently run programs lost money overall but still produced a profit for ETS could only be pushed so far. The client system was crucial to ETS' long-term economic and political interests and could not be endangered for short-term gain. In February 1972, the ETS Programs and Services Planning Committee concluded that "The financial health of our clients is inextricably intertwined with the overall health of ETS. It is critical that we assist clients with their immediate problems by identifying potential reductions in services, even if a short-term loss for ETS may be necessary."[141]

In addition to internal cost-cutting, ETS began shifting client contracts from a cost plus percentage fee to a cost plus incentive fee basis.[142] Under cost plus incentive fee, the contractor is still entitled to recover costs, but no longer has an incentive to inflate them. Instead, the profit received by the contractor is tied to the profitability of the program as a whole. As the profit margin of the program itself rises, so does the percentage of that profit the contractor, ETS, is allowed to keep. Whereas under the old contract system, ETS had no incentive to keep down costs, under the new system cutting costs would increase not only the total profit of the program, but ETS' share of that profit. If it performed well, ETS would be able to bank even larger shares of ever greater profits.

Profit Margins and "Non-Profit" Margins

The 1977 ETS Annual Report is exceedingly modest in matters of pecuniary gain. "It was a sound year financially," notes ETS.[143] The Coopers and Lybrand-approved financial statement reports an "Excess of Revenue Over Expenditures" of $901,022 on an income of $70,006,846.[144] This works out to a percentage of profit on gross revenues or what Vice President Samuel Messick calls "nonprofits"[145]--of 1.3 per cent, a modest figure which would be evidence of a very poor year at a major corporation.*

Despite its phenomenal growth, ETS has always reported profits of roughly this magnitude. In 1976 the percentage was 1.6 per cent, in 1975 it was 1.9 per cent. These would seem to indicate hard times after the relatively prosperous years of 1972--3.9 per cent--and 1971--4.1 per cent.[147] By its Annual Report accounting, ETS has never enjoyed a profit of over 10.3 per cent (in 1955).[148] And, indeed, in 1956 it is reported to have lost money.[149]

ETS gives a similar accounting to the U.S. Internal Revenue Service (IRS), the agency which granted ETS its non-profit status in 1948 and which is responsible for monitoring non-profits to assure that they continue to deserve their privilege. ETS' 1976 form 990, the public tax return filed by all non-profit organizations, indicates a profit of 1.2 per cent on gross revenues of $70,106,660.[150]

---

*In 1978-79 ETS reported a profit on gross revenues of $1.1 million, or only 1.2 per cent of total income.[146]

The IRS rules on non-profit corporations were written to deal with service organizations such as colleges or hospitals, or membership groups such as local civic clubs. The rules were not designed for large-scale producers and marketers of products; thus, the IRS forms do not require the non-profit to disclose how much profit it makes from sales.* The IRS is primarily concerned with assuring, first, that the organization issue no stock nor make similar payments to officers and, second, that it not accumulate large hoards of uninvested cash. ETS qualifies on both counts: it issues no stock and reinvests assiduously, maintaining only a relatively small $4 million liquid reserve of stocks and cash which David Brodsky dismisses as "ludicrous, it's not enough for two weeks payroll; the Trustees Finance Committee has taken us to task for our lack of liquidity."[152]

Neither the public--nor the IRS--knows how much profit ETS makes on its various product lines. This information is not required on the 990 and is not volunteered in the Annual Report. The one per cent profit figure which ETS discloses to the public is of little significance. It merely reflects the excess funds left on hand after management has reinvested the profits derived

---

*The information on the 990 form is essentially the same as that in the Annual Report statement. The only major differences are that the IRS requires non-profits to list their stockholdings, largest expenditures for professional services, and officer's salaries. Although the form is a public document, the most recent form available for inspection at the IRS is usually two to three years out of date, and often requires two to six months for retrieval. (In September of 1979, ETS' 1976 return was the most recent form available.)[151]

from the sale of ETS tests and services. This overall corporate profit figure indicates nothing more than the amount of profits left unspent by the end of the fiscal year. Unlike a profit-making firm where dividends and reinvestments are declared, non-profit ETS can choose to report a low profit margin--even if its products do well--or a high one, all simply by deciding how much of the profits it wants to spend and how much it wants to keep in hand to be revealed to the public and to the IRS.

When asked to disclose the profit margins of various programs, ETS financial executives replied that they had been advised by their attorneys that this was "not an appropriate topic."[153] Even the IRS has never been given such information, according to Brodsky.[154]

In 1974, when Steven Brill reported in New York magazine that "profits of 10 per cent on gross revenues are chalked up on all ETS /programs/,"[155] ETS responded quickly. Public relations head Jenne Britell flatly denied the ten percent figure and invoked the Annual Report financial statements, suggesting that ETS was operating on the margin of survival.

> The statement that "Profits of 10% are chalked up on all ETS programs" is erroneous. The 10% figure is incorrect with regard to ETS' total income. ETS net income in 1973-74 was $1,414,000 or about 2-1/2 per-cent on gross income of $53,902,000. This represents one of the organization's two most successful years in the past quarter-century.[156]

However, ETS' internal Project Operating Statement and other confidential records reveal what ETS financial statements and public relations executives try to conceal: the programs of non-profit ETS are as profitable as many of the nation's most success-ful profit-making businesses.[157]

"ETS," wrote Forbes magazine in 1976, "has easily racked up a record as one of the hottest little growth companies in U.S. Business."[158] In 1976, ETS' two largest programs (ATP Testing and the College Scholarship Service) each had profits on gross revenues of 12.3 per cent. These profits were consistent for all major ETS programs. With one exception, none of ETS' ten largest programs had profits on gross revenues of less than 9.9 per cent in 1976.[159] Of those ETS national testing and service programs that were doing over $100,000 worth of business, almost ninety per cent returned profits in 1976.[160] For 1977, all ETS testing programs and services combined were budgeted to produce an overall profit on gross revenues of 9.3 per cent.[161]

Substantial though they are, in many cases these figures understate the overall profitability of ETS tests, for they only include the share of the profits which ETS retains and do not include the share which is passed on to the client group.* In the case of the Admissions Testing Program (SATs and Achievement Tests), for example, roughly twenty per cent of the candidate's fee goes to test company profit.

ETS officials have frequently attempted to deny the profitability of the SAT. In a July 5, 1979 memo for the press, ETS public relations director Robert Moulthrop asserted that the

---

*If the program suffers an overall loss, of course, these ETS-only figures will be deceptively high. But, as discussed on p. 331, since the advent of incentive fee contracts, ETS has had a strong incentive to insure the overall profitability of programs.

Admissions Testing Program returned a yearly profit of only 0.8 per cent.[162] In November of 1979, ETS Senior Vice President for Finance David Brodsky denied a statement (by the author) that SAT profits have exceeded twenty per cent and said that "the testing service earned about 10 percent, or 83 cents, above direct administration cost on each $8.25 student fee for the Scholastic Aptitude Test."[163]

The two claims contradict each other. Moulthrop's is demonstrably false; Brodsky's statement, while true for <u>ETS alone</u>, gives only half the story, for it fails to include profits kept by the College Board.

The student's ATP fee can be divided into four categories: ETS costs, College Board costs, ETS profit and College Board profit. The payment system works as follows: the student pays a fee to ETS. Out of that fee, ETS bills the College Board for its cost of running the ATP program plus a profit margin. The money left over after ETS has deducted its share is passed on to the College Board. The College Board in turn deducts the costs that it has incurred overseeing ETS' administration of the program. The money which remains is the College Board's profit.[164] Thus, both ETS and the College Board spend some of the fee to run the programs and keep some of it as profit.

The most recent year for which internal ETS budget records on the costs and profits of the SAT are available is 1975-76. By combining these records with the College Board's published figures, the division of the candidate's fee between cost and profit can be estimated. The breakdown is as follows:

Admissions Testing Program, 1975-76[165]

ETS Costs	$10,079,000	(62.0%)
College Board Direct Costs	1,742,474	(10.7%)
College Board Indirect Costs	805,738	(5.0%)
ETS Profit	1,411,000	(8.7%)
College Board Profit	2,222,440	(13.7%)
TOTAL ATP Revenue	$16,260,652	

Overall, twenty-two per cent of the candidate's fee went to ETS-College Board profit, and seventy-seven per cent went to the cost of running the ATP program in 1975-76. This amounts to a profit of more than $3.6 million earned by ETS and the College Board.

The breakdowns for 1978-79 can also be estimated:

Admissions Testing Program, 1978-79[166]

ETS Costs	$13,717,854	(63.9%)
College Board Direct Costs	2,311,480	(10.8%)
College Board Indirect Costs	1,026,785	(4.8%)
ETS Profit*	1,524,206	(7.1%)
College Board Profit	2,898,335	(13.5%)
TOTAL ATP Revenue	$21,478,660	

For 1978-79, ETS-College Board profits stood at approximately twenty-one per cent of gross revenues from the Admissions Testing Program, a sum equal to more than $4.4 million.

---

*The ETS profit of $1,524,206 represents ten per cent of the bill it submitted to the College Board but only seven per cent of overall program revenues.

However, there is evidence to suggest that ATP profit margins may have been even higher in the past than they are today. **After allowing for inflation, the current fee is** actually lower than the one which prevailed in the mid-1950s.[167] Higher costs of test production may in part explain the higher fees of the past. The need for setting profit margins at least as high as those of today to accumulate capital for rapid growth is another likely explanatory factor. The possibility that past profit margins were higher is suggested by the situation which existed at that time. First, revenues from ATP fees were apparently sufficient not only to cover ETS test production costs and profit margins but also to return enough funds to the College Board for building up its New York office. Second, there was enough money in the College Board account left over to cover capital gifts from the Board to ETS ranging from $200,000 (in 1957-58) to $900,000 (in 1969-70).[168]

The commitment of the College Board and ETS to maintaining their profit margin is illustrated by their response to New York's 1979 Truth-in-Testing law. According to an estimate submitted by ETS to the New York Senate Higher Education Committee, an estimate later repeated in Moulthrop's memo, it would cost $1,092,000 (a figure which can be questioned) for the ATP program to comply with Truth-in-Testing and insure, in Moulthrop's words, "maintenance of the current level of service in New York."[169] This cost estimate amounts to only about one-quarter of the 1978-79 estimated $4.4 million profit margin on the ATP. Yet, rather than absorb the cost of compliance with a modest cut in their margins, the College Board and ETS have announced their intention to raise ATP fees for New York students and cut back special test administrations for handicapped students and those who cannot attend Saturday test sessions for religious reasons.[170]

The profits generated by ETS' major testing and service programs are used to subsidize other ETS activities. According to the 1977 budget figures in the Project Operating Statement, the largest shares of the subsidies go to general unallocated administrative expense (thirty-two per cent) and the development of new products and programs (twenty per cent). These two categories account for more than fifty per cent of the spending of ETS' profits.[171] Other substantial subsidies go to, in descending order, psychological research, educational research, and courses and seminars for educators.[172] ETS also subsidizes the operation of the Henry Chauncey Conference Center.[173] A favorite example used by ETS executives for describing where the profits go is the company's studies in infant learning. The Project Operating Statement, however, indicates that infant research projects were budgeted to receive a subsidy of only about $100,000 (or roughly two per cent of the total distributed) in 1977.[174]

In sum, although it enjoys the legal privileges of a non-profit educational institution, ETS also enjoys the financial returns of a large and profitable corporation.

The Two Class System

The official company history likens ETS to a university. Its charter is similar and, according to the ETS account, the commitment of the professional staff to "teaching, research and public service . . . is [one] traditionally associated with the academic community."[175]

"It used to be like a family," recalled G. Dykeman Sterling, retired ETS vice president in charge of personnel and finance (1958-1971), in a 1974 interview. There was "leisure time to sit down and discuss things. . . . They have always had the feeling, which is pretty well justified that they can do most anything and do it better than anyone else." "They are all extremely well educated," Sterling said of his ETS colleagues, "and their motivation and integrity are second to none."[176] The climate at ETS, Sterling said, was not that of a business but "much more academic, even the people who come and do lower things will tell you that."[177] Nonetheless, beyond the oft-repeated imagery of ETS as a sort of massive, pipe-puffing Ivy League colloquium, ETS is an industrial organization. It is, in the words of internal ETS personnel reports, "a two class society,"[178] in which the growth of a group of well-paid professionals and the sustenance of the academic image so vital to corporate expansion have rested on the labor of low-paid women in clerical jobs. Beginning with Henry Chauncey, ETS executives have sought to boost the productivity and decrease the relative numbers of ETS' non-professional clerical staff while increasing the professionals' share of the company's income.

In 1949-50, when ETS tested 378,575 candidates, four times as many non-professionals as professionals worked at ETS.[179] Test forms and registration materials were collated, sorted, mailed, and opened by hand. Temporary employees were brought on during peak periods for tasks such as stapling and packing 1,100,000 test booklets to be mailed to 4,900 test centers and typing, printing and sending 850,000 pieces of ETS promotional material to 97,000 institutions and individuals across the country.[180] It was a prodigious accomplishment. "The volume of papers processed, tests shipped, reports issued, is impressive," Henry Chauncey observed, "even to one who has lived fairly close to the work."[181]

By as early as 1951-52, the ETS operation was running smoothly: "the setting up and administering of testing programs, no matter how large or how complex, is now essentially a matter of routine, while the ability of the staff to make necessary procedural adjustments from program to program and in the same program from time to time, as changing conditions require, is now taken for granted."[182]

Between 1949-50 and 1965-66, professionals and administrators grew from slightly less than twenty per cent to over thirty-five per cent of ETS staff. Even though the number of candidates with forms to be processed increased thirteen-fold during this same period, professional staff grew twice as fast as nonprofessional.[183]

The drive for an organization that would produce consistently under "the requirements of minute and endless detail, dovetailed and synchronized schedules, and speed and accuracy,"[184] was powered by two key objectives: the expansion of production and the relative reduction of costs paid out in clerical wages. In the company's second year of operation, Chauncey was able to report a reduction in the total payroll of over $30,000, "despite a slightly higher level of activity."[185] In 1979, ETS reported that over the past five years, the staff size had grown by only nineteen per cent while the information processing workload "has increased at almost double that rate."[186]

This increasing efficiency in paper handling, which is based on automation and the high productivity of ETS' non-professional staff, has helped generate income and profits which enable ETS to bid for some of the more highly paid professionals in the educational market. The salaries of ETS executives compare favorably with those of their counterparts in the educational institutions ETS serves. In 1979, ETS distributed to Members of Congress a chart purporting to show that ETS professional salaries were comparable to or lower than the average at universities and government agencies. The ETS chart, however, neglected to list the salaries of the entire top echelon of ETS management. It compared, for example, the salaries of university deans--the highest officers of universities--with the salaries of ETS "Test Examiner/s/" and "Program Administrator/s/" who rank near the middle of the ETS hierarchy.[187] A more complete comparison of salaries at the top indicates that ETS executive salaries are roughly twice as high as the national average at colleges and universities:

Average Annual Salaries of Selected College and University Administrators, 1976-77 (from: National Center for Education Statistics)		ETS Officer Salaries, 1976-77	
College President:	$35,135	ETS President:	$75,000
Dean of Graduate Programs:	31,281	ETS Executive Vice President:	67,500
Dean of Arts and Sciences:	29,021	ETS Senior Vice President for Administration:	53,500
Dean of Business:	28,221	ETS Vice President for Research:	52,500
Chief Academic Officer:	27,757	ETS Senior Vice President for Testing Programs:	50,100
Chief Business Officer:	25,413	ETS Vice President for International Programs:	49,256
Director of Admissions:	19,411	ETS Senior Vice President for Development:	49,000
Registrar:	18,845	ETS Senior Vice President for Advisory Services:	46,000

SOURCE: Digest of Educational Statistics, 1979, and IRS form 990, 1976, filed by ETS.[188]

According to the most recent available information on file with the IRS, in fiscal 1977 ETS' top eighteen officers were paid $815,856 for an average of $45,325 per person. The top ten officers received an average salary of $52,886.[189] President Turnbull's 1979 salary stood at $88,000.[190]

By contrast, in 1979, yearly pay for clerical workers began as low as $5,990.[191] The salaries for ETS staff as a whole were such that, despite the presence of a well-compensated community of executives and professionals, the _average_ 1979 ETS salary stood at only $13,600 which was below the average for "wage earners nationwide."[192] The ETS Personnel manual gave explicit instructions that in order to maintain "a proper relationship between the salary of a staff member and that of his supervisor, "the _salary of the supervisor_ should be at least 5% and usually 10% _above_ that of his highest paid _subordinate_."[193] (Emphasis in original.)

Executive salary figures do not include emoluments like the house provided and maintained for President Turnbull at ETS expense, nor the expense reimbursements for ETS officers.[194] Nor does it include the liberal benefits program which was systematically oriented to serve those who needed it least. ETS, for example, would help pay home moving expenses for employees joining the ETS staff _if_ they started at a salary (around 1970) of more than $10,500.[195] Tuition aid for dependents had originally been available to all ETS employees after five years,[196] but between 1967 and 1973 the policy was changed so that higher-paid staff would be eligible immediately. Employees earning less than $15,000 had to wait the five years. Two supervisors commented on this point in a confidential personnel policy meeting:

> /I/s it more reasonable for the highly paid professional to be entitled to tuition aid for dependents in his first year at ETS as opposed to secretaries and other lesser-paid staff having to wait five years . . .? It

seems to be an inequitable spending of available funds. Mr. Goldberg shed some light on this, noting that this benefit was initiated as a recruiting device /for recruiting professionals/. The program costs ETS a large amount of money each year, and if the five-year restriction were lifted the program could explode.[197]

Preferential treatment for professionals sometimes extends across generational lines. When an ETS personnel officer was having difficulty locating a job at ETS for a well-connected but not clearly employable young Ivy-leaguer, ETS Executive Vice President Robert J. Solomon personally interceded with a quick reminder about ETS priorities:

> Can't we do better than send this routine reply? For example, why the interview business for the kinds of jobs described when both Dave and I can vouch as references? Did /the personnel officer/ try to find out if other areas, such as /Test Development Division/ can use him? Myles Goldberg is doing a better job for Dartmouth students. Can't the Harvard son of a Princeton Dean get the same attention?[198]

Management expectations for lesser-paid staff are thoroughly spelled out in some cases. The ETS Secretarial handbook, for example, gives office workers precise instructions on what to do if their boss has scheduled a meeting. "Help prepare your supervisor for a meeting with all the appropriate reference materials," the handbook advises, "several sharp pencils and a pad of paper."[199] And lest there should be any confusion, the handbook gives secretaries step-by-step instructions on "How to serve coffee if desired":

> Keep a list of coffee preferences of the staff members who regularly visit your office.
> It might be helpful to keep coffee and a supply of paper cups on hand. Serve to a small group in paper cups; to a large group in china cups. . . .[200]

With such attention to hierarchy and ceremony Rosedale is kept a comfortable, efficient, and coffee-filled place to work for the professionals who carry on the science of mental measurement. ETS professionals are encouraged to lend an appropriate tone to Rosedale transactions. President (then Executive Vice President) Turnbull in his October 9, 1963 memo, "A Note on Semantics" described a code of verbal restraint as a guide:

> The other day two or three of us got into a brief discussion of ETS terminology when I expressed the view that the words we use are important in several ways. Take the word "company," for example. In recent years this term has cropped up increasingly in internal memos, referring to ETS, rather than the more customary word "organization." My own opinion is that "company" is an inappropriate word for ETS, just as it is for Princeton University. If it comes into general use, our own staff members will find the difference between ETS and commercial enterprises beginning to blur in their minds. And anyone outside ETS who found us referring to ourselves as a "company" could hardly be blamed for a little cynicism about our claim that we are an institution integral to the educational community--a part of it, not a vendor of materials and services to it.
>
> I include on my mental blacklist the term "customers." "Client groups" is a step forward but not a sufficiently long one. . .
>
> While I'm at it, let me inveigh against "Management" as a collective noun. . . . Insofar as a collective noun is called for, I'd prefer "the officers" or "the administration."
>
> Two other terms I dislike for ETS are "sales volume" and our "volume of business." Whenever anyone says anything about "other test publishers," I shudder, since it implies that ETS is properly classified as one test publisher among many, whereas I think we are on a different planet. "Competitors" is a particularly objectionable word. I suspect there are others that

trouble you. If so, and if you think its worthwhile to campaign for verbal purification, let's pool ideas on better terminology and see what we can do to clean up local usage.[201]

In 1970, when one young executive wrote a memo requesting an assistant for "Planning, selling and implementing" some new programs, he was set straight by Executive Director for General Programs (now Vice President for Personnel) Robert E. Smith. Smith returned the memo with each mention of the word "selling" crossed out and the word "developing" penciled in in its place. "While I believe I understand your meaning," Smith admonished in his cover memo, "I think the connotations of the word 'selling' are inappropriate for this organization--'developing' might be a better word. Please redraft with this change."[202]

The People Who Do the Work

From the earliest days of the corporation, nonprofessionals at ETS have been, above all, a cost to be controlled--through speedups, efficiency studies, and careful monitoring of their activities. The reality of Rosedale is far different from the collegial family atmosphere suggested by ETS pronouncements. As veteran systems analyst Shephard Kimberly noted in an April 1972 study of ETS personnel, the "pervasive myth . . . /that/ ETS . . . is 'permissive,' 'democratic' and 'one big family'" was just that--a myth.[203] "The reverse is the case," he wrote, "for most of the staff. The two-class system has evolved a bureaucracy that is neither democratic nor for that matter familial in any but the most patriarchal sense."[204]

Though the report was confidential, and its results never released, what Kimberly found was no secret to the wage-earners processing ETS paper. The two class system was a part of their lives every day. It led to predictable conflict.

During the early 1970s, the ETS Personnel Office began warning company officers that Rosedale was ripe for a union movement. A confidential report to Vice President Scholl and Executive Vice President Solomon portrayed the mood of Wood Hall clerical workers with a series of anonymous quotes:

> It's run like a school, you know? You need little slips signed by somebody to explain where you were.
>
> We're second class citizens, always have been.
>
> When Building E was going up /ETS research building/, a lot of Research and Test Development people went through Wood. The people in Wood got burned up seeing them wander in any old time, or wander out, while they must get in on the dot and stay til the last minute, like kids in a classroom waiting for the bell. . . .
>
> We never hear what Vice Presidents do. . . .
>
> Everyone is pretty well locked in - no chance to do anything.
>
> Look at some of these women that have years and years of experience, and they bring in these young guys to supervise that don't know what's going on, probably never will.
>
> I've talked to 3 different people in Personnel. I don't think they care at all. One man told me if I didn't have an MA the best thing I could do was learn to type.
>
> Even the people who work for the professionals are better off. They get paid the same, but have much better quarters. That place /Wood Hall/ is like a factory.

> Sweat shop. Wonders they don't pay piece-work.
>
> You get little ripples now. Starting to talk union.[205]

A professional staffer, the memo noted, gave the other side: "I agree that we do, well, treat professionals differently but what do you suggest doing? I mean how could that be changed?"[206]

Mailroom workers, after more than a year of grievance meetings with personnel representatives concerning "school-room treatment" and chronic eyestrain and headaches resulting from poor lighting and ventilation, were compelled in March of 1974 to respond publicly in a letter to the editor to what they felt was a derogatory characterization in the company paper.

> It's about time that a situation existing here at ETS be clarified.
>
> Time and again the Mail room -- Preparation, Incoming/Outgoing -- have been considered an unimportant group of low intelligence people. It has taken us years to gain respect and dignity, and the recent Examiner article on temps /ETS temporary employees/ has tended to destroy this. . . .
>
> Now to add insult to injury, your article appears calling the temps in our department "middle aged women."
>
> Let us remind you that these so-called middle-aged women from Pennsylvania have the lowest average of time lost, produce the most in volume and are most competent.
>
> The Mail room is the Alpha of ETS and should be placed in a category of respect. We so-called middle aged women came here as young women and have matured with ETS.[207]

The Examiner printed the letter along with a ready response. "The Examiner understands the Mail room workers' concern. . . . Further checking shows that the Mail room temp force includes young adults and a number of staffers who are New Jersey and not Pennsylvania residents."[208]

Personnel officers also sensed discontent among non-clerical workers who assisted the professionals, but whose lack of certain formal academic credentials precluded them from professional status. A confidential February 16, 1973 meeting of the ETS Personnel Committee considered the complaints of research assistants about their status relative to research psychologists, their professional counterparts.

> Several research assistants feel that they are in fact performing the work of research psychologists but are not recognized or compensated accordingly. . . [T]hey felt that they were either underemployed or underpaid. The requirements of their job were too high for the work, or, if they were employed for their skills, they were being underpaid."[209]

According to the minutes of the meeting, there were other complaints. Lack of a contract which, unlike the research psychologists, made them vulnerable to being fired when there was no work was a complaint that ran through other departments, including operations. Sex discrimination was another.[210]

The officers of ETS did not take these warnings sitting down. Instead, they formed committees. Even before the highly critical report by Shephard Kimberly came in, ETS created several "Planning Committees" to be chaired by officers and comprised of representatives from all levels of the organization.[211] The aim, in the words of a memo from Vice President Solomon's aide David Fox, was "interactive vertical communication on problems of real importance to the organization."[212] (Original emphasis.) In other words, ETS officials were trying to get managers to talk to their subordinates.

The committee's final report proposed a six-month "calendar of events" to familiarize ETS staffers with their leaders and their role in "the organizational hierarchy." Among the scheduled activities were tours of other ETS divisions and even neighboring corporations, videotaped presentations of "A day in the life of" an ETS officer, staff opinion polls in the ETS Examiner, and, at the conclusion, a dinner in the cafeteria among "Selected Officers" and "Selected Personnel" after which questionnaires would be distributed to employees asking them what they had learned from the event and soliciting their opinions.[213]

Despite such energetic plans, the committees were not able, concluded an analysis by Solomon's staff, "to force a democratic involvement of the staff in decision-making where the decision makers do not really want or need advice from the group."[214] (Emphasis added.)

If sharing power with nonprofessionals was not an interest of ETS officials, keeping down their expenditures in this area remained a prime concern. In January, 1972, ETS executives faced a New Jersey State law making temporaries potentially eligible for unemployment benefits--which would be charged to ETS.[215] Up until that time, temps had been considered a corporate godsend. They were a stable, low-paid workforce, rooted to the area by family ties, which ETS could call in and lay-off at will. Concentrated in the lowest-paying ETS hourly wage jobs, the temps handled the night shift at keypunch; the switchboard that handles candidate calls; the file, document and mail rooms; in short, the mass production centers that are the core of ETS' business operations.[216]

Though they often worked more than 1,400 hours per year, some for many years at a time, temps were not eligible for most ETS benefits.[217] Even more important, until the new law was proposed, their temporary classification made them ineligible for unemployment compensation during their frequent lay-offs from ETS. Temps had proven so attractive to the corporation that from the time of its founding through the mid-1970s, thirty to forty percent of the ETS workforce had consisted of these temporary employees, eighty-five percent of whom were women (in 1974).[218] (In 1978, women comprised sixty-seven percent of the total ETS staff. About thirty-three percent of officials and managers, and fifty-three percent of professionals were female. On the other hand, ninety-four percent of office and clerical workers, and eighty-four percent of service workers were women.[219])

The situation of the temporary workers may have been attractive to the ETS officials watching the bottom line, but it was less so to the workers themselves. Temporary employees had already begun to complain about their situation in the <u>Examiner</u>. In a letter, one worker wrote that despite the many surveys, reviews and studies, little of substance had been done to improve the conditions for clerical workers and temps. The bonus she received for 1,300 hours of work, she wrote, could cover neither sick-days nor one year of Blue Cross-Blue Shield health insurance.

If a woman raising a family on a temp job got sick, she wrote, "Would she have to go on welfare because ETS could not give her the benefit of adequate health coverage?" The organization, she reminded ETS executives in closing, "could not function without us /temps/--we are valuable."[220]

The value of temporary workers was, indeed, of concern to ETS executives. A detailed economic analysis--prepared for Vice President Scholl with the advice of Operations Vice President E. Belvin Williams and Financial Vice President David Brodsky found that temporary labor was the most profitable possible arrangement for ETS--<u>unless</u> too many of them started collecting unemployment compensation under the New Jersey law. The study found that the right of employees to collect the unemployment benefits to which state law entitled them could be an expensive proposition for ETS. The study looked at the creation of a subsidiary ETS "manpower" or "Kelly Girl" corporation to "allow for maximum control and flexibility in dealing with temporary-type employees,"[221] and then analyzed the possible financial benefits of this route; using "two extreme cases, (everyone collects all unemployment benefits, and no one collects unemployment)":[222]

<u>NO ONE COLLECTS</u>

<u>Cost Per Year</u>

<u>ETS Temps</u>	<u>Contracted Manpower</u>
$5,245,312	$6,234,375

<u>Corporate Cost Differential</u>

$989,063

ALL COLLECT FULL UNEMPLOYMENT BENEFITS

Cost Per Year

ETS Temps   Contracted Manpower

$7,645,312 $6,234,375

Corporate Cost Differential

$1,410,937

SOURCE: ETS internal memo, August 2, 1972.[223]

"In general," the study concluded, "if experience demonstrates that less than 42% of terminated employees qualify and apply for UC [Unemployment Compensation], then temp. manpower costs less."[224]

ETS responded with a two-part strategy to deal with its temporary workers' unemployment compensation. First, when hired, they would be asked to sign an "availability card" indicating they were "not available for full-time work,"--even if they intended to work all the hours ETS would give them.[225] This action would make them legally ineligible for compensation.[226] The ETS labor consultant recommended that the "significance of the cards . . . not [be] fully explained to the signers."[227]

In a confidential March 14, 1972 memo Robert E. Smith, then Executive Director of General Programs, ordered that all offices hiring temps refer them to Personnel, where they would be asked to sign an "Availability Record."[228] And, a new termination policy was applied to all ETS employees, permanent as well as temporary:

> If questions are raised about eligibility for coverage under Unemployment Compensation, the employee should be instructed to file a claim with the state unemployment office in the appropriate state or regional office. No

> <u>other information is to be given the terminating employee regarding unemployment compensation.</u>[229] (Original emphasis.)

ETS workers quickly discerned the new unemployment policy's true intent. A confidential memo from an operations supervisor who was "seeing and talking to a lot of very unhappy people" reported the sentiments of a meeting of nightshift keypunch workers with "near verbatim quotes" regarding the Availability Record policy:

> ETS is trying to pull something on us and we don't like it.
>
> This is intimidation (one individual said) and we don't like it (most of the group chimed in simultaneously). These are our jobs and we need them. You are taking them from us and we don't like it.
>
> Are you training extra new people in training classes so that you can replace the ones of us who refuse to sign this form?[230]

"As we gain more and more experience with the phenomena of Unemployment Compensation the problems look increasingly ominous," one ETS presonnel official told Vice President E. Belvin Williams in a confidential memo.

> The simple fact is this: we will either have to allow UC payments to nearly all temps or we will take a tremendous beating from the employees for being the "bad guys."
>
> I'm very concerned that the feelings of the employees toward UC will rapidly turn into pro-union sentiments.
>
> We, naturally, want to pay as little as possible in UC taxes while the employees feel UC payments are an unequivocal right. . . .
>
> [A]s we call employees back we will be asking them to sign an Availability Card which will relieve us of much of the potential tax liability next year.

> Employees have already expressed in advance their
> intention to refuse to sign the cards which indicate
> their limited availability.
>
> The conflict we will then face is going to be
> difficult. . . . If we make even a single exception
> to requiring a signed card as a condition of employ-
> ment we will have set the precedent for employee
> rebellion. On the other hand, if we decide to accept
> the risk of a reduced labor pool by insisting on
> compliance and later relent we will also lose face
> and credibility . . . and perhaps control over
> the situation.[231] (Ellipsis in original.)

The personnel director posed two options for ETS management: (1) "dispense with the availability cards and pay the vast majority of UC claims," or (2) "enforce the requirement of the cards as a condition of employment and take the risks of a limited labor pool and union-fostering resentment."[232]

This official was later joined by operations manager B.L. Tchorni in urging that ETS give the workers their benefits. In a confidential memo to Vice Presidents Williams, Brodsky, and Scholl and Executive Vice President Solomon, they concluded that "use of the AC ultimately will not save us money but will certainly cost us much in an increasingly bitter staff."[233]

A letter from a temporary night keypuncher finally delivered the issue to the desk of President Turnbull. Expressing her "displeasure with the methods ETS has employed to try and disqualify all part-time employees from being eligible for benefits," she charged:

> [T]he motive is purely monetary on ETS behalf.
> . . . I am completely exhausted and tired of fighting
> this battle. I refuse to stand in another line at
> Unemployment or have one more person connected with
> that office talk down to me. . . . I have enjoyed my
> two years association with ETS, but I feel very strongly
> that Management quite simply "blew it." I hope in some

way this letter will help my co-workers who can't speak up because they have a much greater personal need for the job.[234]

"I am very sorry that your experience with the Unemployment Compensation program has been so upsetting," President Turnbull replied to the temporary employee two weeks later.

> I can certainly appreciate your frustration. To a large extent, as I'm sure you realize, our actions are determined by New Jersey law. . . . I appreciate the time you took to bring this matter to my attention. Hopefully, future events will not be so distressing.[235]

The attempt to deny the company's lowest-paid workers their legally mandated benefits is a sobering example of the ETS management approach which Shephard Kimberly dissected in his 1972 memo. Aiming to "avoid hyperbole and to keep the level of rhetoric cool,"[236] Kimberly reported, "At ETS a distinction is made between 'professional', and 'non-professional', and, although there is some fuzzy ground, the distinction is, literally, academic. Once made, the distinction creates a basic two-class society where the inequality is profoundly felt by the 'lower' class."[237] A "simple example" of the inequality, Kimberly wrote, was the different situations of the personnel employees hiring professional staff, and those hiring the non-professional staff. He wrote,

> The "professional" personnel hiring staff enjoys better quarters, offices, secretaries, titles like "Recruiter, Recruitment and Placement" and much higher salaries than the people hiring "non-professional" staff, who are called "interviewers" and whose secretarial help doubles as receptionist and errand girl for the rest of the Division.[238]

With an argument designed to appeal to the self-interest of the corporation's management, Kimberly contended that debilitating effects grew from such distinctions in the organization.

> A corporate double standard that will function for 250 people or for 500, or for a thousand becomes increasingly invidious as the size increases, the structure becomes more rigid, and the communications clog. . . . In some sense, the issue is a moral one, especially underlined in the context of Equal Employment Opportunity: ETS <u>ought</u> not operate with a double standard. But the issue is really more pragmatic. With the increased size and resulting intensification of hierarchical authority, both communications and initiative suffer. The organization becomes less responsive to change and innovation in a time when flexibility and enthusiastic welcome to change are necessary for survival.[239]

Besides cutting down the corporation's flexibility, Kimberly asserted that the morale problems associated with the hierarchy may be a factor in the "number of . . . accidents /at ETS/ . . . /and/ the number of extended ill /leaves/."[240]

Though there were medical services available for staff members, Kimberly "was surprised" to find that no psychiatric referral "at least as far as the nurse is concerned" was available for employees. More importantly, he concluded that

> ETS should have available . . . the services of a social guidance person who could advise staff members who are below or near the poverty level concerning services available to them. <u>ETS has large numbers of its staff who have the same kinds of problems as persons on welfare</u>, and who have even less access to competent advice and counseling.[241] (Emphasis added.)

Reconciling the differences between a staff which at one end earned salaries tied to the highest paying universities in the country, and at the other end was filled by large numbers of people living on low-wage incomes would be no easy task. Kimberly recognized. He believed that the friction was not the fault of the Personnel department itself. "The problems of communications, of morale, and high levels of anxiety within the Division are symptomatic of the larger corporate environment, rather than deficiencies within the Division itself."[242]

ETS, Kimberly counseled, could either ignore the dissatisfaction he had unearthed, or recognize that "there must be some flame in all that rhetorical smoke" and move to change the way the company was run. Kimberly wrote:

> The former is much easier and more satisfying, confirming as it does two decades of successful operation. The latter is enormously difficult and time consuming and cannot be delegated, nor accomplished by any conceivable reorganization.[243]

Kimberly believed that the conflict could be dampened by a change in attitudes. The discord, he wrote, "is probably irreversible unless the whole executive level of ETS changes, in ways that are somehow clearly perceptible to the staff, the way it views the majority of the staff."[244]

The experience of ETS minority employees indicates that the problem goes far deeper. For here, even after an apparent change in the receptiveness of ETS executives to employing minority people in top positions, mass discontent with ETS practices has persisted.

In March 1970, ETS President Turnbull hired C. Sumner "Chuck" Stone, author, former newspaper editor, and education aide to Congressman Adam Clayton Powell, as the first non-white executive in ETS or College Board history. Stone was brought on to deal with problems of racial discrimination, both internal--in hiring and personnel policies--and external--in testing and education.[245]

Stone quickly established deep support among the company's minority employees: "There is only one member of ASSETS [Afro-American Society for Soul at ETS] who has the ear of all Blacks at ETS--Mr. Chuck Stone--and for him most of us would put our arms in the fire. . . ."[246] wrote one ETS employee. Stone also drew a strong reaction from the company's top officials, to whom he directed a series of often blistering memos that minced no words about the status of black employees at ETS.

In a somewhat staid, self-consciously restrained and academic corporation, Stone's memos and proposals must have raised more than a few eyebrows. Stone titled one sharply-worded memo to Solomon, a "Blue-print for Black Progress in a White Organization of Red-Blooded Americans." As he, and other minority staff members would argue repeatedly, Stone challenged ETS' assumption that it was not responsible for the use of its tests. In fact, Stone said, ETS should only allow institutions to use the tests, if they agree "to use the test for the limited purposes stated." ETS, he argued, had to face up to the effects of its policies.

> ETS must insist on a more strict accountability in the use of its tests and the purposes for which they are constructed. To prevent inadvertant misuse and in some instances, deliberate misinterpretations of scores for minority groups, ETS should develop a signed agreement in which the user agrees to use the test for the limited purposes stated. There would be no contractual agreements to administer and develop tests or forward test scores to institutions which do not comply with ETS guidelines on the use and interpretation of scores.[247]

About a year later, as its top priority recommendation, the PEOPLE committee echoed Stone's call for accountability. In a memo signed by Stone, the committee called on ETS to include in test literature a condemnation of "misuse of tests." The committee also urged the corporation to "monitor test score use in each program and institute corrective action."[248]

In a July, 1971 memo, Stone scored the company's refusal to establish an independent component within ETS and the College Board to implement President Turnbull's comprehensive plan--known as the HEAR plan--to increase minority admission at colleges and universities:

> It reflects what I call the "Black chain of command syndrome," a genuine fear within predominantly white institutions of an independent Black administration, not only intellectually authoritative, but operationally efficient. Administrative independence is, of course, organizationally impossible, but this still does not reassure white racist predilections.[249]

Stone had been pushing for the development of an authority within ETS, in one form or another, to deal with minority problems--both within and outside the corporation--since his first days at the corporation. In the August 18, 1970 memo to Solomon, Stone proposed the establishment of a Division of Urban and Minority Affairs that would, among other things, promote accountability in the use of ETS tests, undertake new research projects--"under minority direction"--to analyze the effects of the tests on minority students, and recruit more qualified minority employees.[250] (Emphasis in original.)

One barrier to that last goal--increasing the percentage of minority employees--was what Stone called "the persistent practice at ETS of selectively secret employment." Stone observed:

> This is the discovery of a person outside of ETS
> with whom ETS is impressed and either hires the
> person by tailoring job specifications to his
> experience and capabilities, or, as is equally
> true in several instances, an executive or manager
> simply decides he or she wants a particular ETS
> staff member and effects the transfer.[251]

Both of which meant that potential minority applicants would never even hear about the job openings, much less be eligible to apply for them: "I don't think it hyperbolic--or just some more 'rhetoric'--to suggest that the majority of black professionals at ETS would view both procedures as deeply rooted in racist attitudes."[252] J. Bradley Williams, a member of ASSETS who later became ETS' personnel chief, voiced a similar complaint in a 1972 memo. "ASSETS," he wrote, "is increasingly concerned with the discrepency between the philosophical position of ETS (as an equal opportunity employer) and the organization's actual practice."[253]

Equally disturbing was the treatment of minority employees once they were hired. In his November 2, 1971 memo to Solomon and Turnbull, Stone laid out the problems:

> 1.) Minority input was solicited on a general program and then completely ignored. . . .
>
> 2.) Minority input into programs and projects <u>directly</u> related to minority problems has not even been solicited. . . .
>
> 3.) Minority professionals, by and large--and there are some exceptions--are simply not treated with the same professional respect accorded other professionals. In a few instances, some of the minority professionals are over-indulged in their incompetence, a fact which other minority professionals regard as demeaning and patronizing. . . .[254]

Finally, on February 7, 1972 a little under two years after he came to work at ETS, Stone tendered his resignation in a two page letter to Turnbull, with whom he had developed a close relationship.[255] Turnbull urged Stone to stay and head up a new division of minority and urban affairs. "Your leadership is important not only to members of the minority staff at ETS," Turnbull wrote in a memo imploring Stone to stay on, "but certainly to majority staff and most importantly to the educational efforts throughout the country that can be enhanced significantly if ETS's part in them reflects the Black experience and that of other minorities."[256]

Turnbull agreed to support all the reforms Stone proposed in a "Memorandum for the Record" he wrote in February--the establishment of the new division, the establishment of a research center within the division, and six other points--except for one recommendation, the one Stone considered most important. As one of his nine points, Stone proposed that the head of the new division report directly to the President of ETS--Turnbull--instead of to the Executive Vice President--Solomon--like the rest of the corporation. This, Turnbull, despite his glowing praise for Stone, could not support. "I believe that the Center should report to the Executive Vice-President. Any other structural arrangement would interfere with rather than enhance the communicating--coordinating--energizing interaction with the rest of ETS. . . ."[257]

Since the early 1970s and the two-year tenure of Chuck Stone, ETS has made some numerical progress in the recruitment of minority staff. According to figures compiled by Stone at the time, 3.9 per cent of the ETS officers and managers in 1971 were black. Blacks comprised 4.9 per cent of the professionals—but absolutely none of the executive and division directors.[258] According to figures in the 1978 ETS *Annual Report* minorities made up 9.4 per cent of the officials and managers in 1978 and 7.2 per cent of the professionals. By comparison, they made up almost nineteen per cent of the laborers and over fifty-five per cent of the service workers.[259]

However, the increased number of black employees—some like J. Bradley Williams and E. Belvin Williams being placed in top positions—has not had a clearly perceptible effect on the policies faced by ETS minority consumers. Almost a decade after Stone was hired, ETS still officially maintains that its tests are not biased and that the discriminatory consequences of its tests cannot be traced to the actions of ETS. For example, President Turnbull continued the ETS tradition of representing itself as a mere agent of the institutions when he said recently, while discussing law school admissions: "What I want the tests to do is not as important as what the law schools have found in past practice."[260]

Despite some progress in opening executive positions to minority professionals, in 1979 many of the same employment problems outlined by Stone still remained. In May 1979 a group of over 100 black ETS employees signed a stinging four-page memo to Turnbull and Solomon:

> We are especially concerned that the organization has not recognized the promotability of its own Black staff. For example: there has never been a Black staff member

elevated to the position of officer at ETS, there is a
paucity of Black representation at the levels of
administrative directors, area directors, division
directors, program directors and managers of operating
departments. . . .

Why are so few members of the Black staff holders of
the salary grades 43 and above, and relatively few Black
staff members in the upper ranges of the salary brackets?
Surely it is not an issue of credentials or long-term
association with the organization. . . .

Looking at ETS' organizational structure, one is
struck by the fact that the shortage of Blacks appears
to be widespread with the usual exception: those jobs
considered by all to be menial, low status, and low paying. Why is it that when one sees Black people working
at the Henry Chauncey Conference Center, one sees them
working as waitresses and maids? . . .

Along these same lines, we have taken particular note
of the long maintained and loudly proclaimed policy of
the ETS Research Division that allegedly encourages the
hiring of Blacks: "We will hire them if we can find them."
This policy has certainly not produced Black staff members.
Even when one is found and hired, tenure in the Research
Department by any Black is routinely short-lived. Where
is the loudly proclaimed commitment?[261]

The black employees who signed the May 25 memo feared reprisals from management. In a June 7, 1979 message to "Concerned Black Staff", twenty-five of the signatories of the earlier memo reported that some black staff were already having problems with their bosses:

Already, we are learning of problems some of the
Signatories are having with their bosses. We expect
more reprisals to come! We have learned that our
May 25, 1979 memorandum to Turnbull and Solomon has
been xeroxed many times and all of the officers and
most supervisors have a copy with the list of
signatories.[262]

The memo also gave a two-paragraph course in some of the ways ETS has diffused the criticism of its minority employees:

> All of us have been extremely careful not to have
> leaders for this movement, because we are fearful
> that the corporation will attempt to fire or transfer
> some of them, or attempt to work out individual deals
> through the use of promotions or raises for a few. . . .
>
> It is important that you do not listen to or
> participate in rumors regarding the effort to end the
> discrimination at ETS. The purpose of some of those
> rumors is to divide and diffuse our effectiveness and
> block our ultimate goal of ending discrimination
> against Blacks at ETS. . . . If your boss approaches
> you about your <u>Concern for Black Progress at ETS</u>, or
> if you are harassed, report it to the Group.[263]

Minority employees in many companies have had difficulty reforming the practices of top executives. But, ETS' invulnerability to basic change on any major front is more remarkable. It took an ambitious personal project, authorized by ETS President Turnbull, to demonstrate the singular momentum of the corporate machine which resisted the initiatives of even its highest executives.

The project was Turnbull's HEAR proposal--the Higher Educational Ability Recognition Program--which started making the rounds of Rosedale officers in August 1969. As discussed briefly in Chapter III, Turnbull's proposal began with a strongly worded condemnation of the inequities of the United States higher education system:

> The trouble is that at present the number of minority
> group children who gain access to higher education is
> pitifully small. This is not for the most part
> because malevolent men are working to block their
> path. Rather, it is because the . . . system is
> designed to work easily and fairly for the students
> who constitute the bulk of its clientele: the tradi-
> tional college-goers. They are . . . white, middle-
> class youngsters. . . . The system is simply not
> designed to handle the ghetto child.[264]

Turnbull recognized that ETS tests played a role in this system and, as President of ETS, he said he was going to do something about it.

> The tests are built to describe the academic development of the traditionally prepared student, but not to uncover the depth and variety of skills and abilities possessed by the bright student who has come through a vocational program, or an academic program in a school where the college-going tradition is weak or non-existent.[265]

President Turnbull called for a fundamental overhaul of the ETS test system with "a concerted and sustained attack on six fronts simultaneously."[266] He proposed major changes in the fields of guidance, testing, admissions, curriculum, financial aid, and educational research. Under the HEAR proposal, the role of ETS in college admissions would be significantly expanded: ETS would establish and run counseling centers in ghettos around the country, and would coordinate a national program for identifying and giving academic and financial help to promising minority students. But most of all, according to the proposal, ETS would overhaul its biggest selling product line: the SAT.[267]

The President's proposal received immediate top-level attention. A HEAR Task Force of key officers and trustees of the College Board and ETS began a series of meetings that would extend through 1971. Chuck Stone, who in a little over a year was promoted to the newly created post of ETS Director of Minority Affairs and later offered an ETS vice-presidency, assumed primary responsibility for the HEAR proposal.[268]

The HEAR proposal never got beyond the words of Dr. Turnbull's memo. Despite explicit endorsement by the presidents of ETS and the College Board,[269] each of the proposal's six components was abandoned. Chuck Stone and his HEAR counterpart from the College Board staff, Steven Wright, quickly found themselves in possession of a flood of memos from ETS staffers explaining in detail why some proposed alteration, especially of the SAT, was infeasible and undesirable given ETS' current structure. President Turnbull's call for change and overhaul of the SAT was not echoed by the ETS executives who actually managed the program.[270]

In a fourteen page memo dated July 7, 1971, Stone and Wright tersely noted objections to the proposal: "The assumption that the special needs of the target populations require new and special instruments is questioned."[271]

HEAR's failure to survive as an intact, omnibus program did not surprise its advocates. The original Turnbull plan proposed such an imposing new role for ETS in college admissions and society that, as Stone candidly points out, implementation of the program with Stone as director "would have made me the most powerful black man in America."[272]

The opposition HEAR met on every single count was thorough and vigorous. In one memo Stone and Wright complained that "the proposal has generated opposition unrelated to its merit."[273] The HEAR Task Force discovered a growing consensus around the position that the SAT and the college admissions system could be tampered with only at the risk of endangering ETS' current position of strength.[274] The HEAR proposal, President Turnbull reflected in 1977,

> . . . turned out to be more ephemeral than I wish it had been, because we never found a way of getting organized and moving on that, except in bits and pieces. But the proposal as a whole I kind of liked as a whole.[275]

Chuck Stone's verdict, as recorded in a personnel memo recounting the **confidential** ETS exit **interview** given when he resigned months after HEAR died on Mr. Solomon's desk, was more emphatic: A major problem at ETS is, he said, ". . . institutional non-change. The officers are creating their own opposition."[276]

But the effective resistance by the status-quo forces at ETS to proposals for change from within the organization was not similarly successful in opposing reform pressures which have been mounting from the outside during the late 1970s. In the history of ETS, 1979 will be remembered as the year when those examined began to turn the rays of sunlight on the examiners. An organized consumer perspective on the Educational Service began taking shape. One expression of this orientation was the struggle by students for routine disclosure of information about the tests they are compelled to take. Their drive made major news in 1979 with the enactment of New York State's Truth-in-Testing legislation.

CHAPTER IX

RAYS OF SUNLIGHT, WINDS OF CHANGE

It began quite inauspiciously in the New York State legislature. A coalition led by the New York student Public Interest Research Group (NYPIRG) proposed the enactment of a truth-in-testing bill in 1976.[1] During the three years the bill was pending, it had drawn virtually no attention. At the first hearing on the bill, in May 1978, before a state Senate committee, the testing-education establishment opposed the bill strenuously and successfully. It never moved out of committee.[2]

But the testing industry was worried, nonetheless. In a May 15, 1978 memo to the professional staff, S.P. Marland, Jr., president of the College Board and former U. S. Commissioner of Education, warned of "a systematic movement afoot which calls up the sympathies of law-making bodies in the presumed interest of consumers, notably students, who take standardized tests. The generality behind the thrust calls for making test publishers more accountable by state or federal regulation."[3] Mr. Marland took note of College Board communications to all its members in California (where a similar bill was pending) as well as to 1,500 secondary schools. "These mailings," he said, "are part of a major coordinated effort between the New York office . . . and Palo Alto office to call the attention of legislators to the dangers posed by this legislation."[4]

After consultation with testing technicians, chief sponsor State Senator Kenneth P. LaValle revised the bill for the 1979 session, but this did not make it any more acceptable to the

test companies. S. 5200-A contained three major provisions--
none of them imposing regulatory standards. Instead, disclosure
was their touchstone. First, the bill required the testing
industry, including ETS, to make public internal studies on the
tests' validity and data relating to possible cultural and class
biases contained in the tests. Second, it required the companies
to give students specific information on what their scores meant
and how their scores would be presented to academic and other
institutions. Third, the bill required the companies to provide
students--on request--with a copy of the questions, correct
answers and the student's own answers thirty days after the scores
had been received.[5]

Both supporters and opponents of the bill girded for a
major lobbying struggle. The ETS-College Board forces took the
customary corporate lobbying strategies: retain two of the best-
connected corporate law firms in Albany, mass distribute letters
and telegrams to education officials, high school principals,
administrators, and professors urging them to oppose the bill,
and confront the legislature with the specter of horrendous
consequences for test takers should the bill become law.[6] Truth-
in-testing supporters came from diverse constituencies--student,
labor, consumer and minority groups, teachers, parents, and some
testing specialists. The two adversaries brought their views to
the joint hearings on the legislation held by the Senate and
Assembly higher education committees on May 9, 1979. Thirty-one
people testified or submitted written statements.[7]

ETS and its allies alleged that the requirement to disclose questions would necessitate annual rewriting of questions, thereby increasing the price of tests. They added that this state law would place New York students at a disadvantage in admission decisions and would bring the government into an area where it did not belong.[8] Backers of the bill countered by describing ETS' arguments as either factually erroneous, or part of a contrived bluff. Dr. Vito Perrone, president of the National Consortium on Testing told the legislators:

> I am particularly distressed by the threats of dire circumstances--the trebling of the cost, more limited test administration, fewer test administration sites, reduced credibility of results, poorer tests. There is some degree of intimidation in all of this that is unacceptable. There is little evidence that any of the dire circumstances need to prevail, unless, again, the testing industry refuses to bring already existing knowledge and fresh commitment to bear on the new circumstances.[9]

Lewis Pike, a former ETS official, now with the National Institute of Education, responded to a College Board statement against the bill in a letter to Senator LaValle: "What disturbs me most about some of the statements in the memorandum dated May 11 /the ETS memorandum opposing the bill/ is that they continue to emphasize issues that were well-answered during your committee's hearings prior to that date, and that were already well-resolved by provisions built into the testing bill."[10]

One of the major ETS allegations was that the legislation, through its disclosure provision, would disrupt equating (ETS' practice of balancing scores from more difficult test forms with scores from less difficult ones, often by using, repeatedly, the same questions in different exams) and increase fees. Despite the bill's specific exemption of ungraded questions (such as the ones used to equate the SAT) from disclosure, a May 11, 1979 College Board mailing warned educators that the bill would "seriously disrupt the equating procedures."[11] The mailing also neglected another important fact: two days earlier at the hearing, in response to a direct question, ETS' Executive Vice President Robert Solomon had testified that "I would not say it would be impossible /to equate tests under this bill/. . . . There are other ways of equating tests. Undoubtedly, if faced with passage of the bill we would have to look at those."[12]

The other stance ETS and its satellite organizations took was to threaten decreased services. The New York Public Interest Research Group (NYPIRG) responded to the charge that the bill will increase costs: "According to the internal cost studies of ETS, only about 5% of the fee paid by the student goes to the cost of question development compared to 22% to 27% which goes to the test company profit margin."[13] ETS had estimated that the LaValle bill would cost them $1,092,000 in increased development costs for the Scholastic Aptitude Test. By their own figures, that left them and the College Board with more than $2 million* in annual profit on that test alone. There was, NYPIRG argued, no legitimate reason for ETS to reduce services or increase fees.[14] Clearly, ETS was developing an opposition tactic rather than making a supportable claim.

Nonetheless, the May 11th memo had its desired effect: mail from College Board representatives and other educators

---

*The 22-27% figure refers to the range of ETS/CB profits over a three-year period. Recent figures indicate that the dollar profit margin may be even greater than the $2 million figure. See Chapter 8.

opposing the bill began to flood the legislature. "A lot of the professional community did not take the time to really explore the issue beyond what the opposition said in their memo," observed Senator LaValle.[15]

The truth-in-testing forces, led by Senator LaValle and Assemblymen Albert Vann of Brooklyn and Ivan Lafayette of Queens, guided their bill through step after step of the legislative pathway during the last hectic days and hours of the session in June of 1979.[16] The bill had bipartisan backing, drawing support at crucial junctures from such diverse legislators as Republican Senator John Caemmerer and Democrat Alan Hevesi, the Assembly Deputy Majority Leader. On the Assembly floor, John J. Flanagan, a Republican lawmaker from Huntington, Long Island, made one of the most effective speeches: "Standardized tests are taking over our evaluation of people," Flanagan said. "Maybe we can't get rid of **that** but what we have to do is open up the process. Let the people who are being standardized by it look at it and find out what the standards are and why they don't meet with them."[17]

After the legislation passed the two houses, the testing industry turned its lobbying and letter-writing forces on Governor Hugh Carey, urging him to veto the bill.[18] Ralph Nader had a conversation with the Governor and learned that he was favorably inclined to the bill, but had not reached a decision. Finally, despite the opposition of some of his staff to the disclosure bill, Governor Carey signed it into law on July 13, with these words: "The bill's requirements open to public scrutiny, review, criticism, and possible correction, a very important element in the process by which one of the most crucial determinations in a young person's life is made."[19] The Governor continued: "Further public discussion of the uses and abuses of testing seems highly desirable. This bill will provide an opportunity for this to occur in a reasoned and intelligent fashion."[20] The new law went into effect on January 1, 1980.

"Reasoned and intelligent" consideration got a quick jolt. Four days after Carey signed the bill, the Association of American Medical Colleges and the American Dental Association announced that they would cease administering their tests in New York State;[21] these tests are required for admission in most medical and dental schools in the country. Several publishers of low-volume tests, primarily the Psychological Corporation, the testing subsidiary of Harcourt Brace Jovanovich, Inc., announced during the fall that they too were taking their tests out of New York.[22] Although ETS did not withdraw any of its major programs from the state, service reductions and fee increases were announced.[23] In November, the Association of American Medical Colleges (AAMC) escalated its campaign against the law by filing suit in federal court, charging that the measure violated federal copyright law.[24]

Like truculent auto insurance companies who do not get their way, these test administrators appear to be engaging in a pull-out maneuver to force revision or repeal of the law. Many legislators do not like such blatant intimidation even if they agree with the vested interest exercising such a ploy. More subtle pressure may be applied by Gordon Ambach, the New York State Education Commissioner who was opposed to the bill all along. Ambach's preliminary impact statement on the law read something like a testing company broadside against truth-in-testing. And, in December, Ambach's supervisors, the Board of Regents, voted unanimously to gut, by amendment, the bill's key provision--the question disclosure requirement.[25]

These tactics, however, are not likely to roll back the gains made by the passage of truth-in-testing. Senator LaValle and Governor Carey have said that they intend to stand firm. Already, the testing industry is beginning to divide over this issue. The Law School Admission Council has announced that it will voluntarily disclose questions and answers to candidates across the country. In an internal memorandum for trustees of the Law School Admission Council, dated July 24, 1979, ETS Vice President for Law Programs Thomas O. White even conceded that "a totally 'open' testing and admission processing system for legal education is technically and economically feasible . . . our credibility and the quality of our program can be regained and maintained only if we move, as quickly as possible, to full disclosure of all aspects of the Law School Admission Services Programs."[26] The Dental Schools may continue to administer their tests in New York after all. New York's medical colleges have informed Senator LaValle that they were not consulted on and do not endorse the decision by the national association to pull out of New York or file suit in opposition to the law.[27] And, even within ETS, the company line is being eroded. E. Belvin Williams, the senior vice president in charge of testing programs, told the New York Times this fall, "Clearly, there are some arguments we couldn't sell. Students didn't believe our arguments on cost, some of which were inflated and constituted shooting from the hip." Williams even told the Times: "That consumers should have a right to know is fundamental to the effective exercise of public accountability."[28]

The effect of Truth-in-Testing will not be restricted to New York. Senator LaValle believes that by focusing new attention on testing, the bill will prompt schools across the country to "look at the whole student rather than place such an emphasis on the test."[29] Other state legislatures (as many as twenty) and the Congress will be considering similar truth-in-testing proposals.[30] A national bill modeled on the New York law with the addition of a strong financial disclosure provision was introduced in the House of Representatives in July, 1979. Sponsored by Representatives Ted Weiss of Manhattan, Shirley Chisholm of Brooklyn, and George Miller of California, the bill was the subject of hearings in the fall of 1979, and will be the subject of additional consideration this year.[31]

The rise of the truth-in-testing movement sets the stage for the emergence of a new national issue. For close to eighty years the power to define potential--to define the kind of behavior that institutions with the power to grant advancement will recognize as evidence of intellectual merit--has been gradually accumulating in the hands of an academic sub-specialty, the science of psychometrics, and its institutional leader, the Educational Testing Service. This concentration of power has occurred under conditions that have not been conducive to democratic inquiry and debate. So long as the tests and much of the information about their characteristics remained secret, the circle of informed discussion, in turn, remained close to those outside the orbit of the psychometric profession.

Without the means to evaluate the standards by which they were being judged, the people whose lives were altered by the verdicts of the mental testers could be easily dismissed as emotional and ill-informed complainers if they questioned the place assigned to them. "Many people have an aversion to being the subject of mental diagnosis," former ETS trustee John Gardner once explained, "In some this aversion to the tests is defensive: they fear precise appraisal of their own (or their children's) capacities."[32]

Now that the tests which form the basis of the psychometrician's claims are open to public analysis, such condescending dismissals will no longer suffice. The manner in which the Educational Testing Service decides who has "aptitude" and, through institutional intermediaries, accordingly advances or retards their careers and belief in their own potential, is no longer a subject of mere corporate policy or academic dispute. For years ETS' power has been an inescapable and mostly unquestioned aspect of people's lives. Now, it is time for this power to become the conscious and critical focus of their most careful and serious thought.

An institution which presumes to run on the principles of reason and persuasion, as opposed to fiat and force, has an extra burden of proof in justifying each additional increment of its power to the people who will be most affected. For thirty years ETS has been accumulating its power and asserting its reasonableness. But, the justification of that power to a public beyond its own employees, colleagues, corporate and institutional cohorts is only now beginning.

ETS is well aware of these conditions and is preparing a revealing response. On August 14, 1978, ETS President William Turnbull presented a confidential twenty-one page memorandum to his senior staff entitled "Public and Professional Attitudes Toward Testing and ETS: Relations With Key Publics." The Turnbull memo was a painstaking political analysis; it included thirteen pages of charts enumerating criticisms of ETS and testing "and how to invalidate, obviate, counter, rebut them."[33] It also contained lists of various constituencies and groups according to their positions on the issue with remarks about their susceptibility to influence by ETS.[34]

Turnbull began by tracing ETS' quiet rise to power: "We grew to be a large, omnipresent organization . . . by the early '70s ETS stood as a powerful, little-known organization that many people had to deal with involuntarily in order to gain (or be denied) access to educational opportunities."[35] Then, he described how growing public realization of that power had "ushered in the era of angry, hostile, and sometimes paranoid attacks on testing and on ETS."[36] ETS was about to enter an epoch of public questioning, Turnbull wrote, when reasoned discussion would not be adequate to sustain the corporate defense.

> ETS has traditionally taken a rather dignified--even lofty--and apolitical approach to matters of public controversy. I believe we need to retain our dignity but realize that the problems lie much more in the realms of communications and politics than in logic and that the solutions are going to be found (or the battles lost) in those hot arenas rather than in cool reason.[37]

Signs of ETS' "hot arenas" strategy are already beginning to surface. The New York Truth-in-Testing campaign, during which an ETS lobbying memo stated flatly, "Equating . . . would be destroyed by passage of S. 5200,"* was only the start.[38] In Washington, where the federal bill is under consideration, College Board Vice President Lois Rice** has circulated a memo saying that "the Weiss /Truth-in-Testing/ bill is a mysterious piece of proposed legislation. There are no self-evident reasons for its introduction, no known scandals it is to correct, and no apparent basis for the federal intervention proposed. All of which suggests there may be a hidden agenda that will in time be revealed."[40]

---

*By contrast, four months later, after the bill had been enacted, ETS statistician Gary Marco explained to the New York Times how equating procedures were being continued, with modifications, in order to comply with the law.[39]

> "The legislation has caused us to do some creative thinking," said Gary L. Marco, director of statistical analysis for College Board programs. "And there are a lot of people around here who all along favored things like letting a student see his /test/. Now that the competition has to do it, we can."

**Before the lobbying capability of ETS' Washington, D.C. office was bolstered, Rice served jointly as Washington lobbyist for both ETS and the College Board. She is now working together with ETS in lobbying against the federal truth-in-testing bill.

The suggestion that those who question the power of the current ETS test system are somehow pursuing a hidden agenda, which culminates with goals such as the abolition of all evaluation and educational standards, is a centerpiece of the ETS gameplan. ETS strategists are determined to make it seem that defense of the principles of standards, excellence and the intelligent use of information is necessarily equivalent to defense of the ETS test system. The strawman tactic is plain to see in the comments of ETS officials, "I don't happen to believe," affirms ETS Executive Vice President Robert J. Solomon, "that a lack of information results in wiser decisions."[41] "Education and society," notes the Turnbull memo, "would suffer if testing were done away with."[42]

The consumers of ETS have too much at stake to let the corporation define the terms of the debate, particularly to define it in these terms. The Turnbull memo is premised on the assumption that reason and public discussion do not mix well, and that, as the debate over the future of ETS moves from the board room to the lunchroom, logic must give way to a public relations strategy. This condescending approach may, indeed, be the best for safeguarding the interests of ETS. But it is one which ETS consumers cannot afford to let stand unchallenged.

The implications of each aspect of the testing and information system which ETS now controls must be assessed with utmost care. Those aspects which serve consumers and society, rationally and equitably, should be distinguished from those which serve the purposes only of a particular class, and again from those which serve no rational purpose at all. ETS should not be given an intellectual monopoly to complement its economic one by being allowed to define the choices in terms of ETS or nothing. Rather, the choices should involve the question of **which elements of the current testing and information system**, or **which elements of alternative systems**, should be retained or incorporated, and which should be discarded.

There are observers who say that various important services could not be performed without the current ETS test system. Some of those mentioned include providing a network of convenient test centers, a means for applicants from little known schools to become known to universities across the country,[43] and a means of describing inequitable social conditions.[44]

Convenience is provided by the logistical apparatus, which should be distinguished from the substance of the instruments (be they biographical questionnaires, essays, or tests of any form) which happen to be administered in the test centers. The function of calling applicants to the attention of schools depends simply on having instruments which schools recognize, a function which is hurt rather than helped by restricting the instruments available to a single, narrow multiple-choice test. Information on inequitable social conditions can easily be gathered by sampling and need not involve tests which affect the future of individuals. In short, none of these functions depends on maintaining a selective aptitude testing system of the kind now run by ETS.

Some have even gone so far as to argue that the ETS test system is needed to gather information on how well applicants can read and write. Quite clearly, however, ETS' self-styled uniqueness is not premised on tests designed simply to show whether students can read and write. Its uniqueness is based, instead, on the claim that ETS tests measure the basic quality of aptitude and predict future performance.

From the earliest papers of the founders of mental measurement[45] to the most recent aptitude test literature sent to millions of parents and students, the psychometric profession has assumed a role for itself which went far beyond objectively reporting how people had performed on assortments of multiple-choice test questions. In an ideological leap of faith, exceptional in the history of any scientific discipline, psychometricians made the journey from the objective information that individuals had answered a certain number of questions right and a certain number wrong to the subjective judgment--presented as authoritative, scientific finding--that the test had measured a basic quality of their mind.

For the early mental testers it was "intelligence," for ETS it has more typically been "aptitude." But, the message to individuals and to the institution judging them has been the same. "No test of any kind is infallible," wrote Henry Chauncey, "/but/ the fundamental fact is that the good instrument will pick the good **man** far more often that it will err."[46]

This claim and the ensuing practice of using multiple-choice tests to guide crucial decisions about educational and career opportunities form the fundamental issue in the challenge to the reign of ETS. They are the source of ETS' power to hurt individuals and entire classes of people. It is this power which takes ETS out of the league of the conventional $94 million corporation (about the size of the Schwinn Bicycle Company)[47] to make it one of the world's most powerful organizations.

Growing consumer interest and knowledge of the workings and power of the Educational Testing Service are likely to reach a critical mass before long. To direct such energy effectively, an agenda of inquiries to be pursued and alternatives to be considered is needed, one shaped from the perspective of the people who will feel the consequences of the decisions that are reached. We intend to take a leading role in the coming national examination of the examiners and, in this spirit, urge that the following considerations have a prominent part on the agenda.

1. <u>What are the effects of restricting the information system (that is, the test center network and information processing facilities now controlled by ETS) to multiple-choice tests developed and chosen by a single organization?</u>

The question to be asked about the information system as currently constituted should not be just "who should run it?" (for example, should there be consumers on the board?) but "should it be run this way at all?"

Limiting the information gathering instruments to multiple-choice ETS tests restricts, unfairly and unnecessarily, the means by which individuals can demonstrate their skills and potential. "Applicants have an enormous range of special skills, sometimes developed to a remarkable degree as a result of hobby, which the present test programs mask, leaving them unable to show what they are best at and failing to give the college a full view of the individual capabilities of the student," wrote Johns Hopkins sociologist James S. Coleman, in the report of the College Board Commission on Tests. "Beyond the standardized testing that allows colleges to make direct comparisons of a few characteristics of applicants," Coleman argued, "the applicant should have the opportunity through selection from a very wide number of special tests . . . to exhibit his special capabilities . . . that may be relevant to the colleges' interest in him."[48]

The available test and other instruments should not only challenge a broad range of interests but should do so from a diversity of cultural viewpoints. This is particularly important for discovering the potential of minority and working class applicants whose talents may now be masked by the biases that, regardless of the efforts of the testmaker to avoid them, are necessarily inherent in any single test. One way to get an idea of what people can do is to face them directly with demanding tasks, using language and cultural assumptions most familiar to them. However, this approach does not fit into an information system which is dominated on each of its levels (college, graduate and professional school) by a single instrument and a single organization.

A narrowly based multiple-choice test is hardly the most thorough method of discovering the extent to which applicants have mastered tasks they will be expected to perform in school, such as scientific problem-solving or essay writing. On the contrary, as many educators have contended, reliance on multiple-choice tests can actually work against the development of these skills. Such reliance creates incentives for students to master, and schools to encourage the mastery of, the peculiar requirements of multiple-choice test-taking. The proliferation of test coaching courses in many of the nation's high schools (in addition to a multi-million dollar a year commercial business) is testament to the search by students for the test-taking skills they need in order to display "aptitude."[49]

Thomas Wheeler, a writing professor and author of The Great American Writing Block, made the point eloquently in a New York Times article in 1979: "Compositions, essay questions, term papers--vigorous thinking--all have yielded to one right answer out of four, to boxes to be checked, blanks to be filled. . . . The American language--supple, imaginative and alive--has lost ground to the pretense of measurement."[50] Christopher Jencks has also noted the effect of an academic lifespan with standardized tests:

> neither the SAT nor other multiple-choice tests measure students' ability to synthesize diverse information or to generalize from it. Schools and colleges ordinarily try to develop and measure these abilities by having students write essays. If today's high schools were putting more emphasis on writing, and if students were producing more coherent essays as a result, many people would feel this gain more than offset a decline on multiple-choice tests. . . . If secondary school students are writing more, it is a well kept secret.[51]

ETS has argued against the practicality of instruments such as essays and problem-solving exercises which do not use multiple-choice because they are not objective, that is, they do not offer unquestionably right or wrong answers and are difficult to score centrally.[52] But, why must all reflections of student talent be centrally processed through ETS? Cannot essays, for example, be sent to individual schools that could decide for themselves what they were looking for--be it creativity, facility with the language, or analytic ability? The nation's universities and especially ETS owe students whose skills are obscured by the current testing system the answers to these questions.

2. <u>What are academic and other institutions trying to accomplish with their admissions policies? Precisely what goals and whose interests do those policies actually serve?</u>

Any attempt to analyze and reform the test system must begin with ETS; it is more effective to focus on the single organization which creates and promotes the tests than on the thousands of institutions which use them. But, the importance of these institutions must also be recognized. As testmaker, ETS develops the rules about how people will be ranked. It is the institutions, however, which enforce those rules by using the ETS rankings as the basis for admission decisions. Reliance on ETS tests raises basic questions about an institution's purposes, and students, parents, workers and taxpayers should be asking them directly.

The significance of ETS tests in the admissions process is difficult to deny. A student cannot attend an ABA accredited law school without taking the LSAT;[53] 80% of business schools require the GMAT;[54] 74% of graduate departments require or recommend the

GRE;[55] test scores were identified by 80% of undergraduate schools in a 1976 College Board poll as "the most important" factor in admissions.[56]

The justification for such reliance on ETS scores can be seriously questioned. Validated against the criterion of first-year grades, the tests have been shown to improve efficiency of prediction by an average of only three to five per cent.[57] Against longer range criteria which presumably are better reflections of a school's final standards--that is, grades over the entire school career, or ability to graduate, or ability to improve one's knowledge and skills during the school career[58]--the validity of the tests is lower still. When it comes to performance beyond the classroom, such as outside accomplishments and eventual occupational performance, even the testmakers themselves are reluctant to argue that the scores are significant predictors.[59] When such tests are used to exclude people from a school, or an entire profession, as in the case of graduate and professional schools, and particularly law school,[60] it is time to ask why conditions of this kind should be tolerated.

From campus to campus, the first step toward opening up the admissions process is to open up its workings by analyzing the admissions practices of individual universities and colleges and making them the subject of community-wide debate.

Students, parents and concerned citizens generally should hold meetings about and request precise information on questions such as the following:

(a) How important are the tests in the admissions process? What are the actual formulas used for determining admissions and how heavily do these weight the tests? How does the school take into account the tendency of the tests to distribute scores systematically along class and ethnic lines?

(b) Who is excluded through reliance on the tests? ETS provides colleges, for example, with precise breakdowns of the scores and income levels of their applicants.[61] By combining this information with information about the actual admitted class, investigators can attempt to determine which groups tended to be excluded from the school by use of the test.

(c) What does the institution claim to gain from requiring the test and using it in the manner it does? Schools establish a criterion--such as improved prediction of first-year grades--to justify use of the ETS tests. How well does the ETS test predict performance on this criterion? And, for those affected by the admissions process, does the criterion itself constitute a valid or meaningful standard?

3. <u>Should applicants have to bear the cost of the tests?</u>

One reason why colleges and universities have come to rely so heavily on the tests is that the tests do not cost them anything. When deciding whether or not to require the test, the question they are faced with is not "why?," but rather "why not?" For low-income students, on the other hand, the College Board has acknowledged that "test fees themselves constitute a barrier to higher education."[62] Though fee waivers are available, ETS studies have noted that the system misses many of the students who actually need waivers.[63]

In addition, when applicants pay the fees, the test companies gain the political weapon of the threatened fee increase which was used in the truth-in-testing battle. They would likely use this weapon with much more discretion if those fees had to be borne by the universities which decide whether to use (or not use) ETS tests, instead of by defenseless consumers. The question is this: would not a system in which institutions bore the costs (at least the direct economic costs) of their decisions, and in which fee waivers were allocated among dozens of less well endowed schools rather than among hundreds of thousands of poor applicants, be more equitable and efficient?*

4. <u>Is the ETS ranking really a meritocratic ranking? What is the purpose of claiming that it is? What is the purpose of demanding that alternative admission standards rank candidates in a similar fashion?</u>

The assumption that any admissions instrument must be centrally scored is based on the assumption that schools must have a scale on which they can rank their applicants from top to bottom. The purpose of constructing such a scale is to rank the

---

*The mechanics of such a system have already been worked out and used in the case of the ETS Secondary School Admission Test (SSAT), a test which, ironically, serves perhaps the wealthiest pool of ETS consumers, applicants to prep school.[64] Fees can be prorated among schools based on their share of the national applicant pool.

applicants by some standard of merit, a standard which is validated by its ability to predict future success.

This is the theory behind the practice of using national multiple-choice admission tests and the claim that the rankings and admissions decisions they produce are based on merit. It is a theory, however, which is not sustained by the evidence. Thousands of test validity studies and hundreds of research reports indicate that no single numerical standard, or combination of numerical standards (such as scores and previous grades) can predict future success with any confidence.[65] This should not be surprising. Success in any kind of endeavor, academic or post-academic, requires a variety of skills, most of which standardized tests cannot even purport to measure.

This question is not, as ETS would frame it, a political one, but rather one of simple rationality. Is it rational to rank applicants and thereby affect their long-term prospects with tests that provide only an 8 to 15% improvement[66] over blind chance in the prediction of a short-term criterion such as first-year grades?

While the challenge to the current test system can be posed in strictly rational terms, the consequences of that system have clear political implications. For ETS aptitude tests have been shown to produce rankings which systematically reflect the test-taker's social class. By promoting this ranking as one based on merit and using it to deny opportunities and depress aspirations, the ETS test system routinely damages the poor, the working class, and the middle class relative to the more affluent and privileged.[67]

It is sometimes argued that, although all standards of merit are imperfect, the ETS aptitude test is at least a standard, by some definition of merit, and is therefore better than abandoning the attempt to judge merit at all. This argument is misleading for it ignores the availability of other standards and the fact that the selection of a standard has direct bearing on which social classes the admission system will reward and which it will penalize. Jencks has pointed out, for example, that a shift from an admission system based on test scores to one based on previous grades, certainly a legitimate measure of merit by traditional educational standards, would increase the proportion of working class students admitted.[68] ETS' own research has noted that judging candidates by the standard of previous <u>accomplishments</u>--things they have actually <u>done</u> in their school, community and in artistic and scientific endeavors--would virtually <u>eliminate</u> the elements of class and ethnic discrimination which prevail in the ranking by ETS scores.[69] The evidence suggests that the choice of the standard of merit may depend on which class one is interested in serving.

Questioning of the meritocratic presumption, however, must go beyond asking which standard of merit is used, to inquire <u>how</u> those standards are used. The evidence shows that whichever standard is chosen, the elements involved in determining success are too complex to be effectively predicted by any single index number.[70] Some educators have argued that experienced evaluators can take a wide range of unquantifiable information into account and arrive at reasonable agreement about the relative merits of the candidates.[71] If they do, however, little credit is due to ETS. The incentives of its test system push in the opposite direction, offering administratively convenient and politically defensible ways of evading the responsibility of judgment.

For schools, the difference between selection based on assessment of a broad range of information and assessment based on an ETS ranking can mean the difference between sixty minutes of work and sixty seconds of work. In sharp contrast, for many applicants placed low by the ETS ranking--including the working class and minority students who are placed low systematically-- it can mean the difference between selection and rejection.

Availability of a broad range of information is still not enough. Rational and equitable use of such information in the admissions process requires an institutional framework of accountability at each individual school. This can help avoid the biases which are now built into the centralized national ETS test system.

If the people with a stake in the actions of that school are informed and determined to hold it accountable for its choices (as they cannot now do, since schools are simply able to avoid blame for problems which originate with ETS), the issue of which classes and what kinds of people will be favored or penalized by a school's admissions policy can become the subject of free ranging public discussion.

Regardless of how such ultimate questions are resolved, the ETS test system, with its meritocratic pretense and its class-biased practices, is firmly in place and changing lives every day. It should be subjected to wide and careful analysis.

5. <u>Can significant reforms be implemented given ETS' current position</u>?

The final question is the most important. Apart from the choices made and the alternatives proposed, how can they be implemented? More pointedly, can they be implemented given the current structure of the Educational Testing Service and its position in the national system of educational and occupational advancement?

Though never metabolized by a comprehensive movement for fundamental change, a remarkable number of the ideas now being considered for test system reform have been previously proposed within the ETS orbit. Among them:

------Conversion of the SAT, in effect, to a truth-in-testing system, with full disclosure of questions and correct answers was proposed by B. Alden Thresher, Vice Chairman of the College Board Commission on Tests, former MIT Admissions Director, incorporator of the College Board, and Trustee of ETS, in the 1970 Report of the College Board Commission on Tests.[72]

------Abandonment of the claim to be measuring global constructs such as "scholastic aptitude" was recommended in the June, 1972 report of the ETS Committee on Testing of Minority Groups, chaired by Dr. Norman Fredericksen, the company's senior psychological researcher.[73]

------Turning ownership of test scores, and thereby control over how they are converted and used by ETS, over to candidates was proposed in the June, 1970 report of the ETS PEOPLE Committee.[74]

------Monitoring "test score use in each program and institut- /ing/ corrective action," was proposed by the PEOPLE committee.[75]

------"Phasing out of the Scholastic Aptitude Test in favor of a variety of diagnostic instruments to measure particular skills and competencies" was proposed by B. Alden Thresher in the 1970 report of the College Board's Commission on Tests. Seventeen of the nineteen members of the Commission supported his proposal to experiment with new tests; sixteen members backed his call for phasing out the SAT.[76]

Taken individually, each of these proposals is an incremental reform proposed by test-system insiders. Taken as a whole, they would constitute the beginning of a sweeping challenge to the ETS test system as presently constituted. Yet, even as individual ideas, they went nowhere inside ETS. As Thresher recognized when he filed his recommendations, "any proposal to phase out the SAT, the mainstay of the Board's income, must raise serious financial questions."[77] The ETS test system has operated for years as a large, powerful, and entrenched mechanism which served the interests of its managers, offered convenience, prestige and political justification to its clients and, as long as consumers were not organized, made no powerful enemies.[78] ETS has an overwhelming economic and political interest in maintaining the current test system. Any suggestion to alter it more than superficially must be backed by more than the force of reason. As the College Board Commission on Tests recognized:

> The College Board . . . has a history of having responded to change in its environment only after considerable and often prolonged agitation by those of its members who themselves felt the pressure first, or only after considerable pressure was brought to bear by outside forces.[79]

In 1978, Kathleen Brouder, the College Board executive in charge of improving the organization's relationship with student groups was asked, in an interview, about the prospects for basic change from within. There were three succinct answers to three basic questions. Would the Board, and the colleges it represents, ever consider having an agency other than ETS run its information system? "Remotely possible." Would the Board ever consider urging ETS to phase out the SAT? "Bloody unlikely." Would ETS and the Board, as non-profit educational service organizations, ever consider dismantling their organizations if a new, better national admissions information system could run without them? "You've gotta be out of your mind."[80]

The guardians of the ETS test system have obvious vested interests in maintaining the system as it is. In carrying out their campaign of corporate defense, they have at their disposal a network of influence as extensive as it is subtle. It ranges from the highest reaches of government (where ETS has had connections with each of the four Commissioners of Education who served from 1962 to 1972, as well as with the current Secretary of Education)[81] to the estimated 2,000 paid consultants ETS has retained[82] on campuses across the country, to the thousands of universities, colleges, educational associations and local school districts which are members of the College Board and its other client groups.[83]

Of the forty-four individuals identified as most influential in higher education by a 1975 Change magazine survey, fourteen, as the ETS Examiner pointed out, "have present or past ETS connections."[84] When the American Psychological Association, the National Council on Measurement in Education (NCME) and the American Educational Research Association (AERA) convened a committee to write their guidelines on test construction and use--the guidelines which would serve as the ethical and technical benchmark for the profession--the committee was chaired by a former ETS trustee and included an ETS vice president; in all, more than a third of its members had at one time been on the ETS payroll or board.[85]

Similarly, when the National Academy of Sciences (NAS) convened a panel to prepare a report on the social consequences of standardized testing, it included an ETS vice president, more than a quarter of its members had ETS associations, and its first executive director later left to become a visiting scholar at ETS.[86] Thus, it was not surprising that when ETS Executive Vice-President Robert Solomon testified against the Truth-in-Testing bill in Congress, he chose to recommend that no federal action be taken until the issue had been objectively studied--by the NAS panel.[87] On a more grass roots level the ETS network of influence extends to an estimated 28,000 high school guidance counselors who have gone through training programs of the College Board.[88]

ETS realizes that the matter of its future has moved into arenas outside of its domination. For President Turnbull, this makes it all the more necessary to form alliances with groups whom ETS has something to offer. His confidential 1978 strategy memo elaborated this point.

> Within each of the key groups identified as critical of testing (minorities, students, education groups, social critics), there are elements that in fact are well disposed. We should seek out and develop alliances with those elements.[89]
>
> . . . In pursuing a cooperative project with another group, we should select a topic of particular interest to that group and involve them in all phases of it, from planning through dissemination of the results. . . . We

are likely to be most influential with key groups if we succeed in helping them accomplish their purposes.[90] (Emphasis in original)

However, Turnbull recognized, not all groups would be so amenable to the attentions of ETS. The corporation had defined a mission for itself and created a position of power in the lives of millions which had set it on a confrontation course with the people whose lives it shaped. Turnbull appreciated that once the people turned their powers of analysis and their energies of political action onto the target of ETS, the future of his corporation would be very much an open question. "We have a broad choice to make between a relatively active and a relatively passive approach," Turnbull wrote in his recent strategy memo. "If the problems and criticisms were without foundation, the furor pretty well confined, the concern likely to be transient, a passive stance would seem called for."[91] But, he cautioned his associates, these were not the prevailing conditions. "In fact, although many of the criticisms grow out of ignorance and some are wrong, others have substance. Moreover, the furor is widespread and shows no signs of going away."[92] "The situation," President Turnbull concluded, "is most unlikely to blow over."[93]

FOOTNOTES

Key:

1. Abbreviations are used for major organizations (ETS, ACT, CEEB, ACE, LSAT, FTC, etc.) and test programs (SAT, LSAT, GRE, GMAT, etc.). Consult glossary and abbreviations.

2. Several brochures, booklets and some reports cited are prepared and published by ETS with no individual author listed. In these cases ETS is listed only once, as the author. The date of publication is given after the title; the location of ETS (Princeton, New Jersey) is not usually given.

3. After the first reference to a particular work, author and brief title are given for subsequent cites. Many of the sources are internal documents. This fact is noted on the first cite, and thereafter only author and title are given.

4. Particular references:
    a) The *Examiner* is the ETS staff newspaper. It is published weekly.
    b) *ETS Developments* is a quarterly ETS newsletter sent to educators, ETS clients, the media, etc.
    c) "Brief Look at ETS Activities" is an internal newsletter.
    d) The Law School Admission Council Annual Reports are not public documents and are cited as "Annual Council Report."

5. In some cases the authors or recipients of internal memoranda or letters are not listed in order to preserve confidentiality. Recipients of copies of memoranda ("cc") are not usually listed.

FOOTNOTES, CHAPTER I

1. ETS, Annual Report to the Board of Trustees, 1949-50, p.10.

2. Anna Rothe, ed., Current Biography: Who's News and Why,(New York: H.H. Wilson, 1951), pp. 105-106.

3. Marjorie Dent Cardee, Current Biography: Who's News and Why, (New York: H.H. Wilson, 1953), pp. 298-99.

4. ETS, ETS Charter and By-Laws,1973, p.3, and "Agreement Dated December 3, 1947, between American Council on Education, College Entrance Examination Board, The Carnegie Foundation for the Advancement of Teaching, and Carnegie Corporation of New York," filed by ETS with the Internal Revenue Service accompanying application for 501 (c) (3) tax-exempt status. Although the Carnegie Corporation, under Devereux Josephs, coordinated and helped fund the merger, it did not have any testing program to transfer to ETS. The three organizations which transferred testing programs were the American Council on Education, CEEB, and the Carnegie Foundation for the Advancement of Teaching.

5. Increasing Productivity in Higher Education: Proceedings of the Conference to Mark the Dedication of the Henry Chauncey Conference Center, May, 1974, (Princeton: Educational Testing Service, 1974), p. 105. The quotation is from a speech by Henry Chauncey.

6. ETS, Annual Reports,1948-49 through 1955-56. These organizations were all clients of ETS or had representatives on ETS advisory boards. For specific references for names listed in text, see: 1953-54, p.5 (IBM); 1948-49, p.27 (Pepsi); 1948-49, p. 19 (AAMC); 1949-50, p.4 (Harvard); 1949-50, pp.63-64 and 1950-51, p. 73 (State Dept.); and 1948-49, p. 26 (AEC).

7. "Agreement dated December 3, 1947." This is the founding agreement between the organizations which established ETS. It states (p. 8) that Carnegie Corporation shall contribute $750,000 to ETS, that the American Council on Education shall contribute at least $360,000 worth of its testing assets (p. 9) and that the College Board shall contribute testing assets worth an unspecified amount (p. 12). The first year in which the ETS annual report disclosed financial information was 1952-53. In that year, ETS assets stood at $1,816,301.(ETS, Annual Report to the Board of Trustees, 1952-53, p. 126). According to the Annual Report to the Board of Trustees, 1948-49 (p. 8), ETS had 111 employees, all of them previously employed by the founding organizations.

8. ETS, Annual Report to the Board of Trustees, 1949-50, pp. 10-14.

9. Ibid., pp. 9-10.

10. CEEB, About Your PSAT/NMSQT Scores, 1975, 1975, p. 3

11. Letter from "Sam Harrison." to a law school admissions committee, April 24, 1978.

12. Ibid., pp. 2-3.

13. *Pre-Law Handbook: Official Law School Guide, 1973-74*, (Association of American Law Schools, The Law School Admission Council, Inc., ETS, 1972), pp. 26, 62-65. In the year Harrison applied, there was one accredited law school which did not require the LSAT. In 1979-80, all accredited law schools required the test. See Chapter II, footnote 18.

14. The 1973-74 *Pre-Law Handbook* states that the LSAT is a measure of "certain mental capabilities important in the study of law," p.18.

15. LSAC,"1973 Annual Council Report,"p. 149.

16. *Ibid.*,p. 173.

17. *Ibid.*,p. 149.

18. *Ibid.*,p. 128.

19. LSAC internal manual, "Law School Admission Test Operations Reference Manual," Sept., 1975, Sec. 2, p. 8A.

20. Letter from a law school Associate Dean to a campus Affirmative Action officer, Sept. 21, 1977.

21. ETS, *1977-78 Law School Admission Bulletin*, 1977, p.9.

22. Letter from Robert G. Wiltsey to Dianne DeWitt, Feb. 12, 1974, p.3. Copies to "Law schools approved by the American Bar Association." Wiltsey was an ETS Associate Program Director; DeWitt was president of a university student bar association.

23. Letter from ophthalmologist at State University Hospital, December 26, 1973.

24. Interview with Robert Solomon, ETS Executive Vice-President, June 19, 1975.

25. Interview with William Turnbull, ETS President, May 3, 1977.

26. Interview with Robert Solomon, June 19, 1975.

27. Frank Bowles, *The Refounding of the College Board 1948-63*, (New York: CEEB, 1967), p.246.

28. Sidney P. Marland, "A Proposal for a Comprehensive System of Testing for Job Entry," in *Report of the Commission on Tests: II. Briefs*, (New York: CEEB, 1970), pp.68-69.

29. Interview with Robert Solomon, June 19, 1975.

FOOTNOTES, CHAPTER II

1. David F. Sloan, "ETS--Testing, Testing, Testing," College Management, Feb. 1974, p.36. Another article in the New Jersey School Leader ("ETS: Just Testing," March/April 1975) has lengthy passages apparently copied virtually verbatim from Sloan's. The style is typified by the passage "Every department, every office, every enclave at ETS holds fresh surprises and exciting educational challenges," Sloan, p.35. The difference between the two articles is that the College Management piece, directed at college administrators, describes ETS programs for colleges, while the New Jersey School Leader article, directed at elementary and secondary school educators, describes ETS elementary and secondary programs.

2. "Out With the Old and In With the New," (photo caption) Examiner, September 14, 1978, p.1. For more background see "Computer Center--A World of Its Own," Examiner, October 26, 1972, p.1; and "Brief Report of ETS Activities," May 1974 (ETS internal newsletter).

3. Wizard quote: "Computer Center--A World of Its Own," p.1. From published and internal ETS figures it can be estimated that ETS had tested more than 90 million candidates by 1979. A precise figure is hard to find since some people take ETS tests more than once and because ETS has not published complete test volume figures since its 1966-67 annual report. Some ETS tests, such as the elementary and secondary school Cooperative tests, are scored by the institutional users and do not generate files at ETS. (See Appendix I for candidate volume information).
    The 32 million figure is a conservative estimate made privately by an ETS executive in 1975. This figure was used by the author in November, 1976 testimony before the federal Privacy Protection Study Commission and was not rebutted by ETS. ETS told the House Subcommittee on Government Information and Individual Rights: "[I]t would be a major undertaking to produce an accurate count of the number of individuals represented in our files, large portions of which are in any case inactive and are obtained because they constitute a valuable historical record," quoted in transcript, "Educational Recordkeeping Practices," Privacy Protection Study Commission, November 12, 1976, p.317. In addition to files from test programs, ETS has files on millions of families which have used its financial need analysis services (College Scholarship Service, and Graduate and Professional Financial Aid Service), and on individuals who have served as subjects in psychological experiments by the ETS research division. According to the ETS Privacy Commission testimony, some research files are held in a form identifiable with individual subjects, and others are not.

4. Information obtained from ETS Public Information Office, October 1979. See also "Computer Center-- A World of Its Own," p.1.

5. Institute for Educational Development memorandum, "Rough Notes on a Meeting Held at IED on December 13, 1972 with ETS on: 'Possible Cooperation between IED and ETS on the Uses of Educational Technology and in Developing Educational Management,'" December 20, 1972, p.6. The full quote reads: "The Systems Division has the largest capacity for information collection, storage and retrieval in U.S. [sic] education community today. Maybe only the C.I.A. has greater and better capacities."

6. The most recent year for which reasonably complete figures on ETS test volume are available is 1974-75 from ETS, ETS In Fact, 1975. 6,938,300 candidates were tested that year, but even this figure is incomplete since ETS In Fact does not list all ETS test programs. In 1975, according to "1976 Market Data Book Issue," Automotive News, April 28, 1976, p.28, total domestic new car sales for Ford and GM were 5,483,164. This comparison is by main line of business. It does not include ETS financial analysis services, publications, occupational tests, School and College Ability Tests etc.; neither does it include Ford and GM trucks, locomotives, appliances, etc. See Appendix I for discussion of candidate volume.

7. February 24, 1979 was an ETS test date. All the locations listed are ETS test centers. See ETS, GRE 1978/79 Information Bulletin, National Administrations Edition, 1978, pp.41-43.

8. About ETS, an ETS public relations pamphlet (circa 1977) says ETS has more than 5,000 test centers. The U.S. Department of Defense, in "Principal Military Installations or Activities in the 50 States," and "Selected Military Installations or Activities Outside the 50 States," lists 743 defense outposts. Both documents are dated December, 1975. The former "excludes those installations and activities announced for closure, disestablishment, or reduced to Reserve status or inactivated;" the latter excludes Thailand. ETS, Annual Report 1975: Pathways to Quality, p.15, says the centers extend from "Antarctica to Zaire." Test centers are established temporarily, usually in schools and public buildings, and are staffed by local people who receive stipends and instructions from ETS.

9. ETS, Supervisor's Handbook: A Guide for Administering the Testing Programs of the Educational Testing Service, Revised Edition, 1972-73 (1972). See also ETS, Supervisor's Manual 1974-75: Scholastic Aptitude Test, Test of Standard Written English and Achievement Tests, College Board Admissions Testing Program, 1974. Information was also obtained from Paul D. Williams, then Director of the ETS Office of Test Security, July 11, 1975.

10. In 1975 a private investigator was hired to investigate a candidate suspected of falsifying LSAT score reports and Law School Data Assembly Service (LSDAS) grade transcripts. See LSAC, "Annual Council Report 1975," p.100. According to Paul

Williams, one of ETS' main handwriting analysts is a captain with the Pennsylvania State Police. (Interview with Williams, July 11, 1975.) ETS computers are programmed to identify candidates who take a test more than once and whose scores change by the following amounts:
    ATP(SAT, etc.): Verbal-250, Math-250, Total-350
    GRE: Verbal-200, Quantitative-200, Total-300
    GMAT: Total-150
    NTE: Weighted Commons-150
    LSAT: Total 150
All such cases are investigated by Test Security. Robert F. Smith, "Board of Review Recommendations," Oct. 12, 1976; obtained from ETS by Privacy Commission. Williams headed ETS test security.

11. Paul Williams spent more than 20 years with the Office of Naval Intelligence. According to Williams, Jan Beck, a Seattle Washington "Examiner of Questioned Documents" who analyzes the handwriting of ETS candidates suspected of impersonation, is a former CIA documents analyst. (Interview with Williams, July 11, 1975). Robert Van Arsdall, Director of overall ETS Security, was formerly head of the Trenton, New Jersey FBI field office.

12. ETS, *Supervisor's Handbook*, 1972-73, pp.12-14.

13. LSAC, "Annual Council Report 1974," p.26. In "Report of the Legal Affairs Committee" section. The FBI knows of no other non-governmental organization which does mass fingerprinting of the public according to an interview with the FBI press office, January 25, 1979.

14. David Ray Papke, "Cheating the System," *Juris Doctor*, May 1975, p.12.

15. LSAC, "Annual Council Report 1973," p.31, contained in "Report of the Legal Affairs Committee" section.

16. Interview with Paul D. Williams, July 11, 1975.
    Q. Have thumbprints been helpful to you in your investigations?
    A. In this case, it was the only thing we could really rely on because if we hadn't had thumbprints we couldn't have gone with this response mark stuff, that, the Board of Review simply won't accept it. But they did accept the thumbprints.
    Q. Uh huh. Have you ever considered using thumbprints for other tests?
    A. Oh, I imagine it's under consideration by all the program directors, now, yes. It's not my decision, of course, the program directors...
    Q. But just in, in your professional opinion, do you think that might be a good idea?
    A. Well, uh, I think that it would be quite effective. I think it's been quite effective with LSAT. I think, I think that the results such [as] the number of cases that we are able to establish of impersonation have dropped off _radically_ since they started using them. So obviously, it would be a good selection.

Q. When you say they've dropped off radically, about what do you mean? In terms of numbers or percents.
A. Oh, it's been cut in half, at least.

17. "Myrdal Star of Invitational Conference," <u>Examiner</u>, Nov. 7, 1974, p.1.

18. a) Of over 2000 colleges listed in Karen C. Hegner, ed., <u>Annual Guides to Graduate and Undergraduate Study: 1980 Edition</u>, 6 vols., (Princeton: Peterson's Guides, 1979) (known as Peterson's <u>Guides</u>), 52% require applicants to take ETS' Scholastic Aptitude Test (SAT). Seventy-one percent require or recommend the SAT for at least some applicants. Many of these will accept scores on the American College Test (ACT). In 1978-79, 1.5 million SATs were given (ETS, "Legislation on Standardized Testing," p.2; memo circulated to Members of Congress). According to Bob Elliot, Coordinator of Information Services, American College Testing Program, ACT 1978-79 test volume was approximately 954,000 (Interview, December 10, 1979). This means ETS had about 60% of the market, measured by test volume.

b) According to the GREB, <u>Graduate Programs and Admissions Manual 1979-1981</u>, 4 vols., (Princeton: ETS, 1979), a survey of 700 graduate schools with over 12,000 departments, over 75% of the departments or programs require or recommend the GRE aptitude or advanced test or both. Almost 70% of the schools and universities surveyed required the GRE aptitude or advanced test for at least one department. These figures include all departments surveyed (Volume A--agriculture, forestry, the biological sciences, the health sciences and home economics; Volume B--the fine and applied arts, including architecture, the classics, philosophy, religion and languages; Volume C--the physical sciences, mathematics and computer science and engineering; Volume D--education, history, and the social sciences, except business and management, which are excluded because many of those schools require the GMAT instead of the GRE.)

c) ETS, <u>1979-80 Law School Admission Bulletin</u>, 1979, p.72 lists the 168 ABA-approved law schools, all of which require the LSAT.

d) Illinois insurance salesmen are required by the state to take the ETS Multistate Insurance Licensing Qualification Examination. An ETS representative told a June 12, 1978 insurance industry meeting in Washington, D.C. that Delaware, Massachusetts, Pennsylvania, Wisconsin, Colorado and Indiana also require the test. Two small Illinois insurance companies have filed suit against ETS on civil rights grounds (Golden Rule Life Insurance and Congressional Life Insurance, 7th Circuit Court, Illinois, Case #419-76). The case was dismissed October 26, 1978 on technical grounds, without having reached the merits of the arguments against ETS (The Measuring Cup, Vol.1, No. 1, January, 1979 p.5.) Golden Rule is refiling the case.

e. Both the Philadelphia police and fire departments use an ETS multiple choice test for hiring. Interview, Ms. Geri Ellis, Examinations Division, City of Philadelphia Personnel Office, June 25, 1979.

f. The Republic of Liberia, which registers more foreign merchant marine ships than any other nation, uses an ETS test for certifying officers. See "New Tests Put ETS on the Briny Deep," Examiner, October 18, 1973, p.1.

g. According to the National Bar Examination Digest, 1979 edition (Harcourt Brace Jovanovich, 1979), 42 states, the District of Columbia, and some territories use the ETS Multistate Bar Examination, a multiple-choice test usually used in conjunction with a state essay test. See p.36, "Multistate Bar Exam Information." The states that do not are Arizona, Indiana, Iowa, Louisiana, Minnesota, Montana, Washington, and West Virginia.

h. These organizations are among the dozens of corporations, unions, foundations, state agencies, and churches which pick winners of their National Merit Scholarships using the ETS PSAT/NMSQT. See chapter II, pp.47-48, or the PSAT/NMSQT Student Bulletin.

19. ETS, Assessing Occupational Competence, COPA/Center for Occupational and Professional Assessment/Educational Testing Service, (undated, circa 1975), p.3. See Appendix I for discussion of number of annual test-takers.

20. ETS internal report, "Manual of Information for Test Development Professional Staff." The foreword is dated Sept. 1969; materials added to the looseleaf-bound manual have later dates. An internal ETS memo from David L. Fox, "Starter Document for Planning," April 6, 1972, notes how ETS tests are made according to a standardized format: "ETS tests are frequently duplicative in nature because they are custom designed with minor variations for different clients," p.5. Though some small or experimental research, elementary school or occupational tests may be designed with different techniques, the major ETS aptitude, achievement and occupational tests are all built according to the speeded, multiple-choice model. (Fox was an executive associate to Robert Solomon at the time.)

21. Most ETS tests, such as the SAT, LSAT, and NTE, are scored at ETS in Princeton, N.J. Some ETS tests, such as the Cooperative tests for elementary schools and a number of occupational tests, are scored by the users and are not returned to ETS.

22. Public tour of ETS taken by the author, July 1974; "New Scanner Promises Wonders," Examiner, July 8, 1971, p.2.

23. "Mail Department Divides Into Two," Examiner, June 7, 1973, p.1.

24. Among the test programs offered by ETS are the Scholastic Aptitude Test, the College Board Achievement Tests, the Law School Admission Test, which is advertised to measure "certain mental capabilities important in the study of law," [Pre-Law Handbook: Official Law School Guide, (AALS, LSAC, and ETS, 1976-77), p.23], and the National Occupational Competency Testing Program.

25. Report of the Commission on Tests: I. Righting the Balance (New York: CEEB, 1970) p.32. On Further Examination: Report of the Advisory Panel on the Scholastic Aptitude Test Score Decline (New York: CEEB, 1977) p.4, Table 1.

26. Report of the Commission on Tests: I. Righting the Balance, p.30.

27. "CEEB President Sees Expanding Role for College Board in Society," The College Board News, June 1974, p.2.

28. "Conference Center Event Honors Chauncey," Examiner, June 6, 1974, p.1. Robin Kerney, "'Hotel' Classified for Liquor Permit," Trenton Times, May 7, 1974, p.10.

29. Increasing Productivity in Higher Education: Proceedings of the Conference to Mark the Dedication of the Henry Chauncey Conference Center, May 1974 (Princeton: ETS, May 1974) p.111.

30. Ibid., p.11.

31. For the quotation, see "ETS Dedicates Center in Honor of Chauncey," *The Princeton Packet*, May 8, 1974, p.29. For the value of the hotel-conference center, see "Finances...Where The Money Comes From and Where it Goes," ETS (Fall, 1979). This paper was circulated to Members of Congress.

32. List of trustees in *Increasing Productivity*, p.112. Biographical information from *Who's Who 1978-1979* (New York: St. Martin's Press, 1978); *Who's Who in Government*, 3rd edition (Chicago: Marquis Who's Who, Inc., 1977); *Who's Who in America 1978-1979*, 40th edition, 2nd volume, (Chicago: Marquis Who's Who, Inc., 1978); ETS, *Annual Report*, editions for years 1949 to present; and other sources.

33. ETS, *The Farmhouse at ETS*, brochure, (circa 1977).

34. "'Labor of Love,' Author Calls Building History," *Examiner*, Feb. 20, 1975, pp.1-3. Contains excerpts of a history by Helen Weidenmiller of ETS building projects.

35. "Rosedale's Arboreal Wonderland," *Examiner*, July 27, 1972, p.3; "'Labor of Love,'" p.3. According to ETS internal documents, "Cost Center Organization Charts," May 1978, ETS has a staff of seven full-time grounds workers. The Rosedale maintenance staff totals 60.

36. "Rites of Spring," (photo caption), *Examiner*, July 15, 1971, p.1.; "'Labor of Love,'" p.3.

37. ETS, *An Invitation to the ETS Henry Chauncey Conference Center*, (ETS promotional brochure mailed to education groups and prospective clients, circa 1974); *The Henry Chauncey Conference Center...to serve education...* (brochure, circa 1974); *The Farmhouse at ETS*; internal planning memo, "Planning for the Henry Chauncey Conference Center: Things Not to Forget to Remember," Sept. 29, 1971. At one point (p.42) this memo asks: "Though a little swank, should we have a paved and painted helicopter landing pad adjacent to the buildings? (We are already an approved landing site.)" As far as we know, the pad was never built. See also internal report by Kay Sharp, "The Henry Chauncey Conference Center--an overall description," November 1972.

38. "Conference Center Manager Arrives," *Examiner*, Jan. 18, 1973, p.3. "Planning for the Henry Chauncey Conference Center," p.27, said that the manager of the new center should be "Someone with considerable training and experience in managing commercial hotel/convention/club facilities rather than educational or not-for-profit facilities such as college dining halls/dormitories." It also directed that "the quality of Center food services" should be "equivalent to that of a fine restaurant, rather than to that of typical institutional food processors," (p.34).

39. ETS, The Farmhouse at ETS. Many issues of the Examiner have noted the visitors to the Conference Center. See, for example, June 22, 1972, p.1; July 22, 1971, p.1.

40. ETS, The Farmhouse at ETS.

41. In 1974 a local realtor who handles ETS properties estimated the house's value at $250,000. According to the building contractors, construction bids ranged from $130,000 to over $250,000; ETS ended up paying about $150,000. The quotation is from "Christmas in Princeton," Lawrence Ledger, Nov. 12, 1973, p.11. See also blueprints and building inspection reports filed with the Lawrence township (New Jersey) Assessor. After ETS moved from downtown Princeton to Rosedale in 1958, President Chauncey began using "The Farmhouse" as the official residence. When President Turnbull assumed office, ETS built the new house. ETS representatives say the house is comparable to the official residence provided to many university presidents.

42. Sharp, "The Henry Chauncey Conference Center," p. 1.

43. "ETS Conference Center Attracts Groups to Pastoral Setting," ETS Developments, Fall, 1978, p.6.

44. "Brief Report on ETS Activities," March, 1971, p.3.

45. Walter Wriston is Chairman of Citibank. William Colby is former Director of the CIA. Other participants included editors of the New York Times, the Washington Post, ABC News, and WNET. Proceedings of the Ford Foundation conference are published in Howard Simons and Joseph A. Califano, Jr., eds. The Media and Business, (New York: Random House, 1979). ATT meeting: visit by the author, July, 1975.

46. "ETS Conference Center Attracts Groups to Pastoral Setting," p.6; Ed Kiersh, "Testing is the Name, Power is the Game," Village Voice, Jan. 15, 1979, p.53; "N.J. 'Summit' Muffled," Albany (N.Y.) Times-Union, April 23, 1978. Information also obtained from interviews with ETS staff who worked at the conference. For quotation see Sharp, "The Henry Chauncey Conference Center," p.1.

47. Form 990 of the Internal Revenue Service, "Return of Organization Exempt from Income Tax," 1976, filed by ETS; Edward B. Fiske, "Student Testing Unit Assailed as Influence Grows," New York Times, November 14, 1979, p.1.

48. Interview with Samuel Messick, June 20, 1974. According to figures from an internal ETS memo, total costs of developing, producing, and administering the 1970-71 Preliminary Scholastic Aptitude Test were $.54 per student, 27% of the $2.00 price. Some of the profit is kept by the College Board,

the test's sponsor, and some by ETS. See Herman F. Smith to Executive Directors, Program Area Directors, Program Directors and Associate and Assistant Program Directors, "Activity Analysis," Jan. 31, 1972. See Chapter 8 for discussion of ETS profit margin.

49. ETS, Annual Report to the Board of Trustees, 1952-53. See all other Annual Reports through 1973-74. See also Chapter VIII.

50. "The Pleasures of Nonprofitability," Forbes, Nov. 15, 1976, p.90.

51. IRS Form 990 filed by ETS, 1976, Statement 8.

52. Samuel Bowles and Herbert Gintis, Schooling in Capitalist America, (New York: Basic Books, 1976) p.198.

53. The ETS Annual Reports list numerous business leaders who have served on ETS advisory committees. Of those cited in the text, five served on the Advisory Board on Research Related to Industry: Watson (1953-1956), Sheperd (1954-1961), Roy Larsen, President of Time, Inc. (1954-1961), Benjamin Buttenwieser of Kuhn Loeb (1953-1961), Paul Mazur of Lehman Brothers (1953-1961); see Annual Reports of 1953-54 (p.5) and 1954-55 (p.5). Two served on the Standing Committee on Finance: Norton Smith of Johnson and Johnson (1950-57) and Albert Hettinger of Lazard Freres (1953-58); see Annual Reports 1950-51 (p.3) and 1953-54 (p.3).

54. The quotation is from a "boilerplate" General Statement of Competence used by ETS for soliciting grants. This is taken from "Career and College Guidance for Minority Students," a joint proposal from the Los Angeles Unified School District, California State University at Los Angeles, Los Angeles Community College, and Loyola University at Los Angeles, (ETS, 1972) p.22.

55. ETS internal report, "Proposed Goals for ETS, 1967-1977," May 1967, pp.3,8. The report was "prepared for discussion by the Board of Trustees."

56. ETS, Annual Report 1973, 1974, pp.49,11. From Dyer's essay "ETS and the Test of Time/ A 25-Year Review."

57. ETS internal memorandum by William Turnbull, "Public and Professional Attitudes Toward Testing and ETS: Relations with Key Publics," August 14, 1978, pp.1-2. See Ch. 9 also.

58. ETS internal report by Nona G. Johnson, "Report on Free Administration and Fee Waivers," August 1971, conclusion.

59. ETS internal memorandum for six ETS executives, December 16, 1971, p.7. Confidential source.

60. ETS internal report by David Loye, "Cultural Bias in Testing: Challenge and Response," January 12, 1973, p.35.

61. ETS, *Bulletin of Tests and Services: 1973-74 Elementary and Secondary Schools*, p.4.

62. ETS, *Annual Report to the Board of Trustees, 1955-56*, pp.31-32.

63. *Ibid.*, pp.34-35.

64. ETS, *1978 Annual Report*, p.8.

65. ETS, *SSAT/1977-78 Bulletin of Information for Candidates*, 1977, pp.2-3. The schools listed as SSAT Board Members on page 2 use the SSAT.

66. ETS, *1978 Annual Report*, p.7.

67. ETS, *ETS In Fact* (brochure, circa 1975). The edition containing 1974-75 test volume figures says 575,000 took the GED test that year. The GED Testing Service of the American Council on Education confirmed in an interview that the 1978 level was comparable. See GED Testing Service of the ACE, *Examiners Manual for the Tests of General Educational Development*, (Washington, D.C.: ACE, 1971), p.1 for reference on use of GED scores. In an interview, Lois Wade in the Office of Personnel Management (formerly the Civil Service Commission) said many federal government agencies let employees take the preparatory course and the test on government time.

68. Educational Records Bureau, *Catalog of Programs and Services, 1973-74*, (ETS, 1974), p.7.

69. ETS Public Information Office confirmed these approximations in an interview, October 1979.

70. CEEB, *Your PSAT/NMSQT Scores*, 1972, pp.2,5.

71. See for example, CEEB, *PSAT/NMSQT Student Bulletin, 1973*, pp.45-70, or CEEB, *1975-76 Admissions Testing Program Student Bulletin, 1975*, p.15; "Scholarship Selection a Painstaking Process," *Examiner*, April 6, 1972, pp.1-2.

72. "SAT To Get First New Look in Years," *Examiner*, February 28, 1974, p.1. As cited in footnote 18, chapter II, of the 2008 colleges listed in Peterson's *Annual Guide to Undergraduate Study*, 1979 Edition, 1038 require the SAT. (Many of these will accept the ACT instead.) An additional 147 require some applicants to take the SAT, and 241 more recommend applicants take the SAT. Thus, 1426 colleges require or recommend the SAT for at least some applicants. The total number of schools requiring either the SAT or ACT is 1366, or 68%. Those schools that require the SAT or ACT for some or all applicants total 1649, or 82% of the total. For SAT volume figures, see ETS, *1978 Annual Report*, p.7.

73. Lucky Abernathy, "Highlighting What's New in Admissions," College Board Review, Summer, 1976, p.32.

74. College Board, Your Student Report 1978-79, Admissions Testing Program of the College Board, 1978; Ella Mazel, The New York Times Guide To College Selection (Chicago: Quadrangle Books, 1971).

75. Johnson, "Report on Free Administration," p.5.

76. ETS, 1978 Annual Report, p.7.

77. See College Scholarship Service of the College Board, Explaining Financial Aid to Students and Parents, (CEEB, 1978) and Financial Aid Form: Academic Year 1979-80 (CEEB, 1978). See also ETS, 1978 Annual Report, p.7.

78. Gerald V. Lannholm, Graduate School Departments Requiring or Recommending GRE Scores for Admission, GRE Special Report No. 71-1, (ETS, 1971). See also GREB, Graduate Programs and Admissions Manual 1979-1981, 4 vols., and Chapter II, footnote 18.

79. See ETS, 1977-78 GRE Information Bulletin, National Administration Edition, 1977, p.28 for a sampling of agencies which require the GRE.

80. Gerald V. Lannholm, The Use of GRE Scores and Other Factors in Graduate School Admissions, Special Report, (ETS, 1968) p.6.

81. ETS, GAPSFAS: Information for Students, 1976, and GAPSFAS: Application for Financial Aid for the Academic Year 1977-78, 1976.

82. ETS, GMAT Bulletin of Information for Candidates, 1978-79, 1978, pp.26-27. According to Graduate Business Admissions Council, Graduate Study in Management, 1973-74, (ETS, 1973) pp.220,252,259, the business schools of the University of Capetown (South Africa), the University of Nairobi (Kenya), and the University of New South Wales (Australia) all require the ATGSB (now the GMAT).

83. Nancy Rubin, "Test-Coaching: Is It Worth It?", New York Times, September 9, 1979, Section 12, p.1.

84. ETS, 1978 Annual Report, p.8.

85. 1979 Congressional Directory, 96th Congress, 1st Session, (Washington: Government Printing Office, 1979), pp.4-197; Governors of the American States, Commonwealths and Territories, 1979: Biographical Sketches and Portraits (Washington: National Governor's Association, 1979).
   To our knowledge, there are no comprehensive government or private surveys of lawyer income. The best estimate we obtained was from James A. Kilmer of Kilmer & Associates who

said the average salary of attorneys was probably in the $30,000 range. Kilmer & Associates, located in Chicago, is one of the best known consulting firms concerned with lawyers in the country. According to the U.S. Bureau of the Census, 6.4% of the labor force earned $25,000 or more in 1977.

These figures understate the earning power of lawyers, especially those who do well on the LSAT. High LSAT scores are necessary for admission to the better law schools (see Chapter VI), and graduation from the better law schools is frequently a prerequisite for entry into the larger and wealthier firms, where starting salaries in 1978 were in the $20,000 to $30,000 range. According to the Internal Revenue Service, partners in law firms earned an average of at least $47,000 in 1976 (Bill Mudd, December 11, 1979, IRS. This figure represents the total declared net income of all partnerships divided by the number of partners; outside earnings would not be included.) When we asked the American Bar Association for the average annual income of lawyers, they referred us to a study by Altman and Weil, Inc., a management consulting firm, cited in Docket Call, Summer 1978, p.12. The study found that average net income for lawyers in firms in cities of more than one million was $58,000 in 1977; the average net income for lawyers in cities of 250,000 or less was $46,303. In contrast, only 2% of families and unrelated individuals earn more than $50,000 a year, according to the Census Department. The Census Department does not even publish figures on the income of individual wage earners above the $25,000 cut-off, because the numbers are too small.

86. Pre-Law Handbook, 1975-76 (AALS, LSAC, and ETS, 1975) pp.9-16.

87. For citation on law school requirements, see footnote 18, Chapter II. Warren W. Willingham and Hunter M. Breland and associates, "The Status of Selective Admissions," in Selective Admissions in Higher Education: Comment and Recommendations and Two Reports (San Francisco: Jossey-Bass, 1977), Appendix C-3, p.185. 1728 applicants had a grade point above 3.50 and LSAT scores below 500; 856 of these gained admission to at least one LSDAS-ABA accredited law school; 872 applicants, or 51%, failed to gain admission to a single LSDAS-ABA accredited law school.

88. LSAC confidential manual for law school admissions officers, "Operations Reference Book," September 1975, Section VI, "Validity Study Service." The predictions are known as the "Predicted First Year Average" (PFYA). See chapter 6 for a discussion of the decision not to disclose such information to the applicant.

89. The National Bar Examination Digest, 1979 Edition (Harcourt Brace Jovanovich, 1979) p.36.

90. National Education Association, "1974-75 NTE Test Users From ETS Bulletins of NTE Test Users," mimeograph, (circa 1975).

91. Occupations are from ETS, Assessing Occupational Competence; international information is from ETS, ETS International Activities, (brochure, circa 1978). p.3.

FOOTNOTES CHAPTER III

1. Thomas F. Donlon and William H. Angoff, "The Scholastic Aptitude Test," in Angoff, ed., *The College Board Admissions Testing Program*, (New York: CEEB, 1971) p.16. They quote D.G. Ryans and N. Frederiksen, "Performance Tests of Educational Achievement," in Lindquist, *Educational Measurement* (Washington: ACE, 1951).

2. Donlon and Angoff, "The Scholastic Aptitude Test," p.16. They quote L.J. Cronbach, *Essentials of Psychological Testing*, 2nd ed., (New York: Harper and Row, 1960).

3. ETS internal document, "Project Operating Statement By POS-Category/Project Arch 1977," April 19, 1977. According to data in this internal financial analysis of ETS programs, aptitude tests held the following positions in a ranking of ETS programs by amount of income produced in 1976:
   #1. Admissions Testing Program (SAT and College Board Achievement Test).
   #3. Graduate Record Examinations (GRE).
   #4. Law School Admission Test (LSAT).
   #8. Preliminary Scholastic Aptitude Test/National Merit Scholarship Qualifying Test (PSAT/NMSQT).
   #9. Admission Test for Graduate Study in Business (ATGSB--now called the Graduate Management Admission Test, GMAT).
   See Chapter VIII, note 159 for the complete ranking. For the Admissions Testing Program and the Graduate Record Examinations, the income figures in the Project Operating Statement include income from both the aptitude tests and the supplementary achievement tests (known in the GRE program as "Advanced Tests"). Although there are no more detailed breakdowns available for these two programs, the aptitude test component of each can be expected to provide a substantial share of program income. In 1976-77, for example, 1,359,500 candidates took the SAT, compared to 277,700 who took the Achievement Tests (from ETS, *1978 Annual Report*, p.7.) No such figures are available for the GRE program.

4. ETS internal report, "Proposed Goals for ETS, 1967-1977," May, 1967, p.19. "Prepared for discussion by the Board of Trustees."

5. Admissions Testing Program of the College Board, *Taking the SAT: A Guide to the Scholastic Aptitude Test and the Test of Standard Written English*, Admissions Testing Program of the College Board, 1978, p.3.

6. ETS, *1979-80 Law School Admission Bulletin*, 1979, p.17.

7. ETS, *1977-78 GRE Information Bulletin*, 1977, p.4.

8. Time figures are derived from an ETS Statistical Report by Rebecca Bullock and June Stern, "College Entrance Examination Board February 1974 Scholastic Aptitude Test WSAI 3, SR-75-03," January 1975. The SAT Verbal had 90 questions in 75 minutes; the SAT Mathematical had 60 questions in 75 minutes. Content information is from an ETS Research Bulletin by Christopher C. Modu and June Stern, "The Stability of the SAT Score Scale," ETS RB-75-9, April 1975, pp.22-23. Their content descriptions are for tests given in 1973, which had the same item types as the 1974 SAT.

9. See Chapter III supra and footnote 15 for discussion of studies on predictive validity of ETS aptitude tests.

10. ETS internal memorandum from Vice-President Richard S. Levine to several ETS executives including Messrs. Turnbull and Solomon on "Indices of Test Bias," September 24, 1971. See p.130 of this chapter for discussion.

11. FTC memorandum from Albert H. Kramer, Director of Bureau of Consumer Protection, to "Commission" on "Unnamed Test Preparation Services, File 772 3000, et al.," May 15, 1979, p.9. See pp. 107-8 of this chapter for discussion.

12. Quoted in Diane Ravitch, "The College Boards," New York Times Magazine, May 4, 1975, p.13.

13. College Board News, September 1976, p.3. Psychometricians have defined various kinds of validity including "content validity" (which concerns the kind of subject matter sampled by the test), "construct validity" (which concerns the kind of thinking the test purports to measure) and "criterion" or "predictive" validity (which concerns how accurately a test predicts standing on a particular criterion, such as first year college grades). "Predictive validity" is the one kind of validity which is easily subject to empirical study with a method accepted within the profession. This is the definition of validity which underlies statistical research on aptitude test validity. See Hunter Breland with Shula Minsky, Population Validity and College Entrance Measures, RB-78-19, ETS, pp.1-4. See also Samuel Messick, "The Standard Problem: Meaning and Values in Measurement and Evaluation," American Psychologist, vol. 30, no. 10, October 1975, p.957.

14. William W. Turnbull, "On Educational Standards, Testing, and the Aspirations of Minorities," text of speech at Columbia University, December 8, 1974, p.6.

15. The statistic used in this report for describing the accuracy of a predictor is the square of the Spearman correlation coefficient, or the "r squared." According to F.W. Carlborg, Introduction to Statistics, (Glenview, Illinois: Scott Foresman, 1968), p.163, "the square of the correlation coefficient is the percent reduction of the total variation that can be attributed to observing X." It is the "improvement in accuracy of prediction" over prediction by chance. J.P. Guilford, Fundamental Statistics in Psychology and Education, 4th edition (New York: McGraw Hill, 1965) p.379, describes "r squared" as "the coefficient of determination." "This statistic is also sometimes symbolized as d. When multiplied by 100 the coefficient r^2 gives us the percentage of the variance in Y that is associated with, determined by, or accounted for by variance in X." Of the two standard statistics "used to indicate accuracy of prediction" described by Guilford (p.376), the "r squared" is the more conservative. That is, it puts the accuracy of a predictor in the most favorable light. For example, if a test has a .4 correlation coefficient with grades, the first method, the "index of forecasting efficiency" (which equals the square root of $1-r^2$) credits the test with an 8.3% "reduction in errors of prediction." The second method, the "r squared," assigns it a percentage of 16%, which means that the test accounts for about 16% of the variance in grades. Thus, we are using the method which depicts the predictive power of the test in the most optimistic manner possible. In the text, this r squared statistic will be referred to as the percentage of perfect prediction.

Most of the data cited in the text on score-grade correlations come from two compilations of validity studies: for the SAT, Susan F. Ford and Sandy Campos, "Summary of Validity Data from the Admissions Testing Program Validity Study Service" which is contained in the volume of appendices to On Further Examination: Report of the Advisory Panel on the Scholastic Aptitude Test Score Decline (New York: CEEB, 1977); for the GRE, LSAT and GMAT, Warren W. Willingham and Hunter M. Breland, "The Status of Selective Admissions" in Selective Admissions in Higher Education: A Report of the Carnegie Council on Policy Studies in Higher Education (San Francisco: Jossey-Bass, 1977), p.132, Table 15. Ford and Campos summarize the results of more than 2000 validity studies conducted for individual colleges by the ETS Validity Study Service over the period 1964-1974. Their table giving the median correlations for each year's studies for male samples, female samples and combined samples is probably the largest and most reliable data base ever assembled on the predictive validity of the SAT. A 1978 CEEB research report summarizing published validity studies, Hunter M. Breland with the assistance of Shula Minsky, Population Validity and College Entrance Measures, RB-78-19, (ETS, 1978), presents the median correlations of Ford and Campos alongside its own, noting that "the medians offered by Ford and Campos...are offered for comparison because they probably represent better sampling than the other medians based only on published reports " (p.38). For the combined sex samples, which are the ones the charts and figures in this chapter are based on, the studies summarized by Breland and Minsky show the same correlation between SAT Verbal and college grades as do those of Ford and Campos; Breland and Minsky show a slightly lower validity for SAT Math. The Ford and Campos figures will be used in this chapter. Their combined sex sample data include 827 college validity studies. The Willingham and Breland validity coefficients for the GRE, LSAT, and GMAT are based on similar compilations of validity studies. They are described by Willingham and Breland as "characteristic validity coefficients."

The Ford and Campos combined sex sample validity coefficients for the SAT are as follows:

Year	SAT-Verbal	SAT-Math
1964	0.37	0.32
1965	0.36	0.29
1966	0.33	0.28
1967	0.36	0.28
1968	0.40	0.33
1969	0.39	0.33
1970	0.37	0.29
1971	0.34	0.28
1972	0.35	0.33
1973	0.38	0.36
1974	0.42	0.39

A weighted average, based on the number of studies from which each year's median was derived, was calculated for each column. The averages were .37 for SAT-V and .32 for SAT-M. These were then averaged and squared to obtain the 11.9 percentage of perfect prediction figure.

For the LSAT, GRE and GMAT, the Willingham and Breland median validity coefficients were squared to obtain the percentages of perfect prediction.

Psychometricians often attach several caveats to the use
of validity coefficients. See, for example, Willingham and
Breland pp.131-134; Hunter M. Breland, "DeFunis Revisited:
A Psychometric View," (ETS, August 1974) pp.10-14. Although
the coefficients reported in the research literature reflect
the actual correlations that were found between the scores of
a school's students and the grades they earned (or their eventual
graduation or whatever the criterion is), psychometricians
argue that hypothetically the correlations would have been
higher had it not been for several technical factors which
tended to attenuate them. Two of the most frequently mentioned are unreliability in the criterion and restriction
of range. They argue that since the criterion, first year
grades, may vary for reasons unrelated to actual performance,
this makes prediction more difficult for reasons that have
nothing to do with shortcomings in the test. In Guilford's
words, "If the tests from which we wish to predict something
else are not perfect, that fact must be faced, and our predictions are reduced in accuracy accordingly. But we should
hardly expect to be asked to overlook the fallibility of the
criterion we are trying to predict." It could be argued that
the assertion that validity coefficients should be "corrected"
to account for criterion unreliability is somewhat beside
the point, given the fact that, regardless of its faults,
first year grades (or whatever criterion) is the criterion
which psychometricians have themselves chosen to demonstrate
the predictive validity of their tests and is the criterion
by which institutions ultimately judge their students. Nevertheless, even if unreliability is taken into account, the
change in correlation size is modest. Guilford continues,
"The reliability of ratings, even of the better ones, is
characteristically about .60. With such criteria, validity
coefficients are about 25 percent underestimated." (pp.487-488).

The second problem, restriction of range, arises from the
fact that score-grade correlations can only be calculated for
those students who were actually admitted. If the school is
very selective and most of those admitted go on to earn
grades which cluster around the top of the scale, it will
be difficult for the test to distinguish among them. The
theory goes that if those who were rejected due to their test
scores had been admitted instead, they would have earned low
grades and thereby given the test more of a chance to demonstrate its predictive power. According to Willingham and
Breland "In a highly selective program there is typically a
fairly narrow range of ability among those students selected,
particularly on those measures that were used in selecting
the students. This narrow range can substantially lower the
apparent validity of a selection measure, though the accuracy
of estimating the students' likely criterion performance is

not thereby affected...If most admitted students cluster at
the higher score levels, there will clearly be little difference among those students in probability of degree attainment that is associated with test score level." (p.134).
Professor Robyn Dawes, in a mathematical paper in Science
(Robyn M. Dawes, "Graduate Admission Variables and Future
Success," Science, February 28, 1975) p.721, has noted how
for highly selective institutions the predictive validity of
a predictor is ultimately impossible to know conclusively:
"The result is a dilemma. Studies involving admission
variables will yield low correlations of necessity, and hence
these low correlations cannot be used to determine whether
the admissions veriables are any good. They may be. Or on
the other hand, they may be unfair and invalid--and their use
may merely perpetuate an unfortunate status quo." (p. 723)

Another consideration often introduced by psychometricians in
the discussion of validity coefficients is the selection ratio
of the institution. In the words of Willingham and Breland,
"it is also important to note that the effectiveness of a
predictor depends not only upon the magnitude of the validity
coefficient but also upon the proportion of the applicants
selected." (p.132). This is based upon a model known as the
"Taylor-Russell Tables" after H.C. Taylor and J.T. Russell
of Western Electric who in 1939 sought to develop an alternative
way of interpreting correlation coefficients to supplant the
r squared and the coefficient of alienation, which, they
noted " /⎯have⎯/ brought about a considerable pessimism with
regard to the validity coefficients which are ordinarily obtainable when tests are tried out in the employment office of
a business or industry or in an educational institution."
(H.C. Taylor and J.T. Russell, "The Relationship of Validity
Coefficients to the Practical Effectiveness of Tests in Selection: Discussion and Tables," Journal of Applied Psychology,
vol. 23, 1939,pp.565-566). Their model showed that the more
selective an institution, the more useful a predictor was
in telling who would succeed and who would fail, regardless
of the size of its validity coefficient. Their tables depend on three variables: the size of the validity coefficient, the proportion of applicants considered capable of
succeeding, and the proportion of applicants selected. By
their theory,at, say, a moderately selective college where
70% of the applicant pool was considered capable of succeeding
and 60% of the applicants were selected, the use of a test
with a validity of .40 would increase the percentage of admitted applicants who succeeded from 70% (the number which
would succeed if admissions decisions were made by blind
chance) to 79%. (Taylor & Russell, p.576). At a more highly
selective institution, the gain in percentage of successful
admittees would theoretically be higher. Willingham and
Breland use the Taylor-Russell tables to make the following

claim: "If only 20 percent of the applicants could be accommodated, a predictor with a validity of .45 would increase the overall success rate from .50 [50%] to .75 [75%]." (p.132). These figures, however, are drawn from the table (Taylor, Russell, p.575) which assumes that only half of the students applying are capable of succeeding. While an applicant pool with this composition might be found at a relatively unselective college, it would be rare to find an institution which had such applicants while at the same time having a selection ratio of only 20%. Such selection ratios are characteristic mainly of the highly competitive graduate and professional schools which, as Willingham and Breland themselves acknowledge in their discussion of restriction of range, are often faced with a glut of qualified applicants. (See Chapter VI for a discussion of this phenomenon in law school admissions.) At a graduate department, for example, where the selection ratio was 20% and the percentage of qualified applicants was 80%, a predictor with validity of .45 would theoretically increase the percentage of successful admittees from 80% (the level obtained by chance selection) to 95%.

Even when taken into account, the effect of these various considerations on the validity coefficient is modest. In the case of a hypothetical restriction of range model presented by Willingham and Breland, for example, (p.240) even if all students who had been admitted to college (a population considerably less qualified than the typical graduate school applicant pool) were admitted to graduate school and ranked with a test with a .44 validity, that test would still provide only 36% of perfect prediction in predicting their graduate school grades.

Perhaps the most important thing to bear in mind about these various caveats is that validity coefficients which are "corrected" to account for them are based on assumptions about events that never occurred (e.g., the availability of a perfectly reliable criterion, the admission of the entire applicant pool, etc.). This may be a reason why such "corrected" coefficients are rarely reported in the empirical research studies which form the basis of the testmaker's claims to predictive validity, and of the charts and discussion of the text of this chapter.

16. ETS, Your Student Report, 1979-80, Admissions Testing Program of the College Board, 1978, p.3. The "2 out of 3" figure refers to the test's reliability, i.e., its consistency of difficulty from one form to the next. This figure reflects the candidate's chances, if they took the test again, of earning a score within a band of 30 points around the average score that they would in theory earn if they took the test an infinite number of times. The ETS phrase "measure your ability with perfect accuracy" implies that these figures

tell something about the test's validity, i.e., its relationship to later performance. In fact, they do not.
   The 1979-80 student bulletin makes the same point in slightly different words: "Because no test measures with perfect accuracy and consistency, think of ATP scores as approximate rather than exact measures of your abilities." (Emphasis added). The 1979-80 bulletin is more clear than the 1978-79 bulletin in explaining that the two-thirds figure refers to reliability. (See ETS, Your Student Report, 1979-80, Admissions Testing Program of the College Board, p.3.)

17. CEEB, Guidelines on the Uses of College Board Test Scores and Related Data, 1977, p.5. See also William H. Angoff, "A Reminder to Educators: Seven Points to Remember About the SAT," in College Board Review, Winter 1973-74, p.5. ETS, Law School Admission Bulletin, 1979-80, p.17.

18. Angoff, "Seven Points to Remember," p.5.

19. See footnote 15 of this chapter and Ford and Campos, "Summary of Validity Data." Percentages of perfect prediction are derived from Ford and Campos' correlation coefficients by squaring the coefficient and multiplying by 100.

20. Ibid. Derived from Table 5, p.6. See footnote 15 of this chapter for discussion.

21. Figures derived from Willingham and Breland, "The Status of Selective Admissions," p.132. Percentages are derived by squaring the coefficients and multiplying by 100. See footnote 15 for further discussion.

22. Ronald L. Flaugher, "Some Points of Confusion in Discussing the Testing of Black Students," in L.P. Miller, ed., The Testing of Black Students: A Symposium (Englewood Cliffs, N.J.: Prentice Hall, 1974) pp.12-13.

23. Carl C. Brigham, "The Scholastic Aptitude Test," in The Work of the College Entrance Examination Board (Boston: Ginn and Co., 1926), p.52. He uses what is today called an "efficiency of prediction" formula, described in note 36.

24. William R. Shane, Malcolm D. Talbott, et al., LSAT Handbook (Princeton: ETS, 1964), p.45.

25. Paul van R. Miller and John A. Winterbottom, The Admission Test for Graduate Study in Business: A Handbook for Deans and Admissions Officers (Princeton: ETS, 1966), p.114.

26. ETS, Short-Cut Statistics for Teacher-Made Tests, Evaluation and Advisory Series, 1964, p.36.

27. Ibid.

28. Alexander W. Astin, *Predicting Academic Performance in College* (New York: Free Press, 1971) p.19.

29. Willingham and Breland, "The Status of Selective Admissions," p.132.

30. Ford and Campos, "Summary of Validity Data," p.11. The 1971 SAT Math correlation is for females only; the 1969 SAT Verbal correlation is for males only.

31. Dale Tillery, *Distribution and Differentiation of Youth: A Study of Transition from School to College* (Cambridge, MA: Ballinger, 1973), p.83. Since the actual correlations between ETS test scores and grades average considerably less than .50 they improve the betting odds over chance by considerably less than even 25%.

32. Ford and Campos, "Summary of Validity Data," (for the SAT); and Willingham and Breland, "The Status of Selective Admissions," p.132 (for the GRE, LSAT, GMAT). Correlation coefficients are squared and multiplied by 100 to yield percentages of perfect prediction. These numbers are then subtracted from 100 to give the percentage in which random prediction is as accurate as an ETS test. See also footnote 15.

33. Breland and Minsky, *Population Validity and College Entrance Measures*, pp.149,153. The coefficients found in the studies (0.64--New Jersey, and 0.02--Indiana) are squared, multiplied by 100, and subtracted from 100 to yield the percentages in the text.

34. Ford and Campos, "Summary of Validity Data," p.11.

35. Dr. Jay Berger, Director of Admissions, University of California at Berkeley, in a telephone interview with Ronald Brownstein, September, 1979.

36. Ford and Campos, "Summary of Validity Data," p.11. These percentages of incremental predictive effectiveness are calculated in the manner described in a CEEB pamphlet by Cameron Fincher, *Is the SAT Worth Its Salt? An Evaluation of the Use of the Scholastic Aptitude Test in the University of Georgia System over a Thirteen-Year Period*, 1974, distributed by the American Educational Research Association. On page 299 the following formula for calculating efficiency indices, derived from general textbooks, is presented:

$$E = 100\left(1 - \sqrt{1 - r^2}\right)$$

where r represents the coefficient. Efficiency indices for both high school record and combined high school record and scores are calculated. The difference equals the increase in predictive efficiency because of test scores. See also Guilford, *Fundamental Statistics*.

37. Leo Munday, *Comparative Predictive Validities of the American College Tests and Two Other Scholastic Aptitude Tests*, ACT Research Report #6, (Iowa City: Research and Development Division, ACT Program, August 1965) pp.4-7; Oscar T. Lenning and E. James Maxey, "ACT Versus SAT Prediction for Present-Day College Students," *Educational and Psychological Measurement*, 1973, 33, pp.397-406. ACT brochures do not say that their test measures "aptitude," but that it is "a test covering four subject areas--English, Mathematics, Social Studies, and Natural Sciences." American College Testing Program, *Taking the ACT Assessment, 1978-79 Edition, Eastern Region*, (ACTP, 1978) p.2.

38. O.T. Lenning, *Predictive Validity of the ACT Tests at Selective Colleges*, ACT Research Report #69, (Iowa City: Research and Development Division, ACT Program, August 1975).

39. Gene M. Smith, "Usefulness of Peer Ratings of Personality in Educational Research," *Educational and Psychological Measurement*, 1967, 27, pp.967-984. See especially p.974.

40. *Ibid.*, p.977.

41. Anne Anastasi, M.J. Meade and A.A. Schneiders, "The Validation of a Biographical Inventory as a Predictor of College Success," CEEB Research Monograph No. 1, 1960, p.1, quoted in Angoff, *The College Board Admissions Testing Program*, p.159.

42. *Ibid*.

43. *Pro Forum*, October 1979, pp.4,7. This newsletter published by the National Center for the Study of Professions (Washington, D.C.) reviewed ETS, "Using Self-Reports to Predict Student Performance," 1976.

44. *Pro Forum*, October 1979, p.7.

45. John R.P. French, Jr., "Quantification of Organizational Stress," in *Managing Organizational Stress: Proceedings of the Executive Study Conference*, November 29-30, 1967, Princeton, (Princeton: ETS, 1968) p.31.

46. *Ibid.*, p.36.

47. See L.G. Humphreys, "The Fleeting Nature of the Prediction of College Academic Success", *Journal of Educational Psychology*, 1968, 59, pp.375-380.

48. Lloyd G. Humphreys and Thomas Taber, "Postdiction Study of the Graduate Record Examination and Eight Semesters of College Grades," *Journal of Educational Measurement*, vol. 10, No. 3, Fall 1973, pp.179-184.

49. *Ibid.*, p.182.

50. *Intellect*, November 1972, p.76.

51. See for example Leonard L. Baird of ETS, "Biographical and Educational Correlates of Graduate and Professional School Admissions Test Scores," *Educational and Psychological Measurement*, 1976, 36, pp.415-420.

52. Alexander W. Astin, "Racial Considerations in Admissions," in David C. Nichols and Olive Mills, editors, *The Campus and the Racial Crisis* (Washington, D.C.: American Council on Education, 1970) p.87.

53. *Ibid.*, p.88.

54. *Ibid.*

55. Astin, *Predicting Academic Performance in College*, pp.14-15.

56. *Ibid.*, pp.17-18. Percentages of perfect prediction are calculated from Astin's coefficients in the manner noted earlier. See footnote 15.

57. *Ibid.*, p.20.

58. Astin, *Predicting Academic Performance in College*, p.18 (for SAT); Baird, "Biographical and Educational Correlates," p.419 (for LSAT); Willingham and Breland, "The Status of Selective Admissions," p.235 (for GRE).

59. E. Nicholson, *Predictors of Graduation From College*, ACT Research Report #56, (Iowa City: Research and Development Division, ACT Program, March 1973). The quotation is from "Abstract."

60. "Selecting College Material," *New York Times*, April 4, 1976, p.E-7; Interview, Thomas W. Bleezarde, Editor, *Williams Alumni Review*, December 12, 1979.

61. College Board, *Taking the SAT*, back cover.

62. *College Board News*, June 1978, p.5.

63. Willingham and Breland, "The Status of Selective Admissions," p.135.

64. Comments by Shelly Martucci, College Board representative, to the author at a college recruitment fair at the New York Coliseum, Fall, 1978.

65. David C. McClelland, "Testing for Competence Rather Than for 'Intelligence,'" *American Psychologist*, January 1973, p.3.

66. *Ibid.*

67. Nettie H. Seabrooks, "Tests: Gate Openers or Gate Closers?" *G.M. Quarterly*, Spring 1976, p.15.

68. Leonard L. Baird, *Development of an Inventory of Documented Accomplishments for Graduate Admissions*, GRE Board Research Report GREB No. 77-3R (Princeton: ETS, June 1979), pp. 15, 17, 18, 24.

69. Albert R. Marston, "It Is Time to Reconsider the Graduate Record Examination," *American Psychologist*, vol. 26, No. 7, July 1971, pp. 653-654.

70. Willingham and Breland, "The Status of Selective Admissions," p. 135. The undergraduate thesis referred to is J.W. Kallop, "A Study of Scholastic Aptitude Test and Eminence," Princeton University, 1951.

71. W. Coffman and M. Mahoney, "A Follow-Up Study of Yale Phi Beta Kappa Graduates," in ETS, *Annual Report 1966-1967*, pp. 98-99.

72. See Samuel Bowles and Valerie Nelson, "The 'Inheritance of IQ' and the Intergenerational Transmission of Economic Inequality," *The Review of Economics and Statistics*, vol. 56, No. 1, February 1974. Cited in Samuel Bowles and Herbert Gintis, *Schooling in Capitalist America: Educational Reform and the Contradictions of Economic Life*, (New York: Basic Books, 1976) pp. 122, 289-297.

73. Ibid., pp. 289-297.

74. Ibid., pp. 121-148.

75. Richard DeLone, *Small Futures: Children, Inequality, and the Limits of Liberal Reform* (New York: Harcourt Brace Jovanovich, 1979) p. 12. For the Carnegie Council on Children.

76. Christopher Jencks, *Who Gets Ahead? The Determinants of Economic Success in America*, (New York: Basic Books, 1979), pp. 81, 110, 112, 219.

77. Donald P. Hoyt, *The Relationship Between College Grades and Adult Achievement: A Review of the Literature*, ACT Research Report (Iowa City: ACT Research and Development Division, 1965) p. 1.

78. McClelland, "Testing for Competence," p. 2.

79. Ibid.

80. Ronald L. Flaugher, *The New Definitions of Test Fairness in Selection: Developments and Implications*, GRE Board Research Report GREB No. 72-4R, (Princeton: ETS, May 1974), p. 8.

81. Interview with William Turnbull, May 3, 1977.

82. Lewis W. Pike and Franklin R. Evans, *Effects of Special Instruction for Three Kinds of Mathematics Aptitude Items*, CEEB Research Report I (New York: CEEB, 1972) p. v.

83. Kramer, "Unnamed Test Preparation Services," p. 5.

84. Interview with William Turnbull, ETS President, May 3,1977.

85. Letter from Karl U. Smith, University of Wisconsin Professor of Psychology, to the Wisconsin State Journal, November 18,1976, pp. 1-2.

86. ETS, Moderator Variable Study: The Effect of Background Factors on the Prediction of Performance in Graduate Business School, Admission Test for Graduate Study in Business Research and Development Committee, Brief Number 3(Princeton: ETS, 1969) pp. 5, 17.

87. Ibid., p. 5.

88. ETS, Program Research Progress Report, August 1979, p. 29. Cites a study by Joan Baratz and Terry Hartle, "Older Students and the Graduate Record Examinations: A Preliminary Investigation."

89. ACT, Highlights of the ACT Technical Report, ACT Research and Development Division (Iowa City: ACT, 1973) p. 23.

90. ETS "Research Memorandum" by James F. Wohlhueter on "Fatigue in Testing and other Mental Tasks: A Literature Survey", June 1966, pp. 27-8. Cites a 1961 ETS study by John French. The document is at the ETS library (open to the public on request), but is noted:"This memorandum is for interoffice use."

91. Marjorie C. Kirkland, "The Effects of Tests on Students and Schools, Review of Educational Research,vol. 41, no.4, Oct.1971 p. 318.

92. French cited in Wohlhueter, "Fatigue in Testing", p. 28.

93. Kirkland, "The Effects of Tests", p. 318.

94. ETS research bulletin by Bruce Bloxom on "Test Anxiety and Test Performance", RB-68-30.

95. Wohlhueter, "Fatigue in Testing", p. 26.

96. Kirkland, "The Effects of Tests", p. 318.

97. Glenn L. Rowley, "Which Examinees are Most Favored by the Use of Multiple Choice Tests?" Journal of Educational Measurement, Spring,1974, p. 21.

98. M. Kogan and M.A. Wallach, Risktaking: A Study in Cognition and Personality (New York: Holt, Rinehart and Winston, 1964), cited in Rowley, "Which Examinees",p. 21.

99. Seabrooks, "Tests: Gate Openers or Gate Closers?" p. 15.

100. Samuel Messick and Nathan Kogan, "Category Width and Quantitative Aptitude," Perceptual and Motor Skills, 1965, 20, pp. 493-497 (Southern University Press, 1965). The hypothetical questions are from the article. The authors are listed as affiliated with ETS.

101. Rowley, "Which Examinees," p. 15.

102. Messick and Kogan, "Category Width," p. 494.

103. Ibid., pp. 496-497.

104. Dayton Axtell, A Brief Study of Those Not Completing the Mathematical Part of the School and College Ability Test, 1974, cited in ERIC Abstracts, ED 092 584.

105. Report of the Commission on Tests: I. Righting the Balance (New York: CEEB, 1970) p. 76.

106. Report of the Commission on Tests: II. Briefs, (New York: CEEB, 1970), p. 137.

107. Ibid. Thresher quotes an unpublished analysis of the January 1967 administration of the College Board Achievement Tests.

108. Ibid., pp. 137-138.

109. Ibid., p. 142.

110. ETS internal report by Arthur M. Kroll, "A Proposal for the Development of a Test Orientation Publication," May 24, 1973, pp. 1, 10.

111. Ibid., pp. 1-2. Kroll quotes Jason Millman, Carol Bishop and Robert Ebel, "An Analysis of Test-Wiseness," Educational and Psychological Measurement, vol. XXV, No. 3, 1965, p. 707.

112. Ibid., p. 9.

113. Ibid., pp. 11-12.

114. Ibid., p. 12.

115. Ibid.

116. Ibid., pp. 12-13.

117. Lewis W. Pike, Short-Term Instruction, Testwiseness, and The Scholastic Aptitude Test: A Literature Review with Research Recommendations, CEEB Research and Development Report, RB-78-2, (Princeton: ETS, January 1978) p. 28.

118. Henry A. Alker, Julia A. Carlson, and Margaret C. Herman, "Multiple Choice Questions and Student Characteristics," paper presented at the American Psychological Association, September 1967.

119. ETS test-familiarization materials such as <u>Taking the SAT</u> and <u>1979-80 Law School Admission Bulletin</u> include none of the strategic advice cited in Kroll's memo about trying to solve questions susceptible to a quick response or about answering items as the test constructor intended. The LSAT bulletin does urge candidates to answer every question, regardless of whether they have an idea of the answer or not (p. 20). The SAT, which uses a different scoring formula, requires a different guessing strategy.

120. Federal Trade Commission, "Staff Memorandum on The Effects of Coaching on Standardized Admission Examinations," from Arthur E. Levine, Boston Regional Office, to FTC Bureau of Consumer Protection, Sept. 11, 1978, pp. 31-41.

121. See for example, the ad for John Sexton's GMAT and LSAT courses, New York newspapers, September 1978, or FTC memo by Levine, "The Effects of Coaching," pp. 170-173.

122. FTC memo by Levine, "The Effects of Coaching," p. 41.

123. Donald L. Alderman and Donald E. Powers, <u>The Effects of Special Preparation on SAT-Verbal Scores</u>, CEEB Research and Development Report, RDR 78-79, No. 4 (Princeton: ETS, February 1979) p. 4.

124. Angoff, <u>The College Board Admissions Testing Program</u>, p. 7.

125. LSAC, Minutes of the Joint Legal Affairs and Finance Committee meeting, November 8-9, 1974. /LSAC,"1974 Annual Council Report," pp. 284, 285_/

126. LSAC, Minutes of the Test Development and Research Committee meeting, April 13-14, 1973. /LSAC,"1973 Annual Council Report", p. 262_/

127. Richard E. Harpster, "Company Unlocks Mysteries of College Entrance Exams," <u>Morris County Daily Record</u>, July 30, 1978, p. C-2.

128. FTC memo by Levine, "Effects of Coaching," pp. 32-33.

129. Joint hearing of the New York State Legislature Senate and Assembly Higher Education Committees, May 9, 1979, attended by the author.

130. Federal Trade Commission, Bureau of Consumer Protection, <u>Effects of Coaching on Standardized Admission Examinations: Revised Statistical Analyses of Data Gathered by Boston Regional Office of the Federal Trade Commission</u>, March 1979, p. 8.

131. Interview with Lewis W. Pike, former director of ETS Verbal Test Development and senior ETS researcher, February 1979.

132. Peggy Carroll, "Numbers Still Count In The Battle for School Admission," *Morris County Daily Record*, Feb. 22, 1977, p. 11.

133. *Ibid.*

134. LSAC, Minutes of the Joint Legal Affairs and Finance Committee Meeting, November 8-9, 1974.

135. Steven Levy, "ETS and the 'Coaching' Cover-Up," *New Jersey Monthly*, March 1979, p. 4. Levy says the West Point study involved 714 subjects, more than any study included in the ETS-College Board booklet.

136. Pike and Evans, *Effects of Special Instruction*, p. 4.

137. Levy, "ETS and the 'Coaching' Cover-Up," p. 4.

138. LSAC, Minutes of the Joint Legal Affairs and Finance Committee Meeting, November 8-9, 1974, /p. 284/

139. Letter from William Turnbull, ETS President, to Ralph Nader, July 12, 1977, p. 3.

140. FTC memos by Levine, "Effects of Coaching," pp. 23-30; and Kramer, "Unnamed Test Preparation Services," p. 1.

141. FTC memo by Levine, "Effects of Coaching," p. 185.

142. *Ibid.*, p. 186.

143. *Ibid.*

144. *Ibid.*, p. 180.

145. *Ibid.*, p. 257.

146. *Ibid.*, pp. 221-223.

147. *Ibid.*, pp. 224-225.

148. Interview with Michael Pertschuk, Federal Trade Commission Chairman, Sept. 15, 1979.

149. William E. McKibben, "FTC Study Backs Coaching for Tests," *Harvard Crimson*, November 17, 1978, p. 1.

150. Mitchell C. Lynch, "Probe of Coaching for Scholastic Tests Raises Issues About Exams Themselves," *Wall Street Journal*, December 4, 1978, p. 31; Larry Kramer, "FTC Sees Cram Courses as Helpful," *Washington Post*, March 28, 1979, D-7.

151. FTC internal memorandum from Ken Bernhardt and Michael Sesnowitz to Chuck Shepherd on "Differences Between The Analysis Conducted In The Boston Regional Office ETS Report and In Our Report," March 22, 1979. Shepherd is Albert Kramer's assistant.

152. Interview with Pertschuk, September 17, 1979.

153. FTC memo from Kramer, "Unnamed Test Preparation Services," p. 6.

154. Ibid.

155. Ibid., p. 3.

156. Ibid., pp. 2-3.

157. Interview with Pertschuk, Sept. 15, 1979.

158. See FTC memo by Kramer, "Unnamed Test Preparation Services," p. 1; and National Education Association, "NEA Calls Upon FTC to Release Testing Data, Investigate Entire Testing Industry," press release, March 28, 1979.

159. Federal Trade Commission, "FTC Releases Staff Study on Effect of Coaching on Scholastic Aptitude Test Scores," press release, May 29, 1979.

160. Staff Memorandum of the Boston Regional Office of the Federal Trade Commission, The Effects of Coaching on Standardized Admission Examinations, September 1978. The disclaimer is contained on a page stapled to the cover entitled "Notice to Recipients of the Boston Regional Office Report on the Effects of Coaching on Standardized Admission Examinations," May 1979.

161. The reissued report ends on page 174, thus deleting the original findings concerning ETS' potential deceptive trade acts.

162. ETS press release on FTC coaching report, May 1979.

163. College Board, "Backgrounder: The Effects of Coaching on a Student's SAT Scores," press statement, September 1979, p. 2.

164. Letter from Robert J. Solomon, ETS, to the Editor, Science, vol. 206, no. 44, October 19, 1979. pp. 274-5.

165. FTC memo by Kramer, "Unnamed Test Preparation Services," p. 5.

166. Ibid.

167. Ibid., pp. 5-6.

168. *Ibid.*, p. 9.

169. *Ibid.*, p. 10.

170. Interview with Pertschuk, September 15, 1979.

171. College Board, *Taking the SAT*, p. 3.

172. Interview with Pertschuk, September 15, 1979.

173. William W. Turnbull, ETS President, "On Educational Standards, Testing, and the Aspirations of Minorities." Speech made at the Conference on Academic Standards and Their Relationship to Minority Aspirations, conducted by the American-Jewish Congress at the Kellogg Center of the School of International Affairs at Columbia University, December 8, 1974, p. 2.

174. *Ibid.*, p. 13.

175. Junius A. Davis and George Temp, "Is the SAT Biased Against Black Students?" *College Board Review*, Fall, 1971, no. 81, p. 8.

176. Willingham and Breland, "The Status of Selective Admissions," in *Selective Admissions in Higher Education*, p. 192

177. *Ibid.*

178. George H. Hanford, *Minority Programs and Activities of the College Entrance Examination Board: A Critical Review and a Brief Look Ahead* (New York: CEEB, 1976) p. 38.

179. Statement of Robert J. Solomon, Executive Vice President, ETS, before the Subcommittee on Elementary, Secondary and Vocational Education and Labor of the U.S. House of Representatives, July 31, 1979, p. 10.

180. Levine, "Indices of Test Bias," p. 1.

181. Astin, "Racial Considerations in Admissions," p. 92. A number of schools have found that, when admitted, low-income students whose scores would normally exclude them meet or exceed the school's academic standards. For an early discussion of this kind, see "Limitations of Admissions Testing for the Disadvantaged," *Personnel and Guidance Journal*, November 1964, p. 301.

182. American Bar Association, "ABA Says Millions More Needed to Assist Disadvantaged Students to Attend Law School," press release, October 31, 1979.

183. Admissions Testing Program of the CEEB, *College Bound Seniors, 1973-74*, 1974, p. 27.

184. All of the following are by the Admissions Testing Program of the CEEB, published by CEEB in 1974: <u>Southern College Bound Seniors, 1973-74</u>, p. 14; <u>Middle States College Bound Seniors, 1973-74</u>, p. 14; <u>New England College Bound Seniors, 1973-74</u>, p. 20; <u>Midwestern College Bound Seniors, 1973-74</u>, p. 14; <u>Western College Bound Seniors, 1973-74</u>, p. 14.

185. Admissions Testing Program of the CEEB, <u>National College Bound Seniors, 1979</u>, 1979, p. 16. See Chapter V.

186. David M. White, "Estimates of the Relative Ability to Identify the Race of a Law Student by Referring to Various Measures," 1979. Unpublished analysis of data from W. Schrader and B. Pitcher, "Predicting Law School Grades for Black American Law Students," Law School Admission Council Annual Report 530, 567, Table 10 (1973).

187. Baird, <u>Development of an Inventory of Documented Accomplishments for Graduate Admissions</u>, p. 24.

188. Donald M. Medley, University of Virginia, and Thomas J. Quick, ETS, "Race and Subject-Matter Influences on Performance on General Education Items of the National Teacher Examinations," ETS Research Bulletin RB-72-43, September 1972, p. 3.

189. <u>Ibid.</u>, p. 15.

190. <u>Ibid.</u>, p. 20.

191. Robert L. Williams, "The Bitch-100: A Culture-Specific Test," paper presented at the American Psychological Association, Honolulu, Hawaii, September 1972, pp. 1, 8.

192. <u>Ibid.</u>, p. 9.

193. <u>Ibid.</u> Derived from Table 1.

194. <u>Ibid.</u>, pp. 10-11.

195. David M. White, "Whom Do You Trust?" 1979 manuscript prepared for publication in <u>The Measuring Cup</u> (forthcoming).

196. See, for example, Kirkland, "The Effects of Tests." The FTC coaching study found that students who attended coaching courses were generally from the upper income brackets. See chart on p. 98 of text.

197. Chuck Stone, "The End of Colonialism in the College Admissions Office," condensation of a paper delivered before the 27th Annual Conference of the National Association of College Admissions Counselors in San Francisco, September 30, 1971. See especially pp. 3-4. Stone was Director of Minority Affairs at ETS.

198. Robert L. Williams, "The Problem of Match and Mis-Match in Testing Black Children," paper presented at the annual meeting of the American Psychological Association, Honolulu, Hawaii, September 1972, p. 3.

199. Robert L. Williams, "Abuses and Misuses in Testing Black Children," reprinted from Counseling Psychologist, vol. 2, no. 3, 1971, p. 5.

200. Robert L. Williams, "Danger: Testing and Dehumanizing Black Children," unpublished paper, pp.1-2.

201. Ibid. Quotes "Statement on Testing" adopted by the Association of Black Psychologists at their 1969 Annual Meeting in Washington, D.C.

202. George D. Jackson, "On the Report of the Ad hoc Committee on Educational Uses of Tests with Disadvantaged Students," American Psychologist, January 1975, p. 88.

203. Quoted in Esteban L. Olmedo, "Psychological Testing and the Chicano: A Reassessment," paper presented at the First Symposium on Chicano Psychology, University of California at Irvine, May 15-16, 1976, p. 1.

204. Ibid., p. 2.

205. NAACP Report on Minority Testing, (NAACP Special Contribution Fund, May 1976) pp. iv, v, 7-8.

206. The number of groups critical of standardized testing may be far greater than what is presented here, based on a limited sampling. No one has a current count of the total number of organizations opposing standardized testing in its present form. In October 1979, at the National Consortium on Testing Meeting in Arlington, Va., we interviewed representatives of the following organizations opposed, in varying degrees, to current test practices. National Association of Elementary School Principals, National Congress of Parents and Teachers, National Parents and Teachers Association, National Association of School Psychologists, National Association for the Advancement of Colored People, American School Counselor Association, National Education Association, Association of Black Psychologists, Workshop for Open Education, Association for Supervision and Curriculum Development, Center for Study of Evaluation of the UCLA Graduate School of Education, Council for Basic Education, United States Student Association.

207. David C. McClelland, "Testing for Competence Rather than for 'Intelligence'," American Psychologist, vol. 28, no. 1, January 1973, p. 1.

208. ETS internal report by David Loye, "Cultural Bias in Testing: Challenge and Response," January 12, 1973, pp. 25-26.

209. Bernard W. Harleston, "GRE Programs and Tests: Comments and Suggestions," p. 2, unpublished report attached to internal memorandum from Harleston to Richard L. Burns, ETS Program Director, on "Report of recent visit to ETS to review GRE Programs in relation to Minority-group Students," received February 14, 1972. Harleston was Dean of the Graduate School of Arts and Sciences at Tufts University and a consultant to ETS.

210. Ibid., p. 1.

211. ETS internal report by Thomas F. Donlon, Charles W. Daves, et. al, "Statement on Educational Testing and Minority/Poverty Group Needs: A Report to the ETS PEOPLE Committee," June 1970, pp. 14-15. No one with whom we spoke could remember what PEOPLE stood for.

212. College Board, Taking the SAT, pp. 17, 31, 20.

213. Steven Brill, "The Secrecy Behind the College Boards," New York Magazine, October 7, 1974, p. 69.

214. Donlon and Daves, "Statement on Educational Testing," pp. 33-34.

215. Ibid., p. 33.

216. Transcript of speech by George Schlekat of ETS before the Border College Consortium, p. 8. The text is undated, but Schlekat thought the date was in late 1972 (interview, Dec. 17, 1979).

217. Ibid., p. 10.

218. Ibid., p. 3.

219. Turnbull speech to Conference on Academic Standards and Their Relationship to Minority Aspirations, pp. 3, 11.

220. ETS internal report by W.W. Turnbull and G.H. Hanford, "A Proposal for a HIGHER EDUCATION ABILITY RECOGNITION Program to Promote the Entry of Minority Group Students into Higher Education," draft, August 18, 1969, p. II-1.

221. Thomas C. Oliver, "What About Test Bias and Discrimination?" ACTivity, December 1975, p. 6. Oliver was an ACT regional vice president, Educational Services Division.

222. Turnbull, speech to the Conference on Academic Standards and Their Relationship to Minority Aspirations, p. 12.

223. Ibid., p. 10.

224. W.W. Turnbull, "Socio-Economic Status and Predictive Test Scores," *Canadian Journal of Psychology*, vol. 5, no. 4, December 1951, pp. 145-49.

225. T. Anne Cleary, "Test Bias: Prediction of Grades of Negro and White Students in Integrated Colleges," *Journal of Educational Measurement*, vol. 5, no. 2, Summer 1968, p. 115.

226. *Ibid.*, p. 123.

227. Computed from figures in Table 5 of C. Michael Pfeifer, Jr. and William E. Sedlacek, "The Validity of Academic Predictions for Black and White Students at a Predominantly White University," *Journal of Educational Measurement*, vol. 8, no. 4, Winter 1971, p. 258. Both authors are from the University of Maryland.

228. Ronald L. Flaugher, "Bias in Testing: A Review and Discussion," ERIC TM Report 36, ERIC Clearinghouse on Tests, Measurement and Evaluation, ETS, December 1974, p. 1. See also Breland and Minsky, *Population Validity and College Entrance Measures*.

229. Both sources are cited in David M. White, "Culturally Biased Testing and Predictive Invalidity: Putting Them on the Record," *Harvard Civil Rights-Civil Liberties Law Review*, vol. 14, 1979, p. 127. White quotes Linn, "Test Bias and the Prediction of Grades in Law School," 27 J. Legal Educ. 293, 304 (1975) and University of California, *Final Report of the Task Force on Graduate and Professional Admissions* 43 (1977).

230. Turnbull, speech to Conference on Academic Standards and Their Relationship to Minority Aspirations, p. 6.

231. CEEB, *College Board Guide for High Schools and Colleges 1972-73*, Admissions Testing Program, 1972, p. 14.

232. Astin, *Predicting Academic Performance in College*, p. 18.

233. Robert L. Thorndike, "Concepts of Culture Fairness," and Richard B. Darlington, "Another Look at 'Culture Fairness,'" in *Journal of Educational Measurement*, vol. 8, no. 2, pp. 63-82.

234. ETS internal memorandum from Dr. F.M. Lord to Richard Levine on "'Cultural Fairness' and ETS Tests," September 22, 1971, p. 2.

235. Levine, "Indices of Test Bias," p. 1.

236. Flaugher, "Bias in Testing," p. 4.

237. Lord, "'Cultural Fairness'," p. 2.

238. *Ibid.*, p. 5.

239. *Ibid.*, p. 2.

240. See for example Melvin R. Novick and Dorsey D. Ellis, Jr., "Equal Opportunity in Educational and Employment Selection," *American Psychologist*, vol. 306, May 1977, pp. 306-320; or Melvin R. Novick and Nancy S. Petersen, "Towards Equalizing Educational and Employment Opportunity," *Journal of Educational Measurement*, vol. 13, no. 1, Spring 1976.

241. Nancy S. Cole, *Bias in Selection*, ACT Research Report No. 51, (Iowa City: Research and Development Division of the American College Testing Program, May 1972) pp. 8, 16.

242. Frank L. Schmidt and John E. Hunter, "Racial and Ethnic Bias in Psychological Tests: Divergent Implications of Two Definitions of Test Bias," *American Psychologist*, January 1974, p.4.

243. *Ibid.*, p. 5.

244. *Ibid.*

245. *Ibid.*

246. Brief of the Black Law Students Association at the University of California, Berkeley School of Law as *Amicus Curiae* to the United States Supreme Court at 21, in *Regents of the Univ. of Cal. vs. Bakke*, 438 U.S. 265 (1978).

247. "Minority Admissions Defended by Report," *New York Times*, July 24, 1977, p. 27.

248. Vilma Martinez and Mario Lara, "Who Gets In? Standardized Testing, Special Admissions and the Myth of Reverse Discrimination," *The Self-Determination Quarterly Journal*, vol. 2, no. 1, March 1978.

249. Roy D. Goldman and Mel H. Widawski, "An Analysis of Types of Errors in the Selection of Minority College Students," *Journal of Educational Measurement*, vol. 13, no. 3, Fall 1976, p. 196.

250. *Ibid.*, p. 187.

251. *Ibid.*, p. 189.

252. *Ibid.*, p. 196.

253. *Ibid.*, p. 192.

254. *Ibid.*, p. 193.

255. Ibid., p. 197.

256. Flaugher, "Bias in Testing," p. 6.

257. Chapter 672, Laws of New York, 1979, Effective January 1, 1980. The law is commonly known as the "Truth-in-Testing" Law.

258. ETS unsigned memorandum, "Some Constitutional Issues in the Weiss Bill--H.R. 4949," [circa fall 1979]. Circulated to federal agencies.

259. Cited by Kenneth P. LaValle in New York State Senate debate on Truth-in-Testing bill, June 14, 1978, pp. 5326-5327 of transcript. Copy of letter from T.J. Larkin to Senator LaValle.

260. B. Alden Thresher, "Diversification in Educational Assessment," in Report of the Commission on Tests: II. Briefs, pp. 150-151.

261. Oscar K. Buros, "Fifty Years in Testing: Some Reminiscences, Criticisms, and Suggestions," Educational Researcher, vol. 6, no. 7, July/August 1977, p. 14.

262. Ibid.

263. Ibid.

264. National Conference of Bar Examiners, The Multistate Bar Examination, February 23, 1972, (Columbia, Mo.: Lucas Brothers, foreword, 1972.)

265. Answer sheets from Nacrelli, BRI, Smith-Hartman, and Calif. bar review course, attached to and discussed in letter from Joan Claybrook, Director of Congress Watch in Washington, D.C., to Robert Spanner, Chambers of Justice Boochever, Supreme Court, State of Alaska, October 19, 1973.

266. Letter from Professor Sherman Cohn of Georgetown University BRI Bar Review Institute to Kenneth W. Parkinson, Chairman, District of Columbia Court of Appeals, Committee on Admissions, August 8, 1973, on BRI stationary.

267. Letter from Claybrook to Spanner.

268. Letter from Joe E. Covington, Director of Testing, National Conference of Bar Examiners, to Joan Claybrook, October 29, 1973.

269. Hinman, Straub, Pigors and Manning, "Assembly Bill 7668-A/Senate Bill 5200-A (Synopsis of Opposition)," and attached "Debate Memorandum," June 13, 1979. Hinman, Straub is an Albany (N.Y.) law firm which served as "Legislative Counsel for Educational Testing Service." The statement was circulated in the New York State Legislature.

270. *Ibid.* and New York Public Interest Research Group, (NYPIRG), "Statement of Factual Correction and Rebuttal to Educational Testing Service Memorandum in Opposition," May 18, 1979, pp.5-6. Circulated in New York State Legislature. According to ETS internal financial reports, in 1970-71 test development accounted for only 6.7% of total ETS costs for the College Board program (p.5). This information was first presented by the author in testimony before a Joint Session of the Senate and Assembly Higher Education Committees, May 9, 1979. ETS later admitted that test development costs were in fact a small percentage of total costs. In a statement by Jack Dilworth and Don Grant, "Information for La Valle Bill," May 16, 1979, ETS said that test development costs for the ATP represented 6.9% of total costs on the ATP Program. This covered the SAT and Achievement Tests; the bill exempted Achievement Tests. This statement was submitted to the New York Senate Higher Education Committee. (LaValle was the Senate sponsor of the bill.)

271. ETS, "Finances...Where the Money Comes From and Where It Goes," paper distributed to Members of Congress, (circa fall, 1979), p.2.

272. ETS, *Annual Report to the Board of Trustees, 1949-50.* Estimated from staff list on p.5.

273. ETS Personnel Services Division internal documents, "Cost Center Organization Charts, October 1974."

274. ETS Personnel Services Division internal documents, "Cost Center Organization Charts, May 1978." See Appendix II for description of ETS Test Development Offices Staff Allocation.

275. See Appendix I for annual candidate volume figures.

276. Interview with Dr. Marion Epstein, ETS Vice-President and test development specialist, June 27, 1975.

277. *Ibid.*

278. *Ibid.*

279. ETS internal document, "Manual of Information for Test Development Professional Staff," black looseleaf binder--see section entitled "Item Writing and Review," pp.6-7. Hereafter cited as "Test Development Manual." /preface is dated 1969_7.

280. Interview with Epstein, June 27, 1975.

281. "Where Did You Ever Get All Those Questions?" *ETS Developments*, Fall 1978, p.2.

282. "Test Development Manual." See section entitled "The Test Development Examiner," p.2.

283. Ravitch, "The College Boards," p.13.

284. ETS, "Cost Center Organization Charts, October 1974."

285. "Test Development Manual." See section entitled "Item Files," pp.1-2, and "Editorial Services Department," p.2.

286. Ibid., section entitled "Editorial Services Department," p.1.

287. Ibid., section entitled "Item Files," pp.1-2.

288. Ibid., section entitled "Editorial Services Department," pp.1-2.

289. Ibid., section entitled "Pretesting," p.2; see also "Item Files" section.

290. ETS internal memorandum by M. French on "Overlap Statistics," January 1970.

291. ETS internal document, "Checklist for Developing Tests," pp.1-11, (circa 1972).

292. Interview with Epstein, June 27, 1975.

293. ETS internal memorandum from Herman F. Smith to ETS Executive Directors, Program Area Directors, Program Directors, Associate and Assistant Program Directors, "Activity Analysis," January 31, 1972.

294. Ibid.

295. Ibid.

296. Ibid.

297. ETS internal memorandum from David J. Brodsky to Advisory Board "A" on "ETS Finances and Management," September 24, 1974, p.4.

298. ETS, Annual Report 1977, "Auditors' Report."

299. ETS, "Statement of Income and Expense, March 31, 1977," April 27, 1977, p.2. (Confidential 3-page document). The category is called "Professional Services" on this document. Proctors correspond to the "test administrators" line. According to ETS' 1976 Tax Return, ETS paid Wilmer, Cutler and Pickering $321,460 in fiscal 1977. (Internal Revenue Service, Form 990, "Statement of Organization Exempt from Income Tax," 1976, filed by ETS.) Covers July 1, 1976-June 30, 1977.

300. See Dilworth & Grant, "Information for La Valle Bill," and footnote III-270 for discussion of this memo.

301. <u>Ibid</u>. This statement says the cost to the SAT program of compliance with the New York law would be $1,092,000. This is about 25% of the estimated $4.4 million profit made by ETS and the College Board on the 1978-79 ATP program. (The ATP includes both the SAT and the Achievement Tests, but only the SAT is covered by the Truth-in-Testing Law.) See Chapter VIII p. and footnotes VIII-165 and 166 for discussion of ETS-College Board profits.

302. Matthew T. Downey, <u>Carl Campbell Brigham: Scientist and Educator</u> (Princeton: ETS, 1961) p.35.

303. <u>Ibid</u>.

304. <u>Ibid</u>. The quote is by College Board Secretary George Mullins.

305. <u>Ibid</u>.

306. Letter from ETS to approximately 225 law schools using the LSAT, February 9, 1978, quoted in Carey Winfrey, "Revision in Test for Admission to Law School Leads to Dispute," <u>New York Times</u>, April 28, 1978, p.A-23.

307. <u>Ibid</u>.; and David Lempert, "Law Schools Question 1977 LSAT Scores," <u>Yale Daily News</u>, April 26, 1978.

308. Winfrey, "Revision in Test for Admission."

309. Lempert, "Law Schools Question 1977 LSAT Score."

310. <u>Ibid</u>.; and letter from Gary Hirsh to author, May 1, 1978.

311. Interview with Vivian Hirsh (Gary's mother), April 28, 1978; letter from Gary Hirsh to author, May 1, 1978.

312. Computed in Lucky Abernathy, "Highlighting What's New in Admissions," <u>College Board Review</u>, Summer 1976, pp. 31-32.

313. <u>Ibid</u>.

314. Cliff W. Wing, Jr. and Michael A. Wallach, <u>College Admissions and the Psychology of Talent</u> (New York: <u>Holt</u>, Rinehart and Winston, 1971) p.56.

315. <u>Ibid</u>., p.41.

316. <u>Ibid</u>. Statistics based on graph, p.39.

317. See for example, ETS, <u>Your Student Report 1979-80</u>, p.3.

318. Wing and Wallach, <u>College Admissions</u>, p.39. Statistics are based on graph.

319. Bullock and Stern, "College Entrance Examination Board February 1974 Scholastic Aptitude Test WSAI3," pp.1,A.

320. CEEB, "Validity Study Service: Data Analysis and Interpretation, Clifford College, Myth City, Any State," 1970, p.10. Circulated to college officials.

321. *Ibid*. See also discussion of average time per question,

322. ETS internal memorandum from George A. Schlekat, Director, College Board Admissions and Guidance Programs, to 15 ETS Officers, 11 CEEB Officers, and CEEB Division Program Staff of ETS, on "Five-Year Proposal for CEEB Division," September 27, 1972, pp.5-6.

323. ETS internal memorandum from John Kramer and Robert Moulthrop for Senior Staff Forum on "Small Group Discussion: Criticism of Testing," April 25, 1978, p.5.

FOOTNOTES, CHAPTER IV

1. Interview with Robert J. Solomon, Executive Vice President of ETS, June 19, 1975.

2. Matthew T. Downey, Carl Campbell Brigham, Scientist and Educator, (Princeton: ETS, 1961), p. 3.

3. Ibid.

4. Henry Chauncey and John Dobbin, Testing: Its Place in Education Today, (New York: Harper and Row, 1963), p. 1.

5. Leon J. Kamin, Science and Politics of I.Q., (New York: John Wiley and Sons, 1974), Chapter 2, "Psychology and the Immigrant." Kamin's history of the politics of intelligence tests is one of the best ever written. This chapter draws significantly on his work as well as on an essay by Clarence Karier, "Testing for Order and Control in the Corporate Liberal State," in N.J. Block and Gerald Dworkin, eds., The IQ Controversy: Critical Readings, (New York: Pantheon, 1976), pp. 339-373. See also Thelma Spencer, of ETS, "Testing and Minorities," speech delivered at the Fifth Annual Teacher Education Conference sponsored by the Teacher Education Liaison Committee and the Southern Regional Board, Atlanta, Georgia, November 9-11, 1975; John Higham, Strangers in the Land: Patterns of American Nativism 1860-1925, (New York: Atheneum, 1974), p. 324.

6. Chauncey and Dobbin, Testing, p. 2. See also Anne Anastasi, Psychological Testing, Second Edition, (New York: MacMillan, 1962), p. 7. According to Anastasi, a winner of the ETS Award for Distinguished Service to Measurement, "It was the English biologist, Sir Francis Galton, who was primarily responsible for launching the testing movement on its course."

7. Sir Francis Galton, "The Possible Improvement of the Human Breed Under the Existing Conditions of Law and Sentiment," Nature, October 31, 1901, vol. 64, no. 1670, pp. 659-665. Galton's article is a reprint of his Huxley Lecture delivered to the Anthropological Institute on October 29, 1901. The Huxley Lecture was established in honor of Thomas Henry Huxley (1825-1895), the biologist whose grandson, Aldous Huxley, wrote Brave New World, (1932).

8. Ibid., p. 661.

9. Sir Francis Galton, "Eugenics: Its Definition, Scope and Aims," American Journal of Sociology, July 1904, vol. 10, no. 1, p. 3.

10. Galton, "The Possible Improvement," pp. 663-664.

11. Ibid., pp. 664, 665.

12. Galton, "Eugenics," p. 5.

13. Chauncey and Dobbin, *Testing*, p. 3; Kamin, *Science and Politics of IQ*, p. 5.

14. Chauncey and Dobbin, *Testing*, p. 3; Kamin, *Science and Politics of IQ*, pp. 5-10. The test currently in use is the Stanford-Binet.

15. Chauncey and Dobbin, *Testing*, p. 3.

16. Kamin, *Science and Politics of IQ*, p. 5.

17. ETS, *Annual Report, 1963-64*, p. 17.

18. Chauncey and Dobbin, *Testing*, pp. 3, 4.

19. Kamin, *Science and Politics of IQ*, p. 7.

20. *Ibid.*, p. 10.

21. Chauncey and Dobbin, *Testing*, pp. 13-14.

22. *Ibid.*, p. 5.

23. *Ibid.*, p. 6.

24. *Ibid.*

25. Kamin, *Science and Politics of IQ*, p. 6.

26. *Ibid.*, p. 6.

27. Lewis M. Terman, *Intelligence Tests and School Reorganization*, 1923, quoted in Karier, "Testing for Order and Control," p. 350.

28. *Ibid.*, p. 345.

29. Kamin, *Science and Politics of IQ*, p. 12.

30. Karier, "Testing for Order and Control," p. 344.

31. *Ibid.*, p. 345.

32. *Eugenical News*, 1920, p. 110.

33. Henry Andrews Cotton, *Some Problems in the Study of Heredity in Mental Diseases*, Bulletin #8 (Cold Spring Harbor, New York: Eugenics Record Office, 1912).

34. According to Nicholas Murray Butler, "How the College Entrance Examination Board Came to Be," in CEEB, *The Work of the College Entrance Examination Board 1901-1925*, (Boston: Ginn and Co., 1925), pp. 2-3. "At the Toronto meeting /of the National Council of Education/ in 1891 a commmittee of conference between representatives

34. (cont.)

of secondary schools and colleges was authorized, and I had the honor to be designated its Chairman. The members of that committee conferred by correspondence during the year, held a meeting, and drafted a report which it was my function to present to the National Council when it met at Saratoga on July 9, 1892. That report and the favorable action upon it by the National Council of Education and by the Board of Directors of the National Education Association, which took the then unprecedented step of appropriating $2,500 toward meeting the expenses of the conferences that were proposed, marked the formal beginning of the movement which resulted in the organization of the College Entrance Examination Board more than seven years later." Also see this report for a discussion of the founding of CEEB. For a discussion of the Committee on Racial Well Being, see Eugenical News, December, 1916, p. 87.

35. Chauncey and Dobbin, Testing, p. 7.

36. Ibid.

37. Carl Campbell Brigham, A Study of American Intelligence, (Princeton: University Press, 1923), pp. 13, 29.

38. Chauncey and Dobbin, Testing, p. 7.

39. Eugenical News, March, 1928, p. 40.

40. Eugenical News, May, 1917, p. 37.

41. Eugenical News, August, 1923, p. 79.

42. Eugenical News, May, 1917, p. 38.

43. Eugenical News, February, 1916, p. 6; Karier, "Testing for Order and Control," p. 345.

44. Eugenical News, July, 1920, pp. 52-53.

45. Kamin, Science and Politics of IQ, p. 19.

46. Madison Grant, The Passing of the Great Race, or the Racial Basis of European History, (New York: Charles Scribner's Sons, 1916).

47. Kamin, Science and Politics of IQ, p. 19.

48. Ibid., p. 19.

49. Chauncey and Dobbin, Testing, p. 12.

50. Higham, Strangers in the Land, p. 267.

51. Ibid.

52. Kamin, Science and Politics of IQ, p. 19.

53. Ibid.

54. "Flow of Immigration," Eugenical News, January, 1921, p. 3.

55. Kamin, Science and Politics of IQ, p. 17.

56. Ibid.

57. Robert Yerkes, Foreword to Brigham, A Study of American Intelligence; Kamin, Science and Politics of IQ, p. 20.

58. Brigham, A Study of American Intelligence, p. XX

59. Ibid.

60. Ibid., p. 31.

61. Ibid., p. 154.

62. Ibid., p. 171.

63. Ibid., p. 124.

64. Ibid., p. 157.

65. Ibid., p. 178.

66. Ibid., p. 192.

67. Ibid., p. 207.

68. Ibid., p. 182.

69. Ibid., p. 190. Note: the order of sentences has been reversed for clarity.

70. Ibid., p. 192.

71. Ibid., p. 205.

72. Ibid., p. 209.

73. Ibid., p. 210.

74. Ibid.

75. Downey, Carl Campbell Brigham, p. 27.

76. Kamin, Science and Politics of IQ., p. 22.

77. Downey, Carl Campbell Brigham, pp. 26-27. Note: final phrase is presented slightly out of order for the sake of clarity.

78. Kamin, Science and Politics of IQ, p. 27.

79. Eugenical News, January, 1924, p. 1.

80. Irme Ferenczi, International Migrations, vol. 1 (New York: National Bureau of Economic Research, 1929), p. 393.

81. Kamin, Science and Politics of IQ, p. 24-25.

82. Ibid., p. 25.

83. Ibid., p. 23.

84. Ibid.

85. The 1924 quotas were eliminated by the Repeal of the National Origins Quota System Act (Public Law 89-236) which was signed on October 3, 1965 and took effect in 1968. Source: Immigration Subcommittee of the U.S. House Judiciary Committee; interview October 10, 1979.

86. Chauncey and Dobbin, Testing, p. 2.

87. "Membership Roster of the Eugenics Research Association," Eugenical News, January 1, 1926, p. 17.

88. "Report of Sub-Committee on Ultimate Program to be Developed by the Eugenics Society of the United States of America," Eugenical News, August, 1923, p. 73.

89. Butler, "How the College Entrance Examination Board Came to Be," p. 3.

90. Ibid, p. 1.

91. Julius Sachs, "The College Entrance Examination Board, Pioneer in the Solution of Educational Problems by the Cooperation of Those Concerned," in The Work of the College Entrance Examination Board, p. 16.

92. Eliot quoted in Wilson Farrand, "A Brief History of the College Entrance Examination Board," in The Work of the College Entrance Examination Board, p. 21.

93. Sachs, "The College Entrance Examination Board," p. 16.

94. Farrand, "A Brief History," p. 23.

95. Ibid., p. 27.

96. Downey, *Carl Campbell Brigham*, p. 19.

97. *Ibid*.

98. Henry S. Pritchett, "Has the College Entrance Examination Board Justified its Quarter-Century of Life?" in *The Work of the College Entrance Examination Board*, p. 15.

99. *Ibid*., p. 13. According to Pritchett, in 1925 only ten colleges in the country screened all their applicants with the College Board examinations: Harvard, Yale, Princeton, MIT, Haverford, Mount Holyoke, Smith, Vassar, Wellesley, and Radcliffe.

100. Downey, *Carl Campbell Brigham*, p. 12.

101. *Ibid*.

102. *Ibid*., p. 13.

103. *Ibid*.

104. *Ibid*.

105. *Ibid*., p. 39.

106. *Ibid*., p. 39, 40.

107. *Ibid*., p. 19.

108. According to a College Board survey of 144 representative colleges cited in Lucky Abernathy, "What's New In College Admissions," *College Board Review*, Summer, 1976, p. 32.

109. Downey, *Carl Campbell Brigham*, p. 20.

110. *Ibid*., p. 21.

111. ETS, *Annual Report, 1961-62*, p. 12.

112. Downey, *Carl Campbell Brigham*, p. 14.

113. Carl Campbell Brigham, "Intelligence Tests of Immigrant Groups," *Psychological Review*, March, 1930, p. 165, cited in Downey, *Carl Campbell Brigham*, p. 27.

114. *Ibid*., p. 27.

115. *Ibid*., p. 29.

116. Kamin, *Science and Politics of IQ*, p. 27.

117. "Eugenical Sterilization in Germany," *Eugenical News*, September-October, 1933, pp. 89-90.

118. *Ibid.*, pp. 91-93.

119. "German Population and Race Politics," *Eugenical News*, March-April, 1934, pp. 33-43.

120. Karier, "Testing for Order and Control," p. 352.

121. Geraldine M. Joncich, *The Sane Positivist: A Biography of Edward L. Thorndike*, 1st edition, (Middletown, Conn.: Wesleyan University Press, 1968), p. 375.

122. Edward L. Thorndike, *Individuality*, (Boston: Houghton-Mifflin, 1911) cited in Samuel Bowles and Herbert Gintis, *Schooling in Capitalist America*, (New York: Basic Books, 1976), p. 196.

123. Edward L. Thorndike, *Human Nature and the Social Order*, (New York: The Macmillan Co., 1940), p. 959.

124. Edwin G. Boring, Alice A. Bryan, Edgar A. Doll, Richard M. Elliot, Ernest R. Hilgard, Calvin P. Stone, Robert M. Yerkes, "Psychology as Science and Profession," *Psychological Bulletin*, vol. 39, no. 9, November, 1942, p. 761.

125. *Ibid.*

126. Downey, *Carl Campbell Brigham*, p. 32.

127. *Ibid.*, pp. 35, 36.

128. *Ibid.*, p. 22.

129. Carl C. Brigham, "The Place of Research in a Testing Organization," *School and Society*, vol. 46, no. 1198, December 11, 1937, p. 756.

130. ETS, *Establishment of the Educational Testing Service, A Statement by the Board of Trustees*, December, 1947.

131. Downey, *Carl Campbell Brigham*, pp. 22-23.

132. Brigham, "The Place of Research," pp. 756-758.

133. Downey, *Carl Campbell Brigham*, p. 45.

134. ETS, *Annual Report to the Board of Trustees, 1948-49*, pp. 20-21. ETS tested 767,625 candidates in 1948, compared to probably more than eight million in 1978. See Appendix I for discussion of volume figures.

135. "Testing is Big Business," *The American Psychologist*, vol. 2, no. 1, January, 1947, p. 26.

FOOTNOTES   CHAPTER V

1. Frank W. Ashburn, "How Do You Test a Student?," Atlantic Monthly, July 1950, 186: p.55.

2. Letter from Robert Moulthrop, ETS, to Preston T. Edwards, Editor of the Black Collegian, January 7, 1976.

3. Ronald L. Flaugher, "Some Points of Confusion in Discussing the Testing of Black Students," in L.P. Miller, ed., The Testing of Black Students: A Symposium, (Englewood Cliffs, N.J.: Prentice Hall, 1974), pp.11,12.

4. Michael Schudson, "Organizing the 'Meritocracy': A History of the College Entrance Examination Board," Harvard Educational Review, vol. 42, #1, February 1972, p.37.

5. ETS, Annual Report 1960-61, p.25.

6. Ibid.

7. John W. Gardner, Excellence, (New York: Harper and Row, 1961), pp.53-56.

8. William W. Turnbull, "On Educational Standards, Testing and the Aspirations of Minorities," Speech made at the Conference on Academic Standards and Their Relationship to Minority Admissions, conducted by the American-Jewish Congress at the Kellog Center of the School of International Affairs at Columbia University, December 8, 1974, p.11.

9. There are 73 pages of text and sample tests in: Student Bulletin, 1978-79, Taking the SAT: A Guide to the Scholastic Aptitude Test and the Test of Standard Written English, and Your Student Report, 1978-79. None of these documents makes mention of the score-income correlation.

10. College Bound Seniors, 1973-74, Admissions Testing Program of the College Entrance Examination Board, Table 21, p.27.
    The use of mean scores is another way of looking at the score-income relationship. When SAT averages are compared with mean income, as in the tables above, the incomes of people falling within a given score range are obtained and averaged together. This tells you, for example, that people scoring 550-599 on the 1973-74 SAT came from families with an average income of $19,481. When the other technique is used and average income is compared with mean scores, the scores of people falling within a given income range are obtained and a mean score is calculated. This tells you, for example, that for people from families

earning $9,000-11,999, all their scores averaged together had a mean of 455. The second method tends to produce mean scores which cluster around the mean score of the entire population, even if the relationship between scores and income is strong. The score means for the 1973-74 average incomes are as follows:

Mean Income	Under $6,000	6,000-8,999	9,000-11,999	12,000-13,499	13,500-14,999	15,000-17,999	18,000 or over
Mean Score	403	435	455	464	469	473	485

The first technique helps you understand the meaning of a particular ranking. It helps answer the question: What does this 580 score mean, what income class is this person likely to come from? The second technique helps you understand the odds against a particular group. It helps answer the question: what middle point will the scores of people with $9,000-11,999 family incomes tend to cluster around, and how will this midpoint compare with that of other groups?

11. Ibid.

12. Southern College Bound Seniors, 1973-74, Middle States College Bound Seniors, 1973-74, New England College Bound Seniors, 1973-74, Midwestern College Bound Seniors, 1973-74, Western College Bound Seniors, 1973-74, College Entrance Examination Board, 1974.

13. College Guide to the ATP Summary Reports on 1972-73 College Bound Seniors, p.35, Note #1. As the text of the manual makes clear, these tables are designed primarily to help the institution shape its recruiting and financial aid policies by showing what kinds of applicants will be able to afford the school, who will be eligible for federal scholarship money, and how to identify those exceptions to the rule whose families earn little but who still score high. The tables are not presented as data which shed light on the significance of the test itself, nor are institutions encouraged to tell applicants the extent to which they are being ranked by income as a result of reliance on the scores. The most recent publicly circulated version of these tables, in National Report, College Bound Seniors, 1978, breaks down scores by estimated parental contribution to college expenses and sets up the categories in a way that reveals much less about the score-income relationship than the earlier tables. Whereas the '73-'74 college manual tables distinguish among four different groups below 350, for example, the 1978 booklet groups them all together as "below 350."

14. *National Report, College Bound Seniors, 1979*, Table 11, p.16.

15. The figures are derived from Humphrey Doermann, "Lack of Money: A Barrier to Higher Education," in *Barriers to Higher Education*, (CEEB: 1971) p.131.

Table 1. Estimated Joint Distribution of All United States Male High School Graduates, 1969-70: Verbal Scholastic Aptitude and Family Income:

Family Income (Possible Family Contribution to Son's College Costs)	Verbal SAT Scores 200-299	300-449	450-800	Totals
Less than $4,600 (Less than $270)	116,000	113,000	25,000	254,000
$4,600 to $7,499 ($270- $729)	102,000	139,000	44,000	285,000
$7,500 to $10,699 ($730 to $1,419)	89,000	143,000	60,000	292,000
$10,700 to $16,199 ($1,420 to $3,079)	78,000	146,000	82,000	306,000
$16,200 and over ($3,080 and over)	59,000	131,000	123,000	313,000
Totals	444,000	672,000	334,000	1,450,000

16. Humphrey Doermann, *Crosscurrents in College Admissions*, (New York: Columbia Teacher's College Press, 1970), pp.147-49, 162. There are a number of technical problems involved in calculating score-income correlations, some of which result from the fact that information on aptitude test scores is collected and reported primarily by the test industry itself. The ranking of test-takers by income has not been a function which ETS has chosen to publicize widely. The 1979 College Bound Seniors report, for example, presents no score-income tables. Instead, it offers a table relating SAT scores to applicant's estimates of "Parental Contribution Toward Applicant's Education." Over thirty percent of the applicants are lumped into a single contribution category. The text discussing parental contribution and scores is headed "Poor and Rich" in accord with the ETS practice of presenting the scores' systematic reflection of income for _all_ classes as a simplistic dichotomy between the haves and the have-nots.

Jencks has pointed out (Christopher Jencks, "_Inequality, A Reassessment of the Effect of Family and Schooling in America_," Harper and Row, New York, 1972) that "Considering the vast sums that have been spent testing millions of American students, reliable data on the relationship between test scores and economic status is remarkably hard to find" (p.78). Jencks notes that applicant's estimates of their parent's income--which is what the ETS tables quoted in the text are based on--may be of questionable reliability. It seems that the most reliable estimate of an applicant's family income would appear on the parent's federal tax returns. There are only two agencies in the United States possessing large numbers of federal tax returns from people across the country: the IRS and ETS. Through its College Scholarship Service (CSS) and Graduate and Professional School Financial Aid Service (GAPSFAS), ETS requires financial aid applicants to submit a detailed (in some categories, more detailed than the IRS return) accounting of their families' finances and urges them to send ETS a copy of their IRS 1040 form for verification. Were any data relating federally reported income to ETS scores to be released, it could thus be presented only within the assumptions and format chosen by ETS or its consultants.

Jencks (p.78) estimates that the correlation between family economic status and various elementary and secondary school standardized tests is about .35. Bowles and Gintis (_Schooling in Capitalist America_, Basic Books, 1976, p.319) estimate the correlation between socioeconomic background and early IQ scores at .399, which they say increases slightly with age. In a study of the class of 1969 at 47 Boston area high schools, Dennis J. Dugan ("Impact of Parental Educational Investment on Students' Achievement," _American Statistical Association Proceedings of the Social Statistics Section August 19-22, 1969_) found a correlation between family income and mean Verbal SAT of .353. Dugan found a lower correlation with mean Math SAT, .275. Some researchers (see John B. Miner, _Intelligence in the United States_, Springer Publishing Co., N.Y., 1957) have presented data which suggest that on some "IQ" tests although scores correlate with income most of the way up the income scale, the pattern may tend to break down within certain reaches of the upper classes with more income no longer being associated with chances of a higher score.

Jencks argues that when all the factors that go into determining how much schooling a person will get are considered, social class shapes one's chances in ways that go beyond test scores. The ranking of who finally ends up with how much schooling is even more closely linked to economic background than is the ranking by test scores; he estimates the correlation between economic background and final amount of education obtained at .55 (p.175). In addition to various indirect effects of class background, such direct factors as tuition costs, the need to get a job and earn money, institutional favoritism for the children of rich contributors and other institutional factors can add up to an element of class discrimination apart from that introduced by test scores. It should be noted, though, that in his text Jencks presents this point in a potentially misleading way. He writes that if "America adopted a certification system based on standardized tests of the kind now used in college admissions...(s)uch a system would benefit white working-class children and reduce the disadvantage now enjoyed by white middle-class children by about a third." (p.159). What this means is that if all other elements of class discrimination were removed and only the portion transmitted by test scores remained, working-class children would have a better chance. This is certainly true, but it is only a way of saying that if the U.S. economic and educational system were restructured to eliminate all aspects of class inequality except for aptitude tests, then class discrimination in amount of schooling attained would be less. Contrary to the tone of his passage, these facts are far from a testament to the equity of the test system; they merely indicate that the scores are not the whole basis of class discrimination, just a substantial part of it.

In a later study (Who Gets Ahead?: The Determinants of Economic Success in America, Basic Books, New York, 1979) Jencks argues that test scores are not simply proxies for family background, pointing out that scores can vary within families and thereby have differential effects on the family members' economic prospects (p.219). Addressing the fact that background affects test scores which in turn affects opportunities Jencks reports that:

> Men from advantaged backgrounds have higher test scores than men from disadvantaged backgrounds, but this does not explain most of their occupational advantage. This is partly because the background characteristics that affect test scores are somewhat different from those that affect status...Test performance accounts for 40 to 60 percent of demographic background's effect in three samples with reliable scores. But when we also take account of all the unmeasured background characteristics that make brothers alike, controlling test scores only accounts for a quarter of these shared background characteristics' eventual impact on occupational status.
>
> Controlling education as well as test scores accounts for 65 to 92 percent of the effect of measured background on status and 56 to 77 percent of family background's overall effect. Five background characteristics consistently influenced occupational status independent of educational attainment: race, ethnicity, religion, father's occupational status, and farm background...
> The fact that demographic background affects test performance accounts for between 25 and 50 percent of demographic background's impact on earnings in the four samples with test scores. (pp. 214-215,218).

In terms of action, it should be remembered that many aspects of class discrimination will only change when the fundamental rules of the current economic system change. But the use of ETS aptitude scores to influence advancement, while rooted in the economic system (both through the structure of education and the support of ETS by powerful interests), has its impact on people's lives through a practice which is more immediate, specific, and subject to rapid change: the perennial ranking, occuring every Spring in colleges across the country, of applicants according to their SAT scores and, thereby, roughly by their family income. The effects of a change in the test system on class opportunities could be considerable. For example, in a more immediately feasible hypothetical case, Jencks points out that: "A system in which credentials were distributed entirely on the basis of grades, and in which standardized tests played no part, would improve the position of working-class students and reduce the advantage of the middle classes even more than a system based entirely on test scores." (_Inequality_, p.159).

The practice of ranking by ETS scores and, perhaps more important, the institutional claim (and public belief) that this is in some sense a ranking by _merit_, is something which people can begin to understand and change _before_ they succeed in constructing a society with a new definition of economic justice.

17. Susan F. Ford, Sandy Campos, "Summary of Validity Data from the Admissions Testing Program Validity Study Service," June 1977, Figure 3, in Appendices to _On Further Examination: Report of the Advisory Panel on the Scholastic Aptitude Test Score Decline_ (New York: CEEB, 1977).

18. Doermann, "Crosscurrents," p.162. He wrote, "Thomas F. Pettigrew, Associate Professor of Social Relations at Harvard University and a member of the advisory committee for the U.S. Office of Education survey cited above, believes that the sociological and psychological factors working against low-income Negro families may be such that the coefficient of correlation between family income and measured aptitude for Negro students may be higher than the 0.4 estimate used for the larger population. It may be, he thinks, as high as 0.5 and 0.6, but probably not 0.7 or higher. Since there are no directly comparable studies to test this, it remains a reasonable but untested estimate to be considered when using the table."

19. Albert Beaton, Thomas Hilton, William Schrader, "Changes in the Verbal Abilities of High School Seniors, College Entrants and SAT Candidates Between 1960 and 1972," June 1977, Tables 26 and 27, in Appendices to "On Further Examination: Report of the Advisory Panel on the Scholastic Aptitude Test

Score Decline," (New York: College Board,1977). In his book, Small Futures, Richard deLone, offers possible reasons for the disparity in test scores among social classes. He writes, "Abundant journalistic and scholarly studies suggest, on the basis of intensive classroom observation, that many teachers behave differently toward children from different socioeconomic and racial backgrounds and adjust educational goals, teach different material, and reward or punish behavior differently by class and race as well. Typically, such studies have found that teachers of low-income children minimize cognitive discussion and interaction with children while emphasizing pure rote learning. When low-income children ask questions that are tangential to the point, they are rebuked or ignored. Middle-class children, on the other hand, receive answers; their questions are taken seriously. Teachers ridicule students frequently in classrooms with predominantly low-income children. One study found that when lower-and middle-class students were mixed in one first-grade classroom, they were divided within the social class into ability groups ('Cardinals'and'Tigers') that reflected social class differences perfectly and treatment differed accordingly. Another found that when teachers of low-income children were asked about their educational goals, the ones they put first were behavior control and adjustment of children to the norms of the school, and sometimes academic goals were not mentioned at all. By contrast, teachers of predominantly middle-class children stressed cognitive growth and students' satisfaction in learning as their major goals. Small wonder, then, if test scores differ!...The point, it should be stressed, is not that teachers are overtly racist or class-biased. Rather, teachers typically adopt the assumptions of the society to which they belong--and how could they do otherwise? Given the way our society works, it can be argued that teachers who treat children differently on the basis of social class or racial background are performing a good job of helping their students make a 'social adjustment.'" Richard H. deLone, Small Futures (New York and London: Harcourt Brace Jovanovich, 1979), pp.108-110.

20. S.A. Kendrick, "The Coming Segregation of Our Selective Colleges," College Board Review, Winter 1967-68, No.66, p.13; Ronald Flaugher, "Report on Project Access Research Report #2," May 1971, p.2.

21. National Report, College Bound Seniors, 1979, Table 10, p.16.

22. Ronald Flaugher, "The New Definitions of Test Fairness in Selection: Developments and Implications," GRE Board Research Report, GREB No.72-4R, ETS Research Memorandum RM 73-17, September 1973, p.8.

23. Alexander W. Astin, Predicting Academic Performance in College (New York: Free Press, 1971), p.14.

24. Leonard L. Baird, "Development of an Inventory of Documented Accomplishments for Graduate Admissions," (ETS: June, 1979), p. 23.

25. Ibid.

26. Henry Herbert Goddard, Human Efficiency and Levels of Intelligence, Louis Clark Vanuxem Lectures at Princeton University, delivered April 7,8,10,11, 1919, Princeton University Press, Princeton, 1920, p.vii.

27. Ibid., p.22.

28. Ibid., p.28.

29. Ibid., p.48.

30. Ibid., p.116.

31. Ibid., p.101.

32. Ibid., p.42.

33. Ibid., p.97.

34. Ibid., p.vii.

35. ETS, Annual Report 1956-57, p.14. The order of some sentences has been rearranged for clarity.

36. Dan Zegart, "The Educational Testing Service: Who Tests the Testers?" Politics and Education, Summer 1978, p.5.

37. Interview with William Turnbull, May 3, 1977.

38. Ibid.

39. Richard Herrnstein, IQ in the Meritocracy (Boston: Little, Brown & Co., 1973), p.117.

40. Lloyd Humphreys, "Race and Sex Differences and Their Implication for Educational and Occupational Equality," Educational Theory, vol.26, No.2, Spring, 1976, p.145.

41. Lee J. Cronbach, Essentials of Psychological Testing, (New York: Harpers & Bros., 1960), p.174. Cronbach prints a table which purports to show "Expectancies at Various Levels of Mental Ability." The chart shows, according to your IQ, whether you can expect to have, for example, a "50-50 chance of graduating from college" or whether you should expect to learn to "operate (a) sewing machine (or) assemble parts." Cronbach was a member of the ETS committee on research from 1949-53 and 1956-67. He was a recipient of the ETS Award for Distinguished Service to Measurement.

42. Scarvia B. Anderson, Martin Katz, Benjamin Shimberg, *Meeting the Test* (New York: Four Winds Press, 1965), p.26.

43. Moulthrop, letter to Edwards, *Black Collegian*, January 7, 1976.

44. Martin R. Katz, *You: Today and Tomorrow*, Cooperative Test Division, ETS, 1959, p.14; see also Katz, *Teacher's Guide to You: Today and Tomorrow*, Cooperative Test Division, ETS, 1959.

45. *Ibid*.

46. *Ibid*.

47. *Ibid*., p.17.

48. *Ibid*., pp.20,21.

49. *Ibid*., p.30.

50. Moulthrop letter to Edwards, January 7, 1976.

51. Matthew T. Downey, *Carl Campbell Brigham, Scientist and Educator* (Princeton, New Jersey: ETS, 1961), p.15.

52. Marjorie C. Kirkland, "The Effects of Tests on Students and Schools," *Review of Educational Research*, October 1971, Vol.41, No.4, pp.308,329,335.

53. Orville Brim, David Glass, John Neullnger, Ira Firestone, *American Beliefs and Attitudes About Intelligence* (New York: Russell Sage Foundation, 1969) p.1.

54. *Ibid*., p.55.

55. *Ibid*., p.192.

56. *Ibid*., p.107.

57. *Ibid*., p.145.

58. Dale Tillery, *Distribution and Differentiation of Youth: A Study of Transition from School to College*, (Cambridge, Mass.: Ballinger, 1973), p. 83.

59. Tillery, "Distribution," p.93.

60. Dennis J. Dugan, "Impact of Parental Educational Investment on Students' Achievement," *American Statistical Association Proceedings of the Social Statistics Section August 19-22, 1969*. Papers presented at annual meeting of the American Statistical Association (New York, 1969), under the sponsorship of the Social Studies Section, pp.138-148.

61. *Ibid*.

62. James Crouse, "The Effects of Academic Ability," in Jencks, *Who Gets Ahead?* (New York: Basic Books, 1979), p.106.

63. Kirkland, "The Effects of Tests," p.311.

64. Brim, et al., "American Beliefs," pp.55,62.

65. Clarence J. Karier, "Testing for Order and Control in the Corporate Liberal State," *Education Theory*, Vol.22, spring 1972, No.2, p.67.

66. *Ibid*.

67. *College Board News*, September 1978, p.1.

68. Commission on Financing Higher Education, *Who Should Go To College?* (New York: Columbia University Press, 1952), p.138.

69. *Ibid*., p.1.

FOOTNOTES   CHAPTER VI

1. "Law Admissions Aided by Computers," ETS Developments, Fall, 1977.

2. Martin H. Redish, Preferential Law School Admissions and the Equal Protection Clause: An Analysis of the Competing Arguments, prepared for the LSAC, (circa 1974), p.17.

3. LSAC, "1973 Annual Council Report," p.70.

4. Federal Trade Commission internal report by Arthur Levine, Boston Regional Office, "Staff Memorandum on the Effects of Coaching on Standardized Admission Examinations," September 1978, p.13. Submitted to the FTC Bureau of Consumer Protection.

5. Ibid.

6. ETS, 1979-80 Law School Admission Bulletin, 1979, p.72.

7. National Bar Examination Digest, 1979 edition, (Harcourt Brace Jovanovich, 1979), p.36, "Multistate Bar Exam Information."

8. Ralph Nader, "Lemming-Like Lawyers," Washington Star-News, July 29, 1973; interviews with Julie Gitto, Pennsylvania Board of Law Examiners, December 11, 1979; and Stephen Townsend, Secretary to the Board of New Jersey Bar Examiners, December 12, 1979.

9. Carnegie Council on Policy Studies in Higher Education, Selective Admissions in Higher Education: Comment and Recommendations and Two Reports, (San Francisco: Jossey-Bass, 1977), Appendix G-6, p.237. Correlation figures compiled in 1976 which are presented in this report show the LSAT as a better predictor than college grades, with LSAT providing a 13 percentage of perfect prediction compared to 6% for college grades. This would give the LSAT greater weight in most admission formulas. According to attorney David White, who is conducting a study of law school admissions for the National Conference of Black Lawyers, the relative predictive validities of LSATs and college grades fluctuate every few years: for a few years studies will show the grades to be a better predictor, then a few years later the LSAT will show higher correlations, then grades will prove better again. This statistical phenomenon, called the "bouncing beta" by some, is due to the fact that the more one factor, such as the LSAT, is emphasized in the selection decision, the harder it becomes to distinguish among admitted applicants by using that factor, since only those with relatively high scores will have been admitted. Thus, as predictors are increasingly relied upon, they tend to "cancel out" their own measured predictive validities.

10. Vilma Martinez and Mario Lara, "Who Gets In? Standardized Testing, Special Admissions, and the Myth of Reverse Discrimination," The Self-Determination Quarterly Journal, March 1978, p.18.

11. FTC report by Levine, "Effects of Coaching," pp.15-16.

12. Carnegie Council, Selective Admissions, p.185; ETS, 1979-80 Law School Admission Bulletin, p. 15.
 The following chart is derived from a chart on page 185 of the Carnegie Council report. It indicates the estimated percentage of candidates in each category who were offered admission to an ABA accredited law school. The references in the above text to the scores of 425 and 475 come from taking the midpoints of the 400-450 and 450-500 categories.

	Below 300	300-350	350-400	400-450	450-500	500-550	550-600	600-650	650-700	700-750	750-800
3.5 - 4.0	17%	28	40	40	57	76	88	93	95	96	99
3.0 - 3.5	4%	12	17	25	38	56	75	86	90	91	90
2.5 - 3.0	1%	5	12	19	25	40	55	70	78	81	86
2.0 - 2.5	2%	4	6	10	15	23	36	51	61	71	76
Below 2.0	0	0	2	4	8	9	24	27	48	41	75

 A very rough estimate of the number of points decided in a given time can be calculated by:
 a. dividing the number of points on the test (600; on a 200-800 scale) by the number of questions (190). This equals 3.16.
 b. Dividing the number of questions (190) by the number of minutes (215). This equals .884.
 c. Multiplying the two to obtain the number of points per minute. This equals 2.79. By this method 50 points would be determined in 18 minutes. Thirty is thus a conservative estimate. This method is very rough since the LSAT uses a scoring formula which takes into account the relative difficulty of the test and performance of the group.

13. Carnegie Council, Selective Admissions, p.185. Appendix C-3.

14. Barbara Lerner, "Equal Protection and External Screening: Davis, DeFunis, and Bakke," Educational Measurement and the Law: Proceedings of the 1977 ETS Invitational Conference (Princeton: ETS, 1977), p.6.

15. Ibid.

16. Hunter M. Breland, "DeFunis Revisited: A Psychometric View," research paper supported by the Law School Admission Council, August 1974, p.32.

17. Robert Stevens,"Law Schools and Law Students," 59 *Virginia Law Review*, 1973, pp.572-73. Stevens also notes that " [even] allowing for inflation the schools we studied appear to draw students from more affluent families than in the past." For the class of 1970, students from Yale, Pennsylvania, Boston College, University of Michigan, Iowa, Stanford, University of Southern California, and the University of Connecticut law schools were surveyed (p.558). For the class of 1972, questionnaires were administered at all these schools, except USC and Pennsylvania (p.557).

18. ETS internal report by Franklin R. Evans and Donald A. Rock, "A Study of the Effects of Moderator Variables on the Prediction of Law School Performance: Final Report to the LSA Council," May 25, 1973, p.428.

19. *Ibid*.

20. Carnegie Council, *Selective Admissions*, p.192.

21. Rex E. Lee, "The Economics of Law School Admission: Legal Education as a Scarce Resource," *Law and Social Order*, vol.65, 1971, p.71. See footnote 35.

22. Cited in Breland, "DeFunis Revisited," p.27.

23. *Ibid*.

24. *Juris Doctor*, July/August 1977, p.28.

25. LSAC, "1973 Annual Council Report," p. 71.

26. Lerner, "Equal Protection," p.16.

27. *Ibid*., p.15.

28. Leonard L. Baird, "Biographical and Educational Correlates of Graduate and Professional School Admissions Test Scores," *Educational and Psychological Measurement*, vol.36, 1976, p.419.

29. Brief of Joseph H. Gordon and Grant Armstrong as *Amici Curiae* at 7, *DeFunis v. Odegaard*, 82 Wash. 2d 11, 507 P. 2d 1169 (1973).

30. *Ibid*., pp.1,2,7. Gordon was Treasurer of the American Bar Association and Armstrong was Washington State Delegate to the House of Delegates of the American Bar Association. The brief was submitted "on their own behalf and on behalf of counsel" which included Harry B. Reese of the LSAC. "In addition, *amici* share the concern of several professional organizations in the instant litigation--the American Bar Association, the Association of American Law Schools, the Council on Legal Education

Opportunity, and the Law School Admission Council. The interests of these four organizations are put forth more particularly in an Appendix to this brief," p.1.

31. See, for example, an LSAC internal report, "Reports of the Annual Council: Summary of Responses, 1975 Law School Admission Council Survey," 1975, p.330.

32. Stevens, "Law Schools and Law Students," p.573.

33. National Conference of Bar Examiners, "The Multistate Bar Examination, February 23, 1972," (Columbia, Mo.: Lucas Brothers, 1972), pp.2,4,24,32.

34. See ETS, <u>1979-80 Law School Admission Bulletin</u>, pp.23 ff.

35. Millard Ruud, "Summary, Conference on the Future of the LSAT Program", paper presented at LSATC /LSAC/ meeting, November 12-13, 1971, p.6. Ruud noted that "There is apparently only one published study of the connection between success in law school and 'success' in practice." He claimed that the study "shows a reasonably good correlation."

In fact, the study in question (M.K. Distefano, Jr., and Bernard M. Bass, "Prediction of an Ultimate Criterion of Success as a Lawyer," <u>Journal of Applied Psychology</u>, 1959, p. 40) reports no correlation coefficients. The study is a one and one-half page long summary of a Louisiana State University master's thesis. It is based on such sparse data as to be statistically unreliable. In the words of Distefano and Bass:

> Preliminary interviews with lawyers . . .agreed with the ETS conclusion that the ultimate criteria of success as a lawyer were fuzzy. Yet some degree of concensus /sic/ was found in the evaluation of specific individuals by judges. . . . In the first area, three district judges were asked to rate 10 lawyers in their district on the basis of their impressions of the lawyer's legal ability. . . In the second area, seven practicing lawyers were rated by two district judges.

One lawyer was eliminated from the sample when the judges reported that they did not know him. The sixteen lawyers were then divided into two groups, ten rated "high" and six rated "low." The "high" group was found to have a higher mean LSAT score than the "low" group.

36. <u>Griggs v. Duke Power Co.</u>, 401 U.S. 424, 1971.

37. <u>Ibid</u>.

38. <u>Ibid</u>.

39. Ruud, "Summary Conference," p. 6.

40. Interview with Gertrude McQuade, Office of U.S. Deputy Associate Attorney General for attorney personnel, December 10, 1979.

41. "FTC Drops LSAT," <u>The Testing Digest</u>, Summer, 1979, p. 10.

42. LSAC internal document, Minutes of the Joint Meeting of the LSAC Legal Affairs and Finance Committees, November 8-9, 1974.

43. David White, "The Definition of Legal Competence," Santa Clara Law Review, vol. 18, No. 3, 1978, p.662. He is citing <u>Proceedings, Association of American Law Schools, 1947 Annual Meeting</u>, 76-69, 1947.

44. <u>Ibid</u>., pp.663-664, note 108. White quotes Braden, "Use of the Law School Admission Test at the Yale Law School," <u>3J. Legal Educ.</u>, 202, 203, 1950.

45. <u>Ibid</u>., p.667.

46. <u>Ibid</u>., p.647, note 27. White is citing Reese, "The Standard Law School Admission Test," <u>1 J. Legal Educ.</u>, 124, 125, 1948.

47. ETS, <u>1979-80 Law School Admission Bulletin</u>, 1979, pp.21-47.

48. ETS, "LSAT Research Summary: Score Relations Study," 1963. William B. Schrader is listed as "investigator."

49. ETS, "LSAT Research Summary: The Advanced Tests of the Graduate Record Examinations as a Predictor of Law School Grades," 1970, p.1. W.B. Schrader and Barbara Pitcher are listed as "investigators." See also <u>Pre-Law Handbook, 1975-76</u> (AALS, LSAC, and ETS, 1975) p.18.

50. Patricia W. Lunneborg and Donna Radford, "The LSAT: A Survey of Actual Practice," Journal of Legal Education, vol. 18, 1966, pp.313-314. The tables (pp.315-324) show how many schools placed little emphasis on the LSAT, or less in relation to GPA.

51. ETS internal memorandum by Barbara Pitcher and Marilynn Binkley, "A Summary of the LSDAS Optional Calculations Used by Law Schools during 1974-75," July 29, 1975, p.1.

52. LSAC internal report by Albert R. Turnbull, William S. McKee and L. Thomas Galloway, "Law School Admissions: A Descriptive Study," (circa 1972) p.56. Some of the material was prepared for November 1972 publication in the Virginia Law Review; this report also contains confidential information from the law schools surveyed for circulation among the LSAC membership.

53. ETS, 1979-80 Law School Admission Bulletin, 1979, p.72; and 1979-80 Law School Admission Bulletin Supplement, 1979, p.1.

54. Ibid., p.1.

55. E. Gellhorn and D.B. Hornby, "Constitutional Limitations on Admission Procedures and Standards--Beyond Affirmative Action," Virginia Law Review, 1974, p.978, reprinted and distributed by the LSAC.

56. Warren W. Willingham and Hunter M. Breland, "The Status of Selective Admissions," in Carnegie Council, Selective Admissions, pp.101-102.

57. LSAC, "Summary of Responses, 1975 Law School Admission Council Survey," p.339.

58. Interview with William Turnbull, ETS President, May 3, 1977.

59. Carnegie Council, Selective Admissions, p.100.

60. Turnbull, McKee, and Galloway, "Law School Admissions," p.40.

61. Carnegie Council, Selective Admissions, chart on p.237.

62. Turnbull, McKee, and Galloway, "Law School Admissions," p.40.

63. Redish, <u>Preferential Law School Admissions</u>, p.17.

64. Lerner, "Equal Protection," p.6.

65. <u>Ibid</u>., p.16.

66. <u>Ibid</u>.

67. Brief of Gordon and Armstrong as <u>Amici Curiae</u> at A-6, A-7, <u>DeFunis v. Odegaard</u>, 82 Wash. 2d 11, 507 P. 2d 1169, 1973. See also note 30 in this chapter.

68. <u>Ibid</u>., at A-7, A-8.

69. Cited in Lerner, "Equal Protection," p.15.

70. <u>Ibid</u>., p.5, footnote 6.

71. In 1959-60 about 21,000 people took the LSAT (this slightly overstates the number of applicants since some take the test twice) and there were about 17,500 enrolled first year law students. This is a ratio of 1.2 to 1. In 1969-70 about 75,000 people took the LSAT and there were about 37,000 enrolled first year students, for a ratio of 1.99 to 1. Figures from LSAC,"1973 Annual Council Report," p. 91.

72. LSAC internal report by W.B. Schrader and Barbara Pitcher, "Effect of Differences in College Grading Standards on the Prediction of Law School Grades," September 1973, p.472-73.

73. White, "The Definition of Legal Competence," p.667.

74. ETS, <u>Annual Report to the Board of Trustees, 1948-1949</u>, p.26.

75. ETS, <u>Annual Report to the Board of Trustees, 1959-1960</u>, p.54.

76. ETS internal memorandum from Henry Chauncey to Messrs. Turnbull, Ebel, and Winterbottom, "Law School Admission Test Program," June 4, 1962, pp.1-2.

77. ETS internal memorandum from Robert L. Ebel to Messrs. Chauncey, Turnbull and Winterbottom, "Law School Admission Test Program," June 12, 1962, p.1.

78. Chauncey, "Law School Admission Test Program," p.8.

79. ETS internal documents by M. von Mendelssohn, "Master Calendar for Program Divisions," November 29, 1971 and November 1, 1972 editions. See also LSAC, "1972 Annual Council Report," p. 141.

80. Interview with Ms. Ballato, N.Y. State Department of Education, December 14, 1979. The LSAC was incorporated June 21, 1968.

81. After a series of ETS cost overruns and service breakdowns in the 1970s, the law school council began pressing for more control and eventually obtained ownership of the LSAT program. See p. 257 of text.

82. LSAC internal document, "Law School Admission Council, Minutes of the Special Committee on Legal Affairs Meeting," October 13, 14, 1972, p.350, from the LSAC 1973 Annual Council Report. The name change application was filed with the New York Board of Regents on August 14, 1972.

83. LSAC News and Notes, vol. 3, no. 9, May 1974, p.4.

84. M. von Mendelssohn, "Master Calendar," November 29, 1971.

85. LSAC internal report, "Operations Reference Book," September 1975, section 3, p.1.

86. Ibid., section 3, p.3.

87. Ibid., section 3, p.28.

88. Ibid., section 5, p.29.

89. Ibid., section 6, pp.6-8.

90. Castro v. Beecher, 334 F. Supp. 930, 943 (D.C. Mass. 1971)

91. Letter from Harold N. Moorman, Director of Student Services, Dartmouth College, to William W. Turnbull, President, ETS, December 28, 1972.

92. Turnbull, McKee, and Galloway, "Law School Admissions," p.43.

93. "Common Questions and Answers About LSDAS, LSAT, and CRS," LSAC Newsletter, December 1972, p.5.

94. LSAC internal report, "Guide to the Interpretation of Undergraduate Transcripts," November 1972.

95. Pitcher and Binkley, "A Summary of the LSDAS Optional Calculations."

96. LSAC, "Guide to the Interpretation of Undergraduate Transcripts," p.1.

97. R.F. Boldt, "Efficacy of Undergraduate Grade Adjustment for Improving the Prediction of Law School Grades," in Reports of LSAC Sponsored Research: Volume III, 1975-1977 (Princeton, New Jersey: LSAC, 1977) p.376.

98. LSAC internal report, "Guide to the Interpretation of Undergraduate Transcripts," November 1972.

99. "Minutes of the Program Operations Research Committee Meeting, March 24, 1975," LSAC, "1975 Annual Council Report," p.316.

100. "Minutes of the Board of Trustees Meeting (LSAC), May 7-8, 1976," LSAC, "1976 Annual Council Report," p. 64.

101. R.F. Boldt, "Efficacy of Undergraduate Adjustment for Improving the Prediction of Law School Grades," in Reports of LSAC Sponsored Research, Volume III, 1975-77 (Princeton, New Jersey, LSAC, 1977), p.371.

102. LSAC,"1974 Annual Council Report," p. 184.

103. Ibid., pp.184-185.

104. "Minutes of Programs Operation Research Committee," March 24, 1975, p.316.

105. "Educational Recordkeeping Practices," Transcript of Testimony before the Privacy Protection Study Commission, Independence Reporting, Inc., November 12, 1976, testimony by L. Orin Slagle, pp.172-176.

106. Interview with William Turnbull, ETS President, May 3, 1977.

107. Letter from William Turnbull to Ralph Nader, July 12, 1977.

108. Gellhorn and Hornby, "Constitutional Limitations on Admissions." Reprinted and distributed by the LSAC for a June 2, 1974 seminar on "Due Process in Admissions."

109. Ibid., p.977.

110. Ibid.

111. Ibid., pp.1005-1009.

112. Interview with Ernest Gellhorn, December 13, 1979.

113. LSAC internal document, "Law School Admission Test, Minutes of the Services Committee Meeting, February 6-7, 1970."

114. Ibid.

115. LSAC, 1973 Annual Council Report, p.309.

116. ETS, Announcing the Higher Education Admission Law Service, (brochure, circa 1973).

117. LSAC,"Minutes of the Special Committee on Legal Affairs Meeting," October 13-14, 1972.

118. Ibid. Among the studies discussed at the October 13-14 Committee meeting were a "black/white validity study," a study of "application and acceptance rates for men and women," and a study of "the correlation of LSAT scores to job relatedness."

119. Gene I. Maeroff, "Law School Aptitude Tests Backed," *New York Times*, September 29, 1976.

120. *Ibid*.

121. *Ibid*.

122. ETS internal report by Alfred B. Carlson and Charles Werts, "Proposed Relationships Among Law School Predictors, Law School Performance, and Bar Examination Results," February 1973, in LSAC, *1973 Annual Council Report*, p.599.

123. *Ibid*., p.602.

124. The study, as of yet unpublished, is discussed in Douglas E. Rosenthal, "Evaluating the Competence of Lawyers," in *ALI-ABA CLE Review*, vol.7, No. 31, July 30, 1976, p.1.

125. LSAC document, Minutes of Special Committee on Legal Affairs, Subcommittee on Confidentiality, September 15, 1972.

126. Rosenthal, "Evaluating the Competence," p.2.

127. Transcript of testimony by Robert Solomon, ETS Executive Vice-President, before the Privacy Protection Study Commission, p.352. Solomon said, "It is a matter of record—not only a matter of record, a matter of gossip and rumor and everything else, and it is true, that the Law School Admission Council was so dissatisfied with the difficulties we ran into that it came within a hair's breadth of taking its contract to another organization; and the major reason was because of the dissatisfaction in that 1970-71 year of the processing with the LSDAS." (See chapter VIII footnote 137 for LSAC President's report which describes their negotiations with ACT).

128. Interview with Bruce Zimmer, Executive Director, LSAC, December 11, 1979.

129. *Ibid*.

130. *Ibid*.

131. Interview with Orin Slagle, February 27, 1979.

132. Interview with Zimmer, December 11, 1979.

133. Ruud, "Summary Conference," p.16. *DeFunis v. Odegaard*, 94 S. Ct. 1704, 182 (1974).

134. Address by Chesterfield Smith in LSAC, *1973 Annual Council Report*, p.72.

135. Ruud, "Summary Conference," p.4.

136. *Ibid*.

FOOTNOTES   CHAPTER VII

1. Interview with Robert J. Solomon, ETS Executive Vice President, June 19, 1975.

2. According to figures in ETS' "1977 Project Operating Statement," its ten largest testing income sources are the Admissions Testing Program (SAT and Achievement Tests), GRE, LSAT, College Level Examination Program (CLEP), Advanced Placement Program (AP), Test of English as a Foreign Language (TOEFL), PSAT/NMSQT, business school admissions test (then the ATGSB, now the GMAT), National Teacher Examinations, and auto mechanics certification test. It has no competitors in the last eight, and has over 50% of the market in both college and graduate school admission testing. See Chapter VIII, footnote 76 for more discussion.

3. ETS internal report, "Review of the Report of the Commission on Tests: A Set of Analyses and Suggested Courses of Action Devised by Staff Teams at Educational Testing Service," March 1972, p.45. The one known exception to the system under which consumers, rather than institutions, pay for ETS admission tests is the Secondary School Admission Test (SSAT). Schools requiring the SSAT are billed according to the number of score reports they receive.

4. Letter from a parent to New Jersy Public Interest Research Group, May 1, 1975.

5. CEEB, Student Bulletin 1979-80, Admissions Testing Program of the College Board, 1979, p.6.

6. George H. Hanford, Minority Programs and Activities of the College Entrance Examination Board: A Critical Review and a Brief Look Ahead, (New York: CEEB, 1976) p.27.

7. ETS internal report by Nona G. Johnson, "Report on Free Administration and Fee Waiver Programs," August 1971, Conclusion.

8. ETS internal report, "Report of the Committee on Hostile Test Center Environment," 1971, pp.13-14.

9. Hanford, Minority Programs, p.28.

10. Johnson, "Report on Free Administration," Conclusion.

11. Letter from Assistant Director for Counselling, Board of Education, School District of Philadelphia, to Ruth Fort, October 5, 1977, containing chart of results of survey conducted in 1977 concerning need for and use of fee waivers by school district of Philadelphia. Ms. Fort worked for Ralph Nader at that time.

12. Edward Fiske, "Test Publishers See Dropping of Exams," New York Times, October 8, 1979, pp.A1, B4.

13. Interview with John Kramer, June 20, 1975.

14. K.D. v. ETS, New York Supreme Court, New York City, July 28, 1976, cited in United States Law Week, 45 LW 2086, August 24, 1976.

15. Nora K. Duncan, "Adhesion Contracts: A Twentieth Century Problem for a Nineteenth Century Code," Louisiana Law Review, vol. 34, 1974, p.1081.

16. Friedrich Kessler, "Contracts of Adhesion--Some Thoughts About Freedom of Contract," Columbia Law Review, 1943, p.632.

17. LSAC, LSAT/LSDAS Registration Form, 1978-79, 1978.

18. Ibid. See also ETS, 1979-80 Law School Admission Bulletin, 1979, p.16.

19. Ibid., pp.16-17.

20. Interview with C. Boyden Grey of Wilmer, Cutler and Pickering, November 10, 1976.

21. The other two law firms are Ropes and Gray of Boston; and Cravath, Swaine and Moore of New York.

22. Interview with Thomas Robinson, an ETS attorney, July 24, 1975.

23. The Family Educational Rights and Privacy Act of 1974 is commonly known as The "Buckley Amendment."

24. "Educational Recordkeeping Practices," Transcript of Testimony before the Privacy Protection Study Commission, Independence Reporting, Inc., November 12, 1976, p.339.

25. ETS, Principles, Policies and Procedural Guidelines Regarding ETS Products and Services, August 1, 1977, p.8.

26. LSAC, Annual Council Report, 1973, p.309.

27. Federal Trade Commission, "Staff Memorandum on The Effects of Coaching on Standardized Admission Examinations," from Arthur E. Levine, Boston Regional Office, to FTC Bureau of Consumer Protection, September 11, 1978, p.219.

28. Kim Masters, "Why Your Daughter Didn't Get Into Law School: ETS's Star Chamber," The New Republic, February 5, 1977, p.14.

29. Ibid., p.15.

30. Robert E. Smith, "ETS Policy and Procedures: Test Scores of Questionable Validity for Candidates in National Testing Programs," February, 1975, p.3. Unpublished statement available to the public. Smith was chairman of the Board of Review (for test security). He quotes the "candidate's Bulletin of Information."

31. *Ibid.*, p.5.

32. ETS internal memorandum from Robert E. Smith, to 35 ETS executives, "Board of Review Recommendations," October 1, 1976 (Revised October 12, 1976), p.2.

33. Interview with Paul Williams, Director of ETS Test Security, July 11, 1975.

34. *Ibid.*

35. *Ibid.*

36. Smith, "ETS Policy and Procedures," attached chart on security investigation procedure.

37. Interview with Williams, July 11, 1975.

38. Smith, "Board of Review Recommendations." Copies of form letters are attached.

39. Interview with confidential source, 1975.

40. Smith, "ETS Policy and Procedures," attached chart.

41. Smith, "Board of Review Recommendations," p.4.

42. *Ibid.*, p.2.

43. Smith, "ETS Policy and Procedures," p.5; interview with Williams, July 11, 1975.

44. *Ibid.*

45. Interview with a confidential source, October 8, 1976.

46. LSAC internal document, Minutes of Special Committee on Legal Affairs, Meeting of October 13 and 14, 1972, p.352.

47. Ibid; interview with the student's attorney, July 1975.

48. Interview with a confidential source, February 1978.

49. Interview with L. Lynwood Aris, Director, ETS Management Services, July 3, 1975.

50. Interview with Bernard Tchorni, ETS Vice President for Operations, June 19, 1975.

51. Interview with Jean Kerr, ETS Director of Testing Services, June, 1974.

52. "In Short: Wrinkled by a Crinkle," Newsday, July 31, 1979, Part II, p.2.

53. ETS internal memorandum from Frederick H. Dietrich to Programs and Services Committee Members, "Minutes of the May 24, 1972 Programs and Services Committee Meeting," August 15, 1972, p.3.

54. ETS internal memorandum from Ann Z. Smith to several ETS executives, "Minutes of IIPC Meeting, May 8," May 12, 1972, p.2. The IIPC is the Information and Instruction Planning Committee.

55. ETS, "Survey of Law School Admissions Services and Publications," submitted to the Privacy Protection Study Commission (late 1976 or early 1977).

56. ETS internal manual, "Operational Services Division Training Program, 1972-73," (circa 1972), section entitled "LSAT/LSDAS Inquiries," p.5.

57. "Computing Error Lowers Some Graduate Entrance Scores," Binghamton Evening Press, January 31, 1978, p.1A.

58. Interview with John Weiss, Director of Project DE-TEST, December 1, 1979.

59. Personal Privacy in an Information Society: The Report of the Privacy Protection Study Commission (Washington: U.S. Government Printing Office, July 1977) p.411.

60. Ibid.

61. Interview with Robert J. Solomon, June 19, 1975.

62. Letter from Hon. Robert F. Drinan, U.S. Congressman, to Thomas E. Kauper, Assistant Attorney General, March 4, 1976.

63. Letter from Thomas E. Kauper to Hon. Robert F. Drinan, U.S. Congressman, April 15, 1976.

64. Ibid.

65. Phone interview with Jeanne Park, Office of Public Affairs, Office of Education, Nov. 6, 1979. The Department of Education, which will begin operations this spring, will not have jurisdiction over ETS, either.

66. According to the 1977-78 United States Government Manual (Washington: Office of the Federal Register, National Archives and Records Service, General Services Administration, 1977) p.542, some of the principal functions of the FTC are:
    --"to promote free and fair competition in interstate commerce"

--to prevent "false or deceptive advertising"

--to prevent "exclusive dealing and tying arrangements, corporate mergers, acquisitions or joint ventures" which may "substantially lessen competition or tend toward monopoly."

--to prevent "interlocking directorates which may restrain competition."

--to regulate labelling to prevent consumer deception.

67. Letter from Daniel Schwartz, Assistant Director for Evaluation, Bureau of Competition, FTC, to Craig Kubey, Legislative Assistant, Office of Hon. Robert F. Drinan, U.S. Congressman, February 25, 1976.

68. Ibid. In 1977, a bill to extend FTC jurisdiction to non-profit organizations was introduced in Congress and passed the House. After heavy lobbying by non-profit trade associations, it was defeated in the Senate. "FTC Seeking Powers to Regulate Activity of Nonprofit Concerns," Wall Street Journal, May 5, 1977, p.36; interview with Michael Pertschuk, FTC Chairman, September 15, 1979.

69. In the Matter of Psychological Corporation, et al., 55 FTC, Docket 6967, Complaint, November 29, 1957--Decision, November 19, 1958, pp. 752-754.

70. Community Blood Bank of Kansas City Area, Inc. v. FTC, 405 F.2d 1011 (8th Cir., 1969).

71. Meeting with Thomas Robinson, Robert Smith, and Jenne K. Britell of ETS, July 23, 1974.

72. Letter from New York State Attorney General Louis Lefkowitz to Tom Sutton, August 27, 1974. Mr. Sutton is an associate of the author.

73. Interview with Michael Edre, Office of Counsel, New York State Board of Regents, Summer, 1974.

74. Ibid.

75. Ibid.

76. Visit to New Jersey Department of the Treasury, Division of Taxation, Corporation Tax Bureau, July, 1974.

77. Ibid. Comment of Supervisor.

78. For a description of Wilmer, Cutler and Pickering, see Mark Green, The Other Government: The Unseen Power of Washington Lawyers (New York: Grossman, 1975) pp.46,52-57,281-2.

79. Interview with Bruce French, June 30, 1975, and Bruce French v. ETS, District of Columbia Superior Court, Docket C.A. 9787, 1973.

80. Interview with French, June 30, 1975.

81. Ibid.

82. Ibid.

83. ETS internal memorandum from Charles E. Consalus and Leforne Sequeira to Messrs. Brodsky, Manning and Solomon, "Attached Memorandum, Fiscal Review of LSDAS, 1970-71," June 1, 1971. The attached quoted memorandum is dated May 28, 1971.

84. Interview with a confidential source, March, 1976.

85. Confidential source, July 19, 1974.

86. Summary of confidential report prepared for ETS by Peat, Marwick and Mitchell on ETS operations, section entitled "Data Processing and Machine Operations: Major Concerns," copy dated March 7, 1973. According to the LSAC's LSAT Newsletter, vol. 5, #1, September 1972, p.3. similar problems occured in 1971-72.

87. Testimony of Robert Solomon before Privacy Protection Study Commission, November 12, 1976, pp.348-350 of transcript. ETS President William Turnbull reaffirmed this claim in an interview with the author on May 3, 1977. Turnbull also stated that a letter was sent to the candidates affected. When asked for a copy of the letter, however, Turnbull's associate, Robert E. Smith, said that he did not believe that one was available. After the interview, Turnbull sent us a letter reiterating that a letter to candidates was sent, but he did not include a copy of the letter to candidates or specific information about its contents or date. Letter from Turnbull to Ralph Nader, July 12, 1977. Discussion of LSDAS is on p.1.

88. "ETS: The Company That Lives Under a Halo," Sunday Times Advertiser, Trenton, N.J., March 28, 1976, p.C3.

89. ETS internal report, "Operational Services Division Training Program: Candidate Services--Telephone Section--1972-73," September 1, 1972, Preface.

90. Interview with Beverly Lipps, December 18, 1976.

91. Ibid.

92. Ibid.

93. Ibid.

94. Ibid.

95. Candidate letter from Richard Terry to ETS, March 9, 1973. Emphasis in original.

96. Solomon, Testimony before Privacy Commission, p.350.

97. Confidential source.

98. Interview with confidential source, June 24, 1975.

99. "ETS: The Company That Lives Under a Halo," p.C3.

100. ETS, Annual Report, 1972, p.24.

101. ETS internal memorandum from Jenne K. Britell to Advisory Board, "Factual Corrections of 'The Secrecy Behind the College Boards' (Steven Brill, New York Magazine)," April 25, 1975, p.12. Distributed to press; interview, confidential source, March 1976.

102. Solomon, Testimony before Privacy Commission, p.350.

103. Interview with Donald Schiariti, Head of ATP Candidate Services, July 11, 1975.

104. ETS internal memorandum from Jenne K. Britell to Advisory Board, "Interviews with Educational Testing Study Group, Mr. Allan Nairn, Director," June 12, 1975, p.2.

105. Interview with Schiariti, July 11, 1975.

106. Letter from Donovan Parker, Associate Registrar, St. Olaf College, Minnesota, to Shirley Tolley, March 27, 1972.

107. Interview with Beverly Lipps, December 18, 1976.

FOOTNOTES   CHAPTER VIII

1. ETS, ETS Charter and By-laws, As amended December 3, 1973, Article 1, Section 11, p.9.

2. The Carnegie Foundation for the Advancement of Teaching, Forty-first Annual Report, 1945-46, (Boston: Merrymount Press, 1946). See pp. 45-46 of "Examinations and Education" by staff member William S. Learned.

3. Ibid.

4. Ibid.

5. ETS, Establishment of the Educational Testing Service: A Statement by the Board of Trustees, December, 1947, p.4.

6. ETS, Annual Report to the Board of Trustees 1948-49, p.3.

7. "ETS--Free Agent or UFO: Neither, Says Visitor," Examiner, February 1, 1973.

8. Ibid.

9. "CEEB President Sees Expanding Role for College Board in Society," College Board News, June, 1974, p.2.

10. Richard Rampell, "Educational Testing: A Disservice?" undergraduate thesis, Princeton University, Department of Economics, 1974, pp.15-20; and ETS, Selected References in Educational Measurement, Evaluation and Advisory Series, 1970, p.37.

11. ETS, ETS Charter and By-Laws, 1973, Article I, Sec. 2, (a)(v), p.5.

12. According to ETS, 1978 Annual Report, p.11, ETS had assets of $45,385,666 on 6/30/78 (current assets, investments, and property).

13. John Kramer, ETS General Counsel, to Joel Seligman, January 10, 1975. Mr. Seligman worked for Ralph Nader at the time.

14. ETS, ETS Charter and By-Laws, 1973, Article I, Sec. 1, p.5.

15. Ibid.

16. Ibid., Article 1, Section 3, pp.6-8.

17. Rampell, "Educational Testing," p.18.

18. Statistics are calculated from total income figures drawn from the 1964-65, 1965-66, 1967-69, 1969-71, 1972, and 1973-74 Annual Reports. Total income for the fiscal year ended June 30, 1965 was $17,707,617. (A.R. 64-65 p.94). Total income for the fiscal year ended 6/30/66 was $23,068,003 (A.R. 65-66, p.70). Total income for the fiscal year ended June 30, 1969 was $30,533,151 (A.R. 67-69, p.127). Total income for the fiscal year ended June 30, 1970 was $34,896,396 (A.R. 69-71, p.94). Total income for the fiscal year ended June 30, 1971 was $39,795,482 (A.R. 1969-71, p.98). Total income for the fiscal year ended June 30, 1972 was $47,894,896 (A.R. 1972, p.76).

19. "The Pleasures of Nonprofitability," Forbes, November 15, 1976, p.89.

20. Internal Revenue Service, Form 990, "Return of Organization Exempt from Taxation," 1976, filed by ETS, part V, line 14. Covers fiscal year July 1, 1976-June 30, 1977.

21. "Textbook Publisher to Market CTS," Examiner, January 29, 1976, p.1.

22. Interview with Lawrence Township Tax Assessor Robert Immordino, July, 1974.

23. The minimum was $500 per year. "DiDonato Claims ETS Assessment Wrong," Lawrence Ledger, October 31, 1973, p.1. The sales of hay totaled: 1971--$871.85 (Frank Cacavio, Vice President, Mercer Sod, Inc. to E.R. Huddy, ETS, September 10, 1971). 1972--$1139.12 (James Cacavio, Mercer Sod, to E.R. Huddy, ETS, September 8, 1972); 1973--$1,124 (John S. Kramer to Robert Immordino, December 21, 1973).

24. "Farmland Assessment Act Revisited," Lawrence Ledger, November 21, 1973.

25. Ibid.

26. ETS internal memo from David Brodsky, (untitled), February 26, 1976, p.2. ETS counsel John Kramer was quoted in the November 21, 1974 Examiner as saying that New Jersey's foreign corporation rule was inconsistent with a 1968 Supreme Court decision. The Examiner said that ETS might bring a court test of its obligation to pay property taxes (p.1).

27. Robin Kerney, "ETS No Farm; Squibb Worth More," Evening Times, Trenton, New Jersey, October 8, 1974, p.12.

28. Examiner, November 21, 1974, p.1.

29. ETS memorandum from Jenne K. Britell to Advisory Board, "Factual Corrections of 'The Secrecy Behind the College Boards' (Steve Brill, New York Magazine)," April 25, 1975, p.1. Distributed to the press.

30. Interview with John Kramer, ETS Attorney, June 20, 1975; ETS, "Finances...Where the Money Comes From and Where It Goes," (Fall 1979), p.1. This paper was circulated to Members of Congress.

31. Thomas Kauper, Assistant Attorney General in the Antitrust Division of the Justice Department, to Robert F. Drinan, U.S. Congress, April 15, 1976.

32. Daniel Schwartz, Assistant Director for Evaluation, Bureau of Competition of the Federal Trade Commission to Craig Kubey, Legislative Assistant, Office of Hon. Robert F. Drinan, February 25, 1976.

33. ETS, <u>Educational Testing Service: Students, Institutions, and Programs</u>, 1975, p.7.

34. ETS unsigned memo, "Legislation on Standardized Testing," (1979), p.4. Distributed to the press.

35. ETS, <u>Annual Report to the Board of Trustees, 1949-50</u>, p.71.

36. ETS, <u>Annual Report to the Board of Trustees, 1953-54</u>, p.60 (LSAT Board) and p.62 (Business Board).

37. Interview with Maryann A. Lear, Secretary of the GRE Board, July 7, 1975. According to Lear, the suggestion for creating such a board originated in 1964 with a group of West Coast graduate school deans.

38. SSAT: Board is listed in ETS, <u>SSAT 1974-75, A Description of the Secondary School Admission Test Program</u>, 1974. ETS receives advice on SSAT policies from representatives who prep schools appoint to the SSAT Board. GAPSFAS: ETS, <u>Graduate and Professional School Financial Aid Service: Manual for Financial Aid Officers 1974-75</u> lists the Steering Committee of the GAPSFAS Council and states on p. 1 that the Council was organized by ETS and the College Board in November 1971. TOEFL: ETS, <u>TOEFL 1978-79 Bulletin of Information and Registration Form</u>, 1978, states on p. 2 that "Educational Testing Service (ETS) administers TOEFL under the general direction of a policy council that was established by, and is affiliated with, the College Entrance Examination Board and the Graduate Record Examinations Board." Auto mechanics test: interview with Benjamin Shimberg of the ETS Center for Occupational & Professional Assessment, July 7, 1975.

39. James Landers and J. Stryker Meyer, "ETS Files Affect Millions... Who Is Accountable?" <u>Evening Times</u>, Trenton, New Jersey, March 31, 1976, p.A-12.

40. ETS, <u>Annual Report 1973, 1974: Flexibility For the Future</u>, p.29.

41. Interview with Confidential Source, August 7, 1974.

42. ETS internal memorandum from Dorothy Urban to Program and Project Directors, Senior Program Directors, "Contract Negotiations Regarding Proprietary Interests: Addendum to Memorandum, December 22, 1967--Program Development Guide," January 10, 1973. The Law School Admission Council, according to Bruce Zimmer, its Executive Director, now owns both the test questions and the test name (LSAT). (Interview, December 11, 1979.)

43. Interview with Lear, July 7, 1975.

44. Interview with Richard Burns, acting Vice President HECP (Higher Education & Career Programs) and Law Programs at ETS.

45. CEEB, *The College Board Today: A Guide to its Programs and Services*, 1978, p.3.

46. Frank Bowles, *The Refounding of the College Board, 1948-1963*, (New York: CEEB, 1967), p.v.

47. *Ibid.*

48. "ETS President Is Ex Officio Trustee," *College Board Review*, Spring, 1971, p.4.

49. "College Entrance Examination Board Application for Voting Membership," Enclosure C, January 1974, coded OS/30a. Included in letter from CEEB to Joel Seligman, 1975.

50. Quoted in memorandum from Joel Seligman to Ralph Nader and Mark Green on "Educational Testing Service (ETS)," February 27, 1975, p.2. Seligman was permitted to examine and make notes about the agreement on February 13, 1975.

51. Memorandum from Joel Seligman to Mark Green on "CEEB, ETS, and Federal Antitrust Laws," p.8.

52. "Summary of the agreement between CEEB and ETS effective July 1, 1975,"July 17, 1975, p.2. Available to the public on request.

53. *Ibid.*, p.1.

54. *Ibid.*, p.2.

55. Inspection of College Board - ETS agreement by Steve Solomon of the New York Public Interest Research Group (NYPIRG) at the College Board offices in New York, November 29, 1979.

56. ETS, "Summary of the Agreement Between College Board and ETS Effective January 1, 1979," January 1, 1979, pp.1,3. Available to the public.

57. <u>Ibid</u>., pp.1-3.

58. "Agreement dated December 3, 1947, between American Council on Education, College Entrance Examination Board, The Carnegie Foundation for the Advancement of Teaching, and Carnegie Corporation of New York," pp.11,12. Signed by George Zook, Edward Noyes, O.C. Carmichael, and Devereux Josephs.

59. ETS, <u>Annual Reports</u> for years 1957-58 through 1969-71. See finance sections and auditor's statements. The yearly contributions, and page references in the appropriate annual report, are as follows:

Year	Capital Gift to ETS	Page in AR same year
1957-58	$200,000	p.70
1958-59	300,000	p.70
1959-60	400,000	p.65
1960-61	400,000	p.70
1961-62	500,000	p.74
1962-63	600,000	p.66
1963-64	700,000	p.88
1964-65	700,000	p.90
1965-66	700,000	p.66
1966-67	700,000	p.62
1967-68	700,000	p.125
1968-69	800,000	p.127
1969-70	900,000	p.90

60. CEEB, "Statement of Revenues, Expenses, and Fund Balance, Year Ended June 30, 1979," October 1, 1979. The ETS-administered ATP, CSS, AP, PSAT/NMSQT, CLEP, SSS, CGP, and Descriptive Tests accounted for 91% of the Board's $61,085,398 revenues in 1978-79. Grants and contracts accounted for 4%, membership dues and meetings for 0.7%, and investments for 0.3%. According to CEEB, <u>The College Board Today</u>, p.3, the College Board had 230 employees in 1978. According to ETS, "Finances...Where the Money Comes From and Where It Goes," (1979) p.2, ETS had more than 2300 permanent staff in 1978-79. This document was distributed to Members of Congress in the fall of 1979.

61. Winton H. Manning, John Summerskill, and John Childress are former College Board Vice Presidents who became ETS Vice Presidents.

62. Internal Revenue Service, "Form 990: Return of Organization Exempt from Taxation," 1973, filed by CEEB. For fiscal year beginning July 1, 1973 and ending June 30, 1974. "Schedule E, Compensation of Officers," lists the salaries and expense accounts of College Board executives. See also schedule E of the 1971 CEEB 990 form.

63. Confidential interview with CEEB employee, July 1976.

64. The College Board has a staff of "about 230 people." (CEEB, The College Board Today, p.3.) Most of the other client groups have no or only a handful of staff. The LSAC, for example, says it has four staff.(Interview, December 18, 1979).

65. Victor Zonana, "Who Gets Ahead? Biggest Testing Service Faces Critical Scrutiny As Its Influence Grows," Wall Street Journal, February 28, 1978, pp.1,18.

66. "Summary of the agreement between ETS and CEEB effective July 1, 1975," p.1.

67. ETS internal memorandum from Arland F. Christ-Janer and William W. Turnbull to "Advisory Board (List B)" on "Joint Statement to Staff from the Presidents of ETS and CEEB," December 15, 1972.

68. "ETS, CB Regional Offices Join Hands," Examiner, April 26, 1973, Vol.2, No.39, p.1.

69. Ibid.

70. ETS, Annual Report 1973, 1974: Flexibility for the Future, p.9.

71. ETS, ETS Charter and By-Laws, 1973. See charter.

72. ETS internal report, "Review of the Report of the Commission on Tests: A Set of Analyses and Suggested Courses of Action Devised by Staff Teams atEducational Testing Service," March 1972, p.45.

73. See the discussion of ETS profit margins on pp. 333-339 and footnotes 157,159,160,161,165,and 166.

74. Edward Fiske, "Student Testing Unit Assailed as Influence Grows," New York Times, November 14, 1979, pp.A1,27.

75. ETS 1978 revenue was $79.6 million (ETS, 1978 Annual Report, p.14); General Motors 1978 revenue was $63.2 billion (Forbes, May 14, 1979, p.288), or 790 times greater.

76. According to figures in ETS, "Project Operating Statement By POS-Category/Project Arch 1977," April 19, 1977, a computer print out of the ETS budget, ETS' ten largest testing income sources for 1977 were the Admissions Testing Program (SAT and Achievement Tests), GRE, LSAT, College Level Examination Program (CLEP), Advanced Placement Program (AP), Test of English as a Foreign Language (TOEFL), PSAT/NMSQT, business school admissions

test (then the ATGSB, now the GMAT), National Teacher Examinations (NTE), and auto mechanics certification test. No other test publisher is known to administer tests which perform the admissions or placement function of the LSAT, CLEP, AP, TOEFL, PSAT, GMAT, NTE, or auto mechanics certification test. According to figures from GREB, Graduate Programs and Admissions Manual 1979-1981, 4 vols. (Princeton: ETS, 1979), over 75% of 12,000 graduate departments in the country require or recommend that applicants take the GRE. ETS' competitor is the Miller Analogies Test, whose volume was 27% of the GRE's. (See note 135.) According to Annual Guides to Graduate and Undergraduate Study: 1980 Edition (Princeton: Peterson's Guides, 1979), 51% of over 2000 colleges listed require the SAT, 71% require or recommend it. See note 77 below and Chapter II, notes 18, 72, 78, and 83. See also note 135 below.

77. Interview with Bob Elliot, Coordinator of Information Services, American College Testing Program, December 10, 1979. Elliot said ACT's 1978-79 candidate volume was approximately 954,000. SAT volume in that year was approximately 1,500,000, according to ETS, "Legislation on Standardized Testing," p.2.

78. Interview with Bob Elliot, December 10, 1979.

79. ETS, "Finances...Where the Money Comes From and Where It Goes," p.2.

80. Interview with Roger Lennon, Associate to the Chairman of Harcourt, Brace Jovanovich, Inc., December 12, 1979; interview with Clay White, Treasurer, Riverside Publishing Company, December 12, 1979. Riverside is a recently formed subsidiary of Houghton-Mifflin.

81. Oscar K. Buros, "Fifty Years in Testing: Some Reminiscences, Criticisms, and Suggestions," Educational Researcher, Vol.6, No.7, July/August 1977, p.10.

82. B. Alden Thresher, "Diversification in Educational Assessment," Report of the Commission on Tests: Vol.II. Briefs, (New York: CEEB, 1970) p.127. The order of sentences has been altered once for clarity.

83. ETS, Annual Report to the Board of Trustees, 1949-1950, pp.5,34.

84. Examiner, May 18, 1972.

85. ETS internal document, "Cost Center Organization Charts," May 1978, pp.27,38,48,49. See Appendix II for discussion of ETS staff allocations for test development offices, and chapter III, footnote 260.

86. Ibid.

87. ETS, Annual Report to the Board of Trustees, 1949-50, p.41.

88. ETS, "Review of the Report of the Commission on Tests," p.45.

89. Zonana, "Who Gets Ahead?" p.18.

90. ETS internal memorandum from Frederick H. Dietrich "For Programs and Services Planning Committee"(19 persons) on "Minutes of the October 14, 1971 Programs and Services Planning Committee Meeting," November 30, 1971, p.2.

91. ETS internal memorandum from Thomas S. Barrows to 73 middle-level ETS executives on "Twenty-fifth Meeting of the Development Planning Committee, May 28, 1971," June 4, 1971.

92. ETS internal memorandum from Herman F. Smith, Robert J. Solomon and William W. Turnbull to "The Record" on "Criteria for the Evaluation of Developmental Plans," July 7, 1970, pp. 1-2.

93. ETS internal memorandum from Ann Z. Smith, on distribution of Spring 1971 *ETS Developments* (circa Spring, 1971).

94. See "ETS Personnel Policies Manual," looseleaf blue binder, General Sections 1101-F-5 and 6, signed C.E. Scholl, Vice President of Personnel, effective February 1973.

95. "Brief Report of ETS Activities," January, 1976. See p.11 for references to Beaton and Zieky.

96. See, e.g., *Walston v. County School Bd. of Nansemond County, Virginia*, 492 F. 2d 919 (4th Cir. 1974); *Baker v. Columbus Municipal Separate School Dist.*, 462 F.2d 1112 (5th Cir. 1972); *U.S. v. State of N.C.*, 400 F. Supp. 343 (E.D. N.C. 1975).

97. Thelma Spencer, Ph.D. dissertation, 1972, chapter V, "Summary Conclusions and Recommendations," p. 231. These pages were obtained from the Justice Department.

98. Brief for Plaintiff, March 20, 1975, at 43, *U.S. v. State of N.C.*, 400 F. Supp. 343 (E.D. N.C. 1975).

99. *Ibid.*, p.48.

100. ETS internal memorandum from George Elford to Mr. Manning on "Plans for NTE Development and Promotion," February 7, 1975, p.2.

101. *Ibid.*

102. ETS internal report by George Elford, "A Concept Paper: The Revision of the NTE Common Examinations," March, 1975, p.8. Elford was Director, Teacher Programs and Services.

103. Ibid., p.10.

104. Ibid., p.12.

105. Ibid., pp.11,13.

106. Ibid., p.17.

107. ETS, Annual Report: ETS '77, p.16. These figures are for the years 1975-76 and 1976-77.

108. Elford, "Concept Paper," March 1975, p.17.

109. ETS internal report by the Office of State Program Development, "Strategy for Illinois," (circa 1972), p.1.

110. Ibid.

111. Ibid., pp.2-3,6-8.

112. Ibid., pp.3,5.

113. Ibid., p.5.

114. Memorandum from Gordon Miller, Darrell Morris, Warren Willingham to Al Sims, "Report of Task Force on Guidance," June 29, 1972, p.1.

115. The figure on 1969-70 SAT volume comes from Table 1, p.4 of On Further Examination: Report of the Advisory Panel on the Scholastic Aptitude Test Score Decline, (New York: CEEB, 1977). The current figure is from ETS, "Legislation on Standardized Testing," p.2.

116. Fiske, "Student Testing Unit Assailed," p.A27.

117. ETS internal memorandum from B.L. Taylor to seven ETS executives, "Hiring Key Staff for New Jersey School Bussing Project," November 10, 1971. The ETS "Staff Directory: Spring 1972" lists Tom Ronchetti, the individual to which Taylor refers, as "School Trans System Associate, Systems Administration."

118. Fiske, "Student Testing Unit Assailed," p.A-27.

119. According to the ETS Annual Report of that year, in 1950-51, ETS test volumes were: SAT--75,375 (p.56); LSAT--6,631 (p.47); GRE--7,926 (pp.47-48); SSCQT--335,838 (p.46).

120. The total candidate volume of the cooperative tests in 1950-51 was 105,180; about 30,000 greater than the SAT. ETS, Annual Report, 1950-51, Table 3, p.48, programs 4-8.

121. Figures are from ETS, Annual Reports for the years 1950-51 (p.48), 1951-52 (p.48), 1953-54 (pp.53-54), and 1954-55 (pp. 90-93). See also Appendix I for further discussion of candidate volume.

122. See ETS, Annual Reports for the years 1954-55 (pp.90-93) and 1955-56 (pp.96-99).

123. See ETS, Annual Reports for the years 1955-56 (pp.96-99) and 1956-57 (pp. 52-58).

124. See ETS, Annual Reports for the years 1955-56 (pp.96-99), 1956-57 (pp.52-58), 1957-58 (pp.58-63), 1958-59 (pp.58-63), and 1959-60 (pp.52-57). See appendix I for further discussion of candidate volume.

125. See ETS Annual Reports for the years 1955-56 (pp.96-99) and 1960-61 (pp.52-57).

126. Ibid.

127. On Further Examination, p.4.

128. Ibid.

129. Ibid. The report gives the following statistics:

	Entering Freshmen*	SATs taken
1963-64	1,224,800	1,163,900
1064-65	1,441,800	1,361,200
1965-66	1,378,000	1,381,400
1966-67	1,439,000	1,422,500
1967-68	1,629,800	1,543,800

* Referred to as "First-time, degree-credit enrollment."

130. Ibid. In 1975-76, the figure was 70.5%; in 1976-77, the figure was 69.8%. These are based on estimates of first-time degree-credit enrollment in On Further Examination, Table 1. After 1975 the National Center for Educational Statistics stopped compiling figures on first-time degree students, and began compiling total figures of first-time students in both degree and non-degree programs.

131. Fiske, "Student Testing Unit Assailed," p.A-27.

132. From auditor's statements in ETS, Annual Reports for years 1952-53 (p.127); 1957-58 (p.74); 1962-63 (p.70); 1967-68 (p.125); 1972-73 (p.76). The 1979 figure is from Fiske, "Student Testing Unit Assailed," p.A-27.

133. The percentages are calculated from total income figures found in auditor's statements, ETS, Annual Reports, 1967-69 through 1978 and see Fiske, "Student Testing Unit Assailed," p.A-27. ETS total income rose from $79.6 million in fiscal 1978 to $94.2 million in 1979, yielding a growth rate of 18%.

134. ETS, Annual Report, 1955-56, p.12.

135. The total volume of the Miller Analogies Test is about 80,000 a year, according to Roger T. Lennon, Associate to the Chairman of Harcourt Brace Jovanovich, Inc., testifying before the New York Board of Regents on November 15, 1979. The volume of the GRE in 1978-79 was 296,000, according to ETS, "Legislation on Standardized Testing," p.2.

136. ETS internal memorandum from David Brodsky to "Advisory Board 'A'" on "ETS Finances and Management," September 24, 1974, p.8.

137. LSAC internal document, "President's Report," (Spring 1974?), p.2.

138. Ibid., p.2. The President's Report cites a 1973 study by Peat, Marwick, Mitchell and Co.

139. Ibid., pp.2-3.

140. ETS internal memorandum from David L. Fox to Mr. Brodsky and ten other ETS officers, "Starter Document for Planning," April 6, 1972, p.5.

141. ETS internal memorandum from Frederick H. Dietrich to Programs and Services Planning Committee, "Minutes of the February 9, 1972 Programs and Services Planning Committee Meeting," March 23, 1972. Also sent to Mr. Turnbull.

142. Brodsky, "ETS Finances," p.1.

143. ETS, Annual Report: ETS'77, p.20.

144. Ibid., p.24.

145. Interview with Samuel Messick, June 20, 1975.

146. ETS, "Finances...Where the Money Comes From and Where It Goes," pp.1,3.

147. Profit refers to the percentage of annual revenue represented by what ETS calls "excess of revenue over expenditures." See Auditor's Statements in ETS, Annual Reports for the years 1976 (p.14), 1975 (p.19), 1972 (p.76), and 1969-71 (p.98).

148. See ETS, Annual Reports, Auditor's Statements, or Finances sections. In particular, see the report for 1954-55, p.138.

149. ETS, Annual Report 1955-56, p.147.

150. ETS Form 990, 1976.

151. On January 31, 1979, we requested the most recent ETS 990 form and were sent the 1976 return.

152. Interview with David Brodsky, June 24, 1975.

153. *Ibid*.

154. *Ibid*.

155. Steven Brill, "The Secrecy Behind the College Boards," *New York*, October 7, 1974.

156. ETS internal memorandum from Jenne K. Britell to Advisory Board, "Factual Corrections of 'The Secrecy Behind the College Boards' (Steven Brill, *New York Magazine*)," April 25, 1975, p.11, point 43. Britell's assertion was directly contradicted by a document circulated by ETS in 1979 (ETS, "Finances... Where the Money Comes From and Where It Goes," p.3) which said that "In order to help support its other charter-mandated activities and to provide funds for the plant and equipment needed to carry on its work, ETS charges a fee beyond costs to its program clients...Fees are negotiated independently with each of its clients and in each of its contracts, but they have consistently averaged between 9 and 10% of program expenses in the last ten years."

157. While the figures are not strictly comparable, the ETS profit margins of 9-12% on programs discussed below are, on a percentage of revenue basis, significantly higher than the "Fortune 500" industrial average of 4.6% (See "The Fortune Directory of the 500 Largest U.S. Industrial Corporations," *Fortune* May 8, 1978, p. 239).

158. "The Pleasures of Nonprofitability," *Forbes*, November 15, 1976, p.89.

159. See ETS, "Project Operating Statement, ETS Period Ended 3/31/77." (Lines 110,170,180,185,210,575.693-01,896,897,899, 510). The exception is the LSAT-LSDAS program. Separate LSAT and LSDAS program lines both showed net income rates of about 10 percent; common LSAT-LSDAS expenses ran a deficit in 1976 (see lines 896,897,899, p.15). See the chart on next page for the ten largest programs by gross revenues.

160. According to the ETS, "Project Operating Statement By POS-Category/Project Arch 1977," the following national testing or service programs with income or expense in excess of $100,000 returned a profit in 1977:
    Admissions Testing Program (College Board), Student Search Service, PSAT/NMSQT, Advanced Placement, CLEP, Testing Academic Achievement, College Scholarship Service, SSAT, School Scholarship Service, Educational Records Bureau, TOEFL, Undergraduate Program, GRE, GAPSFAS, ATGSB/GMAT, LSAT, LSDAS, NTE, Nurses exam, MBE, Association of Certified Social Workers, Auto Mechanics, Foreign Service Exam, NCARB, National Council of Engineers, SABLE.

FOOTNOTE 159

ETS LARGEST REVENUE SOURCES IN 1977

		Revenue ($ 000)		Profit ($ 000)		Percent Profit*	
		'77 Bud.	'76 Act.	1977	1976	1977	1976
1.	ATP Testing	12,396	11,490	1,532	1,411	12.4%	12.3%
2.	College School Service	7,461	6,425	922	789	12.4	12.3
3.	GRE National	3,634	3,844	389	412	10.7	10.7
4.	LSAT-LSDAS	4,192	3,390	388	-(61)	9.3	(1.8)
5.	CLEP	2,498	2,245	309	276	12.4	12.3
6.	AP	2,464	2,146	305	264	12.4	12.3
7.	TOEFL	1,927	1,852	206	198	10.7	10.7
8.	PSAT/NMSQT	1,779	1,729	220	212	12.4	12.3
9.	ATGSB/GMAT	1,568	1,440	155	143	9.9	9.9
10.	NTE	1,289	1,574	91	264	7.1	16.8

* Figures are profit as percentage of revenue.

489

The following lost money:
Cooperative Tests and Services, Multistate Uniform Insurance Agent exam, Pediatrics exam.

161. See ETS "Project Operating Statement," p. 2. Figures are from current full year budget. Revenues from testing programs and services were budgeted for $60,031,000 and profits for $5,586,000.

162. Robert Moulthrop, "Answers to Additional Questions," July 5, 1979, p.1. Moulthrop is Director of ETS' Information Division. Memo available to the public.

163. Fiske, "Student Testing Unit Assailed," p.A-27. The quote is Fiske paraphrasing Brodsky.

164. ETS, "Summary of the Agreement Between CEEB and ETS Effective July 1, 1975," and "Summary of the Agreement Between College Board and ETS Effective January 1, 1979."

165. The information for this table is derived from two sources: the 1977 ETS "Project Operating Statement By POS-Category," April 19, 1977; and the College Entrance Examination Board, "Statement of Revenues, Expense and Fund Balance, Year Ended June 30, 1976 With Comparative Figures for 1975 and for 1977 Current Projections." (See Appendix IV for documents).

The Project Operating Statement gives 1976 fiscal year figures for ETS income, expense and excess of income over expense for each program. ETS figures are rounded off to the nearest thousand. The college Board statement gives 1975-76 figures for College Board revenues and expenses for each program.

The table in the text is calculated from the following detailed presentation of figures on income, expense and profit drawn from these two documents.

Key: CB: College Board
      ETS: Educational Testing Service
      POS: ETS Project Operating Statement
      SREF: College Board Statement of Revenues, Expenses
            and Fund Balance

490

KEY:
CB: College Board
ETS: Educational Testing Service
POS: ETS Project Operating Statement
SREF: College Board Statement of Revenues, Expenses and Fund Balance

FOOTNOTE 165: ADMISSIONS TESTING PROGRAM: ESTIMATED REVENUE, COST AND PROFIT, 1975-76

1) Total Revenue to the ATP Program $16,260,652

ETS
2) ETS Bill to CB $11,490,000[a]
   (ETS costs plus
   ETS profit)
3) ETS Costs   10,079,000
   (ETS Direct
   and Indirect Costs)   —————————
4) ETS profit $ 1,411,000

THE COLLEGE BOARD (CB)
ETS Bill to CB $11,490,000
5) CB Direct Costs   1,742,474
   in overseeing   —————————— +
   ATP Program
7) Reported ATP $13,232,474
   Program Expense
8) CB Indirect Costs   805,738[b]
   in overseeing ATP   —————————— +
   Program (overhead)
9) Total ATP Program $14,038,212
   Expense

                                      $14,038,212
                                      —————————— —
10) CB Profit $2,222,440
    ETS profit (line 4)   + 1,411,000
                                      ——————————
11) TOTAL CB & ETS PROFIT $ 3,633,440
    ON THE ATP PROGRAM

SOURCE:
1) SREF line 1
2) POS category 110 (see a next page)
3) POS category 110
4) POS category 110 (line 2 minus line 3)
5) same as line 2
6) SREF line 14 minus POS category 110
7) SREF line 14
8) Derived from SREF lines 1, 13, 28. Equals the portion of total CB "General and Administrative" expense attributable to ATP Program. See b on next page.
9) Lines 7 plus line 8 (Or, SREF line 14 plus indirect cost figure derived from SREF 1, 13, 28.)
10) Line 1 minus line 9
11) Line 4 plus line 10

165 (cont'd)

Explanation of the chart:

a) These figures are from POS Category 110 which is entitled "Admissions Program Adm." Line 2 equals the full year income "inc" figure (for the "previous year actual"). This does not represent total revenue of the ATP but simply that portion retained by ETS for ETS total costs and profit. (Line 3 equals the expense--"exp"--figure and line 4 the "net.") Six small categories, other than Category 110, which may or may not be included in the ETS ATP bill to the College Board are not included in the figures presented here. (These are #115--/"Admissions Testing Program-Puerto Rico"/, #120 /"ATP Test Construction"/, #130 /"ATP Analytical"/, #150 /"CEEB Program Administration"/, #166 /"ATP Summary Reporting System," a statistical analysis service for colleges/ and #201 /"ATP Development"/.) Together these six categories brought in $1,816,000 in income against $1,303,000 in expenses, for a profit margin of 28.3%. It is unlikely that they are all included in the bill, since when their income is added to the category 110 income the sum exceeds the total amount recorded in the College Board SREF as having been spent on the ATP. If these categories were included in the calculations, however, they would be reflected by a slight increase in the profits of ETS relative to those of the College Board and a slight increase in the overall share of the candidate's fee which goes to test company profit.

b) Director of ETS' Information Division Robert Moulthrop's claim that the ATP profit margin is only 0.8%, and similar arguments by College Board officials such as Albert Sims, are based on attempts to pad the figures for the College Board's indirect costs. (See Moulthrop, "Answers to Additional Questions," July 5, 1979, p.1.) Moulthrop arrives at his profit figure by first taking the excess of ATP revenues over expenses reported on the 1977-78 SREF (the equivalent of line 1 minus line 7 on our chart). He then calculates the percentage of total College Board revenues which are accounted for by the ATP (37% in 1975-76; 36.6% in Moulthrop's 1979 memo). He multiplies this percentage by College Board general expenses to obtain a figure for the indirect costs (or "support services") attributable to the ATP. He then subtracts this figure from the ATP surplus to arrive at the profit figure.

This method is appropriate for calculating the College Board's profit margin (it does not, however, include the ETS profit margin, which Brodsky acknowledged is 10% of the bill ETS submits to the Board); the problem with Moulthrop's calculation is that he includes categories which cannot legitimately be attributed as indirect expenses for the ATP when setting up the general expense figure which is to be multiplied by 37%. Moulthrop writes that this figure must include "such support services as regional office operations, publications, research and development, administrative costs, support for special conferences, the free validity study service, subsidy for test administrations for special populations (such as religious minorities and the handicapped), and scholarships or vouchers for those who cannot afford to take the test." (p.1). To begin with, Moulthrop's list includes two categories which are already included in the College Board's direct ATP expenditures: special tests for religious and handicapped students and vouchers (otherwise known as fee waivers) for low-income students. (See, for example, a 1972-73 pie chart distributed by ETS entitled "Distribution of the Admissions Testing Program Income Dollar in 1972-73" which lists ATP "direction, development, supervision, scoring, reporting, servicing and fee waivers" together as the basic ATP costs.) Four of the categories--regional office operations, publications, research and development, support for special conferences-- do not involve costs required for running the ATP program but rather are areas in which the College Board has elected to spend its profits. While the Validity Study Service perhaps can be legitimately considered an ATP indirect cost, category 165 of the POS suggests it is a small one (ETS billed the College Board $72,000 for VSS in 1976 and budgeted $125,000 in 1977); the VSS, at any rate, is not listed on the College Board's SREF and thus cannot be taken into account for the year (1977-78) in which Moulthrop makes his calculations.

The one category on the SREF which can legitimately be considered a source of indirect cost to the College Board for the ATP program is "General and Administrative" expense. In 1975-76 expenses in this category (line 28 of the 1975-76 SREF) equalled $2,164,781. Since the ATP accounted for approximately 37% of the College Board's income ($16,260,652 from line 1 of the SREF divided by $43,687,555 from line 13), 37% of the College Board's "General Administrative" expenses should be charged to the ATP as indirect costs. Thirty-seven percent (the exact figure is .3722032) of $2,164,781 is $805,738, the indirect cost figure cited in line 8 of the above chart.

A separate line in the chart for ETS' indirect costs is not included, since the ETS bill to the College Board would be drawn up to recover both direct and indirect costs.

The table in the text uses the following lines from the above chart:

    ETS Costs: Line 3
    College Board Direct Costs: Line 6
    College Board Indirect Costs: Line 8
    ETS Profit: Line 4
    College Board Profit: Line 10

Overall profit on the 1975-76 ATP equals $3,633,440 (line 12). This amounts to a 22.4% profit margin on $16,260,652 of total ATP revenue.

Although the figures on how much of this profit goes to ETS and how much to the College Board can only be treated as rough estimates, since the SREF and POS are prepared with different accounting categories and are therefore not strictly comparable, the overall profit percentage is more reliable.

The 1972-73 pie chart distributed by ETS ("Distribution of the Admissions Testing Program Income Dollar in 1972-73") indicates a comparable profit margin, 18.8%. The profits were distributed to, in descending order of size, "Forum and Governance Activities and Unallocated Administrative Expense," subsidies to other operational programs, subsidies to new programs under development, "Educational/Public Service Activities," and Research.

166. A chart similar to that in Footnote 165 is presented on the following page for 1978-79 Admissions Testing Program Revenue, Expense and Profit. (See explanation of methodology and definitions in footnote 165.) Although there is no Project Operating Statement (POS) available for 1978-79, financial breakdowns for 1978-79 can be estimated by working from the College Board's SREF of that year (CEEB, "Statement of Revenues, Expenses and Fund Balance, Year Ended June 30, 1979 With Comparative Figures for 1977-78 and for 1979-80 Current Projections") and by making the following assumptions. First, we assume that the 1978-79 ETS bill to the College Board constitutes the same percentage of Reported ATP Program Expense as it did in 1975-76 (70.66137%). Second, we use Brodsky's statement about the 10% fee which ETS charges the College Board (see p.   )to determine ETS profit.

The table in the text uses the following lines from the chart on the next page:

    ETS Costs: Line 3
    College Board Direct Costs: Line 6
    College Board Indirect Costs: Line 8
    ETS Profit: Line 4
    College Board Profit: Line 10

The estimated overall profit on the 1978-79 ATP equals:

    ETS Profit: $1,524,206
    College Board Profit   2,898,335

    Total Profit: $4,422,541

This amounts to a 20.6% profit margin on $21,478,660 of total Admissions Testing Program Revenue.

See also Appendix IV for financial documents and ETS, "Finances. . . Where the Money Comes From and Where It Goes" for discussion of ETS 10% fee.

FOOTNOTE 166: ADMISSIONS TESTING PROGRAM: ESTIMATED REVENUE, COST AND PROFIT, 1978-79

1) Total Revenue to the ATP Program $21,478,660

2) ETS Bill to CB
   ((ETS costs plus
   ETS profit) $15,242,060

3) ETS Costs
   (ETS Direct and
   Indirect costs)   13,717,854
                              _____
4) ETS profit $1,524,206

THE COLLEGE BOARD (CB)

5) ETS Bill to CB $15,242,060
6) CB Direct Costs
   in overseeing   2,311,480 +
   ATP Program   _____
7) Reported ATP $17,553,540
   Program Expense
8) CB Indirect Costs $ 1,026,785 +
   in overseeing ATP   _____
   Program
9) Total ATP Program $18,580,325
   Expense
                                              -$18,580,325
                                              _____
10) CB Profit $ 2,898,335
    plus ETS Profit (line 4)   + $1,524,206
                                              _____
11) TOTAL CB & ETS PROFIT $ 4,422,541
    ON 1978-79 ATP PROGRAM

SOURCE:
1) SREF line 1
2) Derived from SREF line 16 (Reported ATP Program Expense); multiply this figure by the ratio of the 1975-76 ETS bill to 1975-76 Reported ATP Program Expense (70.66137%)
3) Derived from lines 2 and 4 of this chart
4) Derived from line 2 and ETS Vice-President Brodsky's statement that the ETS fee is about 10% of costs (i.e., profit is calculated as 10% of line 2)
5) same as line 2
6) SREF line 16 minus line 5
7) SREF line 16
8) SREF line 1 divided by SREF line 15 times SREF line 32—see methodology described in footnote 165.
9) Sum of lines 7 and 8
10) Line 1 minus line 9
11) Sum of lines 10 and 4

167. ETS, "Finances...Where the Money Comes From and Where It Goes," Attachment E.

168. See p.309 and footnote 59 of this chapter.

169. Moulthrop, "Answers to Additional Questions," p.2.

170. "SAT Schedule Will Be Reduced Beginning Jan.1," New York Times, October 10, 1979, p.B-3.

171. ETS, "Project Operating Statement, Period Ended March 31, 1977," p.2 of 2 listing "Full Year Budgets." In the "Current" section, numbers in parentheses in the "Net" column represent programs which operated at a loss and hence were subsidized by profitable programs. These subsidies total $6,194,000. "Unallocated" administrative expenses was subsidized for $1,984,000 and Developmental Projects for $1,218,000.

172. Ibid. Courses and seminars for educators refers to "Instructional Program and Materials."

173. Ibid. The Chauncey Conference Center was budgeted for a subsidy of $233,000 in 1977. According to ETS, "Finances... Where the Money Comes From and Where It Goes," p.4, the Conference Center received an actual subsidy of $150,000 in 1978-79.

174. ETS, "Project Operating Statement By POS-Category/Project Arch 1977," lines 756,798-89,817,828,858,865-47, and 530 represent most of ETS' infant research programs, whose subsidies total $85,000. It is difficult to identify from the POS all infant learning research projects, hence the $100,000 is a rough estimate.

175. ETS, Annual Report 1973, 1974: Flexibility for the Future, p.45.

176. Interview with G. Dykeman Sterling, June 1974.

177. Ibid.

178. ETS internal memorandum to three ETS executives, "Some Random, Unedited Thoughts About the Agenda," June 9, 1971, p. 1.

179. ETS, Annual Report 1949-50, pp.5,34,43,44.

180. Ibid., p.41.

181. Ibid.

182. ETS, Annual Report 1951-52, p.44.

183. As of June 30, 1950, the ETS staff consisted of 276 people. Fifty-two of these, the professionals and supervisors, were listed in the annual report. In 1965-66 the staff totalled 1,011 (on June 30, 1966), of whom 368 were listed as professionals. See ETS, Annual Reports for the years 1949-50 (pp.5,34) and 1965-66 (pp.65,76-82).

184. ETS, Annual Report 1952-53, p.46.

185. ETS, Annual Report 1949-50, p.45.

186. ETS, "Finances...Where the Money Comes From and Where It Goes," p.5.

187. Ibid., Attachment C.

188. W. Vance Grant and C. George Lind, Digest of Education Statistics 1979 (Washington: National Center for Education Statistics, 1979), p.105. College and university average salaries given are for men; women's salaries for the same positions are about 15% less. ETS salaries are from ETS Form 990, Tax Return for 1976, statement 5, p.1. This covers fiscal year July 1, 1976 through June 30, 1977.

189. Ibid., statement 5, p.1.

190. ETS, "Finances...Where the Money Comes From and Where It Goes," p.2.

191. "Job Opportunities," Examiner, January 18, 1979, p.2.

192. ETS, "Finances...Where the Money Comes From and Where It Goes," p.2. "Average salary for the total staff was approximately $13,600 compared to about $13,800 derived from the Bureau of the Census' Statistical Abstract which reports income of all wage earners nationwide."

193. "Wage and Salary Administration," ETS Personnel Policies Manual, Section C-2, p.7 of 16.

194. See Chapter II p.38 regarding the ETS President's house and the ETS Form 990 Tax Return for 1976, Statement 5 regarding expense accounts.

195. ETS, Personnel Policies Manual, "Moving and Relocation Expenses," (circa 1970) Section A-6, p.1.

196. Ibid. "Tuition Aid for Staff Dependents," sec. E-6, p.1. This version "supersedes September 1967" policy.

197. ETS internal memorandum by Sandra J. Polk, to Personnel Committee, "Minutes from February 16, 1973, Meeting of Personnel Committee," April 30, 1973 and attached "Working Paper," February 16, 1973, p.20. ETS personnel policy, "Tuition Aid for Staff Dependent Children," 1101-D-3, (circa 1973).

198. ETS internal "Inter-Office Mail Routing Slip" from Robert J. Solomon to Mr. Scholl and Mrs. Townsend, February 22, 1972.

199. ETS internal manual, "Secretarial Handbook," (undated), p.6.

200. Ibid.

201. ETS internal memorandum from William W. Turnbull to six ETS executives, "A Note on Semantics," October 9, 1963.

202. ETS internal memorandum from Robert E. Smith to Mr. Consalus, "Your April 27 Request for a PAN," May 5, 1970; attached internal memorandum from Charles E. Consalus to Mr. R. Smith and Mr. Winterbottom, "Assistant Program Director," April 27, 1970, p.1.

203. ETS internal memorandum from S. Kimberly to Messrs. C. Scholl and R. Solomon, "Survey of the Personnel Division," April 28, 1972, p.9.

204. Ibid., pp.9-10.

205. Ibid., Appendix pp.1-2.

206. Ibid., Appendix p.1.

207. Examiner, March 28, 1974. Letters to the Editor.

208. Ibid.

209. Polk, "Working Paper," February 16, 1973, pp.5-6.

210. Ibid., pp.7-10.

211. ETS internal memorandum from Ann Z. Smith to 19 ETS executives and Planning Committee members, "Minutes of IIPC Meeting, March 13, 1972," March 24, 1972.

212. ETS internal memorandum from David L. Fox to Planning Committees, "Review of Planning Committee Activities," February 3, 1972, p.1.

213. ETS internal memorandum from the Sub-Committee on ETS Programs to Mr. Levine and Ann Smith, "The Sub-Committee Recommendations," August 16, 1971, p.3, and attached "Calendar of Events."

214. ETS internal memorandum from David L. Fox to eleven ETS officers, "Review of Planning Committee Operations," March 28, 1972, p.5.

215. Interview with Bill Schwarz, administrative analyst in the New Jersey Department of Labor, December 10, 1979. Schwarz said that coverage for unemployment benefits was extended to temporaries in non-profit and higher-education organizations, state hospitals, and universities as of January 1, 1972.

216. See "1,000 Temps--A Staff for All Seasons," Examiner, March 21, 1974, p.1, for ETS' description of the temps' world.

217. Ibid. "Temps are ineligible for the usual ETS fringe benefits, although they are now covered by the ETS ill-time program. In lieu of vacation, temps who work more than 700 hours in a calendar year also receive a payment in January of four hours' pay for every 100 hours worked." See also ETS internal memorandum from K. Landgraf and L. Lavine to Mr. Scholl, "Study of Unemployment Compensation and Related Topics," August 2, 1972, p.7.

218. The number of temporary employees as a percentage of the total ETS workforce is calculated from ETS, Annual Reports for the years 1950-51 (p.41), 1951-52 (p.45) and 1964-65 (p.89). The Examiner, March 21, 1974, reports that 85% of temporary employees were women.

219. ETS, 1978 Annual Report, p.20.

220. Examiner, February 10, 1972, p.2.

221. Landgraf and Lavine, "Study of Unemployment Compensation." See esp. p.12.

222. Ibid., p.17.

223. Ibid.

224. Ibid., p.5.

225. Letter from an ETS temporary worker to William Turnbull, August 1, 1972, p.1. Confidential source.

226. ETS internal memoranda: R.J. Gettelfinger to six ETS executives, "Unemployment Compensation," June 27, 1972, p.1; and B.L. Tchorni and J.C. Yeager to Messrs. Brodsky, Scholl, Solomon and Williams, "The Availability Card," August 14, 1972, p.1.

227. Ibid., p.2.

228. ETS internal memorandum from Robert E. Smith to eight ETS executives, "Unemployment Compensation--Hiring and Termination Procedures," March 14, 1972, p.1.

229. <u>Ibid</u>., Appendix entitled "Termination Procedure."

230. Gettelfinger, "Unemployment Compensation," p.1.

231. ETS internal memorandum to Belvin Williams, "Unemployment Compensation Problems," June 27, 1972, pp.1-2.

232. <u>Ibid</u>., p.2.

233. Tchorni, "The Availability Card," p.2.

234. An ETS temporary worker to Turnbull, August 1, 1972, p.1.

235. Letter from William Turnbull to temporary worker, August 15, 1972. Confidential source.

236. Kimberly, "Survey," p.1.

237. <u>Ibid</u>., p.8.

238. <u>Ibid</u>., pp.8-9.

239. <u>Ibid</u>., pp.9-11.

240. <u>Ibid</u>., p.6.

241. <u>Ibid</u>., p.7.

242. <u>Ibid</u>., p.11.

243. <u>Ibid</u>.

244. <u>Ibid</u>., p.12.

245. Interview with Chuck Stone, July, 1974.

246. ETS internal memorandum from Garrison W. Hendrick to an ETS executive, "Keeping in Touch," May 13, 1971, p.1.

247. ETS internal memorandum from Chuck Stone to Mr. Solomon, "Blue-print for Black Progress in a White Organization of Red-Blooded Americans," August 18, 1970, p.7.

248. ETS internal memorandum from the PEOPLE Committee to Mr. Solomon, "Implementing 'The Statement on Educational Testing and Minority/Poverty Group Needs' authored by the PEOPLE Sub-committee on Test Development," June 14, 1971, pp.2,4,5. No one with whom the author spoke, including Chuck Stone, could recall what the acronym PEOPLE stood for.

249. ETS internal memorandum from Chuck Stone to Messrs. Hanford and Solomon, "HEAR," July 7, 1971, p.6.

250. Stone, "Blue-print," p.5.

251. ETS internal memorandum from Chuck Stone to Messrs. Solomon and Turnbull, "Minority Professional Employment Pattern," February 7, 1972, p.1.

252. Ibid., p.2.

253. ETS internal memorandum from J. Bradley Williams to ASSETS, "Progress Report," April 26, 1972.

254. ETS internal memorandum from Chuck Stone to Messrs. Turnbull and Solomon, "Minority Affairs Inside and Outside of ETS--Some Critical Concerns," November 2, 1971, p.3.

255. Letter from Chuck Stone to William Turnbull, February 7, 1972.

256. ETS internal memorandum from William Turnbull to Mr. Stone, "The Minority Experience at ETS," March 1, 1972, p.4.

257. Ibid.

258. ETS internal memorandum from Chuck Stone to Mr. Solomon, "The Ad Hoc Committee on the Status of Women vs. the Non-Ad Hoc Committee on the Status of Blacks," August 10, 1971, p.2.

259. ETS, 1978 Annual Report, p.20.

260. Personal communication between William Turnbull and Ronald Brownstein, October 12, 1979.

261. ETS internal memorandum from "The Attached List of Signatories" to Messrs. Solomon and Turnbull, "Concern for Black Progress at ETS," May 25, 1979, pp.1-2. The memo was signed by 112 staff members.

262. ETS internal memorandum from "25 of the Original Signatories /of the 5/25/79 memo_/ to "Concerned Black Staff," "Progress Report," June 7, 1979, p.1.

263. Ibid., pp.1-2.

264. ETS internal report by W.W. Turnbull and G.H. Hanford, "A Proposal for a Higher Education Ability Recognition Program to Promote the Entry of Minority Group Students into Higher Education," Draft, August 18, 1969, p.5.

265. Ibid.

266. Ibid.

267. Ibid., pp.9-16. See also ETS internal memorandum from Stephen J. Wright to Members of the HEAR Task Force, "Summary of the Fourth Meeting of the Task Force," January 5, 1971. The fourth meeting took place on December 29-30, 1970.

268. Interview with Stone, July 1974.

269. George Hanford, Acting President of the College Board in 1969-70, was listed as co-author of the August 18, 1969 version of the HEAR proposal.

270. Interview with Stone, July 1974.

271. Stone, "HEAR," p.8.

272. Interview with Stone, July 1974.

273. ETS internal memorandum from Chuck Stone and Stephen Wright to the Officers of the College Board and ETS, "The Implementation of the HEAR Proposal," August 12, 1970, p.1.

274. Interview with Stone, July 1974.

275. Interview with William Turnbull, May 3, 1977.

276. ETS internal memorandum to Mr. Scholl, March 15, 1972, pp.1-2.

FOOTNOTES   CHAPTER IX

1. Interview with Steve Solomon, New York Public Interest Research Group (NYPIRG) Regional Coordinator, August 10, 1979.

2. Interviews with Ed Hanley, July 1979, and Steve Solomon, August 1979. Hanley, a NYPIRG intern, was the only person to testify in favor of the bill.

3. CEEB internal memorandum from S. P. Marland, Jr. to "Professional Staff," on "Truth in Testing Legislation," May 15, 1978.

4. *Ibid.*

5. New York State Senate-Assembly Bill, S. 5200-A, A. 7668-A, 1979-1980 Regular Session, known as the "Truth-in-Testing" bill.

6. ETS hired the firm of Hinman, Straub, Pigors and Manning at a cost of about $22,000 (interviews with Mary Churchill, ETS spokesperson, August 29, 1979 and August 30, 1979). The College Board retained McNamee, Lochner, Titus and Williams at a cost of $26,905 (interview, Jim Baker, College Board Vice-President for Public Affairs, August 30, 1979). According to Baker a total of five mailings were sent in May and June to New York educational officials at a cost of $4,341. Claims in the mailings included threats that the law would "place an added financial burden on students in New York state, damage the fairness and availability of tests.../inconvenience/ students generally and special populations such as the handicapped and students who cannot test on Saturday for religious reasons." (CEEB memorandum from Richard D. Rooney, Director of the College Board Middle States Regional Office to CEEB Representatives and Alternates-New York and CSSA Representatives--New York, "New York Senate Bill 5200/Assembly Bill 7668: URGENT," May 11, 1979.)

7. Interview with Mary Ann McLean, counsel to New York State Senate Higher Education Committee, assistant counsel to Senator LaValle, September 13, 1979.

8. Statement of Gordon Ambach, President of the University of the State of New York and Commissioner of Education, Committee Hearing on S5200 LaValle, et al and A7668 Vann, et al, before the New York Senate and Assembly Higher Education Committees, May 9, 1979. The College Board in Opposition to Senate Bill 5200/Assembly Bill 7668, May 1, 1979, p. 1; Hinman, Straub, Pigors and Manning, Memorandum in Opposition/to Assembly 7668/Senate 5200 / Submitted on Behalf of Educational Testing Service, May 14, 1979, p.2.

9. Vito Perrone,"Testimony Prepared for the Senate and Assembly Higher Education Committees Regarding the Examination and Assessment of Standardized Testing in Light of Legislation Currently Before the Senate and Assembly of the State of New York," (May 9, 1979), p.2. Perrone is Dean, Center for Teaching and Learning, University of North Dakota.

10. Letter from Lewis Pike to Senator Kenneth P. LaValle, June 12, 1979.

11. Rooney, "New York Senate Bill 5200."

12. Testimony of Robert J. Solomon, ETS Executive Vice-President, before the New York State Senate and Assembly Higher Education Committees, May 9, 1979.

13. NYPIRG, "Questions and Answers About Truth-in-Testing," (circa summer, 1979), p. 2. Publicly circulated memorandum.

14. Ibid.

15. Interview with Senator Kenneth P. LaValle, August 1979.

16. Interview with Donald K. Ross, Executive Director of NYPIRG. On Thursday, June 14, the bill passed the Senate by a vote of 38-17. The following day it passed the Assembly Ways and Means Committee by a vote of 20-7. On Saturday afternoon -- the final day of the session -- it passed the Assembly by a vote of 88-48.

17. From transcript of New York State Assembly debate, June 16, 1979.

18. Mailgram from Robert J. Kingston, President, The College Board, to "Principals and Headmasters of New York State High Schools,"June 25, 1979. Kingston wrote,"We believe it is especially important that you urge the Governor to exercise an executive veto."

19. Hugh L. Carey, Governor, State of New York, "Memorandum filed with Senate Bill 5200-A, entitled: AN ACT to amend the education law, in relation to standardized testing,"July 13, 1979, p. 1.

20. Ibid.

21. Lawrence K. Altman, "Citing New Law, Medical Schools to Bar Entry Tests in New York," New York Times, July 18, 1979, p. 1; Association of American Medical Colleges, "New York Law Forces Withdrawal of New MCAT From State," news release, July 17, 1979.

22. Edward B. Fiske, "Test Publishers See Dropping of Exams," *New York Times*, October 8, 1979, p. 1.

23. "SAT Schedule Will Be Reduced Beginning Jan. 1," *New York Times*, October 10, 1979, p. B-3.

24. Dena Kleiman, "Truth in Testing Law Faces Legality Test," *New York Times*, November 9, 1979, p. B-3.

25. Gordon M. Ambach, "Memorandum to Chief Executive Officers of All Postsecondary and Professional Institutions in New York State and Other Interested Parties, Subject: Tests used in the admission selection process by postsecondary and professional schools in New York State," October 29, 1979. Ambach's report accepted most of the test company arguments against the bill. For the Regents vote, see Ari L. Goldman, "Regent Board Head May Bar a 2d Term," *New York Times*, December 16, 1979, p. 28.

26. Memorandum from L. Orin Slagle and Bruce I. Zimmer, to Prelaw Advisors, "Testing Legislation and LSAT Program Changes: Actions of the LSAC Board of Trustees," November 6, 1979; "Internal Memo," *Testing Digest*, vol. 1, no. 3, fall 1979, p. 4; and LSAC, LSAC News and Notes, late fall 1979, p. 1.

27. Interviews with Mary Ann McLean, November and December 1979.

28. Edward B. Fiske, "Finding Fault With the Testers," *New York Times Magazine*, November 18, 1979, p. 161.

29. Interview with Senator Kenneth LaValle, August 1979.

30. Interview with National Public Interest Research Group representatives, December 12, 1979.

31. *Washington Post*, October 24, 1979, p. 4.

32. John W. Gardner, *Excellence*, (New York: Harper and Row, Inc., 1961), p. 53.

33. ETS Internal Memorandum by William Turnbull, "Public and Professional Attitudes Toward Testing and ETS: Relations with Key Publics," August 14, 1978, p. 12.

34. *Ibid.*, p. 7, chart 1.

35. *Ibid.*, p. 1-2

36. *Ibid.*, p. 2.

37. *Ibid.*, p. 6.

38. ETS, "Further Discussion on S. 5200/A. 7668: Standardized Testing," June 4, 1979, p. 1, prepared by Robert Moulthrop, circulated in the New York State Legislature.

39. Fiske, "Finding Fault With the Testers," p. 161.

40. College Board memorandum from Lois D. Rice on "The Gibbons Bill (H.R. 3564) and the College Board," July 23, 1979, p. 3. Circulated in the U.S. Congress.

41. Interview with Robert J. Solomon, June 19, 1975.

42. Turnbull, "Public and Professional Attitudes Toward Testing and ETS," p. 3.

43. Report of the Commission on Tests: II Briefs, (New York: College Board, 1970), p. 69.

44. Report of the Commission on Tests: Vol I. Righting the Balance, (New York: CEEB, 1970), p. 48.

45. See Chapter IV for a discussion of the pioneers of mental testing.

46. ETS Annual Report to the Board of Trustees, 1955-56, p. 23.

47. Dun and Bradstreet Million Dollar Directory 1979, vol. I, p. 2359. Schwinn Bicycle Co. had $100 million in sales compared to ETS $80 million in fiscal 1978.

48. Report of the Commission on Tests: II. Briefs, p. 25.

49. Federal Trade Commission, "Staff Memorandum on the Effects of Coaching on Standardized Admission Examinations," from Arthur E. Levine, Boston Regional Office, September 11, 1978, p. 31.

50. Thomas C. Wheeler, "The American Way of Testing," New York Times Magazine, September 2, 1979, p. 40.

51. Christopher Jencks, "The Wrong Answer For Schools Is: (b) Back to Basics," Washington Post, February 19, 1979, p. C-1.

52. "The College Board's English Test Under Fire," Chronicle of Higher Education, October 29, 1974.

53. ETS, 1979-80 Law School Admission Bulletin, 1979, and Chapter VI, footnote 47.

54. ETS, Bulletin of Information: 1979-1980 GMAT, pp. 25-26, or Chapter II footnote 82.

55. See Chapter II, footnote 18.

56. Lucky Abernathy, "What's New in College Admissions," College Board Review, summer 1976, p. 12.

57. See Chapter III for a discussion of improvement of grade prediction.

58. See Chapter III for a disussion of prediction of grades beyond the first year.

59. See Chapter III, pp. 70-82 for prediction of career success.

60. See Chapter VI.

61. See Chapter V, footnote 13 .

62. George H. Hanford, Minority Programs and the Activities of the College Entrance Examination Board: A Critical Review and a Brief Look Ahead, (New York: College Board, 1976), p. 27.

63. See Chapter VII, footnote 7.

64. ETS internal report compiled by Information Services Division, "Omnibus 1973-1974," p. 15.

65. See Chapter III, first two sections.

66. See Chapter III, first section, for discussion of grade prediction.

67. See Chapter V.

68. See Chapter V, footnote 15.

69. Leonard L. Baird, Development of an Inventory of Documented Accomplishments for Graduate Admissions, GRE Board Report GREB No. 77-37, June, 1979, p. 23.

70. See Chapter III, first two sections.

71. Interview with E. W. Kelley, Professor, Department of Government, Cornell University, December, 1979.

72. Report of the Commission on Tests: II. Briefs, p. 146.

73. ETS internal report by William H. Angoff, Charles W. Daves, et al, "Report of the Committee on Testing of Minority Groups," June 1972, pp. 1, 7.

74. ETS internal report by Thomas F. Donlon, Charles W. Daves, et al, "Statement on Educational Testing and Minority/Poverty Group Needs: A Report to the ETS PEOPLE Committee," June 1970, p. 34.

75. Ibid., p. 67.

76. Report of the Commission on Tests: II. Briefs, pp. 136, 139, 142.

77. *Ibid.*, p. 153.

78. See Chapters VI and VIII.

79. *Report of the Commission on Tests: I. Righting the Balance*, p. 62.

80. Interview with Kathleen Brouder, College Board executive, July 27, 1978.

81. The Commissioners of Education were: Francis Keppel, 1962-66, who served as president of the Carnegie Corporation, a founder of ETS; Harold Howe II, 1966-68, who served as a College Board Trustee; James E. Allen, 1969-70, who served as a consultant to ETS; Sidney P. Marland, Jr., 1970-72, who served as president of the Institute for Educational Development (IED), an ETS affiliate, president of the College Board and a trustee of ETS. The current Secretary of Education, Shirley Hufstedler, has served as a trustee of the Aspen Institute for Humanistic Studies, which houses its international division at ETS.

82. Interview with Robert Solomon, June 19, 1975.

83. CEEB, *Members and Officers of the College Entrance Examination Board 1974-75/Charter and Bylaws*, (New York: CEEB, 1975).

84. *Examiner*, April 10, 1975, p. 2.

85. The chairman of the joint committee for the revision of *Standards and Psychological Tests and Manuals* was Frederick B. Davis, a former ETS Trustee. The other ten members included E. Belvin Williams, an ETS vice president; Edmund W. Gordon, director of the ETS Institute for Urban and Minority Education; and Robert L. Ebel, a former ETS vice president. See *Standards for Educational and Psychological Tests*, (Washington: American Psychological Association, 1974).

86. National Academy of Sciences-National Research Council, Assembly of Behavioral and Social Sciences, "Committee on Ability Testing," October 1979; *Examiner*, October 5, 1978, p. 1. The 20 National Academy of Sciences Committee on Ability Testing members included ETS Vice President E. Belvin Williams, former ETS trustee William J. McGill, former ETS researcher Melvin Novick, and former ETS consultants or advisory board members Lee J. Cronbach, Lyle V. Jones, and John W. Tukey. Barbara Lerner, the committee's former executive director, left in October 1978 to become the first ETS Visiting Scholar in Measurement and Public Policy; *Examiner*, October 5, 1978, p. 1.

87. ETS press release (untitled), July 31, 1979. States that Robert Solomon called for "a comprehensive study of proposed federal regulation of standardized testing," by the NAS panel.

88. Notes of Steve Solomon of NYPIRG on a meeting of College Board executives with student and consumer group representatives, July 28, 1978. The estimate of 28,000 was made by Sidney Marland.

89. Turnbull, "Public and Professional Attitudes Toward Testing and ETS," p. 7.

90. Ibid.

91. Ibid., p. 2.

92. Ibid., p. 6.

93. Ibid.

APPENDIX I

ETS Candidate Volume

APPENDIX I

ESTIMATED NUMBER OF INDIVIDUALS TESTED BY ETS, 1948-79

Estimates of the number of individuals tested annually by ETS from 1948-49 through 1978-79 are presented below. These figures sum to over 100 million. The information comes from ETS *Annual Reports* and other ETS documents (see listing of sources below). The figures do not include the number of individuals who used the ETS financial analysis services or the number listed in ETS research files. Nor do these figures include all ETS test programs. (See the explanatory notes following the chart.)

YEAR	NUMBER OF CANDIDATES TESTED
1948-49	767,625
1949-50	378,575
1950-51	644,826
1951-52	325,785
1952-53	327,979
1953-54	334,832
1954-55	355,818
1955-56	496,552
1956-57	646,767
1957-58	823,067
1958-59	1,185,813
1959-60	1,847,616
1960-61	2,163,263
1961-62	2,561,242
1962-63	2,784,639
1963-64	3,416,566
1964-65	3,723,082
1965-66	4,020,471
1966-67	3,748,996
1967-68	4,200,000
1968-69	4,600,000
1969-70	5,000,000
1970-71	5,499,820
1971-72	5,419,063
1972-73	5,900,000
1973-74	6,400,000
1974-75	6,938,300
1975-76	6,209,000/7,200,000 ?
1976-77	5,455,600/6,900,000 ?
1977-78	7,100,000 ?
1978-79	7,400,000 ?

Explanatory Notes

Volume figures for "candidates tested" are given by program in ETS documents. In general, when adding these figures to obtain an annual total, obvious overlaps were eliminated, e.g., the number of candidates listed as having taken the Achievement Tests, the Advanced Placement Tests, and the college "Writing Sample" were not counted since nearly all of them would have been included in the number listed as having taken the SAT. Nevertheless, the number of candidates may slightly overstate the number of individuals tested since some people take the tests more than once or take several tests in the same year. Notes on the totals in particular years are given below.

1961-62	The _Annual Report_ gives figures for "tests administered" rather than "candidates tested."
1967-70 and 1972-73	Because only incomplete public information on candidate volume was available, these figures are estimates calculated by averaging the differences between the preceding and subsequent years.
1974-75	This figure is understated because the source, _ETS In Fact_, an ETS brochure, does not list all test programs. It omits, for example, most occupational tests.
1975-76 and 1976-77	The first figures in the pairs are from editions of _ETS In Fact_. These editions list even fewer programs than does the edition covering 1974-75. The 1978 edition, which has 1976-77 volume figures, does not include, for example, the GED high school equivalency exam which was taken by over 500,000 people in 1974-75 (_ETS In Fact_). _ETS In Fact_ also omits the Multistate Bar Exam, occupational tests, and the Teacher Education Examination Program. Because these figures are incomplete, we have also given estimates of total volume. The second numbers in the pairs are estimates calculated from the rate of growth in certain reported programs. The growth rate for candidate volume in the SAT, GRE, GMAT, and LSAT is calculated; the total volume figure for the first year is then increased by this percentage amount and rounded off to yield an estimate for the second year. (From 1974-75 to 1975-76, the growth rate was +3.2%; in the following year it was -4.3%.)
1977-78 and 1978-79	Information on candidate volume in the SAT, GRE, GMAT, and LSAT is available. The estimating procedure outlined in the previous note is followed.

SOURCES

Sources: Information for the years 1948-49 through 1966-67 is from the ETS Annual Report for that year. See the following pages: 1948-49, p.22; 1949-50, pp. 43-44; 1950-51, p. 48; 1951-52, p. 48; 1952-53, p. 51; 1953-54, pp. 53-54; 1954-55, pp. 90-93; 1955-56, pp. 96-99; 1956-57, pp. 52-58; 1957-58, pp. 58-63; 1958-59, pp. 58-63; 1959-60, pp. 52-57; 1960-61, pp. 52-57; 1961-62, pp. 64-70; 1962-63, pp. 56-62; 1963-64, pp. 78-84; 1964-65, pp. 79-86; 1965-66, pp. 55-62; 1966-67, pp. 51-56.
After that year, ETS stopped publishing candidate volume figures except for a few of its programs. Figures for the years 1967-68 through 1969-70 and 1972-73 through 1973-74 are estimates based on interpolations from the volume figures for the preceding and following years. Figures for 1970-71 and 1971-72 are from internal ETS memorandums which report volume for all programs. See J. McBride and K. Landgraf, "Summary of Program Directors' Volume Estimates for 1971-72" [internal ETS memo], October 20, 1971, to Officers, Division Directors and others (contains figures on actual volume in 1970-71); and S. Kimberly, "Summary of Program Directors' Volume Estimates for 1972-73" [internal ETS memo], September 11, 1972, to Officers, Division Directors, and others (contains figures on actual volume in 1971-72). Figures for 1974-75 through 1976-77 come from ETS In Fact, an annual brochure. This brochure gives figures for only a sampling of ETS programs. In recent years it has included fewer and fewer programs. Hence total volume figures for these years are understated. An estimating procedure, based on growth in the SAT, GRE, GMAT and LSAT, is used to calculate total volume in the years 1975-1979 (see the notes above). Information on those four programs comes from the Annual Reports (1976, pp. 18-19; 1977, pp. 16-17; 1978, pp. 7-8) and from ETS, "Legislation on Standardized Testing," (circa Fall, 1979). This five-page memo distributed to the press contains information on 1978-79 candidate volume in the SAT, GRE, GMAT, and LSAT programs (p.2).

APPENDIX II

ETS Test Development Personnel

Staff Allocations for ETS Test Development Offices, May 1978

Source: "Cost Center Organization Charts, May 1978"
Elementary and Secondary School Programs (Cost Center 3142)

1 Director of Test Development
2 Senior Examiners
2 Examiners
2 Associate Examiners
3 Assistant Examiners
2 Statistical Associates
2 Program Administrators
1 Administrative Associate
3 Administrative Assistants
8 Secretaries   Total Number of Examiners: 9

College Board Test Development (Cost Center 4122)

1 Director of Test Development
5 Senior Examiners
4 Examiners
8 Associate Examiners
5 Assistant Examiners
1 Administrative Associate
1 Administrative Assistant
6 Secretaries   Total Number of Examiners: 22

Higher Education and Career Programs (HECP) Test Development
(Cost Center 5122)

1 Director of Test Development
2 Associate Directors
10 Senior Examiners
6 Examiners
10 Associate Examiners
3 Administrative Assistants
11 Secretaries   Total Number of Examiners: 26

HECP Center for Occupational and Professional Assessment:
(Cost Center 5155)   (Test Development Staff only)

Health Programs

1 Senior Examiner
3 Associate Examiners
1 Assistant Examiner

Government, Occupational and Personnel Management Programs:

1 Senior Examiner
1 Examiner
1 Associate Examiner
2 Assistant Examiners   Total Number of Examiners: 10

Grand Total of Examiners On ETS Staff: 67
Total Size of ETS Staff: 2000

ELEMENTARY & SECONDARY SCHOOL PROGRAMS

JULY 1, 1978

PROGRAM ADMINISTRATION & SYSTEMS
COST CENTERS 3141, 3142, 3144

- E.D. WILLIAMS — SR VICE PRESIDENT
- J.R. CHILDRESS — VICE PRESIDENT

3141
- J. WEISBRODT — DIVISION DIRECTOR
- P. BELICA — DIV DIR PROGR ADMIN
- ADMINISTRATIVE ASSOCIATE

3141 — EVALUATION AND INSTRUCTIONAL MATERIALS & SERVICES

- G. BOGATZ — ACTING PROGRAM AREA DIRECTOR
- A. GERB — ASSOC PROGRAM DIRECTOR
- C. BROLDY — ADMINISTRATIVE ASSOCIATE
- D. OHARA — ADMINISTRATIVE SECRETARY
- G. MORELAND — CLERICAL TYPIST

PROGRAMS FOR VOCATIONAL EDUCATION
- R. WASDYKE — PROGRAM DIRECTOR
- B. SLAUGHTER — ASSOC PROGRAM DIRECTOR
- P. VITELLA — ASSOC PROGRAM DIRECTOR
- V. MADARA — SECRETARY

3141 — ASSESSMENT AND EVALUATION PROGRAMS

- J. GOODISON — PROGRAM AREA DIRECTOR
- W. SCHABACKER — PROGRAM DIRECTOR
- K. SORIERO — ADMIN ASST
- D. RASKE — PROGRAM DIRECTOR
- D. MAKSYMOVICH — SUPV OPNS CLERICAL
- E. CAREY — SECRETARY
- C. DYER — PROGRAM DIRECTOR
- C. WEINER — ASST PROGR DIR
- H. BUTLER — SECRETARY

CONSOLIDATED PROGRAMS SERVICE GROUP
- J. GOODISON — AREA DIRECTOR
- L. FEIGERT — PROGRAM DIRECTOR
- R. ARCIERI — ADMIN ASSOC
- D. WENE — SECRETARY

3141 — INDEPENDENT SCHOOL AND GOVERNMENT PROGRAMS

- J. WOE — PROGRAM AREA DIRECTOR
- E. DALTON — ASSOC PROGR DIR
- S. SHERWIN — ASSOC PROGR DIR
- J. BARTELS — ADMIN ASSOC
- S. REMBE — SECRETARY
- T. ST. CLAIR — SECRETARY
- S. ROESER — PROGRAM DIRECTOR
- P. WHITEHORNE — ASST PROGR DIR
- Z. HARGRAVE — ADMIN ASST
- P. BALLARD — SECRETARY

3142 — TEST DEVELOPMENT

- J. FREMER — DIR TEST DEVELOPMENT
- F. SWINEFORD — STATISTICAL ASSOCIATE
- W. CASE — STATISTICAL ASSOCIATE
- M. SHERMAN — PROGRAM ADMINISTRATOR
- J. TCHORNI — PROGRAM ADMINISTRATOR
- A. MC ALOON — SR EX MATH/SCI.
- M. ZIEKY — SR EX COMM SKILLS
- C. CASAO — EXAMINER
- E. ROBINSON — EXAMINER
- J. DASS — ASSOC EXAMINER
- M. FOWLES — ASSOC EXAMINER
- H. BROCKMAN — ASST EXAMINER
- N. JOHNSON — ASST EXAMINER
- R. WALKER — ASST EXAMINER
- E. CLENSON — ADMINISTRATIVE ASSOCIATE
- D. MAZZA — ADMINISTRATIVE ASSISTANT
- E. KALAPOS — ADMINISTRATIVE ASSISTANT
- V. WALKER — ADMINISTRATIVE ASSISTANT
- S. DUBY — SECRETARY
- M. ISPANKY — SECRETARY
- C. JOHNSON — SECRETARY
- P. KELLY — SECRETARY
- A. MILLER — SECRETARY
- R. MORTENSEN — SECRETARY
- M. SCHWARTZ — SECRETARY
- J. ZAHN — SECRETARY

3144 — SYSTEMS

- F. RUGGIERO — DIRECTOR
- R. KERSHAW — SR STF SYS ANALYST
- R. KATNER — STF SYS ANALYST
- D. BOONE — SR PROG ANALYST
- T. MANN — PROG ANALYST
- T. HARTLEY — PROG ANALYST
- V. MATTHEWS — PROG ANALYST
- G. SCHEIDELL — PROG ANALYST
- S. ZUCCARELLI — SYSTEMS ANALYST
- J. FOX — PROGRAMMER
- J. REVERE — PROGRAMMER
- G. CULP — SECRETARY
- P. BANNISTER — TECH ASST

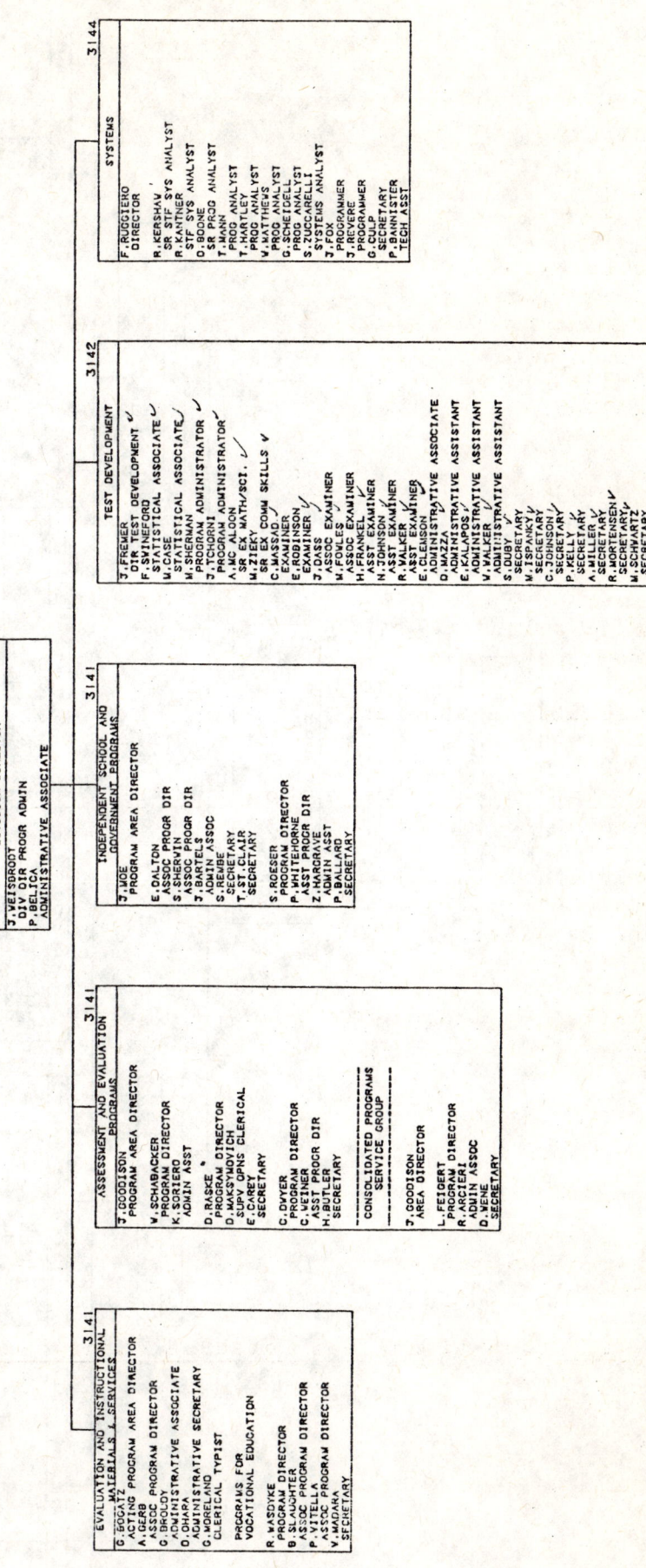

COLLEGE BOARD TEST DEVELOPMENT

COST CENTER 4122

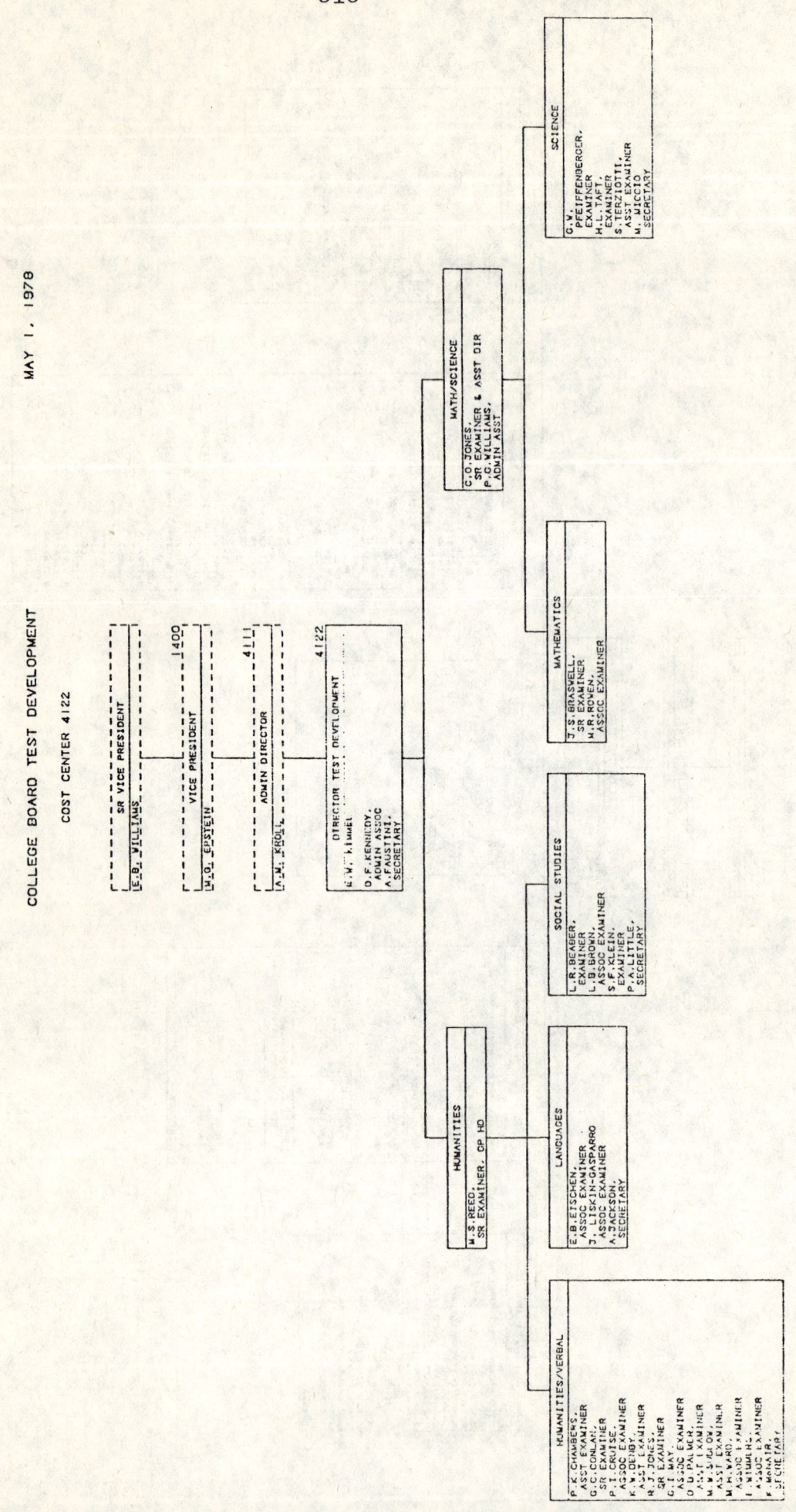

MAY 1, 1978

- SR VICE PRESIDENT — E.B. WILLIAMS
- VICE PRESIDENT — 1400 — L.O. EPSTEIN
- ADMIN DIRECTOR — 4111 — A.M. KROLL

DIRECTOR TEST DEVELOPMENT — 4122
E.W. KIMMEL
D.F. KENNEDY, ADMIN ASSOC
A. FAUSTINI, SECRETARY

HUMANITIES
M.S. REED, SR EXAMINER, OP HD

LANGUAGES
- E.B. EISCHEN, ASSOC EXAMINER
- J. LISKIN-GASPARRO, ASSOC EXAMINER
- A. JACKSON, SECRETARY

HUMANITIES/VERBAL
- P.K. CHAMBERS, ASST EXAMINER
- G.C. CONLAN, SR EXAMINER
- P.I. CRUISE, ASSOC EXAMINER
- K.W. DEINDY, ASST EXAMINER
- H.J. JONES, SR EXAMINER
- G. —, ASSOC EXAMINER
- D.D. PALMER, —
- M.W. SIGLOW, ASST EXAMINER
- M.H. WARD, ASSOC EXAMINER
- I. WIGGINS, ASSOC EXAMINER
- P. MCNAIR, SECRETARY

SOCIAL STUDIES
- L.R. BEABER, EXAMINER
- L.B. BROWN, ASSOC EXAMINER
- S.F. KLEIN, EXAMINER
- P.A. LITTLE, SECRETARY

MATH/SCIENCE
C.O. JONES, SR EXAMINER & ASST DIR
P.O. WILLIAMS, ADMIN ASST

MATHEMATICS
- J.S. BRASWELL, SR EXAMINER
- M.R. ROVEN, ASSOC EXAMINER

SCIENCE
- G.W. PFEIFFENBERGER, EXAMINER
- H.L. TAFT, EXAMINER
- S. TERZIOTTI, ASST EXAMINER
- M. VICCIO, SECRETARY

HECP PROFESSIONAL SERVICES

MAY 1, 1978

COST CENTERS 5101, 5122, 5133, 5144

```
┌─────────────────┐
│ E.D. WILLIAMS   │
│ SR VICE PRESIDENT│
└─────────────────┘
         │
┌─────────────────┐
│ R.L. BURNS      │
│ VICE PRESIDENT  │
└─────────────────┘
         │
┌─────────────────────────┐
│ HECP PROFESSIONAL SERVICES│
│ C. DAVES                │
│ DIRECTOR                │
└─────────────────────────┘
```

5122 — TEST DEVELOPMENT
- P. WOODFORD — DIRECTOR
- A. PICARD — SECRETARY
- M. LEVIN — ASSOC DIRECTOR
- M. McPEEK — ASSOC DIRECTOR
- C. CLAUSS — ADMINISTRATIVE ASSISTANT
- D. JACKSON — SECRETARY

APTITUDE - HUMANITIES
- M. LEVIN — SR EXAM GP HD
- S. JACKSON — SR EXAMINER
- C. TUCKER — EXAMINER
- R. ADAMS — ASSOC EXAMINER
- S. CARLTON — EXAMINER
- C. CHALIFOUR — ASSOC EXAMINER
- R. EBERT — ASSOC EXAMINER
- M. MARGOSIAN — SECRETARY
- S. CIRCH — SECRETARY

EDUCATION - SOCIAL SCIENCE
- J. MATTEL — SR EXAM GP HD
- B. HUMPHRY — SR EXAMINER
- E. WEDLINSKY — EXAMINER
- F. MEREDITH — SR EXAMINER
- A. CRAMER — EXAMINER
- C. NELSON — EXAMINER
- J. FINELLI — ASSOC EXAMINER
- C. SLAUGHTER — ASSOC EXAMINER
- L. NOLAN — ADMIN ASST
- M. BYRD — ASST
- S. GRZIELNIEK — SECRETARY
- D. HENDRICKS — SECRETARY

FOREIGN LANGUAGES
- J. CLARK — SR EXAMINER
- S. STILLER — EXAMINER
- E. LeBARON — ASSOC EXAMINER
- D. ROBINSON — SECRETARY

MATHEMATICS
- T. WILLIAMS — SR EXAM GP HD
- J. McGRATH — EXAMINER
- C. RUE — ASSOC EXAMINER
- B. STARK — SECRETARY

SCIENCE
- F. FORNOFF — SR EXAM GP HD
- B. PIKE — SR EXAMINER
- R. THOMPSON — SR EXAMINER
- R. DeVORE — ASSOC EXAMINER
- G. SANDERS — ASSOC EXAMINER
- M. WARREN — SECRETARY
- E. BYRAM — SECRETARY

5133 — STATISTICAL ANALYSIS
- E. STEWART — DIRECTOR
- R. LaGRUTTA — ADMINISTRATIVE ASSISTANT
- B. PITCHER — SR STATISTICAL ASSOC
- M. WALLMARK — SR STATISTICAL ASSOC
- N. WEXLER — SR STATISTICAL ASSOC
- V. COVELL — STATISTICAL ASSOCIATE
- J. FAGGEN — STATISTICAL ASSOCIATE
- L. WIGHTMAN — STATISTICAL ASSOCIATE
- E. COLCOUGH — STATISTICAL ASSISTANT
- J. DRAKE — STATISTICAL ASSISTANT
- R. DURSO — STATISTICAL ASSISTANT
- J. CRAVENER — STATISTICAL ASSISTANT
- C. SKELTON — STATISTICAL ASSISTANT
- P. AVERRE — STATISTICAL AIDE
- J. CLARE — STATISTICAL AIDE
- B. MARK — SECRETARY
- M. PARKINSON — SECRETARY

5101 — EDITORIAL SERVICES
- R. MILLER — DIRECTOR
- N. PARR — SR EDITOR
- M. KOZMA — ASST EDITOR

5144 — SYSTEMS
- L. TOMPKINS — DIRECTOR
- A. VERNON — SECRETARY
- D. SPADY — SECRETARY

LAW PROGRAMS
- P. LaHOLT — SR STF SYS ANA
- M. JACZKO — SR SYS ANALYST
- SR PROG ANALYST

GMAT, GSFLT
- F. VAN DER LEE — STF SYS ANA
- E. JONES — SR SYS ANALYST
- F. SCHOENTHALER — SR PROG ANALYST
- K. FINCH — PROG ANALYST
- F. McILVAINE — SYSTEMS ANALYST

PROJECT SERVICES
- V. CLARE — STF SYS ANA
- J. ROBINOVITZ — STF PROG ANALYST
- L. CAMERON — STF SYS ANALYST
- C. ZINK — STF SYS ANALYST
- K. BUTLER — SR PROG ANALYST
- M. VACHHARAJANI — SR SYS ANALYST
- R. NETZ — PROG ANALYST

LANGUAGE PROGRAM
- R. McKINLEY — STF SYS ANALYST

GMAT, NTE
- R. HUNTER — STF SYS ANA
- J. SILVESTRO — PROG ANALYST

PROGRAMMING SERVICES
- R. IMATO — SR STF PROG ANA
- C. HOFFMAN — SR PROG ANALYST
- J. KRAINSKI — PROG ANALYST
- C. KRAMER — PROG ANALYST
- J. DOMINICK — PROGRAMMER
- B. PHILLIPS — PROGRAMMER
- C. CRUSER — TECH ASST

HECP CENTER FOR OCCUPATIONAL AND PROFESSIONAL
ASSESSMENT
COST CENTER 5155

MAY 1, 1978

SR VICE PRESIDENT
F.J. VILLAMS

VICE PRESIDENT
R.L. BURNS

COPA
A. MASLOW — DIRECTOR
J. HOUIS — MANAGING DIRECTOR
A. SCHAUGER — AREA FINANCIAL ANALYST
C. KALOKITIS — STAFF ASSOCIATE
C. LUMIA — STAFF ASSOCIATE
J. PELLATON — DIR COPA EDITORIAL SRVCS
D. SAVARY — SECRETARY
B. CISNEY — TEXT PROCESSING SECRETARY

PERSONNEL EVALUATION
O. JENSEN — SR EXAMINER

SPECIAL PROJECTS
U. SHTUBERG — DIR. SPECIAL PROJ.
O. BROWN — ADMINISTRATIVE SECRETARY

TECHNICAL SERVICES
A. CARLSON — DIRECTOR
S. TRAVIA — STAFF PROGRAMMING ANALYST
B. ALLEN — SR PROGRAMMING ANALYST
M. BINKLEY — SR PROGRAMMING ANALYST
R. MARDISAN — STATISTICS ANALYST
J. MITTENHOFER — PROGRAMMING ANALYST
R. TOTH — PROGRAMMER
C. CONSTANTINI — STATISTICAL ASSISTANT
P. NUCHES — STAFF ASSOCIATE
R. MACHUSAK — TECHNICAL ASSISTANT

HEALTH PROGRAMS
T. FRIEDMAN — PROGR.DIR.GROUP HEAD
C. SCHOLL (SIO) ?
A. SHARON — STAFF ASSOCIATE
R. SMITH — PROGRAM DIRECTOR
J. WOOD — PROGR DIRECTOR
R. VARNER — SR PROG RES ASSOC
J. TIMMINS — PROJECT DIRECTOR
B. GRONIKOWSKI — PROGR. DIRECTOR
V. KASTRINOS — ASST. PROGR. DIRECTOR
S. BOCCHIERI — ASSOC EXAMINER
B. COHEN — ASSOC EXAMINER
S. MAGGIO — ASSOC EXAMINER
S. CARLSON — ASST EXAMINER
P. BERWICK — STAFF ASSOCIATE
J. ZITO — STAFF ASSOCIATE
P. HAMMER — ADMINISTRATIVE ASSISTANT
D. DERVIN — PROGRAM ASSISTANT
N. DECK — SECRETARY
O. DERWIN — SECRETARY
Y. FOSTER — SECRETARY
L. LENZ — SECRETARY
J. MCALLISTER — SECRETARY

GOVERNMENT, OCCUPATIONAL AND PERSONNEL MANAGEMENT PROGRAMS
E. WANWARING — PROGRAM DIRECTOR
L. SENECA — PROGRAM DIRECTOR
E. GLOSSBRENNER — ASST. PROGR. DIRECTOR
M. PACK — ASST PROGR DIRECTOR
C. BARR — PROFESSIONAL ASSOCIATE
L. CROOKS — PROGR. RESEARCH SCI.
R. FLAUGHER — PROGR. RESEARCH SCI.
M. ROSENFELD — PROGR. RESEARCH SCI.
R. THORNTON — PROGR. RESEARCH SCI.
L. NORRIS — ASSOC PROGRAM RES SCI.
S. LIVINGSTON — ASSOC. PROGR. RESEARCH SCI.
R. GLAZER — SR PROGRAM RES ASST
C. MEREDITH — SR EXAMINER
G. MONCRIEF — EXAMINER
C. STEN — ASSOC EXAMINER
E. TURNER — ASST EXAMINER
K. FARRELL — STAFF ASSOCIATE
R. HUFF — STAFF ASSOCIATE
L. KELLNER — ADMINISTRATIVE ASSISTANT
J. FARMER — ADMINISTRATIVE ASSISTANT
O. POLIZZI — PROGRAM ASSISTANT
J. HAMILTON — ADMINISTRATIVE SECRETARY
A. MOORE — ADMINISTRATIVE SECRETARY
S. RONDINELLI — ADMINISTRATIVE SECRETARY
P. LEAGERT — SECRETARY
O. EICHINGER — SECRETARY
D. GUMIENNY — SECRETARY
E. WYNINGS — SECRETARY

VOCATIONAL AND TECHNICAL PROGRAMS
L. VALRFO — PROGRAM DIRECTOR
C. TERYEK — PROGRAM DIRECTOR
V. HOGAN — ASST. PROGR. DIRECTOR
E. PEARSON — ASST PROGR DIRECTOR
M. PEABODY — STAFF ASSOCIATE
R. RAMOS — SECRETARY
S. REED — SECRETARY

APPENDIX III

An Analysis of Questions Exemplifying Cultural Bias
from
David M. White

WHOM DO YOU TRUST?
David M. White

Look carefully at the following question. Do you see an ambiguity in it which could cause SAT candidates from low status backgrounds or with certain political perspectives to systematically choose the same wrong answer?

From the first the islanders, despite an outward ----------, did what they could to ---------- the ruthless occupying power.

(A) harmony . . assist

(B) enmity . . embarrass

(C) rebellion . . foil

(D) resistance . . destroy

(E) acquiescence . . thwart

Since most readers are probably relatively certain of their answer, and since much bias is unconscious, few readers are likely to notice two answers which could seem plausible to different groups. These statistics should help you. The chart divides 300 students into equal fifths of 60 according to their overall score on the SAT. It also indicates how many students in each group chose each option.

RESPONSES	LOWEST FIFTH	NEXT LOWEST FIFTH	MIDDLE FIFTH	NEXT HIGHEST FIFTH	HIGHEST FIFTH
Omit		2	4	1	
A				1	
B	4	1			
C	10	7	2		2
D	37	28	16	8	3
E	9	22	38	50	55
Total	60	60	60	60	60

As can be readily seen, the big argument is between those who chose (D) and those who chose (E). Only 1 student chose (A), despite otherwise high test results. Only 5 students chose (B), all from the lowest two-fifths on the total test. Option (C) was somewhat more attractive, drawing 19 of the 300 students. In contrast, the attraction of option (D) is remarkable, with almost a third of the students choosing it.

We are able to make such a careful analysis of this question because it is contained in a booklet entitled "Multiple-Choice Questions: A Close Look," published in 1963 by the Educational Testing Service which develops the SAT. As the ETS authors explain this question: "Examination of the question should indicate that the answer involves two words which are, in a sense, opposite in meaning, since the word 'despite' carries with it the implication that the islanders acted in one fashion, while presenting a somewhat different impression to the 'ruthless occupying power.' With this relationship in mind, (A), (B), (C), and (D) can be eliminated since all of those answers fail to give the sense of contrast that is required."

Yet this explanation fails to answer our main puzzle--Why did most wrong answers indicate (D) if similar logic should have prompted candidates to choose (A), (B), or (C) instead? The ETS explanation is not helpful, since the first three options are disproven with a sentence each, whereas "The same logic holds for 'resistance . . destroy'." is the only text devoted to (D). The results, however, make one suspect that more than logic was involved in the widespread selection of (D).

The key to our puzzle may lie in the perspective of the reader answering the option. Although few readers would identify themselves as members of a "ruthless occupying power," the perspective of the answer (E)--as well as of the explanation given by ETS for the question--is clearly through the eyes of the powerful and not through those of the islanders. Yet it is possible to imagine the sentence in the question as part of a tale told by the islanders.

Almost as soon as the last shot of conquest was fired, the conquerors began to impose their will on the defeated islanders. Soldiers enforced curfews and checked newly-issued ID cards. Political meetings which might give voice to the frustrations of villagers were banned--even the ritualistic ceremonies of the priests were monitored to avoid any mention of political uprising.

Yet political activity did not cease. From the first the islanders, despite an outward resistance, did what they could to destroy the ruthless occupying power. Children taunted the soldiers; adults whispered of an impending uprising.

Whether such a story was running through the unconscious imagination of students answering (D) is impossible to say without personal interviews. Yet is seems clear that the students did not expect the islanders to be duplicitous-- as those scoring the question apparently did. Instead they may have been predisposed to see a conflict facing the islanders. The word "despite" need not carry with it the implication that two words must have opposite meanings, it may also imply opposition between the islanders and the actions of the ruthless occupying power. The reader can try to understand this predisposition by substituting a group with which they personally feel empathy, such as the Polish Resistance or the Irish Republican Army, for the islanders.

A similar situation may appear in a sample question of the Law School Admission Test (LSAT). The question concerns "Samuel Williams, the black manager of a retail shoe store in a large midwestern city,... interested in opening his own business." A 109-line reading passage describes his dilemma of trying to accumulate investment capital while keeping the business ownership among members of the community. "He predicted that these stockholders would bring their business to the store and would encourage their friends to do the same." In addition, the passage notes that "the store was to be located in a business district occupied predominantly by black-owned and black-operated establishments." Just as the store is about to open he has accumulated only one-half the needed capital and faces a decision. As the last paragraph explains: "Williams was reluctant to begin operation of the store without sufficient capital to cover unforeseen problems in operation. However, he was even more convinced that the store would be successful only if it were controlled by community members. He therefore chose the last alternative."

Candidates are given six different statements and asked to classify each as a (A) Major Objective, (B) Major Factor, (C) Minor Factor, (D) Major Assumption, or (E) Unimportant Issue in making the decision. The fifth statement is: "Value of establishing the store's reputation as a community enterprise." The correct designation is (D) Major Assumption and the explanation given makes it clear that a careful reading of the statement is necessary, since "it is the value of the reputation that is at issue and not the reputation itself." To those accustomed to thinking in terms of a corporate framework of value, this explanation may be persuasive.

Yet there may be a value <u>to the community</u> of establishing the store's reputation as a community enterprise. This might be true if only for the symbolic value of demonstrating that a black-owned shoe store is possible. This might be particularly poignant for a black man who has been a "manager of a retail shoe store" but not yet an owner. The value may also strengthen the entire community's reputation as an area in which black-owned businesses exist. If one read the question with this perspective, identifying the statement as a Major Objective would seem plausible. In contrast, the explanation offered would only recognize the statement "Establishing store's reputation as a community enterprise" as a Major Objective. Yet even this similar statement would contain potential bias. Those familiar with a community in which black-owned businesses existed may recognize that local residents are reluctant to patronize a store which is owned by absentee owners even if a "black manager" is prominent on the premises. For those candidates, the designation as a Major Factor would seem plausible.

In either the actual question or a similar hypothetical statement mentioned in the sample book's explanation of the question, the potential of bias against candidates familiar with black-owned businesses exists. There is considerable irony if such a biased pattern of responses were revealed in an item analysis similar to the one provided for the "islanders" question. In this case, the question would have been written with the express purpose of providing reading material relevant to the experience of black candidates. Yet the potential bias arises precisely because of that relevance. Black candidates may have been penalized because of their familiarity with the situation of establishing a community-owned enterprise and their perspective which differs from that of the majority of candidates who continue to view the value of establishing a store's reputation as a community enterprise as an assumption--in part because that assumption has not been tried during the actual experiences of the majority of candidates.

In both of these questions, then, the question arises whether those who fail the question fail because they lack relevant skills in "verbal aptitude" or "data analysis" as the test section names imply. It is possible that some fail because their perspectives on a question differ because their experiences differ. If further analysis confirms these suggestions, then a further dimension of "cultural bias" in testing will have been established. Unfortunately, the possibility of such bias does not surface in published explanations of sample questions on the SAT and the LSAT, raising the further danger that similar unconscious bias persists among those questions not published nor explained.

APPENDIX IV

ETS and College Board Financial Documents

40 COLLEGE BD PROG & SERVICES

PROJECT OPERATING STATEMENT
BY POS-CATEGORY / PROJECT
MARCH 1977
(IN THOUSANDS OF DOLLARS)

PAGE 1
FIS540A7
RUN 04/19/77

CURR MONTH ACTUAL			YEAR TO DATE ACTUAL					YEAR TO DATE BUDGET			FULL YEAR BUDGET			% EXP
INC	EXP	NET	INC	11	10	1	110-17		INC	EXP	NET	INC	EXP	NET	YTD
7	6	1						ESSAY READING PROGRAM							
								PREVIOUS YEAR ACTUAL							
								ITD ACTUAL / CONTR. CEILING							
730	684	46	9,113	8,036	1,077		110	ADMISSIONS PROGRAM ADM.	10,098	8,850	1,248	12,396	10,864	1,532	73
611	536	75	8,500	7,456	1,044			PREVIOUS YEAR ACTUAL				11,490	10,079	1,411	73
			9,264—	8,148—	7,412—			ITD ACTUAL / CONTR. CEILING							
1	1		5	4	1		115	ADMISSIONS PROGRAM-PUERTO RICO	5	4	1	6	5	1	78
			4	4				PREVIOUS YEAR ACTUAL				3	3		119
			4—		8—			ITD ACTUAL / CONTR. CEILING							
							117	COLLEGE LOCATER SERVICE							
								PREVIOUS YEAR ACTUAL							
								ITD ACTUAL / CONTR. CEILING							
2	2		20	18	2		119	INSTITUTIONAL SERVICES	18	15	2	24	21	3	83
2	2		12	11	2			PREVIOUS YEAR ACTUAL				17	15	2	70
			11—	10	21—			ITD ACTUAL / CONTR. CEILING							
15	15		312	275	37		120	ATP TEST CONSTRUCTION	321	282	40	444	389	55	70
39	34	5	223	196	27			PREVIOUS YEAR ACTUAL				332	291	41	67
			213—	187	400—			ITD ACTUAL / CONTR. CEILING							
	1	1—	124	109	15		130	ATP ANALYTICAL	156	139	17	194	173	22	63
20	17	2	142	125	17			PREVIOUS YEAR ACTUAL				183	161	22	77
			137—	120	257—			ITD ACTUAL / CONTR. CEILING							
5	5		43	38	5		140	APPLIED RESEARCH	46	41	6	68	59	8	64
10	9	1	58	51	7			PREVIOUS YEAR ACTUAL				75	66	9	77
			54—	48	102—			ITD ACTUAL / CONTR. CEILING							
18	17	2	140	124	17		142	APPLIED RESEARCH	189	170	19	247	221	26	56
18	16	2	95	84	12			PREVIOUS YEAR ACTUAL				144	126	18	66
			84—	74	157—			ITD ACTUAL / CONTR. CEILING							
26	24	2	234	206	28		150	CEEB PROGRAM ADMINISTRATION	236	211	25	321	286	35	72
31	27	4	258	227	32			PREVIOUS YEAR ACTUAL				332	291	41	77
			253—	222	475—			ITD ACTUAL / CONTR. CEILING							
59	53	6	330	291	39		164	STUDENT SEARCH SERVICE	365	320	45	490	430	60	67
64	56	8	280	246	34			PREVIOUS YEAR ACTUAL				369	324	45	75
			240—	211	450—			ITD ACTUAL / CONTR. CEILING							
2	2		96	85	11		165	COLLEGE BOARD VALIDITY STUDIES	100	88	12	125	110	16	77
5	4	1	47	41	6			PREVIOUS YEAR ACTUAL				72	63	9	64
			48—	42	90—			ITD ACTUAL / CONTR. CEILING							

COLLEGE ENTRANCE EXAMINATION BOARD

Statement of Revenues, Expense and Fund Balance
Year Ended June 30, 1976
With Comparative Figures for 1975
and for 1977 Current Projections

	Actual 1974-75	Actual 1975-76	Current Projections 1976-77
Revenues			
Programs and Services			
Admissions Testing Program	$16,036,276	$16,260,652	$17,640,000
College Scholarship Service	8,473,349	10,073,548	10,508,000
College-Level Examination Program	2,775,571	2,962,842	2,954,000
Advanced Placement Program	2,378,307	2,743,120	3,322,000
PSAT/NMSQT	2,834,586	2,970,615	3,249,000
Student Search Service	1,301,802	1,863,551	1,835,000
Puerto Rico Programs	586,964	626,854	718,000
Comparative Guidance and Placement Prog.	393,761	447,140	489,000
Other	936,200	1,298,106	1,579,000
Grants and Contracts	4,692,798	3,743,678	3,073,000
Membership dues and meetings	393,675	399,202	397,000
Investments	199,713	243,979	225,000
Other	-	54,268	-
	$41,063,002	$43,687,555	$45,989,000
Expenses			
Programs and Services - Direct			
Admissions Testing Program	$12,550,541	$13,232,474	$14,099,000
College Scholarship Service	7,604,774	8,572,262	8,686,000
College-Level Examination Program	2,360,241	2,620,043	2,770,000
Advanced Placement Program	2,101,210	2,543,251	2,866,000
PSAT/NMSQT	1,658,821	1,719,939	1,840,000
Student Search Service	816,993	863,687	908,000
Puerto Rico Programs	500,094	569,908	726,000
Comparative Guidance and Placement Prog.	358,519	373,410	379,000
Other	1,068,589	269,882	461,000
Educational and Public Service Activities	2,807,169	2,665,938	1,811,000
Membership Services - Direct	486,158	491,338	494,000
Support Services			
Regional Office Operations	2,537,620	2,768,498	2,853,000
Publications	1,257,625	1,700,292	1,776,000
Research and Development	1,048,615	1,719,161	2,087,000
General and Administrative	1,846,801	2,164,781	2,717,000
Other	621,901	738,732	877,000
	$39,625,671	$43,013,596	$45,350,000
Excess of revenues over expenditures before cumulative effect of a change in accounting principle	$ 1,437,331	$ 673,959	$ 639,000
Cumulative effect to June 30, 1975 of changing the method of accounting for accounts receivable		921,344	
Net Increase in Total Fund Balance	$ 1,437,331	$ 1,595,303	$ 639,000
Expenditures included above charged to Research and Development Fund			400,000
Net Increase in General Fund Balance	$ 1,437,331	$ 1,595,303	$ 1,039,000
Fund Balance			
General Fund			
Beginning of year	$ 5,655,321	$ 6,342,652	$ 7,937,955
End of year	$ 7,092,652	$ 7,937,955	$ 8,976,955
Research and Development Fund			
Beginning of year		$ 750,000	$ 750,000
End of year		$ 750,000	$ 350,000
Total Fund Balance			
Beginning of year	$ 5,655,321	$ 7,092,652	$ 8,687,955
End of year	$ 7,092,652	$ 8,687,955	$ 9,326,955

September 22, 1976

COLLEGE ENTRANCE EXAMINATION BOARD

Statement of Revenues, Expenses and Fund Balance
Year Ended June 30, 1979
With Comparative Figures for 1977-78
and for 1979-80 Current Projections

	Actual 1977-78*	Actual 1978-79	Current Projections 1979-80
Revenues			
Fees for Programs and Services			
- Admissions Testing Program	$19,205,988	$21,478,660	$22,443,000
- College Scholarship Service	15,267,308	18,819,291	20,332,000
- Advanced Placement Program	3,719,224	4,228,966	5,008,000
- PSAT/NMSQT	3,423,228	3,719,620	4,008,000
- College-Level Examination Program	3,582,263	3,677,820	4,020,000
- Student Search Service	2,134,264	2,574,882	2,767,000
- Puerto Rico Programs	791,753	1,017,589	889,000
- Descriptive Tests	35,570	704,109	478,000
- Comparative Guidance and Placement Program	340,103	304,573	377,000
- Other	1,714,551	1,612,631	1,818,000
Grants and Contracts for Special Services	1,559,774	2,248,870	1,713,000
Membership dues and Meetings	425,697	456,909	507,000
Investment Income	218,702	187,903	225,000
Other	34,896	53,575	108,000
	$52,453,321	$61,085,398	$64,693,000
Expenses			
Programs and services:			
Direct:			
- Admissions Testing Program	$14,964,491	$17,553,540	$17,790,000
- College Scholarship Service	14,112,686	17,248,229	19,576,000
- Advanced Placement Program	3,055,702	3,630,054	4,215,000
- PSAT/NMSQT	1,595,835	1,838,045	1,904,000
- College-Level Examination Program	2,724,071	3,198,548	3,074,000
- Student Search Service	1,007,077	1,141,438	1,412,000
- Puerto Rico Programs	881,140	885,981	1,053,000
- Descriptive Tests	489,107	812,270	752,000
- Comparative Guidance and Placement Program	304,682	264,651	303,000
- Research and Development	1,589,339	2,314,852	2,675,000
- Educational Public Service	1,019,846	878,879	798,000
- Other	896,282	558,430	575,000
Unallocated			
- Regional Office Operations	3,189,223	3,524,511	3,943,000
- Publications	2,111,136	2,317,179	2,636,000
- Other	850,145	1,091,362	1,192,000
Membership Services	546,399	618,753	705,000
General Administration	2,511,100	2,920,181	2,988,000
	$51,848,261	$60,796,903	$65,591,000
Excess of Revenues over Expenses	$ 605,060	$ 288,495	$ (898,000)
Fund Balances			
Beginning of Year	$ 9,787,500	$10,392,560	$10,681,055
End of Year	$10,392,560	$10,681,055	$ 9,783,055

*Certain items in 1977-78 have been reclassified to conform to the 1978-79 presentation.

( ) denotes red figure

October 1, 1979

APPENDIX V

Truth-in-Testing

STATE OF NEW YORK

S. 5200—A
Cal. No. 1215

A. 7668—A

1979-1980 Regular Sessions

SENATE–ASSEMBLY

April 26, 1979

IN SENATE—Introduced by Sens. LaVALLE, ACKERMAN, BABBUSH, BARTOSIEWICZ, BEATTY, BERMAN, BERNSTEIN, BRUNO, CAEMMERER, CONNOR, FLYNN, GALIBER, GOODHUE, HALPERIN, LACK, LEICHTER, MARKOWITZ, McCALL, MEGA, MENDEZ, OWENS, PADAVAN, PISANI, PRESENT, RUIZ, SOLOMON, TAURIELLO, TRUNZO, VOLKER, WINIKOW—read twice and ordered printed, and when printed to be committed to the Committee on Education—reported favorably from said committee and committed to the Committee on Higher Education—reported favorably from said committee, ordered to first and second report, ordered to a third reading, amended and ordered reprinted, retaining its place in the order of third reading

IN ASSEMBLY—Introduced by COMMITTEE ON RULES—(at request of M. of A. Vann, LaFayette, Bianchi, Boyland, Cochrane, Cooperman, Eve, Farrell, Flanagan, Fortune, Gottfried, Grannis, Griffith, Harenberg, Hinchey, Hirsch, Hochbrueckner, Howard, Jacobs, Jenkins, Koppell, Lentol, Lewis, Lipschutz, McCabe, G. W. Miller, Nine, Passannante, Pesce, Proud, Serrano, Siegel, E. C. Sullivan, Virgilio, D. B. Walsh, Yevoli, Zagame)—read once and referred to the Committee on Higher Education—reported and referred to the Committee on Ways and Means—committee discharged, bill amended, ordered reprinted as amended and recommitted to said committee

AN ACT to amend the education law, in relation to standardized testing

The People of the State of New York, represented in Senate and Assembly, do enact as follows:

1   Section 1. The education law is amended by adding a new article seven-A to
2   read as follows:
3   *ARTICLE 7-A*
4   *STANDARDIZED TESTING*
5   *Section 340. Definitions.*
6   *341. Background reports and statistical data.*
7   *342. Disclosure of test contents.*
8   *343. Notice.*
9   *344. Disclosure of test scores.*
10   *345. Regulations.*

EXPLANATION — Matter in *italics* is new; matter in brackets [ ] is old law to be omitted.

S. 5200—A   2   A. 7668—A

   346. Violations.
   347. Severability.
 § *340. Definitions. As used in this article:* 1. *"Standardized test" or "test" means any test that is given at the expense of the test subject and designed for use or used in the process of selection for post-secondary or professional school admissions. Such tests shall include, but are not limited to, the Preliminary Scholastic Aptitude Test, Scholastic Aptitude Test, ACT Assessment, Graduate Record Examination, Medical College Admission Test, Law School Admission Test, Dental Admission Testing Program, Graduate Management Admission Test, and Miller Analogies Test. This article shall not apply to any state, federal, or local civil service test, any test designed and used solely for non-admission placement or credit-by-examination, or any test developed and administered by an individual school or institution for its own purposes only.*
 2. *"Commissioner" means the commissioner of education of the state of New York.*
 3. *"Test subject" shall mean an individual to whom a test is administered.*
 4. *"Test agency" shall mean any organization, association, corporation, partnership, or individual or person that develops, sponsors or administers a test.*
 § *341. Background reports and statistical data.* 1. *Whenever any test agency prepares, causes to have prepared or provides the data which are used in any study, evaluation or statistical report pertaining to a test, such study, evaluation or report shall be filed with the commissioner.*
 2. *If any reports or other documents submitted pursuant to this section contains information identifiable with any individual test subject, such information shall be deleted or obliterated prior to submission.*
 3. *All data, reports or other documents submitted pursuant to this section shall be public records.*
 § *342. Disclosure of test contents.* 1. *Within thirty days after the results of any standardized test are released, the test agency shall file or cause to be filed in the office of the commissioner:*
 a. *a copy of all test questions used in calculating the test subject's raw score;*
 b. *the corresponding acceptable answers to those questions; and*
 c. *all rules for transferring raw scores into those scores reported to the test subject together with an explanation of such rules.*
 2. *After the test has been filed with the commissioner, and upon the request of the test subject, the test agency shall send to the test subject:*
 a. *a copy of the test questions used in determining the subject's raw score;*
 b. *the subject's individual answer sheet together with a copy of the correct answer sheet to the same test with questions counting toward the subject's raw score so marked; and*
 c. *a statement of the raw score used to calculate the scores already sent to the subject, provided that such request has been made within ninety days of the release of the test score to the test subject.*
 The agency may charge a nominal fee for sending out such information, not to exceed the direct cost of providing the information.
 3. *This section shall not apply to College Board Achievement Tests or GRE Advanced Tests.*
 4. *Documents submitted to the commissioner pursuant to this section shall be public records.*
 § *343. Notice.* 1. *Each test agency shall provide, along with the registration form for a test, the following information:*
 a. *The purposes for which the test is constructed and is intended to be used.*
 b. *The subject matters included on such test and the knowledge and skills which the test purports to measure.*

c. Statements designed to provide information for interpreting test results, including but not limited to, explanations of the test score scale, the standard error of measurement of the test, and a list of available correlations between test scores and grades, successful completion of a course of study and parental income.

d. How the test scores will be reported, whether the raw test scores will be altered in any way before being reported to the test subject and whether and how the test agency will use the test score in raw or transformed form by itself or together with any other information about the test subject to predict in any way the subject's future academic performance for any post secondary educational institution.

e. A complete description of any promises or covenants that the test agency makes to the test subject with regard to accuracy of scoring, timely forwarding of information, policies for notifying test subjects regarding inaccuracies in scoring or score reporting and privacy of information relating to the test subject.

f. Whether or not the test scores are the property of the test subject, how long they will be retained by the test agency, and policies regarding storage, disposal and future use of test score data.

2. Any institution which is a test score recipient shall be provided with the information specified in this section. The test agency shall provide such information prior to or coincident with the first reporting of a test score or scores to a recipient institution. Such institution shall be encouraged to provide interpretive processing by qualified personnel where such personnel are available.

§ 344. Disclosure of test scores. The score of any test subject shall not be released or disclosed by the test agency to any person, organization, corporation, association, college, university, or governmental agency or subdivision unless specifically authorized by the test subject. A test agency may, however, release all previous scores received by a test subject on a test to anyone designated by the test subject to receive the current score.

This section shall not be construed to prohibit release of scores and other information in the possession of a test agency for purposes of research leading to studies and reports concerning the tests themselves. Such studies and reports must contain no information identifiable with any individual test subject.

§ 345. Regulations. The commissioner shall promulgate regulations to implement the provisions of this article.

§ 346. Violations. Any test agency which violates any section of this article shall be liable for a civil penalty of not more than five hundred dollars for each violation.

§ 347. Severability. If any provision of this article shall be declared unconstitutional or invalid, the other provisions shall remain in effect notwithstanding.

§ 2. This act shall take effect on the first day of January next succeeding the date on which it shall have become a law.

96TH CONGRESS
1ST SESSION
H. R. 4949

To require certain information be provided to individuals who take standardized educational admissions tests, and for other purposes.

IN THE HOUSE OF REPRESENTATIVES

JULY 24, 1979

Mr. WEISS (for himself, Mrs. CHISHOLM, and Mr. MILLER of California) introduced the following bill; which was referred to the Committee on Education and Labor

A BILL

To require certain information be provided to individuals who take standardized educational admissions tests, and for other purposes.

1 *Be it enacted by the Senate and House of Representa-*
2 *tives of the United States of America in Congress assembled,*

3 SHORT TITLE

4 SECTION 1. This Act may be cited as the "Educational
5 Testing Act of 1979".

6 FINDINGS AND PURPOSE

7 SEC. 2. (a) The Congress of the United States finds
8 that—

(1) education is fundamental to the development of individual citizens and the progress of the Nation as a whole;

(2) there is a continuous need to ensure equal access for all Americans to educational opportunities of a high quality;

(3) standardized tests are a major factor in the admission and placement of students in postsecondary education and also play an important role in individuals' professional lives;

(4) there is increasing concern among citizens, educators, and public officials regarding the appropriate uses of standardized tests in the admissions decision of postsecondary education institutions;

(5) the rights of individuals and the public interest can be assured without endangering the proprietary rights of the testing agencies; and

(6) standardized tests are developed and administered without regard to State boundaries and are utilized on a national basis.

(b) It is the purpose of this Act—

(1) to ensure that test subjects and persons who use test results are fully aware of the characteristics, uses, and limitations of standardized tests in postsecondary education admissions;

(2) to make available to the public appropriate information regarding the procedures, development, and administration of standardized tests;

(3) to protect the public interest by promoting more knowledge about appropriate use of standardized test results and by promoting greater accuracy, validity, and reliability in the development, administration, and interpretation of standardized tests; and

(4) to encourage use of multiple criteria in the grant or denial of any significant educational benefit.

INFORMATION TO TEST SUBJECTS AND POSTSECONDARY EDUCATIONAL INSTITUTIONS

SEC. 3. (a) Each test agency shall provide to any test subject in clear and easily understandable language, along with the registration form for a test, the following information:

(1) The purposes for which the test is constructed and is intended to be used.

(2) The subject matters included on such test and the knowledge and skills which the test purports to measure.

(3) Statements designed to provide information for interpreting the test results, including explanations of the test, and the correlation between test scores and future success in schools and, in the case of tests used

for postbaccalaureate admissions, the standard error of measurement and the correlation between test scores and success in the career for which admission is sought.

(4) Statements concerning the effects on and uses of test scores, including—

    (A) if the test score is used by itself or with other information to predict future grade point average, the extent, expressed as a percentage, to which the use of this test score improves the accuracy of predicting future grade point average, over and above all other information used; and

    (B) a comparison of the average score and percentiles of test subjects by major income groups; and

    (C) the extent to which test preparation courses improve test subjects' scores on average, expressed as a percentage.

(5) A description of the form in which test scores will be reported, whether the raw test scores will be altered in any way before being reported to the test subject, and the manner, if any, the test agency will use the test score (in raw or transformed form) by itself or together with any other information about the test subject to predict in any way the subject's future aca-

demic performance for any postsecondary educational institution.

(6) A complete description of any promises or covenants that the test agency makes to the test subject with regard to accuracy of scoring, timely forwarding or score reporting, and privacy of information (including test scores and other information), relating to the test subjects.

(7) The property interests of the test subject in the test results, if any, the duration for which such results will be retained by the test agency, and policies regarding storage, disposal, and future use of test scores.

(8) The time period within which the test subject's test score will be completed and mailed to the test subject and the time period within which such scores will be mailed to test score recipients designated by the test subject.

(9) A description of special services to accommodate handicapped test subjects.

(10) Notice of (A) the information which is available to the test subject under section 5(a)(2), (B) the rights of the test subject under section 6, and (C) the procedure for appeal or review of a test score by the test agency.

(b) Any institution which is a test score recipient shall be provided with the information required by subsection (a). The test agency shall provide such information with respect to any test prior to or coincident with the first reporting of a test score or scores for that test to a recipient institution.

(c) The test agency shall immediately notify the test subject and the institutions designated as test score recipients by the test subject if the test subject's score is delayed ten calendar days beyond the time period stated under subsection (a)(8) of this section.

REPORTS AND STATISTICAL DATA AND OTHER INFORMATION

Sec. 4. (a)(1) In order to further the purposes of this Act, the following information shall be provided to the Commissioner by the test agency:

  (A) Any study, evaluation, or statistical report pertaining to a test, which a test agency prepares or causes to be prepared, or for which it provides data. Nothing in this paragraph shall require submission of any reports or documents containing information identifiable with any individual test subject. Such information shall be deleted or obliterated prior to submission to the Commissioner.

  (B) If one test agency develops or produces a test and another test agency sponsors or administers the same test, a copy of their contract for services shall be submitted to the Commissioner.

(2) All data, reports, or other documents submitted pursuant to this section will be considered to be records for purposes of section 552(a)(3) of title 5. United States Code.

(b) Within one year of the effective date of this Act, the Commissioners shall report to Congress concerning the relationship between the test scores of test subjects and income, race, sex, ethnic, and handicapped status. Such report shall include an evaluation of available data concerning the relationship between test scores and the completion of test preparation courses.

PROMOTING A BETTER UNDERSTANDING OF TESTS

SEC. 5. (a) In order to promote a better understanding of standardized tests and stimulate independent research on such tests, each test agency—

(1) shall, within thirty days after the results of any standardized test are released, file or cause to be filed in the office of the Commissioner—

(A) a copy of all test questions used in calculating the test subject's raw score;

(B) the corresponding acceptable answers to those questions; and

(C) all rules for transferring raw scores into those scores reported to the test subject and postsecondary educational institutions together with an explanation of such rules; and

(2) shall, after the test has been filed with the Commissioner and upon request of the test subject, send the test subject—

(A) a copy of the test questions used in determining the subject's raw score;

(B) the test subject's individual answer sheet together with a copy of the correct answer sheet to the same test with questions counting toward the test subject's raw score so marked; and

(C) a statement of the raw score used to calculate the scores already sent to the test subject if such request has been made within ninety days of the release of the test score to the test subject.

The test agency may charge a nominal fee for sending out such information requested under paragraph (2) not to exceed the marginal cost of providing the information.

(b) This section shall not apply to any standardized test for which it can be anticipated, on the basis of past experience (as reported under section 7(2) of this Act), will be administered to fewer than five thousand test subjects nationally over a testing year.

(c) Documents submitted to the Commissioner pursuant to this section shall be considered to be records for purposes of section 552(a)(3) of title 5, United States Code.

PRIVACY OF TEST SCORES

SEC. 6. The score of any test subject, or any altered or transferred version of the score identifiable with any test subject, shall not be released or disclosed by the test agency to any person, organization, association, corporation, postsecondary educational institution, or governmental agency or subdivision unless specifically authorized by the test subject as a score recipient. A test agency may, however, release all previous scores received by a test subject to any currently designated test score recipient. This section shall not be construed to prohibit release of scores and other information in a form which does not identify the test subject for purposes of research leading to studies and reports primarily concerning the tests themselves.

TESTING COSTS AND FEES TO STUDENTS

SEC. 7. In order to ensure that tests are being offered at a reasonable cost to test subjects, each test agency shall report the following information to the Commissioner:

(1) Before March 31, 1981, or within ninety days after it first becomes a test agency, whichever is later, the test agency shall report the closing date of its testing year. Each test agency shall report any change in

the closing date of its testing year within ninety days after the change is made.

(2) For each test program, within one hundred and twenty days after the close of the testing year the test agency shall report—

(A) the total number of times the test was taken during the testing year;

(B) the number of test subjects who have taken the test once, who have taken it twice, and who have taken it more than twice during the testing year;

(C) the number of refunds given to individuals who have registered for, but did not take, the test;

(D) the number of test subjects for whom the test fee was waived or reduced;

(E) the total amount of fees received from the test subjects by the test agency for each test program for that test year;

(F) the total amount of revenue received from each test program; and

(G) the expenses to the test agency of the tests, including—

(i) expenses incurred by the test agency for each test program;

(ii) expenses incurred for test development by the test agency for each test program; and

(iii) all expenses which are fixed or can be regarded as overhead expenses and not associated with any test program or with test development;

(3) If a separate fee is charged test subjects for admissions data assembly services or score reporting services, within one hundred and twenty days after the close of the testing year, the test agency shall report—

(A) the number of individuals registering for each admissions data assembly service during the testing year;

(B) the number of individuals registering for each score reporting service during the testing year;

(C) the total amount of revenue received from the individuals by the test agency for each admissions data assembly service or score reporting service during the testing year; and

(D) the expenses to the test agency for each admissions data assembly service or score reporting service during the testing year.

REGULATIONS AND ENFORCEMENT

SEC. 8. (a) The Commissioner shall promulgate regulations to implement the provisions of this Act within one hundred and twenty days after the effective date of this Act. The failure of the Commissioner to promulgate regulations shall not prevent the provisions of this Act from taking effect.

(b) Any test agency that violates any clause of any provision of this Act shall be liable for a civil penalty not to exceed $2,000 for each violation.

(c) If any provision of this Act shall be declared unconstitutional, invalid, or inapplicable, the other provisions shall remain in effect.

DEFINITIONS

SEC. 9. For purposes of this Act—

(1) the term "admissions data assembly service" means any summary or report of grades, grade point averages, standardized test scores, or any combination of grades and test scores, of an applicant used by any postsecondary educational institution in its admissions process;

(2) the term "Commissioner" means the Commissioner of Education;

(3) the term "postsecondary educational institution" means any institution providing a course of study

beyond the secondary school level and which uses standardized tests as a factor in its admissions process;

(4) the term "score reporting service" means the reporting of a test subject's standardized test score to a test score recipient by a testing agency;

(5) the term "standardized test" or "test" means—

    (A) any test that is used, or is required, for the process of selection for admission to postsecondary educational institutions or their programs, or

    (B) any test used for preliminary preparation for any test that is used, or is required, for the process of selection for admission to postsecondary educational institutions or their programs,

which affects or is conducted or distributed through any medium of interstate commerce, but such term does not include any test designed solely for nonadmission placement or credit-by-examination or any test developed and administered by an individual school or institution for its own purposes only;

(6) the term "test agency" means any person, organization, association, corporation, partnership, or in-

dividual which develops, sponsors, or administers a standardized test;

(7) the term "test preparation course" means any curriculum, course of study, plan of instruction, or method of preparation given for a fee which is specifically designed or constructed to prepare a test subject for, or to improve a test subject's score on, a standardized test;

(8) the term "test program" means all the administrations of a test of the same name during a testing year;

(9) the term "test score" means the value given to the test subject's performance by the test agency on any test, whether reported in numerical, percentile, or any other form.

(10) the term "test score recipient" means any person, organization, association, corporation, postsecondary educational institution, or governmental agency or subdivision to which the test subject requests or designates that a test agency reports his or her score;

(11) the term "test subject" means an individual to whom a test is administered; and

(12) the term "testing year" means the twelve calendar months which the test agency considers either its operational cycle or its fiscal year.

EFFECTIVE DATE

SEC. 10. This Act shall take effect one hundred and eighty days after the date of its enactment.

○

GLOSSARY

American College Testing Program (ACT): Test company formed in 1959 based in Iowa City, Iowa; administers college admission tests used primarily by colleges in South, West and Midwest.

American Council on Education (ACE): One of the founders of ETS; ETS charter gives it the right to submit nominees for seats on ETS' board of trustees.

Angoff, William: Leading ETS spokesperson on test development issues.

Binet, Alfred: Developed in 1905 the first systematic "intelligence" test for the French Ministry of Education.

Bowles, Frank H.: College Board President and ex officio ETS trustee 1948-1963; initiated the policy of reporting SAT scores directly to applicants.

Brigham, Carl C.: Developed SAT, Achievement Tests and ETS test development techniques; member of Eugenics Research Association and Galton Society; professor at Princeton University where he developed the first grade prediction method using the SAT. Author of A Study of American Intelligence, a major work which purported to prove Nordic intellectual superiority on the basis of Army test results--had wide repercussions including aiding passage of the Immigration Act of 1924--and was repudiated by Brigham in 1930.

Britell, Jenne K.: Former ETS Director of Information Services and assistant to President Turnbull; head of the new ETS Office of Program Planning.

Brodsky, David: ETS Senior Vice President with responsibility for finance.

Carnegie Corporation of New York: One of the founders of ETS.

College Board: Association of colleges, secondary schools and other institutions, formed in 1900; contracts with ETS to run SAT, Achievement Test, PSAT, CLEP, AP, College Scholarship Service, and other programs; College Board President is ex officio ETS Trustee; ETS President is ex officio College Board Trustee.

College Entrance Examination Board (CEEB): See College Board.

Committee of Ten: Group of University officials convened in 1892; initiated planning for creation of the College Board; chaired by Harvard President, Charles W. Eliot.

Conant, James B.: Former president of Harvard, ETS trustee; suggested creation of ETS.

Eliot, Dr. Charles W.: President of Harvard, Chairman of the Committee of Ten; leader of the early College Board; member of the Eugenics Research Association.

Eugenics Research Association: Affiliated with Eugenics Record office; devoted to the promotion of eugenics through planned marriages, immigration restrictions, and assignment of social roles through mental tests; members included Carl Brigham, E.L. Thorndike, Lewis M. Terman, H.H. Goddard, Charles Eliot, and other leaders of psychometrics and education.

Galton Society: Small eugenic study and strategy group created in 1918 by Madison Grant, author of The Passing of the Great Race; members included Brigham, Goddard and Thorndike.

Galton, Sir Francis: Regarded by many as the father of the intelligence testing and eugenics movements; developed statistical techniques used in modern testing.

Gardner, John W.: Former ETS Trustee, president of Carnegie Corporation, Secretary of HEW, founder of Common Cause; spoke at Rosedale dedication ceremony.

Goddard, Henry H.: Brought Binet tests to the U.S., active eugenicist; anticipated day when a "Mental Engineer" would use tests to assign people to appropriate roles in the class system.

Hanford, George: College Board President, ex officio ETS trustee.

Johnson, Albert: Chairman of the House Committee on Immigration and Naturalization; author of the Johnson-Lodge Immigration Act of 1924; president of Eugenics Research Association.

Josephs, Devereux Colt: Organized and provided funds for creation of ETS; President, Carnegie Corporation and New York Life Insurance Company; Director, J.P. Morgan, American Brake Shoe, American Smelting and Refining.

Kramer, John: ETS Counsel.

LaValle, Kenneth P.: Chairman New York State Senate Higher Education Committee; principal sponsor of New York Truth-in-Testing law; continues to study the role of standardized admissions tests in higher education.

Lord, Frederick: Senior ETS researcher.

Marland, Sidney P.: College Board President and ex officio ETS trustee 1973-78; former U.S. Assistant Secretary for Education.

Messick, Samuel: ETS Vice President with responsibility for research.

Moulthrop, Robert: ETS director of public relations; lobbied in Albany against the New York State Truth-in-Testing bill.

Slagle, Orin: Chairman, Law School Admission Council.

Smith, Robert E.: ETS vice president for personnel; former chairman of ETS Board of review, which investigated candidates suspected of cheating.

Solomon, Robert J.: ETS Executive Vice President.

Stone, Chuck: Former ETS Director of Minority Affairs. First black executive at ETS; resigned from ETS in 1972 and is now an outspoken advocate of testing reform; author, editor and former education aide to Congressman Adam Clayton Powell.

Terman, Lewis M.: Stanford psychologist; produced the first American version of Binet intelligence test; eugenicist.

Thorndike, Edward L: Author of landmark works in psychometrics; developer of Lorge-Thorndike test; eugenicist.

Turnbull, William W.: President of ETS, 1969 - present; began working for College Board while graduate student at Princeton; joined ETS at its founding.

Williams, E. Belvin: ETS senior vice president with responsibility for testing programs.

Wilmer, Cutler and Pickering: (Now called Wilmer and Pickering while partner Lloyd Cutler serves as counsel to President Carter); ETS' Washington, D.C. law firm and lobbyist.

Yerkes, Robert: Harvard psychologist; President of the American Psychological Association; developed WWI Army Alpha and Beta tests; wrote preface to Brigham's *A Study of American Intelligence*; member, Eugenics Research Association.

ABBREVIATIONS

AALS	Association of American Law Schools
AAMC	Association of American Medical Colleges
ABA	American Bar Association
ACE	American Council on Education
ACT	American College Testing Program
AP	Advanced Placement (Program)
APA	American Psychological Association
ATGSB	Admission Test for Graduate Study in Business (became GMAT, July 1975)
ATP	Admissions Testing Program
BRI	Bar Review Institute
CEEB	College Entrance Examination Board: now called College Board
CIRCUS	The title of an assessment program for young children
CLEO	Council on Legal Education Opportunity
CLEP	College Level Examination Program
COPA	Center for Occupational and Professional Assessment
CSS	College Scholarship Service
CTS	Cooperative Tests and Services
EPRI	Education Policy Research Institute
ERB	Educational Records Bureau
ERIC/TM	ERIC Clearinghouse on Tests, Measurement, and Evaluation, which is run by ETS under contract to the National Institute of Education (NIE)
FTC	Federal Trade Commission
GAPSFAS	Graduate and Professional School Financial Aid Service
GBAC	Graduate Business Admissions Council

GED	Tests of General Educational Development
GMAT	Graduate Management Admission Test (formerly ATGSB)
GPA	Grade Point Average
GRE	Graduate Record Examinations
GREB	Graduate Record Examinations Board
HCCC	Henry Chauncey Conference Center
HEALS	Higher Education Admission Law Service
HEAR	Higher Education Ability Recognition Program
HECP	Higher Education and Career Programs
HEW	(Department of) Health, Education and Welfare
IAEA	International Association for Educational Assessment; convened by ETS
IED	Institute for Educational Development
Infant Lab	ETS nursery and research laboratory for study of infant learning
IRS	Internal Revenue Service
JAC	Joint Administrative Committee (CEEB/ETS)
JSAT	Junior Scholastic Aptitude Test
LSAC	Law School Admission Council
LSAS	Law School Admission Services
LSAT	Law School Admission Test
LSDAS	Law School Data Assembly Service
MBE	Multistate Bar Examination
MCAT	Medical College Admission Test
NAS	National Academy of Sciences
NCBE	National Council of Bar Examiners
NEA	National Education Association
NIE	National Institute of Education

NTE	National Teacher Examinations
NYPIRG	New York Public Interest Research Group
PIRG	Public Interest Research Group
PSAT/NMSQT	Preliminary Scholastic Aptitude Test/National Merit Scholarship Qualifying Test
SAT	Scholastic Aptitude Test
SCAT	School and College Ability Tests
SDQ	Student Descriptive Questionnaire
SRA	Science Research Associates
SSAT	Secondary School Admission Tests
STEP	Sequential Tests of Educational Progress
TOEFL	Test of English as a Foreign Language
TSWE	Test of Standard Written English
VSS	Validity Study Service

Your Comments Invited

A national dialogue on as fundamental a subject as standardized testing should involve a broad cross section of the population. Students, of course, face the consequences of standardized testing most directly. Parents, teachers, educational and other administrators, academicians and others are also affected, albeit in different ways. The growing discussion on standardized testing would benefit substantially from their active participation.

We invite their comments on any or all parts of this report, and we welcome information, such as that drawn from their experiences with testing, and ideas for a more equitable testing arrangement. The perspective of each of these groups, and others who are concerned, is essential in developing policies on testing. We shall make use of such comments, information, and ideas in our work on this issue.

Please address your comments to: Allan Nairn, P.O. Box 19312, Washington, D.C., 20036.